STRATEGY IN ADVERTISING

STRATEGY IN ADVERTISING

LEO BOGART

Harcourt, Brace & World, Inc.

New York / Chicago / San Francisco / Atlanta

© 1967 BY HARCOURT, BRACE & WORLD, INC.

Library of Congress Catalog Card Number: 67-17508

Printed in the United States of America

It is far easier to write ten passably effective Sonnets, good enough to take in the not too inquiring critic, than one effective advertisement that will take in a few thousand of the uncritical buying public.

Aldous L. Huxley, *On the Margin*

The consumer isn't a moron; she is your wife.

David Ogilvy, *Confessions of an Advertising Man*

We should spare no effort in the organization of good advertising. Neither should we economize on advertising, because expenditures for it are repaid a hundredfold.

M. Argunov, in *Sovietskaya Torgovlya* [Soviet Trade], February, 1966

PREFACE

Strategy is the art of deploying available resources to attain objectives in the face of active opposition. In a competitive economy, the success of a company often hinges on its ability to master the strategy of advertising. This mastery in turn depends on the company's ability to assemble and to apply information. Advertising men today deal with a greater volume of information than ever before. In every substantial advertising agency and department, specialists are now at work systematically setting forth their knowledge, inferences, and guesses on such subjects as the consumer purchase cycle, the effects of repetition, and the relation between information, attitudes, and buying action. The computer has given the advertiser a remarkable capacity to apply this knowledge to the ever more complicated problems of the marketplace.

Advertising is inevitably a powerful economic force in any complex industrial society where production capacity exceeds effective consumer demand. But advertising is more than an economic force; it is also a profound influence on our culture, on our values, on the quality of our life. Directly, it provides us with constant stimulation, reminders, judgments, and guidance, not only about what products we ought to own but about the kinds of people we ought to consider attractive, the kinds of places we should want to live in, and the standards we should observe in our dress or way of speaking. Indirectly, advertising strongly influences our great mass media; their shape, substance, and style are all profoundly affected by the fact that they are themselves products in a market where the advertiser is the customer.

The assumptions that enter into advertising decisions thus have consequences that go far beyond advertising itself. Not all advertisers operate by the same rules, of course; but bit by bit, as knowledge replaces conjecture about the process of communciation, more and more advertisers come to work from the same basic assumptions. Most of these assumptions, let us hope, are sound and solidly rooted in evidence, and in this book I have tried to set them forth systematically. But the greatest obstacles to effective advertising strategy are assumptions which are faulty, and which because of their widespread acceptance create complacency on the part of business managements and advertising practitioners alike. These questionable assumptions waste the advertiser's money; they also lead to judgments that cause our mass media to be different from what they otherwise might be, and perhaps to fall short of their true potential.

Systematic inquiry is the only way by which evidence can replace conjecture, true or false. Research can transform into science judgments made on the basis of art or intuition. As our information accumulates and our sophistication grows, will we ever get to the point where the scientific aspect of advertising becomes all-inclusive and the aspect which is art unimportant? I don't believe this can ever happen, because no advertising problem is ever exactly like any other. The scientific method may and should be used to approach subjects which are in at least some respects outside the domain of science (and I believe communication is such a subject), but it will not always lead to solutions. Advertisements may be *evaluated* scientifically; they cannot be *created* scientifically.

I shall have little to say in this book about how to write good copy, design good layouts, or produce good commercials. These are highly specialized subjects in themselves; I do not believe they readily lend themselves to generalization, because they involve elements *unique* to the particular product and its manufacturer: its name, packaging, and physical attributes, its established competitive position, its existing reputation and advertising history.

This book deals rather with the *generic* characteristics of mass communication which lend themselves to marketing purposes. It focuses sharply on media strategy: how much money to spend, where, in what kind of message units, with what frequency, directed at what targets. Over these matters the advertising strategist can exercise rational controls. But the symbolic content and style of the advertiser's message may be even more important than the means of communication he uses. The idea behind his ad, original or banal, is at the very heart of strategy, and this idea cannot come from a book on "how to do it."

I am grateful to Austin Nichols Inc. and to their former advertising agency, Hockaday Associates, for permission to reproduce the ads in the Grant's Whiskey campaign, to Papert, Koenig, Lois, Inc. for permission to reprint the Polycrest ad, and to these advertising agencies for permission to reproduce the airlines ads at the end of Chapter 4: Burke Dowling Adams, Inc.; Campbell-Mithun, Inc.; Doyle, Dane, Bernbach, Inc.; Foote, Cone & Belding; Leo Burnett Company; Sullivan, Stauffer, Colwell & Bayles, Inc.; Wells, Rich & Greene, Inc.; Young & Rubicam, Inc.

I appreciate James O. Peckham's willingness to allow me to refer extensively to his recent analyses of advertising and sales; Norman Mackworth's permission to quote from an unpublished manuscript; Herbert Krugman's graciousness in letting me quote the "Hints to Intending Advertisers" after he used them in a speech; briefings from Robert Coen and David Learner on their companies' computer programs; permission from the *Journal of Marketing* and *Management Review* to use some of my writing which appeared earlier in their pages.

Certain chapters of my book profited from the critical readings of William Moran, Charles M. Kinsolving, Jr., Bernard Lipsky, Charles Benesch, and Malcolm McNiven. Mary Lehr supplied many choice bits of information. Joan Lent, my almost infallible secretary, was indispensable to the manuscript's progress, and (with Harriet Wiesner's help) struggled with the typing on far too many weekends.

Agnes Bogart supplied me with what she herself modestly describes as "a completely supportive environment," meaning that she kept Gregory and Michele pretty much out of my hair.

In judging what I have to say, the reader must be alert to the fact that I hold a job with one advertising medium which naturally has competitive problems with the rest. However, while I have indeed drawn heavily on studies I directed at the Bureau of Advertising of the American Newspaper Publishers Association (a number of them sponsored by the Newsprint Information Committee), this book reflects my own time and my own personal opinions.

LEO BOGART

CONTENTS

STRATEGY IN ADVERTISING

ADVERTISING ON THE AMERICAN SCENE

At noon on a summer day in 1916 a media representative called at the
J. Walter Thompson agency and found that his luncheon date was tied
up with a client and would not be able to see him. He was about to
leave, he told Sidney Dean[1] years later, when he found himself being
clapped on the back by the normally aloof Commodore Thompson
himself. To his amazement, Thompson invited him to lunch at the
Duane Hotel across Madison Avenue and even bought the first round
of drinks. He then made a gleeful announcement: "Congratulate me,
Joe! I just sold the business to the Resor boys. They don't know it,
but the advertising agency business has seen its best days!"

Half a century later, sixteen billion dollars were being spent annually on advertising in the United States (ten billion through the media

---

[1] Sidney W. Dean, Jr., a former vice president of the J. Walter Thompson agency,
to whom I am indebted for this anecdote.

of publications, broadcasting, and posters);[2] the "agency business" was handling seven billion dollars worth of accounts; and the J. Walter Thompson agency alone was doing business worldwide at the rate of $558 million a year!

Advertising billings in the United States have expanded fourfold since World War II. Not all of this expansion has been converted into greater advertising pressure on the individual consumer. But even when we adjust for inflation and for the rise in population, the growth of advertising as an economic and social force stands as one of the most remarkable developments on the American scene in recent years.

Since 1950, the number of advertising messages disseminated daily through print media — newspapers and consumer magazines — has grown by a third, and the number in the hands of the average adult has increased by about 11%. During the same period, the number of commercial messages broadcast daily has gone up 145%; the number coming within range of the average adult in his daily radio listening and TV viewing has gone up 61%.

Every day 4.2 billion advertising messages pour forth from 1,754 daily newspapers, millions of others from 8,151 weeklies, and 1.36 billion more each day from 4,147 magazines and periodicals. There are 3,895 AM and 1,136 FM radio stations broadcasting an average of 730,000 commercials a day; and 770 television stations broadcast 100,000 commercials a day. Every day millions of people are confronted with 330,000 outdoor billboards, with 2.5 million car cards and posters in buses, subways, and commuter trains, with 51.3 million direct mail pieces and leaflets, and with billions of display and promotion items.

The main source of messages to the consumer is not within advertising mass media at all but at the point of sale. We are subjected to more product ideas and impressions from packages and store window displays than we get from television commercials or magazine ads.

The signs which identify shops are a form of advertising. Matchbooks, calendars, and a host of other commonplace objects carry advertising messages which are hardly ever out of sight, though they are

---

[2] In 1966, about $16.3 billion was spent on advertising in the United States; $9.9 billion of this was national and $6.4 billion was local. Of the total, newspapers represented $4.8 billion (nearly a billion of it in national advertising); television $2.8 billion ($2.3 billion national); magazines $1.3 billion (all national); radio $1 billion (about one-third national); and outdoor and transit advertising about $200 million (about two-thirds national). The remainder represented industrial, farm, and trade publications, direct mail, and other miscellaneous forms of promotion. About half of *national* advertising investments were made in the four major media. Of this four-media total, television received about 46% of the investment, magazines 26%, newspapers about 20%, and radio 7%.

generally out of mind because we absorb them not as active communications but as part of our visual environment.

Advertising and the business climate

One reason why more advertising messages are disseminated per person today than was the case only a few years ago is that there are more new products than ever and an increasingly competitive business climate. Throughout the world, the marketing function has become increasingly important to corporate managements, and the attention paid to advertising has grown correspondingly.

Because advertising is at the white-hot center of marketing competition, perhaps no other aspect of American business management undergoes so many fluctuations in its focus of attention from year to year. There is a ceaseless search for new formulas to make better use of the advertising expenditures that business finds so hard to evaluate. Fads and fashions are characteristic of advertising as they are of any field that is fraught with an intense competition of ideas and a constant outcropping of new pressures from unpredictable sources.

In advertising, fashions center on key phrases, often ones arising from the vocabulary of research — Motivation Research (M.R.), Operations Research (O.R.), "Demographics" (generally mispronounced). Perhaps because it was vaguely associated with sex, motivation research got more general publicity than most advertising fads and left an indelible impression on advertising's words and illustrations. Fad or no, motivation research reawakened interest in the Great Creative Idea as the heart of successful advertising.

When American business was reorganized in the post-war years, marketing emerged as a major function which coordinated hitherto separate specialties: product development, sales promotion, merchandising, advertising, and market research. Great emphasis was placed on the integrated marketing plan, which attempted to reduce selling to the same cut-and-dried assemblage of budgets, quotas, and completion rates that occur in manufacturing. Motivation research offered a desirable counterpoise to the assumption of the planners that customers could be "manufactured"; it revivified the old P. T. Barnum concept of advertising as the creation of dreams and fantasies.

In contrast to such technical marketing specialties as market research or distribution planning, advertising is one of the most familiar phenomena in modern society. Its very familiarity leads business decision-makers to deal with it in common-sense lay terms and with an illusion of knowledgeability that they would hardly assume on other specialized subjects.   The businessman who fancies himself an advertising expert is not only the bane of professional advertising men, he is also responsible for much of the wasted effort which a surprising proportion of advertising expenditures represents.

Advertising and society

The importance of advertising in American life cannot be measured either by the sheer number of individual advertising messages disseminated or by the substantial expenditures these represent, whether in actual dollars or as a percentage of consumer sales.   It is also necessary to consider the power and influence of advertising institutions and leadership in the business community and — at election time — in politics.[3]   Most of all, the significance of advertising is expressed by the ubiquitous presence of its symbols and slogans throughout the culture.

As a subject of conversation, advertising can generate strong emotions, pro and con.   For several generations advertising has been condemned by intellectuals because of its frequent use of the cliché in language, illustration, and concept and because of its occasional appeal to irrational motives and vulgar tastes. Within the academic community everywhere, though perhaps less in the United States than in Europe, there is also an essential cynicism about advertising's economic usefulness which reflects a sense of malaise about the place of the intellectual in the business system. Charles Horton Cooley, the great social psychologist, once wrote that "only a somewhat commonplace mind will give itself wholeheartedly to the commercial ideal." [4]   To this Mandarin disdain has occasionally been added an aversion on ideological grounds: Marxist revulsion against the social waste involved in economic competition.   For those who hold this view, it is easy to focus on advertising as the most blatant, vigorous, and overt manifestation of that waste.   The combination of these strains of negative criticism persists in America today long after Communist economists have revised their practices and theories about the law of supply and demand and long after marketing

[3] An advertising agency with a political assignment uses the standard operating procedures and terminology of the trade.   On one occasion, a meeting of the "product group" of an agency planning a pre-election advertising campaign was interrupted by the unexpected appearance of the "product," the governor of the state.
[4] Quoted in Richard Hofstadter, *Social Darwinism in American Thought, 1860-1915,* Philadelphia: University of Pennsylvania Press, 1945, p. 121.

principles and advertising's utility have been accepted as part of the natural order in the Soviet Union and other socialist countries.

At the other extreme are those who proclaim the sacred virtue of advertising as the mysterious catalyst of the entire free-enterprise system and who regard even minor criticisms of advertising as an attack on the entire structure of capitalism.

The truth may lie somewhere between the two poles of opinion. Advertising is an indispensable ingredient of the communications system of a modern industrial society in which similar goals are separately pursued by divergent methods and techniques. It is neither nice nor not nice; it is simply there as part of the world we live in.

Social critics often speak of the billions spent on advertising as though this money represented a single lump sum which might better be spent to destroy slums and build schools. But the economy at large has no advertising budget. The sums spent are an aggregate of separate decisions made by many hundreds of thousands of individual enterprises to whom advertising represents an essential cost of doing business.

Not all the attacks on advertising are comprehensive in scope. Some which deal with specific aspects or practices arouse a strong defensive response from most practitioners. During 1966 and early 1967 such attacks and counter-attacks seemed to be coming up every week.

Does heavy advertising lead to corporate concentration? The Assistant Attorney General in charge of the Antitrust Division of the Department of Justice, Donald F. Turner, argued strongly that it does, in a speech which raised the temperature of advertisers large and small.[5] According to Turner, there exists "a significant correlation between the proportion of industry sales devoted to advertising and the average profit rates which were earned." Turner maintained that "what has become important is not so much the context of an advertising message, but rather the mere fact that it has been advertised." He suggested that "to the extent that consumers are unable to evaluate the relative merits of competing products, the established products may have a considerable advantage and it is this advantage that advertising messages tend to accentuate." Since large firms enjoy the advantages of volume discounts from media, Turner insisted that advertising works in the direction of monopoly and should be controlled or limited.

[5] Speech before the Federal Bar Association, June 2, 1966, Washington, D.C. The same argument was taken up in testimony before the Senate Antitrust Subcommittee in September 1966. John Blair, the committee's Chief Economist, analyzed the degree of economic concentration in various product areas involving consumer goods heavily advertised on network TV. He reported increases in the four leading companies' share of market in twenty-five product areas. In eleven other consumer fields concentration declined, although the four leading companies were heavy users of network television.

A strong rejoinder to Turner came from a prominent economist, Jules Backman. In a searching analysis of the evidence, Backman concluded that "the assumption that large companies will continually increase their share of the market because of their financial resources is not supported by experience." He refuted Turner's argument about the advantage enjoyed by the established brand by pointing to the successful introduction of many new brands. Backman presented a convincing statistical analysis to dispute the charges that advertising leads to concentration, price inflation, and excessive profits. From a preliminary analysis of the 125 largest advertisers in 1964 he found that less than one-tenth of the difference in rates of return for these companies could be explained by differences in the percentage of sales that had been spent on advertising.[6]

As for the charge that advertising makes much out of minor brand differences, Backman asked,

> What is the alternative in a competitive economy? Shall we allocate special sectors of the market to different companies as is done under cartels? Or shall we prohibit the introduction of new brands which are not "genuinely new products," however that term is to be defined? Clearly, there are inefficiencies inherent in the competitive process. These must be incurred if the benefits of competition are to be realized.

The innumerable appeals of advertisers simultaneously clamoring for attention are constant reminders of the incessant claims which are made on all of us by the many complex relationships of an impersonal and mechanized society. When once we look at these appeals coldly and objectively, when once we question their meaning and value, many of them appear monstrous or ridiculous.

But the fatuous, absurd, and exaggerated symbols through which some advertisers metaphorically proclaim the virtues of their products are rarely a subject of dispassionate examination by the average citizen of contemporary America. They are accepted as part of the landscape. Does anyone really believe that "Us Tareyton Smokers Would Rather Fight Than Switch"? Of course not; yet no one is indignant at this widely proclaimed statement, because no one assumes it is to be taken at face value.

The Western visitor to a Communist country who is appalled by the countless identical plaster casts of Lenin and the sloganeering drivel adorning places of public assembly inevitably wonders how intelligent people can live seemingly normal lives in the presence of so massive

[6] Speech before the Association of National Advertisers, October 24, 1966, Colorado Springs, Colo.

and continuous an assault on their intelligence. A Pole whose company cafeteria had been festooned with a banner reading, "To Socialism through Collective Eating!" once gave me a convincing answer. He compared the political inanity in question and his own reaction to it with the animated stomach action depicted in TV commercials for analgesics which American viewers similarly "accept" with complete aplomb. The intimation is that neither type of message really influences people directly, though it may have a more subtle effect as part of the environment.

Advertising is one of a modern society's most visible aspects. Its character reflects the state of the civilization from which it springs.[7] The same moral standards prevail in the creation of advertising as in the ordinary conduct of citizens. Most of the rules and regulations (legal or otherwise) which generally apply to the conduct of business carry over to the conduct of businessmen as advertisers. In short, advertising and its values are interwoven with the whole fabric of society.

Individual advertisements for any particular product provide scant basis for assessing the over-all social usefulness of advertising as an institution. The dramatic cases of "bad" advertising in recent years are more often those which involve misleading illustrations of permissible claims than those which involve fraudulent claims *per se*. The shaving cream commercial which showed loose sand being shaved instead of sandpaper (as represented) was, in the producers' minds, not a deliberate deception but an attempt to dramatize a real, though minor, product advantage: "softening" power. In the world of hyperbole, exaggeration, and nonsense — which is the everyday milieu of some kinds of advertising expression — the borderline between the cute and the crooked is often difficult to trace.

Many moral problems in advertising arise with regard to those product categories where brands are actually very much the same or differentiated to such a very minor degree that consumers are unable to distinguish them, as in blindfold tests. Of course, the very notion of a brand name implies some differentiation, since names, even in sound and appearance, carry different connotations, different psychological values for different people. To make its brand stand out a little more from the rest, however, each company is forced to take such minor utilitarian differences as exist and convert them into what appear to be large psychological differences. Small variations in packaging, ingredients, or

[7] The controversy over cigarette advertising is an example of the mistaken tendency to blame advertising for what in fact is a national policy. The persistence of high consumer demand for tobacco products is easier to trace to the Federal crop support program than to cigarette advertising, yet advertising and cigarettes are strongly linked in the minds of people who dislike them both.

other secondary attributes are exaggerated and stressed by copywriters and artists to distinguish the product from its competitors.

It is in the zeal to differentiate that many of the so-called ethical problems of advertising occur. Yet this very differentiation being sought is a visible sign of freedom and one which the social critics of advertising often reject too easily and thoughtlessly. In Communist countries during the Stalin era, one of the most depressing features of the topography for a visitor from abroad was the stores labeled "meat" or "bread" or "men's clothes," all with identical signs and identical window displays and with none of the cheerful variety which is present in the brand displays of merchandise in a free market economy.

The aspect of advertising that may be most vulnerable to criticism is actually one which is rarely associated with ethical problems; that aspect is its relation to the aesthetics of the mass media. Advertising has helped create tolerance for kitsch in taste and for cant in ideas. It has helped devalue the coin of communication by developing a massive, unthinking tolerance for nonsense and vulgarity. While individual ads and commercials are often brilliantly witty, far more tend to blunt our sense of humor. We are forced to take for granted too much that is ridiculous.

However, advertising can hardly be assigned the responsibility for the deficiencies of public taste. The intimate relationship between the institutions of advertising and the control of the mass media has indeed governed much of the shape of popular culture. But, while advertising men should not be proud of the cultural values reflected in much of American broadcasting and the popular publications, neither can they be wholly blamed for those values. The *Reader's Digest*, that greatest of all middle-brow magazines, built its formula for success on the public taste long before it accepted advertising. And motion pictures, which decades ago explored and exploited every inanity on which television programming bases its nightly fare, similarly depended directly upon pre-existing tastes as reflected at the box office — and not on corporate decisions in the advertising industry.

How Americans feel about advertisements: the A.A.A.A. study

Advertising comes in for periodic investigation by congressional committees and federal agencies, but at the same time it enjoys an extremely high level of public acceptance. In spite of occasional specific criticisms and a prevailing suspicion of Madison Avenue "city slickers," the American public, according to many opinion surveys, has put its seal of approval on advertising as a part of the business system.[8]   The most elaborate examination of how people consciously react to advertising was made for the American Association of Advertising Agencies (the A.A.A.A.) under the direction of Raymond A. Bauer of the Harvard Business School.[9]

Bauer concluded that 41% of the people interviewed could be classified as generally favorable toward advertising; 34% had mixed attitudes; 11% were indifferent; 14% were unfavorable.   The unfavorable group were more likely to report seeing or hearing annoying and offensive ads. They also tended to overestimate the proportion of a typical television hour which was taken up by advertising.

A special feature of the study was that the people sampled actually added up all the ads they were aware of during half a day with the aid of hand counters that they carried around with them.   Bauer called the figures resulting from this procedure a measure of "sensitive attention" rather than "exposure."   The respondents also filled out cards with their detailed reaction to unusual ads.   The readings on the counters and the number of cards filled out were then doubled to project a full day's response.   The average person recorded 76 ads a day; 12 of them (or 16%) were considered sufficiently singular to warrant classification on the cards.   Of the 12 ads so categorized, 4.4 were considered informative, 4.2 enjoyable, 2.8 annoying, and 0.6 offensive.

In general, ads were considered "informative" because of the information they gave on a product.   "Enjoyable" ads were categorized as such largely because of their technique.   "Offensive" ads were largely judged so because the product itself was considered in bad taste or uninteresting to the respondent.   "Annoying" ads were reported seen or heard too often, exaggerated, or boring and monotonous.

Two lessons about the public's response to advertising are immediately suggested.   First, constant repetition of ads for inoffensive products may induce a boomerang effect opposite to the advertiser's intention, especially when, as in broadcasting, there is no easy way to avoid the advertising message.   (Getting up from one's chair requires an effort.) Automotive and cereal ads were most often criticized as annoying because they were seen or heard too often.   Drug ads, however, were more often

[8] The relevant polls have been reviewed and digested in Stephen A. Greyser and Raymond A. Bauer, "Americans and Advertising: Thirty Years of Public Opinion," *Public Opinion Quarterly,* Vol. XXX, No. 1, Spring 1966, pp. 69-78.
[9] *Cf. The A.A.A.A. Study on Consumer Judgment of Advertising,* American Association of Advertising Agencies, May 1965.   This research was initiated by two A.A.A.A. researchers, William Weilbacher and Donald Kanter, and conducted by the Opinion Research Corporation.   Bauer summarized the findings in a speech delivered before the Association of National Advertisers, November 11, 1964, Hot Springs, Va.

classed as annoying because of their exaggeration. Coffee, tea, and cocoa ads were often classified as annoying because they were boring or monotonous. Individual advertisements which are repeated often may be repeated, literally, *ad nauseam.*

A second lesson of the study is that many objections to advertising actually reflect a dislike of the product it is selling. Eight times as much criticism of "annoying" ads was directed at the advertising as at the product advertised. However, among ads classified as "offensive," a much higher ratio of criticism was directed at the product (one-fourth as many references as to the ad itself).

For such sinful products as beer and cigarettes, the advertising presentation received only about two-and-a-half times as many mentions as the product itself. For wholesome products — soaps and detergents, cleansers and polishes — criticism of the presentation was seventeen times more frequent than criticism of the product. An unusual proportion of favorable mentions was given to pleasant product categories like canned and packaged goods, cereals, and baked goods.

The method used in the A.A.A.A. study forced the participants to interrupt their normal media experience in order to record their advertising impressions. The effects were inevitably less disruptive for the broadcast media than for print (in which ads are scanned or read as part of a whole communications environment rather than as isolated units). This gave heavy emphasis to TV commercials among the advertising singled out for special and for critical mention. The method may have had another effect: when someone knows he is being used as a guinea pig, his media habits may be affected as well as his exposure to advertising. The average person is exposed to far more ads in a day than the 76 recorded in the A.A.A.A.'s study. However, the proportion of these exposures which create a significant reaction must be far less than the 16% which were written up by the respondents. Presumably, many hundreds of additional messages went "unseen" and unrecorded.

The A.A.A.A. study seems to suggest that people harbor a certain amount of resentment at being subjected to information which carries no useful meaning for them. The resentment may be of a very low level. Most of it probably rises to the level of consciousness only under artificial conditions of exposure, such as those called for by research in which the individual is asked to play the role of advertising critic. Negative opinions are inevitably voiced with disproportionately high frequency when people are asked to play critic.

As a matter of fact, much or most advertising can never be meaningful or interesting to any one person at any one moment of time. There are bound to be ads for products we do not use, some for brands with which we have had poor experiences, and some that we may look down our noses at. The puritan's rejection of cigarette or beer advertising carries with it a *heightened* sensitivity to such advertising. But for most people, most ads are received with great tolerance when they manage to penetrate into awareness. Americans approve of advertising in practice as well as in principle.

Coping with the information explosion

The enormous expansion in the volume of advertising messages represents only one aspect of the twentieth century information explosion. A more complex society demands more and more specialized knowledge. In the United States, the demand for information reflects the steady rise in education, shorter work hours, and more leisure time along with the increased purchasing power to pay for transistor radios, second TV sets, and magazine and newspaper subscriptions. The diversification of interests creates more differentiated occupational, avocational, and social roles, and new media spring up to serve the special needs of hot rodders and art collectors.

Paradoxically, the enormous growth in the over-all volume of advertising complicates the problem of measuring its effects. The more highly competitive the climate, the more advertising works defensively and at cross-purposes. The consumer now has a harder job in differentiating information which is useful to him from the "noise" of advertising which is irrelevant to his needs or interests. Advertising is perceived selectively. It is also perceived differently at various stages of the purchasing process. Because of the variety of forms that advertising assumes in each of the different media, the number of advertising messages disseminated every day provides few clues as to how many come within the average person's range of vision or hearing,[10] or how many actually make a conscious impression on his mind.

The American public is engulfed in an ocean of words, spoken and written, informing, persuading, importuning, cajoling, demanding. The process of scanning, filtering, screening, and squelching the words we don't need is one in which most people are unconsciously engaged every moment of the waking day.

Human beings have developed unconscious defensive reactions to the information explosion and to all the irrelevant messages that assault our senses. We defy their intense stimulation by being indifferent or

[10] A commonly used "guesstimate" is 1,500 a day.

oblivious, by discriminating in the attention we give things, or by deliberately training ourselves through such techniques as programmed instruction and speed reading to cope with the vastly increased output of ideas and facts. Education gives people a better capacity to sift information at the same time that it makes for a bigger supply of information to sift.[11]

We handle excess information by automatically and subconsciously ranking the stimuli with which we are bombarded. The sound of an automobile horn to which we pay no attention on a street crowded with traffic will startle us when we hear it on a country road.

Television and radio newscasts and newspaper and news magazine columns may for weeks and months resound with the names of Indonesian cabinet ministers, Brazilian generals, and Laotian princes. Yet most of this information fails to register with the general public which dutifully exposes itself to it in massive doses each day.

Li'l Abner, Mickey Mouse, and Dr. Kildare are figures of far greater renown and familiarity to most people than the names of their own legislators. A Gallup poll some time after the first announcement of the hydrogen bomb found that only half the public knew what it was and 30% had never heard of it.

When we consider the extent of public ignorance on matters of far greater concern than the merits of competing brands on the market place, the fact that much advertising goes unobserved or unregistered by the consumer is far less remarkable than the fact that so much appears to be remembered.

The consumer is somewhat like an Indian in a forest who hears and sees a thousand things at once, but who brings his attention to bear only on the particular crackle and the particular bent twig that tell him what he needs to know.

---

[11] Better educated people read more newspapers on a given day and read them more thoroughly and intensively. But they actually spend *less* time with each newspaper that they read because they read more efficiently. *Cf.* Bureau of Advertising, ANPA, *The Daily Newspaper and Its Reading Public,* New York, N.Y., 1961.

DECIDING HOW MUCH TO SPEND, AND WHERE

2

The ultimate purpose of *most* advertising is to sell.[1] A sales objective
must be achieved through a devious route. Along the way, advertising
has many intermediate aims: to identify the product, to catalog its
attributes, to surround it with the right emotional aura, to inform people
of its virtues, to remind them of its existence, to persuade them that it
merits use, to reinforce their favorable predispositions against forgetful-
ness. In preparing an advertising campaign, there is often great confusion as to exactly which of these different purposes is intended. Yet
the size of the budget, the selection of media, the media-scheduling
strategy, the copy theming, the creative form of the advertising message,
and every other aspect of advertising depend for their success upon a
clear definition of aims.

[1] There are exceptions to this. Public relations advertising may be basically concerned with the company's survival or its freedom to achieve corporate goals, and
these vital functions may have nothing to do with sales.

Retail and national advertising objectives

Although the layman often indiscriminately lumps all forms of "advertising" together, the term encompasses innumerable subspecies, each with its own characteristics, techniques, and objectives. To begin with, there is a generic distinction between the advertising placed directly by manufacturers to promote their products or services and the advertising placed by retailers to bring in business.

The national advertiser doesn't think in terms of a specific ad, as the retailer usually does. The retailer tends to be mainly concerned with the return on his investment in today's advertising here and now. Yet, like the national manufacturer, the typical retailer advertises on a continuing basis and must be concerned with the cumulative effects of repetitive advertising. While particular ads stress different items with different selective product appeals, the whole continuous progression of his ads serves to create and build his store's reputation. No one item in any one ad can attract all of the readers, but at the same time that the retailer directly appeals to some of his customers with any one ad he is subtly influencing all of them.

Classified advertising in the newspaper represents, perhaps in its purest form, communication for business purposes via the mass media. The reader who seeks out classified ads is highly purposeful, as purposeful, in fact, as is the advertiser who has a specific house to sell or car to trade. The people who see the ad are, by definition, those with a strong buying interest, and they are represented within the total audience of the newspaper in much the same proportion as in the population at large.

Retail display advertising in the newspaper (where most retail advertising runs) is also aimed at the people with potential interest in the product advertised, but at a broader group than those with the avid concern of the classified ad reader. The retail ad's position within the body of the paper lends itself to casual perusal by a great many people who would not trouble to turn to a classified listing of the same merchandise. Such advertising plays upon the vague, unformed, tentative buying interests which, in enormous variety, are latent in the minds of most people at any given moment.

A person who is in the market for a coat, dress, or living-room sofa is apt to shop the retail ads in a purposeful way, much as the prospective purchaser of a house will look through the classified ads in the real estate section. But the bulk of the people whose attention alights on the typical retail display ad are people who have at the moment only the most nebulous interest in the product.

For the national advertiser, the probability of catching readers, viewers, or listeners who are actively in the market for his product is more remote. He may hope to reach people who are actually on the verge of a specific brand purchase decision, but at any moment in time such persons will represent but a fraction of those within reach of his message. His main objective in advertising is to lay a foundation for the purchase decision when the time comes.

A very substantial part of retail advertising (perhaps as much as half) is actually paid for by national manufacturers through the means of cooperative allowances. These allowances are intended to give the retailer an incentive to promote a manufacturer's wares, not only in the retailer's ads but in his internal display and promotion.

For many manufacturers, cooperative advertising is considered as more a sales or promotional expense than as advertising, since the company — though it furnishes copy, artwork, and mats for engraving — loses effective control over the end product. Since the average retailer is less skilled in advertising techniques than the average manufacturer and his agency, "co-op" ads sometimes present a hodgepodge of products from different companies.

However, cooperative advertising gives the manufacturer the positive advantage of associating his merchandise with stores of fine reputation that the customer respects. For an unknown or little-known brand or for a new product, this may be a substantial advantage indeed. There is also a practical advantage for the manufacturer: under the less expensive bulk rates paid by the large retailer who advertises fairly continuously, the same amount of newspaper space may usually be bought for a single ad at less cost than the national advertiser would have to pay if it bought directly through its agency.

Retail advertising serves a number of distinctive purposes. The average person thinks of a retail ad as one designed to sell those particular products which the store has on sale. Most retail advertising does represent this kind of specific promotion of individual items which the store hopes to sell within the next few days at a gross profit that will more than pay for the cost of the ad itself.

Retailers expect such advertising to have a direct pull, to sell more of the product than usual. However, merchants normally do other important things at the same time they advertise a product, like reducing its price and displaying it prominently within the store. It is therefore very difficult in practice to determine how much of the extra sales come from the advertising and how much from other aspects of the promotion. Any store in a good location, with an established reputation and clientele, is going to draw customers in the normal course of events and is going to sell any item featured in the store.

The direct value of a promotional ad is that it draws some customers who might not otherwise be shopping in that store on that day. Once in the store, they will not necessarily buy the advertised product, no matter how much the ad may have attracted them. The item may not live up to the promise in the ads; the store may not have the right color or size; the customer may not get the proper level of attention and service.

But if the customer is in the store, whether or not he buys the item, there is a strong likelihood that he will buy *something*. (A study made by the Bureau of Advertising in association with a large department store found that two-thirds of the women interviewed who had bought a product after seeing it advertised also bought one or more other items in the store. In another similar study we found that women attracted by promotional ads bought 1.3 unadvertised items for every advertised item they bought.)

It follows from all of this that a major objective of every promotional ad run by a retailer is to generate store traffic, because an ad that brings customers to his store will result in the sale of merchandise which is *not* advertised. Among people exposed to the advertising who are not immediately impelled to visit the store and shop for the product, the advertising serves an extra purpose: it reminds them that the store carries this particular kind of item. The illustration, the description, the pricing of the articles — all go to create or strengthen identifications which, over the long haul, bring customers to that store for that type of merchandise.

Promotional ads run by retailers for individual products or product assortments therefore carry an institutional burden. Straightforward institutional advertising, moreover, represents an increasingly important part of retail advertising. Big chains like A & P and Sears Roebuck have joined ranks with those individual department stores which have long-run advertising to extol their intangible merits — service, quality controls, style sense, pricing policy, concern for the individual customer. When the Detroit Art Institute added its magnificent new wing in 1966, J. L. Hudson's ran a brilliant reproduction of the museum's prized Van Gogh self-portrait in a high-fidelity SpectaColor preprinted newspaper page. This kind of celebration of the store's identification with its community represents institutional advertising at a level that must inevitably affect sales results, but to a degree that is impossible to trace.

For the national manufacturer, institutional advertising for general public relations purposes may also take the form of a "special" — as in the televised sponsorship of national political conventions. Often, however, it is carried on over a period of years and with great consistency. The maintenance of an established, consistent schedule of institutional or public relations advertising may give a company a strong pedestal from which to launch its harder-hitting product promotional campaigns. If there is a clear and strong identification of product brand names with the company name (as is true of General Electric but not of General Foods), however, corporate advertising and brand advertising are hard to distinguish.

Advertising objectives for the established product

The communications task of advertising a product which has been around for a while and of which people have an impression, whether or not they have actually used it, is essentially different from that involving a new product. The promotion of an established product may represent a continuing effort to maintain an established market position. It may also be a special event, closely tied to activities of the company's sales department. Such a particular effort may be in support of a trade deal involving extra financial incentives to the retailer to stock the product or to give it extra shelf or display space. It may be backup for a consumer deal involving price-off labels, coupons, or premiums.

In many packaged goods categories, such consumer promotions represent a fact of normal advertising life and occur at predictable intervals, and must, moreover, be built into the year's advertising plans right from the beginning. But special promotions may also represent a company's response to an unexpected competitive development, and the advertising schedule and budget required to support them may have to be created at the expense of the planned advertising program.

Depending on its past history, an existing product may be thought of as unpopular or unsuccessful by those who have never tried it themselves. It may carry negative associations in the case of those who have tried it in the past but found it unsatisfactory. In either case, the communications objective is to remind these people that the product exists and to present it in a light different from the one in which it may have been cast before.

An additional and important job to be done in advertising an established product is to reinforce among past and present satisfied users their existing favorable opinion of the product. They must be given reasons and arguments to support what might otherwise be no more than an emotional tone of relatively low charge.

The term "reminder advertising" applied to transit ads, small print ads, and outdoor advertising properly refers only to advertisements which communicate nothing more than the name or picture of the product itself. "Reminder advertising" describes a technique rather than an objective. Any ad reaching someone who does *not* already know the advertised product obviously does not come as a reminder; any ad reaching someone who *does* know the product is a reminder to some degree, depending on the new information it contains.

Advertising objectives for the new product

Established products rarely make spectacular case histories. Much of the lore in advertising concerns new products which achieve success through a brilliant slogan, theme, or concentrated effort — Lestoil, Mr. Clean, Alberto VO5. Such campaigns attain greatness in the annals of advertising when they manage to put a product's name into common currency and transform that familiarity into actual trial use, repeated use, and, finally, established brand position.

It has been estimated that 25,000 new items are introduced on the American market every year. For the companies that make them, each one is a new venture; for the consumer, it may or may not be seen that way.

The definition of a "new product" is a matter of some confusion. A product may be wholly new in the sense that it does something that no existing product has managed to do up to that point. (An example of this, when it comes, will be the picturephone, or telephone-television — already a technical reality in 1967 but not yet generally available.) Or it may be a substantial improvement on an existing product (like color TV).

Most new products, however, are far less dramatically novel. They merely represent minor variations in products already on the market, improvements in some cases, in others a difference merely in size, packaging, or name or a slight variation in the secondary features. The allegedly high failure rate of new products largely reflects the luck of this type of new brand entry into an existing competitive market rather than that of major product innovations.

A substantial part of new product development occurs under the labels of existing brands. Kellogg's new varieties of dry cereals and Campbell's new varieties of canned soups maintain these companies in strong positions of market leadership, where innovation plays a vital part.

It is the generic brand name, rather than any subvariety of the product, which maintains continuity in the public mind.

James O. Peckham, Executive Vice President of the A. C. Nielsen Company, points out that in the dry-grocery field, manufacturers' advertised brands (as opposed to private store labels, wholesaler brands, and non-advertised brands, mostly of the local or regional variety) account for 18% of the brand choices available, but for 74% of the sales.[2]

Ninety-five per cent of the sales of such brands in 1965 came from labels which were on the market four years earlier, leaving only 5% sales from newer brands. Moreover, in the four-year period checked, the existing brands chalked up a 13% gain.

Apart from this evidence that new brands are not quite as important as they are sometimes thought to be, it should be noted that almost all the money invested by manufacturers in new brands comes from profits made on existing products.

Smashing success stories in advertising are few and very far between. For established brands on the market place, the struggle for survival is keen and never-ceasing. For new products, it is even more desperate. It expresses itself at every step of development, starting with the initial debate over the packaging, the name, and the ingredients to be used in the product. It takes a hard fought battle to get distribution through retail buyers, wholesalers and buying committees, and the innumerable other guardians of the gates to consumer access and consumer awareness.

The new product marketer must traverse a dark and intricate labyrinth before he sees the light of day and gets his product out where people can buy it. Throughout this whole initial process of product planning and introduction, advertising appears as only one of many elements which the marketer must confront.

The brilliance of a planned advertising campaign can never be used to presell it to the trade. The company salesman calling on his accounts takes pains to mention the *size* of the advertising budget for the product. He emphasizes how much money is being spent for the product within the local market. He may stress the use of prestige media which the retailer believes in or which the company believes the retailer to believe in. But rarely (if ever) will he say as he opens his promotion kit, "We've got a great new slogan, a great new unique selling proposition, a great new motivation-research-engendered shortcut to the consumer's libido!"

[2] Address to the Grocery Manufacturers of America, November 9, 1965, New York, N.Y.

Within the market, brand share for established products does not undergo rapid or dramatic shifts from month to month, from one store audit period to the next,[3] or even from year to year.

With new products the story is different because they have no place to go but up or out. A new product must by advertising fight its way into the public's awareness and into a sector of the established market. It must work quickly to get past the initial months of heavy investment and learn to stand on its own feet within the designated pay-out period.

In the case of a new product, the advertiser's objective is twofold. He must create a sense of awareness or familiarity which permits his brand to be anchored as a significant reference point in the consumer's mind. Then he must create from scratch a favorable or positive set of associations which will cause the product to be tried, perhaps even preferred.

If the product has sufficient intrinsic interest, an announcement which is sufficiently striking and vividly presented can accomplish both purposes: arresting the consumer's attention and familiarizing him with both the brand name *and* the product story at the same time. Typically, however, the new brand faces a real problem in making the consumer aware of its existence. There is no purpose in registering copy points if the product itself lacks clear identity in the consumer's mind.

For this reason, it often makes sense for an advertiser to build awareness and recognition for his product before he launches into a full-fledged exposition of its virtues. A decision to proceed in this way has implications for the choice of media as well as for the type of messages to be used at each stage of an introduction. "Familiarizing" the consumer is sometimes done with small-space print ads, with outdoor or transit ads that have high visibility, or with very brief commercials (like the "I.D.'s" which accompany a station's identifying call letters on TV). Such a schedule is designed to place the product name, however fleetingly, before the largest possible number of people. Later, larger units can be directed at the best prospects with a full product story.

The initial advertising push for a new product must bear a disproportionate part of the load in meeting the marketing objectives for the whole first year. It has to be strong enough to provide substantial support for the salesmen during the selling-in period. It must help achieve

---

[3] Store auditing is the most widely used system for measuring changes in a brand's market position. Audits involve the use of a sample of retail outlets in which, at periodic intervals (usually of two months), a count is made of all merchandise on the shelf or in inventory and a record is kept of all shipments received since the last audit date. For each measured brand, shipments minus stocks on hand equals sales for the audit period.

a high level of distribution. It must make the product generally familiar. It must establish the brand's identity and its principal points of advantage in people's minds. It should create trade "excitement"; it must often tie in with merchandising premiums, sampling, or other incentives to get the consumer to try the product. All these things must be done at once. Is it a wonder so many new products never make it?

Peckham's formula

James O. Peckham has analyzed the relation between advertising and sales for a number of new grocery, toiletry, and proprietary drug products, using the A. C. Nielsen Company's vast resources of store-audit data.[4]   Peckham used share percentages rather than actual dollar figures in measuring both advertising and sales. Share percentages do not take into account the element of leverage which is introduced into the total consumption of a product category as new brands are introduced or as existing brands step up their advertising on special promotions. According to Peckham, over a four-year period there was a 35% increase in the total volume of consumer sales in twelve product groups with new or improved brands. In thirty-two more stable product groups the gain was only 20%.

Peckham focused on *successful* new products.[5]   The new toilet goods brands which he classified as successes (because they achieved an established position in the market) had a share of advertising about 60% *greater* than the share of sales which they eventually attained. Those with the highest share of sales also had the highest share of advertising.

Peckham's evidence covered a variety of products, distribution situations, and promotional plans, so there is no way of inferring how an advertising investment should be scheduled or spread out. In one case, a substantial proportion of it was spent in the first few introductory months. In another case, there was a slower buildup to a peak. Once at a peak, sales were sustained at the same level in some instances but not in others.

Peckham advances a "Formula for Marketing Success" which stresses introductory offers to both consumers and the trade, "sufficient

[4] Peckham's work was presented in speeches before the Grocery Manufacturers of America, November 9, 1965, New York, N.Y., and before the Advertising Research Foundation, October 4, 1966, New York, N.Y.

[5] He attributes their success to "a demonstrable consumer 'plus' both recognizable and merchandisable, developed with the benefit of adequate consumer product studies and thoroughly market-tested in the crucible of actual sales conditions at the retail store level."

advertising over a 24-month period to produce a share of advertising about one and one-half times that of the share of sales you plan to attain," and "enough advertising in subsequent months to maintain [the product's] share modestly ahead of its sales position." [6] The question of how much that "enough" will turn out to be is best answered the way Abraham Lincoln answered the question of how long a man's legs should be — long enough to reach the ground.

Although Peckham stressed that the average successful new product has an advertising share one-and-a-half times its eventual sales share over a *two-year* introductory period, his individual case histories also presented convincing evidence of the lack of any consistent *short-term* relationship between share of advertising and share of sales on a national basis. Here are just a few illustrations:

Food Brand Epsilon. This company made a real effort to "buy" the market. Its share of advertising climbed steadily, reaching 82% of the total within eight months. As late as eighteen months after introduction it was spending half the advertising dollars in its field; it was spending a third of the dollars ten months after that. While its sales share first rose steadily and touched 31% within a year after introduction, it was down to about a fifth of the market six or eight months later, and then held at that level.

Toilet Goods Brand Beta. This brand's history is almost a perfect model of what every advertiser dreams about. The product was introduced slowly and selectively with very limited advertising support. In its first eight months on the market its share of advertising did not go above 3%, nor did its share of sales reach 1%. About a year after introduction, a massive advertising campaign was launched, raising the advertising share to nearly 30% of the total corporate budget for a six-month period. Then advertising was slightly reduced, reaching the 23% level two years after the product's introduction; nevertheless, sales share showed a consistent and steady increase during this same period and was over 12% at the two-year mark.

Toilet Goods Brand Theta. This brand got off to a fast start. Six months after introduction it had a 5% market share, and it held on to that 5% share for the next year and a half. During that same period, advertising came and went in the form of successive campaign waves: 12% share after two months, down to 6% after four, up to 12% at eight months, down to 3% in the following six-month period, then up to 9% and down to 2% again. Here, obviously, is a classic demonstration that

---

[6] To the smaller manufacturer who wonders where the money will come from to maintain his advertising pressure at a level one-and-a-half times as great as his sales share goal, Peckham suggests a selective concentration on the parts of the market which the bigger companies are neglecting.

short bursts of advertising pressure, with periods of inactivity in between, can produce sales results which are smooth and consistent. They do not reflect the saw-tooth pattern of the advertising curve itself. Yet sales curves just as smooth resulted in other cases from advertising pressure steadily maintained at an even pace.

These were success stories, but the case history of a failure bears out the general point about the lack of a consistent short-term advertising-sales relationship:

Toilet Goods Brand W. Share of advertising for this product built up to 5% within four months and remained at that level for another four months. During this period the brand share hovered just above the 1½% level. Advertising was cut back sharply (a year after introduction it was practically non-existent). Then a sudden short-run advertising promotion raised the advertising share back up to 3%. This had no effect on sales share, which continued on a slow but steady downward course after the brand's first six months on the market. (Peckham's diagnosis of this particular case is that the advertising promised more than the product could ever deliver in actual performance.)

Peckham stresses the distinction between *share* of advertising and the advertising/sales ratio. He refers to "the fallacy of attempting to link advertising expenditures to product sales on a ratio basis." He cites as an example the sales of one brand which increased 47% during the second year, although the per cent of sales spent for advertising declined to 5%. "Since 10% of one brand's sales may be more in actual dollars than 50% of another brand's sales, obviously the brand with the smaller sales volume must have a higher percentage in advertising or go completely unnoticed by the majority of consumers."

Since "it is readily apparent that sudden increases or decreases in advertising expenditures alone, during a given year, do not prompt similar responses in sales except in a minority of cases," Peckham is pessimistic about the chances of finding an ideal ratio of advertising to sales. He states: "The net conclusion seems to be that the methods used to encourage product growth must be tailored to the individual product and to the market in which the product is competing." [7]

Setting advertising goals

Peckham's analyses emphasize that a company must outspend its competition for every point of market share it hopes to win for a new product. For years, advertising men have encouraged their clients to think of

[7] *Nielsen Researcher*, No. 1, 1965.

advertising as an investment rather than as an expense, since the term "investment" suggests a continuing pay-out over a period of time rather than a recoverable short-run cost. Economist Joel Dean points out that "advertising is now book kept and budgeted as though its benefits were used up immediately, like purchased electricity." The result is that advertising is thought of as a current expense and as part of the operating budget. He suggests that advertising and other forms of promotion belong in the capital budget, since "the hallmark of an investment is futurity." [8]

Regardless of how his "bookkeepers" handle the matter, the typical advertiser is constantly preoccupied with the question of what return he is getting on his advertising "investment," maybe because he is apt to think in conventional cost accounting terms. He would like to be able to say that for a given number of dollars spent on advertising he got back a specific dollar return in sales. But this assumes that advertising is a discretionary expenditure rather than a fundamental cost of doing business, like the cost of raw materials or of labor.

Every business has expenses which are necessary, yet whose amounts are fixed by the laws of supply and demand in only the most general way.[9] Executive compensation is one example of an expense which can rarely be justified in precise terms. The board of a large corporation may pay its president $100,000 a year on the premise that this is what it takes to attract a man of the ability required. How could the board prove that the salary should not be $110,000 or $90,000 a year? If the figure were substantially increased or lowered, judgment would dictate at some point that it was unreasonable, unrealistic, or out of line. But where would that point be?

This kind of judgment about expenses is made in business all the time, and the sense of it is rarely questioned. It is really much like the kind of judgments that people make in their personal spending.

In the imaginary world of early classical economics, the consumer was expected to make rational choices about the comparative utility of his various purchases. Today we are more willing to acknowledge that Economic Man's rationality is often modified by subjective and irrational notions about what is of value to him.

To ask about the return on advertising is somewhat like asking the reader, "Did the last $100 suit you bought really give you $100 worth

---

[8] "Does Advertising Belong in the Capital Budget?" *Journal of Marketing*, Vol. 30, No. 4, October 1966, pp. 15-21.
[9] A marketing conference held by the Department of Commerce with 65 leading marketers and educators concluded, according to the New York *Times*, November 6, 1966, that "the average company knew roughly half its costs were in marketing and distribution, but that was about all it knew."

of satisfaction? Might you not have been better off with a different suit at the same price, or with a $75 suit and $25 worth of shirts and furnishings?"

Advertising is as essential to the functioning of a business as clothes are to the consumer. The answer to the question of how much advertising is needed must therefore be "just the right amount; not too much and not too little." There can be no general laws. Only judgment can prove the answer to the advertiser who is unwilling to experiment with his own product. As the old story goes, a horse which is trained to work without eating will eventually die. A product which has no promotion or advertising to nourish it must eventually die too, but no one can predict just exactly when this will happen.

"DAGMAR"

In his book, *Defining Advertising Goals for Measured Advertising Results*,[10] Russell H. Colley attempted to clarify the "corporate management approach to the advertising investment." His work has been highly influential because of its distinguished sponsorship by the Association of National Advertisers (the ANA).

As his title implies, Colley is out to show advertisers how they can *measure* the return they are getting on the money they spend to advertise. He concludes that "to measure the accomplishment of advertising, a company must first have a clear understanding of the specific results it seeks to accomplish through advertising." This means distinguishing advertising objectives from the more general marketing objectives. For example, Colley distinguishes the *corporate* objective of making a profit from the *marketing* objective of selling goods and the *advertising* objective of creating brand preference.

Colley makes a further distinction between long-run advertising objectives and "goals." In his lexicon, "goals" are objectives that are specific as to time and degree — e.g., earning 10% on invested capital in a given year, or achieving a given brand share or a given brand preference among a certain number of housewives.

He offers the following illustration of an advertising goal that could be "based upon research studies and tests": "To increase among 30 million housewives who own automatic washers the number who identify brand X as a low-sudsing detergent and who are persuaded that it gets clothes cleaner — from 10% to 40% in one year."

---

[10] New York: Association of National Advertisers, 1961.

To set so specific a goal implies that a benchmark piece of research has been done to measure acceptance of the message before the start of the advertising campaign and that a similar study will be made afterwards. "Thus," says Colley, "with defined goals and measured results, we have a basis for both copy and media evaluation. Does copy approach A get the message through to more people than copy approach B, does medium C do a better job at lower cost than medium D? Is the copy theme or major media used for several years beginning to get a little tired? Or is the public just beginning to catch on?"

Colley concludes that current sales are not a final yardstick of advertising performance except under one of three conditions, none of which frequently prevails among so-called [11] nationally advertised products: (a) advertising is the single variable in sales; or (b) advertising is the dominant force in the marketing mix; or (c) there has been an immediate pay-out, with sales closely following the ads, as in mail order or (he says) retail advertising.

Apart from the carry-over effect of today's advertising on tomorrow's purchases of big-ticket items, Colley points out, "the consumer who switches today to a brand of cigarette, toothpaste or coffee because of advertising, may continue to use the brand and pay dividends to the advertiser for several years to come."

Colley concludes that to define advertising goals, information based on research, experience, and judgment is needed regarding the merchandise, the markets, the motives, the messages, the media, and the measurements in question. Moving from this fine alliterative sequence, Colley says, "Information must be translated into strategy, strategy expressed in terms of goals. Measurement then becomes feasible." He cites four stages of commercial communication — awareness, comprehension, conviction, and action.

Unfortunately, most of the examples offered in this widely quoted book are theoretical ones, illustrated with "before" and "after" campaign changes which are rarely encountered by research under normal conditions in the marketplace.

Colley begins quite correctly by rejecting the "hard" evidence of sales results as a criterion for advertising effects because, as he points out, too many marketing forces might interfere with the cause-and-effect relationship. Then he dashes on, courageously assuming that major changes in attitude and awareness can be created by the typical advertising campaign and that these changes can be measured in a clear-cut way.

[11] "So-called" because manufacturers with only regional distribution are normally grouped under this heading.

Colley has provided the "broad outlines" and left it to the technicians to fill in the "operating details." [12] Happily, figuring out "how to do it" is beyond his concern. Tremendous difficulties of research design and experimentation must be overcome in judging whether a particular set of goals have actually been met. Colley does not appear to be especially troubled by the question of whether the goals are realistic in the first place.

Setting the budget total

Every year many words are written and spoken about how to determine the advertising budget. Most of them are ignored in practice.

One tack is to take a fixed percentage of expected sales, derived from past experience with the product (or from the record of competitive products), and peg the advertising budget to that. This procedure can be highly conservative in its effect if the decision on each year's budget is set exclusively in terms of the previous year's showing rather than in terms of future expectations and forecasts.

Another textbook approach (the "task method") is to start with the media schedule required to do the desired job and then calculate what it costs. The next step, which the texts sometimes ignore, is to cut this (generally ambitious) figure back to fit somebody's judgment of how much the company can afford in relation to all its other manufacturing and sales expenses, its overhead, and its profit goals.

The task method of budgeting arose in a pre-broadcast era. This method afforded the advertiser a considerable degree of freedom because of the variety of ways in which print media can be scheduled. In an epoch of large-scale expenditures on network television, the task method loses a good deal of its flexibility. The advertiser who is considering the possible buy (or "participation" buy) of a network "package" (of combined program production costs and air time costs) has only a yes or no choice as to his participation. The inflexibility of these media costs is incompatible with the task method theory that the advertiser should spend whatever is needed to do a particular job.

Essentially, setting the advertising budget is not very different from any other business investment decision. The firm looks at the total market for the product field and assesses its potential for growth. It

[12] The dragonfly on the nose of the hippopotamus suggested that his host learn to fly, and instructed him by flapping his wings. "How can I do it?" asked the hippo. "I've given you the broad outlines of the idea," said the dragonfly. "Surely you can work out the operating details." This summarizes the agency-client relationship.

examines its own competitive position, seeking to evaluate realistically the attributes of its product, packaging, pricing, and distribution relative to what other brands have to offer.

Advertising requirements can be clearly stated only in relation to the total sales and marketing effort, including promotion, display, and publicity. All the judgments a company makes must be based on the best available evidence, which may not be very good at all.[13]   How this can be done systematically was outlined by Robert Weinberg[14] in a paper called "Developing an Advertising Expenditure Strategy." Weinberg begins by positioning the company in its four simultaneous environments: economic, internal, competitive, and institutional. He then undertakes a fundamental consideration of company net profits and their dependence on such factors as general business conditions, the level of industry sales, competitive activity and the company's own reactions to it, and the tax structure.

Weinberg points out that the additional sales the advertiser seeks to create by advertising ought to be *profitable* sales, which return more than they cost to create: "The relative merit of a given *increase* in advertising or sales promotion expenditure may often depend on what fraction of the *incremental* profits generated will remain available to the company after taxes."

In actual practice, Weinberg points out, it is unlikely that a company can increase its ultimate profits through an expansion of its share of market without, at the same time, changing its cost structure and the net profitability of its total sales. This profitability is bound to be weakened by "the actions required to increase the company's share of the market . . . advertising, sales promotion, new customer development, new market development and related expenditures." Thus, he concludes, "the key question in formulating an optimal competitive strategy is that of determining the most profitable trade-off" between an improved share of market for the company and a lower ratio of net profit to company sales.

However, the company's optimal market share depends on its current market position and on the intensity and effectiveness of competitive

[13] One company president told Sidney Dean that a full-dress sales forecasting session (replete with charts and statistics) he had just attended reminded him of a wartime experience he had in the Aleutians. A meteorologist noticed an Eskimo building an igloo with double-thick walls and, impressed by the natural instincts of this primitive man, asked him how he was able to predict that the winter ahead would be a hard one. "I *know*," said the Eskimo, "I see the white man has laid in extra big coal piles this winter." The company's market analysts were not amused by this analogy.
[14] Weinberg is a mathematical economist, formerly with IBM, who is now a vice president of Anheuser-Busch. His paper was prepared in 1962 for an ANA symposium on the computer in advertising.

activity, which are beyond the company's control.   The intensity of competition will reflect both the consumer demand for the product and the production capacity of the company and the rest of the industry.   It does not always pay to advertise when the objective is to win more of an existing market share at the expense of the competition.   This is just one reason for the constant stress on new product development by American business.   Apart from the objective of gaining an immediate competitive advantage, there is always the hope that through a change in the product itself additional sales may be gained by expanding the circle of consumer demand.

There is a considerable difference between the advertising investment decision for an established product and the decision for one about to be introduced.   For a new product, the decision is at once more difficult and more simple, because it is part of a whole series of interrelated policy decisions as to how the product will make its debut.

A new product is commonly taken through a rather elaborate process of research and laboratory development.   This makes it possible to check consumer reactions to the product, packaging, and copy theming and to get some indication of the potential rate of purchase before major investments are committed.   In market tests, advertising schedules can be compared using different levels of expenditure, different mixes of media, and different copy themes.

In the case of an established product for which no major changes are contemplated, the most common procedure is to plan strategy on the basis of what was done the previous year.   An advertising investment and media strategy which has produced successful growth in the past is normally not abandoned without compelling reason.   Most manufacturers and their advertising agencies have a tendency either to maintain the same investment policy or to reinforce the strategy they have been using.

A decline in sales or brand share is always likely to produce a shift in advertising strategy.   This may take the form of a change in the ratio of advertising budget to sales or a change in the mix of media, in the campaign scheduling, or in copy theming or art style.   Not uncommonly it also leads to a change of agencies.

Market tests of expenditure levels

It is common practice today for companies to arrive at an advertising-to-sales ratio by test market experiments in which budget levels are varied and sales results or attitude changes compared.   As I shall emphasize later, this kind of study is hard to do well, and it is difficult to avoid inadvertently testing media and copy at the same time that budget levels are being evaluated.

The Missouri Valley Petroleum Company conducted a three-year experiment in which a large number of cities were divided into three test groups and a control group. As reported by Charles H. Sevin, one test group received half as much advertising as normal while the other two got twice and three times as much.[15]

This company found that reducing advertising by 50% had neither a favorable nor an unfavorable effect on sales compared with the control group. In the double power group, sales at company-owned outlets increased 17% the first year, 23% the second year, and 36% the third year over the base. However, in the group receiving tripled advertising power, the increases were 16% the first year, 11% the second year, and 16% the third year. "Thus company officials expected, within certain limits, that a doubling of advertising would actually foster a greater sales increase than would a tripled advertising schedule."

Can such a conclusion actually be drawn? The more disappointing record in the triple power markets may simply illustrate the difficulty of controlling for competitive activities, distribution conditions and market idiosyncracies which inevitably beset the advertising tester.

From the experience of the Milwaukee Advertising Laboratory, G. Maxwell Ule describes a case where extra advertising input was applied against half the market.[16] The results in the second of four test periods showed a fourfold increase in the extra sales volume generated, compared to the first. In the third test period, the effect was reduced by about a fourth, and it fell again by a third in the fourth period studied. This case shows what Ule calls the "principle of diminishing returns through time" but also a continuing net gain, on balance, in the area with extra advertising.

In another notable study, a DuPont product which is sold only through a relatively short season[17] was tested, using different advertising expenditure levels in separate parts of the country: the same level of expenditures as the base period, and two-and-a-half and four times normal.

[15] "What We Know About Measuring Ad Effectiveness," *Printers' Ink,* July 9, 1965, pp. 47-53.
[16] Address before the 12th Annual Conference of the Advertising Research Foundation, October 1966, New York, N.Y.
[17] This condition simplified the problem of measuring advertising results, since there was no reason to assume that there would be carry-over effects during an extended period. Malcolm McNiven, former Advertising Research Manager of DuPont, has been an outstanding figure in this type of difficult experimentation. DuPont ran

Within each area, three test markets were selected in which the product's market share was either comparatively high, middle, or low.   In the areas which were to receive above-normal expenditures, additional advertising was placed in local media over and above the national network TV schedule.   Therefore, the media mix was inevitably varied as well as the total budget.

As reported by Sevin, "The results showed a range in profit contribution per dollar advertising of 2.5 to 1 as between the highest and lowest areas.   Accordingly, parts of the advertising budget were experimentally reallocated from some of the least profitable territories to the most profitable ones."   In other words, the conclusion from the published evidence appears to be that the effect of increased advertising expenditure weight could not be divorced from the over-all marketing conditions in each area.

In yet another experiment reported by Sevin, a manufacturer varied the level of television and newspaper expenditures in a number of different sales territories and compared the resulting sales and profits. On both these scores there appeared to be an inconclusive set of findings with regard to the media mix.   Total sales went up $3\frac{1}{2}\%$ when advertising expenditures were doubled in both newspapers and TV.   But because of the cost of this advertising, the profit actually went *down* $15\frac{1}{2}\%$.

When the budget was cut in half in both media, the sales went down $1\frac{1}{2}\%$ but the profit went up nearly 7%.   "Accordingly, marketing management adopted the experimental results on a national basis.   TV and newspaper advertising expenditures were reduced by 50% in almost all territories for this particular product.   Long-run profits of this product were soon increased substantially."

No one can quarrel with this kind of experimental method of arriving at the "right" level of advertising expenditure — as long as the research is done properly.   But the assumption that less advertising may be more efficient carries with it an immediate question as to whether the message is right and whether the right combination of media is being used.   The advertising planner may still be reduced to conjecture and to judgment when he tries to answer that question.

---

another interesting experiment, summarized by Sevin, in which it was found that sales of Teflon-coated cookware increased most dramatically when a high level of advertising expenditure (in TV) was maintained, not only through the fall months but during the winter period as well.   When advertising was low both in the fall and in the winter, there were 25 units sold per 1,000 housewives.   When it was high in the fall and low in the winter, the number of units rose to 32 units.   Low fall and high winter advertising doubled sales from 25 to 49, but a high fall and high winter combination brought sales from 32 per 1,000 to 70 per 1,000.

What should the Advertising/Sales ratio be?

We saw, in looking at "Peckham's Formula," that a brand's share of total advertising in its product class is a totally different matter from the percentage of sales it spends on advertising. In most industries, the top brand spends less on advertising in proportion to total sales than is true of its competitors. The smaller firm has the problem of maintaining high visibility for its brand on a lesser budget. At the same time, the smaller firm is usually unable to earn the same volume discounts from the media which permit economies for the larger advertiser, and it is less likely than the larger company to win the most favorable positions for its ads or commercials. For the same reasons, a brand manufactured by a multi-product company starts with an advantage over a competitive brand made by a one-product company.

The Lever and Colgate companies market equivalent products at the same price as Procter & Gamble. But this larger firm, with its gigantic sales volume and advertising power, can put greater promotional support behind each case of soap it sells, at a lower cost per case, and create, in total, greater pressure on the minds of consumers.

In 1965, Procter & Gamble, spending a total of $225 million in advertising to create $2.058 billion in sales, had an Advertising/Sales ratio of 10.9%. Of its smaller competitors, Lever Brothers spent 20.4% on advertising as a per cent of sales, and Colgate-Palmolive 21.8%. On the other hand, Purex, a minor competitor, spent only $10 million on advertising to create $160.8 million worth of sales, or an A/S ratio of 6.2%.

Advertising represents 2.2% of the U.S. Gross National Product, and the proportion has remained at about this level over the post-war period. The ratio of advertising to sales for the leading 100 advertisers in 1963 ranged from 0.3% in the gasoline and oil industry to 19.6% for drugs and cosmetics. The median for the 100 advertisers was 5.8%. (Being the 100 biggest, they naturally spend more on advertising than the average company in absolute dollars, either because they are big or because they are concentrated in consumer product categories where heavy advertising is the norm.)

Of substantial interest, however, is the variation among individual companies in the same category. A 1954 study, conducted jointly by the University of Illinois and *Advertising Age*, analyzed the percentage of sales devoted to advertising by 2,325 companies in 70 business classifications (the average was 2.5%). Among the 27 firms in the cosmetics and beauty aids category, the range was from 0% to 38%. In the proprietary medicine category, the proportion ranged from 0.1% to 49.3% in 1954, with a median of 15.7%. In the gasoline and oil field, it ranged from 0%

to 18%. For small appliances, it ranged from 0.8% to 45% with a median of 5.1%. In the beer, wine, and liquor category, it ranged from 0% to 65%, with a median of 4.9%.

The relatively high percentage of sales income spent on advertising in certain product fields (toiletries, for example) is often cited by critics of advertising as a cost passed on to the consumer. (One such critic, Harry J. Skornia, estimates that a typical family with $5,000 in disposable income is "taxed" $75 a year for broadcast advertising alone.[18]) Actually, A/S ratios are generally found to be high precisely in those categories which are characterized by a strong fashion or style emphasis and frequent introduction of highly competitive new products with their inevitably high advertising investments. The advertising "tax" may be the price the consumer pays for his own interest in innovation, which, at the same time, advertising stimulates.

Allocating the budget

A shift in advertising strategy almost always produces an increase in sales. When an advertiser switches from one combination or mix of media to a radically different one, his sales usually get a shot in the arm. But the immediate effect of such a policy is generally short lived and sales quickly resume their former position or else dip lower.

Why does a change of media add to sales in the first place? The answer might well be that the advertiser is benefiting *both* from the delayed impact his messages had on the audience he reached with his former media schedule and *also* from the effect of his new campaign on people he previously wasn't reaching. As his new media strategy continues, the effect of his earlier media mix becomes more and more tenuous and finally dies out altogether, at which time the effect of the new campaign begins to take over.

A number of case histories from the Milwaukee Advertising Laboratory document the notion that when advertising strategy changes, the resulting effects diminish over time.[19] In one instance, an experimental increase in advertising produced a proportionately much sharper increase in sales, but a subsequent further increase in advertising was accompanied by a drop in sales. And when advertising was maintained at this level, the sales curve returned to a point only slightly above the level at which the experimentation began. In yet another case, the advertiser varied

[18] *Television and Society,* New York: McGraw-Hill Book Company, 1965.
[19] G. Maxwell Ule, *op. cit.*

his media strategy but kept the same budget level. One strategy produced a steady gain in incremental sales over a twelve-week period, but in the subsequent twenty weeks there was no change in the margin of extra sales gained by this strategy over the other.

An analysis of expenditures in 1962 and 1963 shows that there is an annual turnover of about one out of every four national and regional advertisers in both newspapers and spot television and of about one advertiser in every five in network TV. This turnover represents leaving a major medium *altogether* and usually reflects an important shift in advertising policy, without an important change in budget.

Some years ago I analyzed the measurable media expenditures of ten leading U.S. advertisers over a three-year period. In the last year studied, these companies spent, in the aggregate (for all their products), $6\frac{1}{2}\%$ more than the previous year. One of them was spending 51% more and one was spending 12% less. This same wide range of variability is found when we compare the previous year's budgets with those of the year before, making the average rate of increase highly misleading.

When we go beyond these figures and examine the expenditures of these advertisers on individual media, we find even more striking variations. Here are just a few illustrations:

In one year, Company A's budget was up $1\frac{1}{2}\%$ — almost unchanged from the previous year. But it gave up a third of its budget to enter network TV. This meant that it virtually eliminated newspaper supplements and cut its budget for business publications by nearly half, its budget for newspapers by a fourth, and its budget for magazines by a fifth.

In the same year, Company B, already in network TV, decided to greatly increase its effort in that medium. But it did so by raising its total ad budget by 80%, so that TV, while drawing about the same proportional share, was actually getting much more money. It put substantially more effort into newspapers, but raised magazines only slightly, so that their share was nearly 30% less than before. The next year the company cut its advertising slightly, but at the expense of print media, actually raising its share for TV.

Company C raised its budget by 12%, but tripled its expenditures in newspapers, cut supplements by one-half and slashed its network TV commitments from 40% to 30%. The following year its ad volume went up 25%, but the budget for supplements increased fivefold, while the other media maintained about the same balance.

The scheduling of budgets within these media showed similar fluctuations. The last advertiser mentioned, Company C, sponsored or participated in six network television shows in one year. The following year it had thirteen, four of which were retained from the previous calendar year (this representing, in some cases, the same broadcast season). The next year it was back to seven shows, three of which had already been on the air, but only one of which it had sponsored two years previously.

Few competing brands spend their advertising media dollars in exactly the same proportions. This may be illustrated by taking the proportion of advertising expenditures devoted to a single medium — newspapers — among 1963's 100 leading advertisers. In the food field, the range was from 2.6% to 22.8%. In the soft drinks field, it was from 6.4% to 25.5%. In the gasoline field, the proportion varied between 5.4% and 40.4%.

It is apparent that companies with rather similar marketing objectives spend rather different proportions of their available budgets on advertising and distribute their advertising dollars according to different strategies. Yet it is unusual to find a product category in which they use *radically* different mixes of media. Regardless of whether or not they end up with the same media mix, most advertisers appear to operate under rather similar assumptions in devising their strategy for the same product.[20]

Generalizations *are* possible: automotive advertisers rely very heavily on "personality-type" television shows, large newspaper advertisements, and prestige-building color ads in magazines. Many food advertisers use magazine color heavily for appetite appeal and service suggestions. They use TV to show how easy it is to prepare their products and how grateful the children and the husband are to the housewife. Detergent and soap advertisers make strong use of spot and participation strips in daytime TV. Appliance and tire advertisers rely heavily on cooperative dealer-placed advertising in the newspaper, along with network TV (for product demonstration) and magazines.

How drastically can a company change its advertising strategy? It is usually held in check by counterpressures to stay in line with what its main competitors are doing, both in the over-all level of advertising expenditures and in the choice of media. Competitors must contend with similar problems in allocating their promotional expenses. In evaluating media capabilities, competitors and their agencies are apt to start from similar premises and make comparable judgments.

[20] This was vividly illustrated in a program organized at my suggestion for the 1956 meeting of the Eastern Division of the American Association of Advertising Agencies. A marketing problem was set forth for a group of four well-known media directors. All of them were given the facts in the case and asked to prepare a media plan. While the four plans differed in detail, they were highly similar in the selection of media and in the outline of the suggested schedule. A repetition of the same project at a subsequent meeting a few years later produced very similar results for a different product.

If an advertiser keeps his media schedule in a constant state of ferment, should he not benefit by the constant change in his audiences? He would probably run a new danger of confusing people by the rapid shifts of messages and creative techniques. His various campaigns might only confound and contradict each other in the consumer's mind.

In advertising, as in every other aspect of business, there are cautious companies and companies that are willing to take risks; there are followers and leaders; there are operating styles which are consistent and others which are quixotic. At the point when all corporations proceed from the exact same premises in determining how much advertising money to spend and where, there will no longer be any reason to advertise.

ADVERTISING STRATEGISTS IN ACTION

The businessman is apt to be concerned with the over-all effectiveness of advertising before he turns his attention to the detailed questions of advertising strategy. To the extent that he is called on to review particular advertising recommendations, he probably thinks first of all in terms of his rather general opinions about the media which the advertising agency recommends and next in terms of the broad question of what to say about his product and how to say it: sales appeals and themes, copy, layouts, the choice of models or broadcast personalities. He seldom grapples with the tricky problems of how to buy and distribute his units of advertising in any given medium.

When businessmen evaluate media, they are inclined to make three common errors:

1 They don't pay enough attention to the *quality* of communication through each medium.

2 They exaggerate the intensity of the public's experience of the mass media.

3 They assume that advertising comes through at a level of interest and emotion which is somehow comparable with the information or entertainment content which audiences seek in a medium.

Media decisions are often made on the basis of cliché judgments. Each medium is typically considered to be endowed with certain characteristics in its manner of communicating: radio is thought of as a companion, TV as a device for demonstration, newspapers as a way of making announcements, general magazines as colorful showcases.   Such generalities are then, for simplicity's sake, applied as though they operated across the board.

Actually, each medium provides an enormous number of subvarieties of media experience.   Each encompasses many vehicles, and every vehicle evokes different kinds of audience response under different circumstances.   Finally, different segments of society typically use media in different ways.

Impressing the dealers

Any advertiser is subject to pressure from his own organization and dealers as well as from rival media whenever he departs from the conventional media strategy of his product field.   One of the perennial bugaboos in the advertising business is the notion that dealers or distributors insist on a certain type of advertising media strategy.   Their opinions on this subject are generally supposed to be based on "mother-in-law" surveys, or on their own media habits which they naively identify with those of the average man.   According to this theory, national advertisers must use the particular mix of media which their dealers approve and demand.

Both the individual chain-supermarket manager and the chain buying committee are generally impressed by the weight of advertising and promotion behind a product; they consider this when one or the other is deciding whether to stock a product and how much shelf space to give it.   But no grocery retailer can possibly keep in mind the full array of advertising plans which backstop all the competitive products he sells. In spite of this, many advertising campaigns are run to conform with the real or imagined specifications of dealers.   Thus the advertising objective is to assure optimum distribution or display rather than to sell to the consumer directly.

Underlying the faith of many national advertisers in the dealer's judgment is the assumption that somehow the retail merchant is in the best possible position to judge the effect of a specific advertising campaign. The principle behind this is that the dealer is close to the "true" results; his satisfaction with a campaign is determined by the jingle of the cash register as the contented customers respond to successful advertising strategy. In point of fact, most retailers are actually just as uncertain about the sales effects of specific ads and campaigns as manufacturers are.

The advertiser's concern with the sensibilities of distributors and dealers may be based on the common notion that the merchant is an active student of the advertising for the brands he sells. Clearly, such a notion is erroneous in the case of the storekeeper or store manager with thousands of branded articles for sale. But it is even untrue in the one industry where the relation between retailer and manufacturer is closest and exclusive. In a study of 785 car dealers conducted in 1959 by the Bureau of Advertising,[1] only 7% were able to answer the question, "Do you know the approximate breakdown of the factory advertising budget for newspapers, magazines, television, radio, outdoor, direct mail?"

In spite of this widespread ignorance of how their factory's advertising was distributed, three out of five dealers reported that the factory's use of the media was "about right." There were only small differences in this proportion between the dealers who knew how the factory was advertising and those who did not. This is in keeping with what many studies in other fields have shown to be the tendency of most people to believe that those whom they accept as authorities are making the right decisions and doing their jobs well.

Who decides?

Advertising decision-makers at any level of authority do not represent a cross-section of the consuming public they set out to persuade. They are geographically concentrated in a few big centers (47% of all U.S. agency billings are placed in New York, 15% in Chicago, 7% in Detroit, 4% in Los Angeles). They are above average in income and education. Their media habits are atypical. For one thing, they are far less avid viewers of television than the general public. A survey of 513 advertising executives made by the Psychological Corporation in 1965 found that average viewing time on the day prior to the interview was one hour

[1] Reported by Frank E. Orenstein, "Are Automobile Dealers Good Judges of Media Allocations?" *Journal of Marketing.* Vol. 26, No. 1, January 1962, pp. 76-78.

and a quarter, exactly half that of the average person, according to national television viewing surveys.

It is obvious that while the advertising decision-maker may be a conscientious student of the media, he is not an ordinary reader, listener, or viewer. This makes it all the harder for his own subjective judgments to be dissociated from his sober professional ones.

How is the advertising decision of how much to spend and where made in actual practice? This question can provoke highly contradictory answers within the same organization. There is a wide gap between official procedure and actual practice both in companies and agencies. There is also often considerable disagreement among people holding various functions and titles regarding the importance of the roles they play.

Periodically one or the other of the advertising trade publications surveys executives in companies and agencies to find out who is involved in advertising decisions. Invariably there are discrepancies among the reports given by different individuals within the same organization and between the agency on the one hand and the client on the other. These discrepancies reflect more than mere differences in viewpoint; they also reflect the fact that different individuals and departments have key roles to play at different *points* in the decision-making process.

David Stewart, president of Kenyon & Eckhardt, analyzed the progress of a media recommendation made to a national advertiser and found that "counting agency and client executives, the recommendation had to pass through 54 different hands." [2]

A mail survey made by the *Gallagher Report* in early 1964 found that in consumer goods companies, the president had to approve the advertising budget in 72% of the cases. (By contrast, the proportion of presidential approvals in the case of industrial advertisers was 56%.) In 32% of the consumer companies, approval was required from the executive vice president, in 20% by the sales vice president or director, in 16% by the board of directors, and in 12% by the treasurer or comptroller. The advertising vice president or director was the arbiter in only 10% of the companies and the marketing vice president in 10%.

A similar survey conducted at about the same time by *Sales Management*[3] concluded that a company's top marketing executive is generally charged with final responsibility for advertising plans. This suggests that presidential approval may be little more than a rubber stamp in

[2] "Stewart Deplores Bureaucracy That Entangles Ad Programs," *Printers' Ink*, October 2, 1964, p. 9.
[3] "Controlling the Advertising Function," *Sales Management*, July 3, 1964, pp. 69-92.

many cases.   The marketing chief, *Sales Management* pointed out, does not always carry the word "marketing" in his title.

Advertising planning in different product fields ranges from the orderly to the disorderly.   This variation reflects whether or not the business is subject to fluctuations resulting from product innovation or from competitive promotion, merchandising, or other sales activity.

A business whose sales are relatively even and stable from year to year, like the oil business, is able to lay out its plans well ahead of time. The toiletries business, in which companies must respond quickly to competitive product introductions, may experience radical shifts of advertising strategy within short spans of time.

Big advertisers like Procter and Gamble and General Motors generally have strong ideas about how their very large advertising investments should be made.   They have a corporate philosophy about media and how they are to be used.   They generally have a corporate policy regarding media concepts, and about research concepts and techniques as well.

An advertiser like GM or P & G is bound to be a major account, if not *the* major account, for every agency on its list.   In 1965, GM's nine U.S. agencies billed over $830 million.   Procter and Gamble's eleven U.S. agencies (all but one different from GM's) billed over $1.280 million that year.   (Even when an agency has only a minor product, or modest billings from such a big advertiser, it always lives in hope of more, of showing the client what a great job it can do.)

This often means that the practices and preferences of the big advertiser may be adopted as standard operating procedure or as the preferred services of all their agencies.   Once adopted, or once the investment has been made to use a certain service on The Big Account, it is not surprising to find further use being made of it on *all* the agency's accounts. Thus the leverage exerted by the large advertiser is even greater than it might at first appear to be.

The print media are most flexible from an advertiser's standpoint in that they are comparatively easy to get into and out of on short notice. Paradoxically, this very quality makes them a more stable component in the decision-making process than is often the case with network television programming.

The use of available TV program or time positions may be presented to a company for a last-minute rapid decision (with little or no preparation or prior analysis) as part of a complicated web of negotiating relationships among the agency (which may have its own active television department and wide array of accounts), the "package producer" of the entertainment, and the network.

A new show is commonly sold on the basis of a pilot film (or sometimes even a mere outline of intention), and agency and advertiser may be under pressure to move fast before the big opportunity is snapped up by someone else. The network is motivated less by its aspirations for any particular program than by its desire to maintain a large and stable audience from segment to segment of the evening lineup.

The extent to which top company management itself becomes involved in the advertising media decision depends upon the importance of advertising within the total corporate budget. There are few companies indeed where top management does not make at least an over-all review of the allocation of advertising strategy by media budgets. But there are many companies where decisions made by the advertising department are, for all practical purposes, final and where the corporate management merely exercises a formal approval or veto power.

In still other companies, particularly those dominated by a single strong personality, the head of the firm may interject himself into even the most picayune details of the media scheduling or creative strategy in an advertising campaign. His influence may be felt in television programming, even extending to the question of what quiz show contestants should win or lose.[4]

There is also great variation in the respective importance of the agency and of the company's own advertising and sales departments. In some instances, advertising strategy is set by the company down to the finest point of media selection and schedule-building; the agency merely executes the orders. In other cases, the agency may function as the company's advertising department, or a company department may exist merely to review and approve plans worked out in detail by the agency.

Between these extremes is the pattern of give and take which characterizes most agency-client relations. The client comes up with a general statement of direction he wants to pursue; the agency implements these informal directives by preparing a media proposal as part of an over-all advertising plan. This in turn the company's advertising department scrutinizes and modifies in a manner which may range from authoritarianism to democratic partnership.

The different ways in which agencies function in part reflect variations in the status of the corporate advertising director. In many instances, the agency principals have a close personal relationship with the management of the client company. They are accepted as equals and confidants. Where there is such a close relationship, the corporate advertising director may be regarded almost as a clerk, as someone who

[1] *Cf*. Robert Foreman, *The Hot Half Hour*, New York: Criterion Books, Inc., 1958, for an entertaining portrayal of this phenomenon in the thin guise of fiction.

attends essentially to details and deals with his opposite number in the agency, the account man. In such a situation, the latter is also likely to be a person of subordinate status.

In other cases, the advertising director wields real life-and-death power over the agency. The same little drama is played out lower on the scale of power, between the account executive and the advertising director, with the higher-ups maintaining a detachment which reflects disinterest or snobbery or both.

Within the corporate structure, the advertising department may be an autonomous operation with considerable prestige and authority, reporting directly to top management. Or it may be one of a number of subsidiary staff functions reporting to a general marketing or sales management which exercises strong professional control over advertising plans.

Many big companies today use the brand-manager system in which a single marketing executive heads up all aspects of planning a brand's production, sales, and promotion as though he were running his own little business. In such a setup, the advertising department may be merely a coordinating, liaison, and contact operation. The actual decisions in this instance are made by the brand manager, who looks on advertising as merely one of a whole panoply of tools with which he works (including merchandising, promotion, pricing, packaging, and display). To the extent that the brand manager is responsible for the advertising budget and advertising strategy for his brands, the advertising department is reduced in status from a strategy-making unit to a service arm.

Where a strong sales management views advertising primarily as a weapon to support the sales force, the allocation of advertising budgets may be largely determined by the definition of sales districts and by the varying nature of dealer or distributor demand.

Within the advertising agency, there are also variations in the division of responsibility between the account group and the specialized departments which may have a voice in the major decisions. In a large agency, an associate media director works closely with the account group in preparing media strategy. His recommendations may or may not be significant in the over-all determination of how the advertising budget should be divided.

There is always give and take between the account group and the media department, just as there is between the client's advertising department and the agency. Plans are usually discussed informally before they are officially presented.

Almost always a precedent exists in previous practice as a start-

ing point for media strategy. By and large, the account group sets the
broad dimensions for budget allocations by media, but it does so within
the limits described by the media department as realistic requirements
for each medium to be used with the desired weight and coverage. Once
the general outlines have been set, it is the function of specialists within
the media department to prepare detailed plans and estimates based on
specific media vehicles, the frequency of ads or commercials, and the size
units to be employed. A major fixed budgetary commitment to a single
medium like a network television show or a monthly ad in a magazine
may set restrictions on the way in which other media can be used.

Negotiation of TV programming arrangements falls under the
jurisdiction of the media director in some agencies, while in others it
comes under a separate television department which also has charge of
talent and production management. Needless to say, the Television
Department, whose job it is to ferret out promising program ideas, may
exercise strong influence on over-all media planning within the agency,
for it represents the agency's coveted link to show business.

The changing media man

A striking transformation has taken place in the agency media function
since the early post-war years. Fifteen or twenty years ago the media
department was made up of people who might be classified as either
"bookkeepers" or "diplomats." The former kept the files on rates, circulation, and other statistics and used them to work out estimates on
schedules pretty much specified by the account groups. The "diplomats"
were the media relations people whose job it was to listen patiently to
competitive sales pitches and, when the time came, to wangle an ad into
a far-forward position or a commercial into a better time slot.

Today there is a new breed of media specialist who sees himself as
a marketing man. His planning starts with the consumer product his
client is trying to sell and not with the media products his agency is
going to buy.

There are a number of reasons for the New Look in agency media
departments:

1 The internal complexity of the advertising business has grown
   to vast proportions. The job of riding herd on media practices
   and innovations can be handled by nothing less than an agency's
   best minds.

2 Since the war, research has grown several times as fast as advertising billings. There is a vast new reservoir of knowledge about products, consumers, communications, and audiences. To be intelligently used, these data require a new kind of specialized know-how, skill, and training.

3 The computer has emerged as a major influence on decision-making, not so much because it has forced new kinds of decisions as because it has demanded a new discipline on the part of the decision-makers. It has attracted a different kind of technician to the agency media department and has stimulated a whole new wave of technical training.

4 Today it is generally understood that no area of advertising is an island unto itself. The new kind of media specialist must be an advertising generalist who understands consumer motivations, merchandising tactics, and principles of copy and layout. Just as an ad communicates through its total content — copy theme, illustration, and headline — so the kind of schedule a budget buys within a medium cannot be separated from the decision about what to put in the space or on the air. And what goes into an ad or commercial cannot be divorced from its size or length. So the media man has to think in terms of the total advertising plan.

The researcher is a natural ally for the media planner.[5] He turns to him for the data he needs to help him arrive at his more sober judgments and to justify and rationalize his more subjective ones. To many advertisers, in fact, the distinction between the media planner and the market researcher is not altogether clear; in many smaller agencies both hats are worn on the same head.

Among the innumerable petty civil wars of jurisdiction which rage intermittently in every advertising agency, the struggle over media research is an old one. Some large agencies place this function in the media department, others in research; still others give it a separate and independent status altogether. The skill most commonly associated with media research is statistics, for the media analyst's principal task has always been to estimate numbers that do not exist out of numbers that do: the duplication of audiences, the turnover of viewers from one

---

[5] By contrast, a natural enmity pervades the relation of researcher and creative man, but it exists almost entirely on the side of the latter. As for the researcher, it is the creative man's output, laboriously ground out or spun of sudden inspiration, on which he is called to pass his objective judgment. He bears the creative man no grudge. In fact, he may secretly sympathize with the writer's impatience at literal interpretations of his ratings or scores, for he knows that these are the weapons which account men use to defend and rationalize their own plans and convictions when they present them to the client.

program to the next, the reach of a schedule of different magazines over a cycle of weeks or months.

To be sure, the analyst can prepare such estimates only if he knows how to distinguish good numbers from bad ones, so he has always been (more or less in individual cases) a methodologist probing and passing judgment on the studies made by the media for their own selfish purposes.

The media planner has traditionally made use of only a small part of the research spectrum. He is unlikely to be much of a psychologist. This is a serious deficiency, since more and more his job entails passing judgments on the comparative communications capabilities of different media, different vehicles, and different units of space or time. He has dealt primarily in the statistics on media costs, circulation, and audiences. For years, circulation data were looked at in relation to the coverage of households in cities and counties. Audience data were dealt with in aggregates rather than in terms of their component parts. As more and better information became available on the different characteristics of consumer markets and media audiences, the media planner's job expanded beyond the task of maximizing coverage and cost efficiency. It became one of matching media and markets. Broadcasting, with its volatile, constantly shifting public, made him concerned with the duplication of media vehicles and with the accumulation of audiences. In all these assignments the media planner relied on the help of the survey technician, the statistician, and the marketing expert. Rarely, if at all, did he feel the need to call in the psychologists for help.

This changed, to a degree, in the era of motivation research. The media themselves, like advertisers and agencies, called in psychoanalytically oriented psychologists to explain the attraction their products had for the ultimate consumer. Some of these projects were undertaken for reasons of internal planning by the media operators; in this category were Herta Herzog's classic studies of the daytime serial [6] and the Professor Quiz show,[7] and also the extensive efforts by CBS, under Frank Stanton's leadership as research director, to find out how various programs worked, and the roots of their audience appeals. Only a few years later, when W. Lloyd Warner was commissioned to study the daytime serial,[8] the intention was to discover a way of explaining to advertisers that soap operas were *good* for the housewife — that they lessened her

---

[6] "On Borrowed Experience," *Studies in Philosophy and Social Science*, Vol. IX, 1941, pp. 65-94.
[7] "Why People Like the Professor Quiz Program," in Paul F. Lazarsfeld, *Radio and the Printed Page*, New York: Duell, Sloan and Pearce, 1940.
[8] W. Lloyd Warner and William E. Henry, "The Radio Daytime Serial: A Symbolic Analysis," *Genetic Psychology Monographs*, Vol. XXXVII, 1948, pp. 3-71.

anxieties and taught her to cope with her daily lot. By inference, advertising on such programs would be respectable and wholesome.

Continuing in the tradition of qualitative media research, Burleigh Gardner did a series of studies for MacFadden Publications which documented the helpful, prestigious role of *True Story* and its sister magazines in providing readers with models of proper behavior. The lowly confession books could now be seen by the advertiser in a new and warmer light, as the blue-collar housewife's indispensable guide and companion.[9] Gardner did a study for *Good Housekeeping*[10] in 1956 which had a similar objective. It demonstrated to the advertising planner a dimension of readership which ordinarily had to be conveyed over martinis by a space salesman: the emotional feeling that readers had for a publication, its meaning in their lives, their confidence in it, its editorial vitality.

But studies of this kind were early casualties as motivation research retreated from the scene. They were replaced by the more familiar, conventional, and hence more comfortable compilation of statistics on audience size and composition just as suitable to the new jet-age all-purpose plans of electronic data processing as it had been to the pencil and paper calculation of readers per dollar in an earlier era.

For years, marketing research was dominated by a concern with what has always been the principal task of field intelligence — the collection and ordering of data. This descriptive tradition took a considerable buffeting with the advent of social scientists in advertising, for they took the position that the numbers one collected on the facts of marketing life were less important than the analytical interpretation of those numbers. The arrival of the computer was greeted with jubilant cries from the nose-counters. Operations research (O.R.) had, in their view, the merit of being based on numbers, and it arrived on the scene with impressive credentials: a mathematics unfamiliar to most marketers and hardware so expensive that no one who had invested in it could afford to deny its authority. As advertising research developed in the computer era, it produced ever more descriptive, ever more up-to-date compilations and recompilations of similar data. Media research studies were produced essentially to provide raw material for the agency's statisticians. The humanistically oriented social scientists and clinical psychologists faded from center stage and the model-builders took over.

---

[9] *The Meaning and Function of True Story for Its Readers*, Chicago: Social Research, Inc., 1955.
[10] *The Meaning of Good Housekeeping and Its Advertising to Its Readers*, Chicago: Social Research, Inc., 1956.

In some of the largest agencies, media planners were actually far ahead of their counterparts in the research departments in mastering the new technology of the computer.[11]   Historically, the rapid acquisition of proprietary interest in electronic data processing on the part of media departments took place during the years when market and opinion researchers were floundering about, trying to debug their computer programs to make them more efficient than the conventional IBM machines. Initial experiences in the use of electronic data processing for attitude survey data were often disappointing.   Thus the first major applications of computers tended to be achieved not by agency researchers but by their better-heeled counterparts in the corporations, whose work with large masses of sales records lent itself to more straightforward techniques of mathematical analysis.

While the media planner has become more of a figures man than he used to be and these days may even be thought of as one of the Big Brains of his agency, his day-to-day job continues to require cunning, good judgment, and intimate acquaintance with the devious ways of organizations and individuals who can help him get things done.

Media sellers and buyers

The world of media buying and selling is governed by strong interpersonal relationships, just like the relations of agency and client.   Buyers like some media representatives and dislike others, and few people have enough insight to know when their presumably objective judgments are influenced by this fact.

Even in the computer era, the media planner must spend a part of his time holding court, like a medieval baron, for the troops of salesmen who fill his reception room.   They call him to offer new statistics, presentations, research reports, creative suggestions, demonstrations, cocktails, lunches, good fellowship, and all other possible forms of persuasion and influence.

In some quarters of the advertising business, a media sales presentation is met with resistance, or even resentment.   Most advertising prac-

---

[11] As will be described in Chapter 12, computers entered the agency via accounting and billing, an area closely allied to the media department and in some cases under its direct control.   The automated handling of media accounts opened the way for media cost estimating by computer.   This relatively simple operation ate into one of the traditional tasks assigned to media department manpower and in a number of instances caused the estimating function to be shifted from media to accounting. From computer cost estimating for different schedules there was only a small step to computer comparison of value received in terms of reach, frequency, and other criteria.

titioners, particularly media specialists in agencies, assume that they already know the qualifications and characteristics of the various media.

However, no intelligent media planner ever refuses to see a media salesman or representative. These men are occasionally the purveyors of information that can be directly applied to the marketing problems of an account. In every campaign, the buyer runs into highly varying standards of performance from every medium he uses. He never knows when he will next be involved in negotiations over rates, position, timing, exclusivity, or compensation for some dereliction of quality control. On such occasions, it is the media salesman who is the buyer's friend in court, who must plead his case with his own superiors or production people. It is to the salesman that he must go for help and service on matters that sometimes have no bearing at all on the use of his medium.

Media salesmen are the honeybees of the advertising world; they get around from agency to agency and from one dukedom to another within the big, sprawling, impersonal agency empires. They help people find jobs and they provide invaluable reports and rumors of competitors' activities. They carry tidbits of personal gossip on the impending moves of accounts and individuals, tidbits which give the lowliest agency man a sense of having his ear attuned to the most powerful forces in the world.

This particular function both stems from and feeds the illusion that advertising is just one big happy family business. Partly this is in the good old American tradition of Kiwanis, Elkdom, and Odd Fellowship. Partly it reflects the high rate of job mobility among advertising people which gives them a broad acquaintance. And partly it reflects the first-naming which is almost universal in American marketing. The man with whom I once shook hands at a brief meeting is forever Jim to me. The junior account executive who is called Joe by the president of the agency responds by calling him Bill. This makes the trade gossip about Jim or Bill *personal* gossip, involving my own acquaintances, my *friends!*

Media presentations are commonly made at group luncheons. Those on the receiving end are presumably lulled into a state of euphoric acquiescence by the libations which traditionally precede the first spoken word. The canny media man listens and applauds politely and customarily withholds all judgment until he or his "research expert" has had a chance to study the "leave-behind" booklet which sets down in writing everything that was said in the presentation itself.

For the media director who is really in the big time and gets involved in television programming decisions, the glamorous atmosphere of show business may present even greater enticements. Media strategy has been changed as much in the swimming pools of Beverly Hills as in the counting houses of Madison Avenue. (The networks and package producers have long ago learned to include the client's advertising specialists in this part of the act!)

Decisions, reasonable and unreasonable

How much are advertising decisions swayed by emotion rather than by evidence? One could have quite an argument defining emotion and evidence in this connection. It is not surprising that a large part of the research that is done for any medium is designed to demonstrate its virtues rather than its limitations. But the media themselves are not alone in using facts selectively. A substantial part of the workload of any agency media research department has always been to marshal data to support a strategic decision already made on intuition. And much of marketing research generally, including the studies made by large corporations, has the hidden or acknowledged aim of proving somebody in management right — or wrong!

A well-known broadcasting and show business personality was a leading stockholder in a major drug firm, going back to the early days of his relation with the company's current management. Long after his program had lost much of its audience and had ceased to be an efficient buy, it represented a major advertising commitment for the drug corporation.

The television schedule for a major appliance concern was set up to include all cities in which the company had manufacturing plants and in which principal distributors were located. This was true even though the schedule was otherwise set up to cover a limited number of markets, and even though the cities in question rated low in relation to others on the list.

E. Lawrence Deckinger recalls that while he was at the Biow Company he conducted some research for a client which suggested that certain ads would be better if the type were run at an angle. Later, during a meeting in the client's office, the firm's fabled president sat calmly thumbing through a newspaper. All at once he came upon one of his ads with the type set at an angle. He turned purple. "What's this?" he demanded, starting up. Hurriedly it was explained to him that research had been done which demonstrated that the type should be displayed at an angle. "——— the research!" the president shot back, "I want it straight!" Thereafter, "straight" it was.

The client's wife has long symbolized irrationality in media decision-making. No one in the agency business is without his own stories about her, or about her equally terrible spouse (he is the one who used to oppose TV advertising on Sunday afternoon because everyone is out at the polo matches at that time). I know of one such wife who had an aversion to a certain national magazine which, folded in its brown wrapper, she always confused with one of her favorites and then was disappointed when she opened it. She was married to a top executive in a major firm. Although the company was a wide user of magazines, this publication was never included in any of its media lists.

The wife of yet another executive, this one in a giant automotive firm, was particularly fond of Dalmatians (dogs, not people). The order went out to include such an animal in all future truck ads. One day the boss was asked to approve a double-page, four-color spread which showed the heavy-duty line of trucks engaged in heavy construction work in a sand-pit setting. It was a very busy ad, trucks coming and going, a flagman directing traffic, and so forth. The executive took one look and said "N.G." "Why?" cried the ad man. "No Dalmatian," said the client. "My wife will kill me."

In another little-known incident, the copy chief and art director of an agency spent sixteen sleepless hours polishing up the agency's recommended fall campaign for a client meeting. After a two-hour presentation, replete with comps (ads ready for the engraver), finished copy, and media programs, the president leaned back, reached in his jacket pocket, and pulled out a piece of paper. "Here's a little thing my wife happened to scribble down last night," he said to the shocked agency group. "Now for a layout." He proceeded to draw some lines on a yellow pad, and concluded the meeting by saying, "Here's how it should look." The agency had to go along with his wife's copy and his layout.[12]

All three of these stories are not really about wives, of course, but about the irrational element in business decisions, which occurs in realms other than advertising. Why does the agency generally go along with the client's decisions even when the client seems to be out of his mind? The answer may have been supplied by Bill Day, a former plans board chairman at J. Walter Thompson, who once proclaimed, "I'll never sacrifice my principles on the altar of poverty." [13]

[12] David North supplied me with this story.
[13] This profound remark is recalled by Sidney Dean.

PERSUASION AND THE MARKETING PLAN 4

A great deal of confusion and error always result when people are asked to report where they saw or heard a particular advertisement, no matter how vividly they remember the words of the message or the pictures associated with it.   This very disregard for the media involved well serves the advertiser's purpose, which is to give his product unique over-tones of meaning, rather than to connect a particular slogan or sales argument with a certain media environment.   However, it often leads to distortions in the popular view of advertising.

Motivation research revisited

When advertising is discussed by people who are not themselves involved in the buying, selling, or creating of ads, the talk usually centers on an ad's content, rather than the medium through which it is presented.   The tendency is to focus on the strategy of what to say rather than of the strategy of when, where, and to whom to say it.   Most popular books on advertising reflect this emphasis on consumer motives and how to play on them in copy.

In recent years the layman has been told to equate advertising psychology with a subversion of the public will.   This evokes an image of experts armed with mysterious weapons to probe the mind of the consumer.   After first opening his unconscious weaknesses to the cunning manipulations of "hidden persuaders" who prey on secret fears and fantasies, the advertisers then sell him what he does not need and does not really even want.   This view of advertising psychology has attained such wide currency that it may now be taken to represent an integral part of the public view of both advertising and psychology.

Vance Packard, in his best-selling book,[1] sees motivation research as a kind of occult practice, the secret of whose very existence is *hidden* from the consumer.   Moreover, he seems quite convinced that this research, once accomplished, provides the advertiser with magically irresistible powers of *persuasiveness*, and even *control*, over the public mind.

Packard sees us heading into "the chilling world of George Orwell and his Big Brother."   The public is being "treated like Pavlov's conditioned dogs."   "Nothing is immune or sacred. . . .   [A] Chicago ad agency has used psychiatric probing techniques on little girls."

Much of the evidence Packard cites for this resolves into a series of clichés — the by-now classic examples which have long been a familiar part of the literature on consumer behavior.   There is our old friend from Chicago, Mrs. Middle Majority; there is the lazy housewife who uses instant coffee, and her daughter who washes her face to be attractive rather than clean.

The man in the Hathaway shirt and the tattooed man with the Marlboro cigarette are both presented as creatures of the Hidden Persuaders, even though there is no suggestion that they were the products of motivation study rather than advertising inventiveness.

To provide an eyepatch for the man in the Hathaway shirt is inspiration, but it may also be inspiration that leads a researcher to suggest that baking a cake is comparable to having a baby, or that the convertible is to the sedan as the mistress is to the wife.   Both are imaginative and provocative ideas, but both arise from psychological insight or psychological theory, rather than from research.   There are some practitioners who are remarkably skillful at sparking such ideas but who are less

---

[1] *The Hidden Persuaders*, New York: David McKay Company, 1957.   My comments on Packard and Dichter were embodied in reviews of their books that appeared originally in *Management Review*.

concerned with the unglamorous task of putting them to the test of evidence.

In reciting his case histories, Packard draws no distinction between marketing decisions based on research and others which simply reflect creative ingenuity. He offers the following example:[2]

> An Indiana supermarket operator nationally recognized for his advanced psychological techniques told me he once sold a half ton of cheese in a few hours, just by getting an enormous half-ton wheel of cheese and inviting customers to nibble slivers and cut off their own chunks for purchase. They could have their chunk free if they could guess its weight within an ounce. The mere massiveness of the cheese, he believes, was a powerful influence in making the sales.

To Packard's readers this represented psychiatric depth probing, Big Brother, and Pavlov's dogs, but maybe it was nothing more than smart cheese merchandising! Packard appears to believe that it is dangerous and immoral for manufacturers with goods to sell to employ the services of experts who can help them do an effective job. The reader may be somewhat perplexed at this point. Should advertisers *not* try to do a good job? It is hard to see how they could fail to take advantage of the twentieth century's improved understanding of human behavior. To ask today's advertising man to leave psychology out of his ads is like asking him to dispense with photography or with the rules of good layout and design.

In a competitive economy, researchers, like advertising people and businessmen, work for different ends. They are not in conspiracy, though Packard comes close to suggesting that they are. (He even raises the question, "Were some of the resolutely mediocre shows on television that way by design, to increase the impact of the commercials?")

The real job of persuasion rests with the experts in the arts of persuasion. Research does not write copy, redesign packages, or change distribution methods. However, more intelligent decisions on how to persuade may be made with an understanding of consumer motivations, as well as with knowledge of the basic facts about who and where the customers are.

Many of the research reports of the motivation era were brilliant essays, in which assertions and psychological insights of varying plausibility or validity were woven together in a tissue of supporting quotations from the words of interviewed consumers. At their not-so-best, the reports represented a distillation of what went on in the mind of the analyst rather than a synthesis of the data actually collected. The more

[2] *Ibid.*, p. 110.

flamboyant practitioners of "motivation research" did nothing to discourage the myth that there is only one door to the study of buying motives, and only a handful of keys. As shrewd businessmen, they were enchanted by the idea that they were shamans endowed with otherworldly knowledge of the secret workings of the mass mind. After all, with this magical gift, their patrons could mold and control the popular passion to consume.

The most authoritative defense of motivation research, written by one of its best-known practitioners, Ernest Dichter,[3] did not take issue directly with Packard's charges, but dealt more with attacks from another quarter.

The keystone of Dichter's methodological argument is that "each individual represents a motivational universe. . . . To record scientifically how the population is motivated with respect to a specific phenomenon, we must fully understand why each individual as a member of this group behaves the way he does."

But our understanding of one individual's motivation has to be based on principles of behavior that can only be deduced from the systematic study of large populations. To be systematic, some kind of counting is called for, and then there is no choice but to obey the rules of good statistical practice.

Dichter does confront one of Packard's criticisms when he says: "A knife has no morality of its own. Making it sharper thus does not make it more or less immoral. Persuasion techniques are like sharpened knives. They are tools. Of course, the wielder of the tool *has* to have moral standards. As long as they are, however, only borrowed from a given culture or political system, they are relative."

Apart from the fact that this statement might be considered theologically suspect, it fails to take account of the fact that the design of a tool reflects the end for which it is intended. A butcher knife and a butter knife are both specialized instruments whose structures reflect distinctly different purposes. A wide range of instruments is available, and no one has a monopoly on their use or improvement.

Fortunately, or perhaps unfortunately, the secrets, such as they are, of research were and are readily accessible to all who will pay for them. Qualitative research methods had an established place in the armory of social scientists long before they were adapted, glamorized, and publicized by the motivation researchers of the 40's and 50's. The special advantages won by the firm which was first to apply imaginative new research techniques were quickly lost as competitors hired equally

[3] *The Strategy of Desire*, New York: Doubleday & Company, Inc., 1960.

competent consumer psychologists (or often the same ones) to unlock the mysteries on their behalf.

In its heyday the concept of consumer motivation was sometimes broadly applied. The psychologist Herbert Kay refers to an advertising agency research report which included a "motivation type question" which read as follows: "Why do you use this product occasionally?" The most commonly given answer was "because I don't like this product," and the next was "because I just use it occasionally."[4]

Consumer psychology and the making of ads

Motivation research has had some very striking personalities as its spokesmen. They brought the social sciences and social theory into marketing research and gave everyday currency in the realms of business management to terms and concepts which were ignored or disdained by the first generation of market survey technicians.

The market research pioneers of the 20's and 30's were essentially business statisticians who collected consumer data through sampling surveys as an afterthought to their sales and distribution analyses. They were largely preoccupied with the description of the market rather than with an understanding of the forces within it.

This emphasis on description reflected the defensiveness of these early practitioners. They had to protect their discipline from the know-nothing school of hard-boiled business judgment characteristically suspicious of the egg-head in a world where know-how comes from direct exposure to field conditions, impatient with long-winded discussions of method and concerned with conclusions rather than with how they were derived.

The early market researcher was strongly concerned with methodology; the doubts of the know-nothings required that he keep justifying himself by proving that his findings really were valid, that he really could generalize from a few thousand interviews to the buying habits of a whole population. He had to concentrate on producing descriptive data which looked hard and accurate.

Along with the statisticians, occasional psychologists drifted or were pulled into market research. Some, like Daniel Starch and George Gallup, bear names which have become household words (at least in the households of advertising men).

---

[4] Herbert Kay, "How To Get False Media Audience Figures Without Really Trying," address to the Media Research Directors Association, October 19, 1966, New York, N.Y.

The initial preoccupation of advertising psychologists was largely with the evaluation and testing of advertisements rather than with the systematic examination of consumers' "hidden desires."   The use of qualitative techniques of interviewing and data analysis, along with projective methods of psychological testing, did not become prevalent in advertising circles until after the upheaval of the war years.

The subsequent boom in the university output of clinical psychologists and applied social scientists brought into being a cadre of people with more eclectic views and greater tolerance for psychoanalytic theory than had been exhibited by the advertising psychologists of the pre-war period, who came out of a tradition of laboratory experimentation.

The flowering of motivation research during the late 40's and 50's, a period in which U.S. advertising investments doubled in a decade, represented an effort to achieve a mutual accommodation between science and art in advertising.

"Science" in this case was represented by the learned doctors who could speak with authority on why people rejected prunes or were psychologically "threatened" by Brand X's new slogan.

"Art" was represented by the creative people, the writers and art directors who instinctively felt (and feel) that the "Great Idea" is the secret of successful advertising.   In many cases they were (and are) convinced that the Great Idea would come to them more quickly and in purer form if not for the inhibiting interference of clients, account executives, media specialists, and factfinders telling them what to do.

For the "creative man" in advertising who judges ads or commercials according to whether or not they "send" him personally, motivation research was more readily acceptable than copy research that compared consumer reactions to different advertisements and told him, *after* he had knocked himself out, that his creations were good or bad.

Qualitative research methods carry their own special risks and dangers.   The interpretations which are given the data depend very much on the skill and talent of the individual analyst, and brilliant but idiosyncratic interpretations have been known to be just as brilliantly wrong in their implications for action as brilliantly right in their subtlety of insight.

According to Papert Koenig Lois' Arthur Wilkins, a leader in copy research, "If you have a lot of qualitative data about an ad that you know on good authority to be great, you will be ingenious enough to recognize, in the welter of diagnostic data at hand, the reasons why it was so great. But with the *same data* at hand, if you had been told on good authority that the commercial was a 'bomb,' you would see that material in a different light, and would emerge, I am sure, with a no less plausible analysis of the *weaknesses* of the advertising." [5]

The motivation researcher, when he functioned well, could play the part of a benign Muse, stimulating the writer to more exuberant efforts in the direction most persuasive to the consumer and most rewarding to the advertiser.

Sometimes the trained M.R. man can contribute deep psychoanalytical understanding which would never be apparent to a mere layman. I know, for example, of an agency group that worked on the account of a synthetic fibre used in tires. Since construction with this fibre eliminated the slight sag which some tires acquire when they remain in one position for a while, the creative department came up with the copy theme "No Morning Thump." The agency's learned motivation specialist vetoed this because of "negative sexual connotations"!

Motivation research has gone out of fashion, but is has not disappeared, by any means. It has merely gone underground, making significant contributions in the preliminary stages of developing conventional survey research plans. In the new era of operations research the efforts of advertising psychologists have in many cases been diverted from the study of product purchase motivations to the study of reactions to advertising itself.

There has been a fresh wave of interest in new systems of copy testing and concept testing (as the name suggests, this involves evaluating sales ideas before they are embodied in test ads). Imaginative use has been made of such gadgets as eye cameras, which measure pupil dilation, and psychogalvanometers, which measure skin conductivity. One instrument that acquired popularity in 1965 was a pedaling mechanism which the viewer must keep pressing if he doesn't want the test TV commercial he is watching to fade from view. (This interesting device was adapted from its original use with pigeons, who were offered more tangible rewards.)

The prevalence of psychological gadgetry rests on the assumption that while the worth of various advertising ideas can be compared, most of them cannot be evaluated by pure judgment or by instinct. The Great Idea is not likely to be in the sheaf of first sketches which the copywriter submits to his art director; in fact, it is not likely to be out there at all. The free-form consumer interview, qualitatively analyzed under the name of motivation research or under some other heading, remains a predictable source of inspiration for those who create advertisements.

[5] Unpublished communication.

Product familiarity as a goal of advertising

The advertiser must make his product acceptable before he can persuade the consumer to buy it. It can be acceptable only if it seems familiar. To "know" a product may be compared to "knowing" a personality; the single verb may cover a broad range of varied experiences. We may say we know someone who is not even a proper acquaintance because we can recognize and place him or can identify him by name, by his general position in life, or by some trait of character revealed to us through observation rather than interaction. And from there on we move through all the shades of mutual recognition, association, friendship, and intimacy.

We regard it as a commonplace that on some critical occasion we may discover in a loved individual — a spouse, child, parent, sibling, or close friend — characteristics, qualities, or defects that many years of close familiarity have not revealed to us.

Knowing someone is a continuous process. People whom we "knew" in the past are not necessarily among those whom we "know" today. People whom we know in certain well-defined roles or situations are not necessarily recognized, placed, or greeted when we see them out of context.

We feel we "know" political or entertainment personalities who do not know us, because the mass media give us an illusion of insight into their lives and because we have vicariously shared some of their private dramas, if only as anonymous spectators.

The nature of our knowing a person reflects not how often we meet or observe him, but the quality of those meetings and the kind of interaction which takes place. We may be physically in the same room with someone many, many times and yet not feel we know him. Or we may briefly meet someone once and yet recognize this as a significant experience. His salience for us may reflect who he is, how he behaves toward us, or the intensity of common experience.

Sociometrists (those sociologists who study the patterns of human relationships) have been intrigued by the problem of how we come to rank each other in the hierarchy of familiarity that ranges from nodding acquaintance to intimacy. Many things come into play which arise from personal compatibility: common occupational or family role; mutual acquaintances; common social, ethnic, religious, or cultural background; similar intelligence; and compatibility of temperaments. But in large part the quality of acquaintance will depend on purely material factors:

the physical location or propinquity of the parties; [6] the frequency, duration, and circumstances of their contact; and the degree of privacy or impersonality in contact, a reflection of the number of other people present.

All these factors could be set forth in a schematic diagram that would look very plausible and nonetheless utterly fail to capture the uniquely qualitative element in interpersonal relations, the cues and signs that people present to each other, the complex interplay of the elements that make up each personality, and one human being's mysterious interaction with another.

The manufacturer of a product is, at great remove, engaged in a complex process of communication with the product's eventual customers that is in some ways comparable to interpersonal relations. The haggling of buyer and seller in a Levantine marketplace illustrates the most direct confrontation of personalities in the economic process; there the joy of bargaining may be of far greater importance to the eventual transaction than the utility of the goods exchanged. In our society of impersonal mass marketing and mass consumption, the relationship of buyer and seller is greatly attenuated, yet in a sense the advertiser is still constantly trying to establish a relationship with prospective customers or to deepen a relationship which already exists. The reputation of his company or brand is as complex and subtle a product of events and forces as is the impression one human being has of another. That reputation is built from many bits and pieces of personal experience, conversation, and symbolism of name; packaging, pricing, and product attributes; and channels of distribution. But above all, it emerges from the mass media and the way advertisers use them.[7]

The importance of brand identity is shown in a study made by P. E. V. de Bruin and J. H. van Lonkhuysen of Philips Lamp in Holland. They compared a split-run of a full-page, two-color ad for a photo cell in a Dutch industrial publication, "The Engineer." The copy and illustration were identical in both ads except that one carried the logo-

---

[6] In a study of the evolution of friendship patterns in a campus veterans' housing project, Leon Festinger, Stanley Schachter, and Kurt Back found that these could in large measure be explained by the physical location of dwelling units; cf. their Social Pressures in Informal Groups, New York: Harper & Brothers, 1950.

[7] Paul Lazarsfeld and Elihu Katz have described the "two-step flow" of communication by which mass media content is transmitted by word of mouth and thus acquires the more vivid character of interpersonal contact. This process works with advertising as well as with other types of messages, but only rarely can an item of conversation be traced back to any specific ad as it might be to a specific news story or TV program. More usually it is a whole ad campaign, particularly one with some highly distinctive slogan or illustrational flair which, as it gathers momentum, gets talked about and is gradually absorbed into the stream of social currency. Cf. Personal Influence, New York: Macmillan (The Free Press of Glencoe), 1955.

type symbol that identifies "Philips" and the other a logotype for the mythical brand "TAG." The Philips logo created *five* times as much unaided recall, "action scores" which were four times as high, and aided recall which was over twice as high as created by the unknown brand name.

But the reputation of the store may be just as important to the consumer as that of the product. Louis P. Bucklin of the University of California surveyed 506 women shoppers in Oakland.[8] He found that where *no* brand was known and *no* particular store preferred, 31% of the women had made more than one shopping trip for the (unidentified) product in question. Where *no* brand was known but a particular store was preferred, 21% of the women made more than one shopping trip. When a brand was known but *no* store preferred, 16% of the women made more than one shopping trip. When the brand was known *and* a particular store preferred, the proportion who made more than one trip dropped to 15%. Of those women who preferred a particular store and were familiar with all the brand features, only 7% made more than one trip. This proportion was 35% for those familiar with only some of the features. Apparently, familiarity with *both* the brand of merchandise *and* the store which sells it reduces the uncertainty which causes people to shop around before they buy. This sense of familiarity and trust is what every advertiser seeks to establish.

Media strategy, motivational strategy, and brand distinction

National advertising includes many product categories in which different brands have virtually identical physical characteristics. In such product fields as soaps and detergents, soft drinks, cigarettes, beer, liquor, and gasoline, objective tests indicate that many consumers are unable to tell one brand from another when labels are removed.

As a result of research into consumer motivations, advertisers of such products became aware that in making the choice among relatively undifferentiated brands, the consumer buys mainly the satisfactions arising from a brand's unconscious symbolic meanings and associations.

This makes the task for advertising quite distinct from what it is for cars or appliances, where there are large and self-evident differences in the design of various makes and where the commodities are invested with considerable emotion because they represent major expenditures.

[8] *American Druggist*, June 6, 1966.

The planning and strategic thinking of a number of large advertising agencies is dominated by the package-goods clients whose products are of low interest to the consumer and closely resemble those of his ever-vigilant competition. Because these big advertisers are both powerful and unusually thoughtful and exigent, the theoretical assumptions which underlie their kind of advertising may tend to be carried over into the deliberations of agency account groups and plans boards when they deal with less sophisticated and demanding clients.

One objective for any low-interest product is to get a top-of-mind or tip-of-the-tongue association between the generic product category and the individual brand (not "soft drink" but "Coke"; not "facial tissue" but "Kleenex"). Such an identification makes it more likely that the customer will ask for the brand by name or reach for it on a shelf arrayed with identically priced and apparently similar items.

The advertiser wants the customer to feel that his item is a widely advertised, well-known (and therefore respectable) product manufactured by a big company. The company is assumed to be "big" because it is well known. Because it is big, the customer further assumes it cannot afford the risk of distributing merchandise that is not good.

The advertiser must break through the barrier of inattention which confronts a low-interest product. If people are not interested in what he has to sell them, they are not likely to pay attention to the messages which review his points of product superiority.

Behind the widespread use of broadcast spot advertising to promote low-interest products is the assumption that sheer repetition can break through the inattention barrier, that a message repeated often enough to the senses of sight and hearing in a time dimension simply cannot be ignored.

However, competitive brands in such product categories often start out with very similar assumptions and from them derive similar media strategies. The effect of this is the proliferation through the same media (typically spot TV) of an enormous array of competitive messages that are frequently repeated and that reiterate product claims which may be virtually indistinguishable from each other.

This enormously complicates brand decisions for the consumer, who must distinguish meaningful demands on his attention from the surrounding sea of noise which washes over him constantly through all the mass media. In the midst of this clamor, the exact repetition of a message no longer adds to a brand's ability to break the consumer's resistance. It may merely add to the confusion.

When we compare brand share and brand awareness in many product fields, we find that there is no consistent relationship. This fact must be kept in mind in considering Colley's recommendation to the advertiser that to win the market share he wants and expects (because his advertising budget is predicated on achieving a certain sales target), he must make a far larger proportion of the product's potential purchasers aware of his brand's name. In practice, for a widely used commodity he may have to take as his goal making "everybody" aware of it. He must assume that product quality, pricing, distribution, and merchandising efforts will all work at a peak level of efficiency to translate advertising awareness and successful transmission of product claims into actual share of market.

To make a brand stand out from its competitors may require a unique appeal to consumer motivations, but it also requires a media strategy which can make that unique appeal universally familiar to all those who might be persuaded to buy.

Which comes first: creative theme or market strategy?

Many of the most astute practitioners and articulate theorists of advertising today seem to agree that the advertising plan should start with a creative spark.

Rosser Reeves, former board chairman of the Ted Bates agency, expounded this position in his book, *Reality in Advertising*,[9] which proved a success not only in its popular sales, but also in attracting new accounts to his agency. The foundation for a successful campaign, Reeves wrote, was the "Unique Selling Proposition," the embodiment of those qualities (real or putative) which distinguish a brand from its competition and offer the consumer a unique benefit. Marion Harper, Jr., Chairman of Interpublic,[10] had long used a similar concept, that of the "purchase proposition" as the starting point of the advertising plan.

Another influential figure, David Ogilvy, places similar stress in his *Confessions of an Advertising Man* on the importance of beginning with the right creative touch to set a product apart from its competitors. Ogilvy puts it this way: "What really decides consumers to buy or not to buy is the *content* of your advertising, not its form. Your most important job is to decide what you are going to say about your product, what benefit you are going to promise." [11]

In more and more product fields (runs the argument of both Ogilvy and Reeves) the consumer cannot easily tell one brand from another,

[9] New York: Alfred A. Knopf, 1961.
[10] The Interpublic Group of Companies, Inc.
[11] *Confessions of an Advertising Man.* New York: Atheneum, 1963.

We're back where we belong. Serving you. If your plans were disrupted because we were grou

THE GREAT CREATIVE IDEA

The End of the Airline Strike

A day or two after a strike of the major United States commercial airlines ended on August 19, 1966, eight newspaper advertisements appeared heralding the return of planes to the regular schedule. This is a unique instance in which eight agencies worked, under the same time pressures, with identical communications objectives, using the same medium. What made the Eastern Air Lines ad, prepared by Young & Rubicam, so extraor-

…n only apologize. And ask you to let us serve you once again. ▲ EASTERN

dinarily different from the others was its dramatic photograph of a sea gull, which expresses all the excitement, power, and beauty of flight. The symbolism of this magnificent illustration, the associations it evokes on behalf of the client, the subtle long-term carryover of its impact, are all in realms of meaning which are beyond conventional research because they defy verbalization.

65

regardless of whatever minute differences really exist. Every advertiser of beer, gasoline, filter cigarettes, or toothpaste must begin his planning by defining how he would like his brand to be considered "different," either in those tangible attributes which the consumer experiences and tests first hand, or in its "personality." We may note in passing that it was one of the main tasks of motivation research to assist at this stage, by describing the personality characteristics which people already associated with a brand and its competitors and by indicating the directions of possible change and improvement.

One of Reeves' concepts is that everything that an individual learns from an advertising campaign forces out awareness of other advertising campaigns, even those for different products.

He refers to the percentage of people who remember a current advertising campaign as "penetration." He cites a Ted Bates study of the current campaigns of 78 major advertisers which found a range of penetration levels between 78% and 1%.

Reeves insists that frequent change of the advertising campaign message results in a loss of penetration. "Changing a story has the same effect as stopping the money, as far as penetration is concerned. Thus if you run a brilliant campaign every year, but change it every year, your competitor can pass you with a campaign that is less than brilliant — providing he does not change his copy."

It follows that "unless a product becomes outmoded, a great campaign will not wear itself out." This conclusion in part reflects Reeves' assumption that "the consumer tends to remember just one thing from an advertisement — one strong claim, or one strong concept."

Reeves attacks "originality" as the most dangerous word in advertising. He chortles over the fact that when an advertising magazine asked top creative people to pick the three worst television commercials of recent years, they included two of the most dramatically successful. (The fact remains that in few major agencies is the choice of what ads or commercials are to run made by the creative people.)

Unfortunately, the evidence which Reeves introduces amidst his authoritative *dicta* falls considerably short of proving his point that establishing awareness of the slogan is the mark of success in an advertising campaign. In fact, some of the evidence seems contradictory. He himself points out that not only do brands differ widely in public familiarity with their current slogans, but there are similar wide variations in what he calls "usage pull" — the degree to which knowledge of the slogan makes any *difference* in actual product use. One is left with the uneasy feeling that consumer confidence in General Electric or Pillsbury may reflect a long-established, advertising-influenced corporate reputation rather than the Unique Selling Proposition of the current year.

In essence, Reeves' emphasis on the U.S.P. is an appeal for a return to advertising's first principles — simplicity and concentration of effort. This makes great sense when the product is a toothpaste whose special claims to superiority, or even to a separate identity, are circumscribed within a narrow sphere. Yet how useful is the U.S.P. to a manufacturer who sells his product to different kinds of people who buy it with different motives?

Reeves asks, "Is it better to reach a smaller audience, to reach it more times? Or is it better to reach a bigger audience — and reach it less often? The answer is, buy dispersion. Try to reach more homes, not the same homes. Try to reach more people, not the same people."

Implicit in Reeves' position (although he does not come out and say it) is the notion that one must start first of all with the right message, theme, or Unique Selling Proposition and then figure out the right means to get this message around to as many people as possible.

In spite of Reeves' disparagement of "originality" (which he, as a great copywriter, can afford to make), the assumption which governs this sequence of steps is that the key to successful promotion is the Great Idea concerning what to say about the product. *How* to say it best can be learned through copy research, which tests different methods of giving expression to the Great Idea. The job of media selection comes last and entails, first, a judgment about the suitability of each medium to the creative approach already chosen, and, second, a matching of media audiences to the demographic or psychological characteristics of prospective customers.

Herbert Maneloveg, one of advertising's top media practitioners and theorists, also believes that the copy approach is paramount. "In the final analysis it's what you have to say that counts. . . . When an agency or client puts media selection before copy and lays most emphasis on media, it is usually because the product's appeal is low, very low, and the only way to penetrate through the boredom screen of today's tumultuous cacophony of sound and messages is by pounding away with a slogan, any slogan, often a mediocre slogan, but pound, pound, pound." [12]

This strategy demands that the advertiser start with an introspective look at his own reaction to his product. From such introspection may come (if he is lucky) insight into the right thing to say. Once he is saying the right thing, how can people fail to listen?

There are, however, other possible starting points for advertising strategy. For instance, the planner may start by looking at the customers rather than at the product. If he begins with the marketing data, he must first ask where — in what sectors of society — his customers or

---

[12] *Advertising Age,* August 23, 1965.

prospects are, and next how — with what media — they can be reached. Only then will he consider the media context or auspices which promise to find them in the most receptive mood. These considerations would lead him to select a medium or a mix of media. Creative strategy and style would then have to be developed in the terms most appropriate to the medium selected and the audience desired rather than on the basis of fantasy, speculation, or research about the product in an abstract setting.

If media plans were developed in this sequence, it would reduce the problems which arise whenever a campaign successfully developed in one medium is carried over to another. Too often the resulting ads or commercials are mere adaptations which fail to account for the essential differences in form between media, the varying possibilities for attracting (or even overwhelming) attention, the emotional effects of color, the audience's frame of mind and expectations, and the editorial or entertainment context of the advertising message.

In actual practice, few advertising plans are developed exactly in either one of the two sequences described here. Just about every plan submitted is derived from the plans that preceded it and there are generally starting points both on the creative and media sides which modify and shape strategy as it evolves. The Great Idea is often visualized in the context of a particular medium or with a particular audience in mind. And the media plan which emerges in mechanical projections from marketing statistics may be irrelevant to the real communications problem of the product.

Advertising and the decision to buy

Marketing and advertising strategy is almost inevitably (and understandably) devised from the perspective of the seller. The man who has a product to sell generally starts with the idea of placing his message before prospective customers. These may be heavy users of the product or simply people susceptible to persuasion for one reason or another. Generally he hopes to convert or persuade them to try his product the next time they are "in the market" or ready to buy.

He may urge these prospective customers to "rush right out and buy it now." Some of the time this may just be hyperbole, but in the case of the retailer or of a national advertiser with a new or promotional item, there may be an honest expectation that a certain number of people will be persuaded to "rush right out" because of a special incentive or deal which the advertising proclaims.

Implicit in the mind of the advertising planner is the notion of an audience of consumers, real or potential, with varying degrees of propensity for using his product, frequently or in substantial quantities, and in various stages of predisposition to buy it. His ads are placed before customers in the context of messages for products which compete either directly or indirectly with his own. They are intended to persuade or *pull* people toward his product who might not otherwise be receptive to buying it at all or who might be impelled toward a competing brand.

However, the real function of advertising looks very different when seen from the standpoint of the *buyer* rather than the seller. We might start by thinking of the degree to which people in our advanced commercial society live with a constantly changing set of internal and external pressures to consume a great array of products and services. These pressures vary in intensity from moment to moment, from day to day, from week to week. They jostle and compete with each other for the consumer's available resources of disposable income and shopping time. They reflect changes in life circumstances, family relationships, the seasons, the weather.

Considered from this vantage point, advertising must, of course, be numbered among the influences on people's consumption values. But an ad's short-term influence cannot be described, as it is so often, as sensitizing people to the merits of a product or making the product seem more desirable and important. This kind of effect on the way people position products and brands occurs only over the *long* term. Advertising is really inseparable from all the many other long-term economic and cultural influences on personal values.

Few consumer *needs* stem from an individual ad for a particular product. The direct short-term effects that an advertiser may expect from a specific ad are those from the few people who already want the product and who are so close to the act of purchase that the ad *triggers* their decision by reminding them of a brand or style or store. The extent to which conscious readiness to buy is converted to an actual purchase depends on a myriad of accidental factors involving the daily time budget and the pressure of competing interests, activities, and purchase desires.

Most advertisers think of the "pay-out" or yield for an ad or commercial in terms of the carry-over of favorable familiarity into a future purchase period. Our perspective must be quite different when we think of it in terms of the immediate or short-run sales potential that it activates or generates.

When we look at advertising from the perspective of the buyer, it is apparent that most advertising messages are wasted. They *have* to be, because at any given moment only a fraction of even the best customers are on the verge of buying the product. Nevertheless, a correspondence school may use match-book advertising very efficiently even though only a very small proportion of the people to whom match books are distributed have any conceivable interest in taking a correspondence course. It is still worthwhile to put the message in the hands of a great many uninterested people if in the process it reaches the handful who may write for information.

The return to an advertiser from his media investment must be calculated in terms of the very, very small numbers of people to whom he really wants to talk at any moment.

This theory of the "necessary waste" in advertising must work differently for products which are bought infrequently, like refrigerators or cars, and those which are bought daily, like cigarettes or bread. For a product whose frequency of purchase varies from one individual to another, obviously the frequent (or heavy) buyers will be found "ready to buy" in disproportionate numbers at any given time.

This theory also implies that there is value in exposing customers to the message as close as possible to the time they decide to buy. The point of decision often occurs well before the actual purchase. It is reflected in the timing and direction of the shopping trip, as well as in the composition of the shopping list.

A further implication of the theory of wasted messages is that high frequency of exposure is valuable not so much for the purpose of accumulating reach or for building a persuasive impact by message piled upon message, but simply because it maximizes the probability that the story is being told to people who are close to the buying decision.

Introducing a new product

In making the first major announcement or delivering the first major message for a new product, it is desirable that there be some prior subconscious sense of familiarity or acceptance. Thus even before a large investment is made in a large advertisement some kind of minor preconditioning is often called for.

A heavy push for a product that no one has even seen or heard of before may tend to create a degree of disbelief, rejection, or resistance. If the product name has already been placed before the public, such resistance might be diminished.

How can one quickly build up such a sense of familiarity? One way, ~~obviously,~~ is to scatter small ~~unobtrusive~~ messages before the public in a variety of different contexts. For instance, in newspaper advertising, small-space units lend themselves very well to this objective. The first such ad may capture the conscious attention of a very few readers. But when the same ad or a variation of it appears again in a very different context, the very *incongruity* between the second appearance and the first, along with the *similarity* of the basic story, may produce a kind of low-level shock effect. This may jar into awareness readers who might otherwise skim by the same item if they were seeing it for the first time.[13]

A spectacular initial drive may succeed in making a product well known to a high percentage of the public. It is fair to assume that there would be a very rapid attrition of that awareness, particularly among people who are not at the moment in the market for the product advertised, even though those who enter the market in the ensuing weeks may have their familiarity refreshed when they actually go into the store and encounter the merchandise on the shelf.

A major objective for a new product must therefore be to maintain the level of familiarity or awareness for a continuing period *after* the introductory wave of heavy advertising. The rate at which people are being reminded has to compensate for the rate at which they would otherwise forget because of their disinterest in the product category itself.

This argues for the consistent use of reminder advertising to keep alive the memory of both the brand name and its product characteristics. Ideally, one would always wish this reminder advertising to take the form of messages delivered in unit sizes large or impressive enough to assure the high level of attention that was achieved by the initial effort, but this is only rarely feasible within budget limitations. The advertiser thus perennially faces the problem of balancing greater frequency in small doses against less frequent messages strong enough to revive the memory of his whole product story.

When is the right time to give a new product a second big push? A low-key continuity campaign may maintain awareness at a desired

---

[13] These considerations suggest the desirability of using a number of small-space ads on different pages within the same issue of a newspaper. If all the ads were placed before the reader at the same time, i.e., on the same page, the likelihood of intriguing him would be less. If the same ads were scattered over a longer period of time, the normal processes of memory attrition would reduce the probability of this kind of carry-over of attention. If they were spread out over a very long period of time, the probability would also be less. Putting them together within a period of 37 minutes (the average newspaper reading time) heightens the possibility of getting the message across. In the newspaper, the use of small-space units has another advantage: it permits the placement of ads in sections which are known to have particularly high traffic among men or women. Thus the copy, illustration, and headline can appeal to different segments of the total audience reached. (Comparable strategic considerations would obviously apply in introducing a new product through other media.)

level, but beyond a certain point there is apt to be a strong need for full restatement of the product's basic story. This commonly calls for a change of pace within the existing media mix, or a radical, usually temporary, shift of media balance. The timing of such a move is often governed by merchandising requirements but it may also be influenced by traditions such as spring and fall promotions.

The advertiser is always fighting a losing battle over a period of time. Unless he repeats an ad of the same powerful dramatic quality he used originally, there will be fewer and fewer people every day who spontaneously associate his brand with the product category.

He can try to offset this attrition by periodically introducing a more powerful message unit (a bigger ad, a longer commercial). This might restore awareness in people who have become oblivious to the small ads for reasons which have to do either with their lack of interest in the product or with the creative themes of the ads.

The function of advertising is often merely that of a catalyst. Two men with identical buying wants and capacities may pass the window of a store in which shirts are offered for sale. If one of them has seen an ad for these shirts that day, he may be more impelled to walk into the store and buy the merchandise. In practice, however, it is hard to tell whether the positive decision of any one customer reflects the influence of advertising, of greater immediate needs, of purchasing power, or of a private affinity for the styling and color patterns of the shirts in the window.

The consumer decision: a minor purchase[14]

How does the persuasive power of advertising fit in among all the forces that influence the consumer's buying decision? The answer to this question varies, as is illustrated by the case histories of two strikingly different commodities we studied at the Bureau of Advertising. The first is a product category with a broad market, low consumer interest, and high purchase frequency. Interviewers stationed outside supermarkets in Modesto, California, questioned 613 housewives who had just bought one or more paper products — kitchen towels, facial tissue, toilet tissue, wax paper, and napkins.

Eighty-four per cent of the purchases were reported by the shopper to have been planned or thought of in advance. In half these cases she had actually written the item down on a shopping list.

[14] The next three sections are adapted from a talk I made before the New York City Chapter of the American Marketing Association, May 14, 1964.

The study indicated that nearly three women in five believe that one brand in particular is outstanding. While in general they buy that brand, if a price or premium offer is available, it may easily deflect them. Yet only seven in ten said they had looked around in the store to see the prices of other brands.

Four out of five shoppers reported that the item they had just bought was a brand they usually use. When asked why they preferred that brand, the percentage referring to a price advantage ranged from 9% for facial tissue to 40% for napkins, and there were notable differences among individual brands. Of the switchers who did not just buy the brand they "usually buy," between 40% and 50% reported that they had made their purchase on the basis of price.

During the period of the study, a record was kept of actual sales and of changes in shelf facings and displays. In one period, a brand of facial tissue was selling at its regular price in a certain supermarket and was bought by only 2 out of the 35 women who bought facial tissue. A few days later, it went on sale. On two sale days, 13 out of 25 facial tissue purchasers bought it.

When another leading brand of facial tissue was on sale and was prominently displayed in the store, 25 of 33 tissue buyers chose that brand. Its share dropped to 7 purchasers out of a total of 15 when its leading competitor also went on sale. When only the competitor's product was on sale, the leading brand was bought by only 3 out of 10 facial tissue purchasers.

In another supermarket, a brand of paper towels attracted a total of 22 purchasers with a premium offer. In another period, with the premium offer plus a sale price, it got up to 14 out of 16 purchasers. When this brand (with a premium offer only) had the same number of shelf facings as its leading competitor (which had no premium), it was outsold, 11 packages to 16. But when it was later offered at a sale price as well as with a premium, it sold ten packages to every five for the competitor.

Where does advertising fit into such a volatile mix of marketing forces? Paper products as a group are consciously missed when the household supply runs low or out. If the need has registered, the housewife automatically plans a purchase; she even writes it down.

It is not that the subject is of any particular interest to her. Despite the enormous volume of advertising in this category (over $50 million in 1965), only one woman out of four spontaneously recalled any advertising during the past week for the product she had just bought. Yet that advertising, sustained over the years, helps her to make quality distinctions among brands, so that when she comes into the store she has both a preference (not a clear-cut one, but a general tendency perhaps) and also a range of acceptability for other brands, with definite outer limits on how far she can be lured by a premium or price advantage.

When three women in ten say they did not look at the prices of brands other than the one they bought, this does not necessarily mean that they are oblivious to price. It merely indicates that they perceived the pricing of their brand relative to its competition to be within the bounds of expectation and tolerance.

Advertising thus serves the primary function of placing a brand within the spectrum of what is acceptable.

As a second function chronologically, advertising's stress on specific product advantages or its symbolic overtones give the consumer a rationale or an emotional inclination which is reinforced by actual purchase. An imperceptible advantage on a continuum of preference for one brand versus another becomes an absolute yes-no advantage when the consumer must decide in the store on purchase or non-purchase. Once the affirmative act of purchase has been made, the consumer is psychologically committed to support the brand she chose with her preference, and advertising gives her the reasons.

Finally, advertising may alert the consumer to a sale or special offer. This is important in reaching the extremely economy-minded customer or the woman who uses advertising as a reference in making up her shopping list. But to many more customers, the notice of a sale serves as a preliminary cue to be activated at the point of sale, or as a trigger which sets into motion the cumulative effect of much previous promotion.

The consumer decision: a major purchase

If the purchase decision on paper products represents the low end of consumer interest and involvement, the automotive purchase decision, next to that of a home, is usually the biggest and most important one that a family makes.

To understand how people go about buying a new car, we asked the Oxtoby-Smith research firm to conduct intensive interviews with nearly 200 recent purchasers. With the help of some searching questions, the purchasers were asked to retrace the steps they had taken in arriving at the decision to buy. On the basis of their responses, it would seem that the process of buying a car can be visualized in two separate stages, each of which starts in a vague fuzzy way and ends at a hard, sharp focal point.

The first stage is one of "preliminary exploration." It may be described as the gradual evolution of a state of readiness to buy. It culminates in a definite decision, expressed in verbal commitments, to enter the market. This exploration is set in motion almost imperceptibly, in response both to external events and to internal psychological changes. A man arrives at this state, for example, when his car has passed a certain age (which he defines as "old" in comparison with the model year of cars owned by people he considers significant). Or he may be impelled from the stage of unconscious sensitivity to one of active readiness by a change in life circumstances — a marriage, a change of job or residence, the birth of a new child, a death in the family — anything which alters his functional or status requirements. A buildup of tension takes place gradually over months for most people. During this period, anything that goes wrong with the prospect's current car assumes an importance it did not have before. If the car burns oil or gets less mileage to the gallon of gas, or if minor parts have to be replaced, this now becomes a matter of family conversation. (Family discussion, in fact, accompanies all of the subsequent stages in the process of decision-making.)

As the car owner finds himself talking more about cars, he also becomes more sensitive to advertising and editorial matter dealing with automobiles. He pays more attention to new models he sees on the road. Automobile shows and new model introductions intensify the process by creating fresh occasions for conversation and reflection.

As this "preliminary exploration" goes on, the car buyer comes more and more to think of himself as being actively in the market. He may define his interest now in terms of a target date for his purchase. This may be related to the introduction of the new models, to the end of winter, or to the anticipated lowering of prices at the end of the old model year.

Often some decisive incident or event (a major repair job, or an occasion to celebrate) forces the prospect to begin his active shopping. Even before he reaches the point of decision to buy, he has become highly conscious of the different makes and models, and of the dealers in his area of residence.

Once he has made up his mind to buy a car, the customer starts to look into showroom windows and even to browse through floor displays. He starts studying the ads to compare features and prices. He consults the "experts" of his acquaintance — like filling station attendants. He chats with friends about his own past experience. At the final stages he talks to dealers about features, prices, and trade-ins and, on the basis of comparison, closes his deal.   In a majority of cases he makes up his mind within a matter of weeks after he has made the decision to buy.

Throughout these crucial weeks, the prospect's feeling about the reputation of a make is buttressed now by what he sees in the advertising to which he has suddenly become sensitive.   But the ads he sees with new interest produce their effect by reactivating all the other advertising — not to mention all the news and rumor — that has reached him from that company over the years.

This description of the automotive purchase decision holds up nearly universally, but the actual form and timing of the various stages in the process show considerable variation from one individual to the next.

Advertising in perspective

In two examples of the purchase decision as disparate as those for a paper product and a new car, the differences are far more striking than the few common elements — the awareness of a need, the decision to buy, the shopping process, and the choice among brands on the basis of both general reputation and specific price value.

But the two studies together lead to certain conclusions.   They force us to place advertising in a realistic perspective among all the forces that influence a purchase.   Whereas in both cases advertising proved to be an important element, its importance lies not in having elicited a specific purchase response to a specific ad.   The real significance of advertising is its total cumulative weight as part of the culture — in the way in which it contributes to the popular lore of ideas and attitudes toward consumer products.   The information and impressions which people have about branded goods represent folk wisdom: they are part of the landscape of symbols with which people are familiar from childhood on, and which they play back to each other in the discussions that precede a major purchase.

Advertising forces the consumer to recognize the values in a product, or it may create artificial values in the form of a symbolic aura. But these values, material or psychological, are constantly being weighed against the reference point of price.   Advertising may limit the range of choice to a number of acceptable brands.   But the scales can easily be tipped by a price advantage.

Both the studies force us to differentiate among customers according to the way they go about buying.   No realistic model of the purchasing process can apply equally well to all people, whatever the degree of their price motivation and whether or not they pursue novelty or whether or not they are brand-loyal.

Timing, repetition, dominance, reach, and frequency represent strategic considerations of quite different dimensions for advertising which is going to be actively consulted and for advertising whose main purpose is to lay a foundation of imagery or information to which a prospective buyer will subconsciously refer.

The timing requirements are different for a purchase decision in which months have been spent in reflection and one made in a matter of hours or minutes, starting merely with the customer's observation that she is running short on a needed item.

Except in the case of sales or specials, when the advertiser can induce a sense of urgency, the problem of timing his messages may be likened to the management of a municipal water system. The relationship is tenuous indeed between each drop of water that trickles into the reservoir and each drop of water that trickles out through a faucet at the other end of the system. Whether any particular drop gets into the reservoir, or whether any particular drop flows out of the faucet makes little difference to the system as a whole. But should the water stop coming in, there would eventually be nothing to come out at the other end.

In advertising we are, in effect, trickling drops, spoonfuls, or buckets of persuasion into the reservoir of product information and opinion from which consumer actions are drawn. We can rarely trace the flow from any one message put into the reservoir to any one purchase act, and any connection between the two exists almost outside of a time dimension.

Wanted: the Great Creative Idea

Although most advertising messages may lose their individual identity soon after they go forth, no advertiser fails to expect from his agency the unique advertisement which will endure forever; and rarely will an agency refuse this assignment. The struggles to complete it become particularly painful in the case of those low-cost frequently purchased packaged goods which constantly face new competitive brands and product changes. Often the old brands are kept faintly alive as the manufacturer puts new ones on the market, until a fresh infusion of promotional effort returns them to the ranks of the effective contenders, freshly baptized as "new and different." William Weilbacher once reported to me the case of such a product, scheduled for re-introduction:

> Always willing to be convinced, the manufacturer had designed a market test, complete with a fully-produced ad campaign (to be limited to

the test areas). At a meeting with the client, the agency presented the comps for the test campaign. The agreed theme was to be centered on convincing consumers that the re-born product is *changed.* The agency man rolled back the cover sheet from the mounted comp layout. The layout was an orthodox 4-C bleed page, dominated by a Gallup-Robinson formula illustration area, a formula copy block size, a formula logo size — but a *non*-formula headline running diagonally across the illustration. The head read, "Ooh, Boppo! How you've changed!"

"Not bad," said the client ad manager. "Let's see the others."

After a few exchanges of blank looks, the agency men explained that the "others" were eliminated by the account group back at the shop, and that *this* was their concerted choice of their best effort.

"Won't do," admonished the ad manager. "Please bring us some alternative approaches to consider."

After an interval, the same characters met in the same place. The agency man had several veiled comps standing in the chalk trough, leaning against the board. After proper introductions of why the meeting was called, he ceremoniously rolled back the cover sheets on the alternate layout approaches the creative group had produced. As he progressed, a look of disbelief came across the face of the ad manager. All of the layouts were identical to the original one in every respect save one: the headlines. On one layout, the head said, "Ah, Boppo! How You've Changed." Another said, "My Boppo! How You've Changed!" Another, "Goodness, Boppo! How You've Changed!" [15]

Why does the output of extraordinary ads not increase in proportion to the increased volume of advertising? Works of genius are inevitably individual creations rather than the products of collective effort. But the process of producing advertising today is a group activity, both in the initial effort and also in the bureaucratic reviews which are part of the system.

In Albert Lasker's heyday, he could jot a slogan on a piece of paper, show it to a client, and put his advertising in print, just about in that order.

Today's creative ideas are discussed in committee, reviewed with account groups, and traipsed before a series of plans boards within the agency. When they pass this ordeal they are subjected to further scrutiny at the client level.

At every stage of the review process, suggestions and additions are made. The final product is subject to further modification based on copy research. Is there any wonder then that innovation in advertising today must often beat the system to find expression and that Great Creative Ideas are something less than universal?

---

[15] Unpublished communication.

I doubt whether anyone has ever written great advertising copy as a result of reading a book by Claude Hopkins or David Ogilvy on how to do it. Studying the work of such established masters is part of the basic training in any craft, of course. The copy cub who dissects the latest output of this year's Hot Creative Agency is (properly) picking up pointers which he will put to good use later on, but this kind of study can not evoke the copywriting Muse, just as no amount of reading Tolstoy or Proust will train anyone to write a great novel.

Advertising is different from fiction, you may be thinking, and indeed it is, for so much of it is written and forgotten every day. For a writer of routine reports, training can make the difference between copy that is acceptable and copy that gets rejected. But the textbook rules of advertising are constantly being violated by the copywriters who have a Great Idea.

Keep the headline short! Promise a strong consumer benefit! Don't confuse copy claims! Have one dominant illustration! Don't use long sentences or big words! Be specific! Avoid cuteness and unusual references! All of these rules vanish into the air when we look at individual campaigns. The Great Idea that catches the public fancy never comes by the book and never comes from perusal of what worked well in the past.

Every creative man in an advertising agency has the goal of the Great Idea before him every time he confronts a blank sheet of white paper. And yet as a practical matter he is rarely convinced that he is going to achieve it.

Look at and listen to the advertising around you today. What proportion of it is fresh, inspired, or unusual? There is a good reason why the proportion is so small. Unusual ideas carry a strong risk of being unusually bad as well as unusually good.

Advertising plans are made by businessmen, they involve large sums of money, and there is a strong conservative resistance to the offbeat, to breaking with the formula. Why shouldn't there be? Offbeat ideas, especially untested offbeat ideas, have a long record of failure.

There are a number of reasons why Great Ideas are as rarely visible in ads as they are in the fine arts. Most American advertising is placed by retailers cataloguing their wares and offering specific factual descriptions of features and prices. The most brilliant retail advertisements rarely penetrate beyond their own home markets and thus for the most part are invisible to the country as a whole.

Many fine national advertisements also have a highly restricted audience because they are aimed at minor segments of the market and confined to media which reach special small groups of potential customers.

Finally, the Great Idea itself wears out in practice. It is embellished and varied in subsequent repetitions of the same campaign; it is adapted from one media form to another and always loses something of its original vitality in the process. And it is likely to be imitated to the point where it appears overly familiar and hackneyed and generates ridicule or resentment.

Needless to say, the Great Idea invariably has some functional relationship to the product advertised. Even when the Idea involves a gimmick, this becomes meaningful only in relation to the fantasies it releases with regard to the product. Again to take the example of Baron Wrangel, the original model in Ogilvy's ads for Hathaway shirts, the eyepatch represents a mysterious identity, a glamorous suggestion of an adventurous (and perhaps shirtless!) past which contrasts sharply with the crispness of the model's pictured attire.

Advertising ideas misfire when the gimmickry buries or overwhelms the product or contradicts its appeal. One of the hardest elements to introduce successfully into advertising is humor; when it is too robust it threatens or blanks out the product, when it is too gentle or intellectual it carries the risk of being ignored altogether. Context is all-important here; the serious reader is not prepared for levity on the facing page, whereas the entertainment-minded listener or viewer is equally unprepared to change his mood to deadpan earnestness when the commercial comes on.

If Great Ideas in advertising are few and far between, there are even fewer which are considered great by marketing men and copywriters alike. A great advertising campaign is, by definition, one which advertising professionals admire aesthetically or intellectually, and not necessarily one that sells the client's product line. A creatively undistinguished advertising campaign may sell a lot of merchandise as part of an over-all effort which involves far more than the copy theme or execution. (For one thing it probably involves a good product as well as a substantial advertising investment.)

Hard-nosed marketers are fond of expressing disdain for campaigns which win awards but fail at the cash register. They merely choose to ignore the fact that an even higher percentage of campaigns which don't win awards *also* fail at the cash register.

A Great Idea in advertising has coherence, simplicity, and unity. For this reason I think it is inconsistent with the recent tendency — initiated in Colley's famous A.N.A. report and further preached in various learned treatises of the Marketing Sciences Institute — to define advertising goals in highly specific terms which can then be used as yardsticks for scientific evaluation.

Colley's approach embodies the tired businesman's ancient lament (maliciously attributed to John Wanamaker) that half his advertising budget is being wasted but he doesn't know which half. The preoccupation with assessment is, as I shall point out later, at odds with the great difficulty of making a meaningful evaluation of advertising's unique contribution to sales. It causes the goals of advertising to be redefined, shifting attention away from sales or market share statistics (the playthings of competitive action) and focusing on goals involving changes in awareness, information, and opinion of Our Brand — changes which *can* be measured and compared under different conditions or at different points of time.

Alas, advertising agencies are often in business to make the client happy, and many can stay in business only by keeping him happy over the short run. Many a bad commercial or ad has been approved by an agency plans board simply because pretests show it will get a good score from Starch or from Gallup and Robinson (if these be the idols which the client venerates). By similar logic, why cannot advertising campaigns be designed to raise "unaided recall of Our Brand's slogan" from 4% to 6.5% in a three-month period, or to raise its share of mentions as "one of the best" from 23% to 31%?

The Great Idea does not lend itself to such petty and transitory goals, however amenable they may be to measurement. It belongs to the realm of lore and fable, which measurement can only distort and falsify. How can one measure the effects of the Three Bears and Goldilocks, or of Red Riding Hood and the Wolf? Why then measure the effects of Rinso White! Rinso White! Jello again! Burma-Shave, Burma-Shave! Lucky Strike Green has gone to war! or any of the more recent additions to the mythology of American commerce?

The Great Ideas in advertising are indistinguishable from the other elements of popular culture which are deeply embedded in our collective experience of the mass media. In the minds of all who grow up and participate in a world of half-real, half-fictional personalities and symbols, the presence of the Marlboro cowboy's tattoo and the Toni twins are to be taken for granted as much as the Beatles, Willie Mays, or Donald Duck. All alike are regarded as universally known and surrounded by a set of universally understood associations.

The Great Idea in advertising gives a product this kind of commonly known, clearly defined character. It keeps its identity vivid and positive. It gives it new overtones of freshness when it threatens to become tired.

Whatever the unique requirements of the product, the creative idea becomes persuasive only in an appropriate media environment. In a brilliant marketing plan, the message, the medium, the target audience, and the product attributes all fit together like pieces in a Chinese puzzle.

"UNDERSTANDING MEDIA" 5

In the cryptic words of the popular cultural historian, critic, and oracle Marshall McLuhan, "the medium is the message." [1] The content of the medium communicates only in the manner which the form dictates, and symbolic meanings are inseparable from the unique kind of sensory stimulation which the medium employs.

In McLuhan's words, "Our conventional response to all media, namely that it is how they are used that counts, is the numb stance of the technological idiot. For the 'content' of a medium is like the juicy piece of meat carried by the burglar to distract the watchdog of the mind. . . . The effect of the movie form is not related to its program content."

For McLuhan, the "Gutenberg Galaxy" of communication through print, the impersonal symbol, and the individual's eye are giving way to a

---

[1] *Understanding Media,* New York: McGraw-Hill Book Company, 1964.

new era.   Broadcasting brings mankind back to an earlier epoch of communication through the direct contact of speech.

Advertisers have long appreciated that each medium puts its characteristic stamp on the messages it disseminates, although they would be
reluctant to admit that there isn't a little something of the message left
to work just for their benefit!

When we refer to "messages" in advertising, we customarily have
in mind communication units in the major media — newspaper and magazine ads, television and radio commercials, outdoor or transit posters;
we rarely consider window displays and promotion devices, or the brand
names and labels emblazoned on products and packages.   Such casual
reminders represent a very large proportion of the total number of product messages presented to people each day, though few of them represent
direct attempts at persuasion in the sense, say, of a "hard sell" TV commercial.

The influence of conventional media advertising can best be understood if we consider the consumer's response to packaging, store displays,
and sales promotion devices.   A consumer may remain oblivious, for all
intents and purposes, to the advertising message on the wall calendar,
the ash tray, or the match book, however often he looks at it.   He accepts
such messages as part of the environment.   The subtle penetration of
these messages is demonstrated when the consumer encounters the product or brand in another context.   The familiar name encountered in an
unfamiliar setting may produce the little "shock of incongruity" which
trips it into conscious awareness.

Unfortunately, the word "message" applies equally to the brand
name on a soup label seen on the pantry shelf and to the two-minute live
television commercial or the six-page blockbuster gate-fold ad in *Life*.
The advertising lexicon contains no intermediate terms to differentiate
the varieties of communications experience embodied in advertisements
of different dimensions in different media.   In spite of this, advertising
plans characteristically compare media messages by such criteria as coverage, frequency of exposure, and cost per thousand — just as though the
units being compared weighed equally in the balance.

Distinguishing media capabilities

Which medium is best?   No question in advertising is easier to answer,
the answer being, "it all depends."   It depends on the product, on the
marketing target, on the budget available.   Many experts would also
say it depends on the copy theme and creative approach, and in prac-

tice it often does. But there are few copy points, to judge by my own experience, which cannot be well expressed in a variety of media, even though each may make its own special technical demands in expressing the story best.

The larger the advertiser and the more diversified his product line, the less likely he is to think of which one medium to spend his money in and the more likely he is to think in terms of a combination of media to accomplish all the tasks he has in mind. There are exceptions to this rule, of course. Procter and Gamble habitually (and most successfully) puts over 90% of its advertising dollars into television in support of a wide array of new and established products. But most of the time, the big advertiser has to use a number of media simply because his advertising objectives are apt to be complicated.

The small advertiser may also have complex marketing problems, but his ability to spread out among a number of media is sharply limited by his budget. In many media his dollars do not buy him as much as do those of his big competitors, in quantity or in quality of position. If he markets his wares in only a restricted area, he can turn to magazines that issue regional editions. Through the sectional editions now offered by 62 magazines, in up to 75 segments (for *Look*), the regional advertiser now has an extraordinary degree of flexibility, but he will have to pay a premium over the national rate per reader and the distribution of the edition may or may not coincide well with his own sales territory. Above and beyond any financial disadvantages, the small advertiser who divides his budget among the media is apt to be spreading himself too thin to make any substantial impact with any one of them.

In evaluating a medium, the advertiser must think in terms of what *he* will get out of it in terms of position, timing, scheduling, and public attention, rather than of the medium in the abstract. In practice, glamorous media vehicles or the advertiser's own favorites may find their way on to a list because of their aura rather than their inherent suitability.

Comparatively little of the total effort expended to research, promote, and sell media is made on behalf of media as the advertiser and agency consider them. Such efforts are made by the advertising bureaus which every medium has set up to serve its collective interests. Most media research, promotion, and selling is used by one vehicle within a medium in its competitive struggle to win an advantage over other vehicles in the *same* medium — to get on a list ahead of its confreres. Yet rarely (except in network television) is a decision made to use a vehicle until *after* a basic decision has first been made to use the medium of which it is a part.

Advertising planners are strongly tempted to think of media in the idealized and highly differentiated way that is fostered by the media themselves in their promotion and selling. Because each media communications environment is thought of at its prototypical best, the qualitative or psychological differences among the media may be exaggerated.

The true difficulty of sharply differentiating between the qualitative environments of one medium and another appears if we accept two principles: (1) for most people the mass media represent a relatively trivial pastime rather than significant aesthetic or cathartic experiences; (2) much advertising is incidental to, or actually at odds with, the audience's primary purpose in reading, viewing, or listening.

This latter principle must be refined to distinguish between print and broadcasting. In broadcast media, commercial messages are dispersed in time and station position throughout the day. Even through commercials get an excellent response when they are unusually humorous, dramatic, informative, or attractive, it is not ordinarily conceivable that a viewer or listener might tune in to a program for the purpose of hearing or watching a commercial. By contrast, advertising in print media may be as avidly consulted and sought for as editorial content. Classified advertising sections in the newspaper are based on this premise. Newspaper readers, especially women, use the paper as a daily catalogue of merchandise, comparative prices, sales, and style information. Advertising in specialized magazines and industrial publications serves a similar function of keeping the reader informed about products and services in which his occupation or avocation give him a direct interest.

Media may be differentiated in terms of the size and characteristics of their audiences, their communications capabilities, their cost and flexibility of usage by the advertiser, and the environment they provide the advertising message. Today all U.S. media are mass media, although individual media vehicles are not. Ninety-eight per cent of all American households have a radio, and 75% of the adult population are reported to listen, on the average, $2\frac{1}{2}$ hours per day. Ninety-three per cent of the households have one or more TV sets, and 81% of the adults watch TV for an average of $3\frac{1}{4}$ hours on a given day.[2] Eighty-seven per cent of the households receive at least one newspaper on the average day, most of these home-delivered on a regular basis, and 81% of the adults read some paper daily (an average of 1.4 per reader). At least one single weekly or monthly issue of the current magazines is read by 80% of the adults in 87% of the households.

[2] This estimate of viewing hours comes from a 1966 Nielsen report of audience composition, based on the diary method. I shall have occasion to question it later on.

Beneath the surface of these general averages lurk great differences in the audience sizes of individual media vehicles. On a single TV network in prime evening hours (7:30 — 11:00 P.M. E.S.T.) one week in late January (the heaviest viewing period) of 1966, the range of Nielsen ratings was from 12 to 31. Magazines range in size downward from the *Reader's Digest* with a 16.5 million circulation in 1966 to those with only a few thousand subscribers. The New York *Daily News* had a circulation of 2.1 million in the same year, but the median U.S. daily paper was in the 10,000 circulation bracket.

Along with this variation of size goes a considerable variation of audience composition. Generally speaking, the print media make their greatest appeal to those of highest education and social status, while broadcasting's appeal assumes the reverse direction. (In the heaviest TV-viewing fifth of the adult population, 43% of the people in 1963 were in families with under $5,000 income a year and 22% were in families with over $8,000. Among the lightest-viewing fifth the proportions were reversed, with 15% in the low-income bracket and 43% at high incomes. The non-viewers, incidentally, are a curious mixture which includes the very poorest, who don't own TV sets, as well as those at the highest social level who have kicked the habit.)

Of course, such generalizations may cut no ice as far as any particular advertiser is concerned, for within any medium he can seek to be selective in choosing those vehicles which give him the kind of audiences he wants to reach. An exception occurs in single-newspaper or single-TV channel markets, where he has the sole option of using the medium or not using it. Another exception occurs when he buys spot television in evening hours and takes his chances on program/adjacency positions. In that case too, the people he is most apt to reach, and reach most often, are the people who in general watch TV most. And of course with such media as billboards and car cards, the advertiser has only a limited option — by selecting poster locations — to concentrate his fire on less than the whole population at once.

How media define markets

"Market" may well be the most popular word in advertising circles, and yet it is used to mean a number of different things. A market is a place, but it is often also a state of mind which characterizes people of common tastes and buying propensities. As such, it is apt to be made by — and be defined in terms of — the mass media of communication and advertising.

Markets have traditionally been thought of in geographical terms, as focal points of a distribution network. We have always had to define them in terms of the accessibility and availability of various forms of transportation along which both customers and goods could conveniently and economically be brought together.

Historically, markets (like towns) developed at breaks in transportation which became the logical stopping and crossing points for travelers with different types of merchandise and services to exchange. When we think of markets in today's terms, we normally think of towns or cities which, as agglomerations of populations, are reservoirs of buying power and central points of production for the goods and services to be bought and consumed.

A broader definition of the market probably found its first expression in the concept of the "retail trading zone" — the area surrounding any population point within which people tend to do the bulk of their shopping. By extension, a market may be defined not only as a town or town trading zone, but as a region with some geographic homogeneity (held together by a web of transportation and communication or by a common historical and social heritage) like the American South. Markets are also limited by political boundaries. Thus Fort Worth and Dallas make up a metropolitan agglomeration although they are by no means a single market in an economic sense. Providence is a part of Boston's television area, but this only means a greater probability of unused circulation for local advertisers in either market.

A market may correspond to something existing in nature (like an island) or constructed by man's artifice (like a railroad line), but it may also exist in terms that no one can describe in any physical sense at all. It may have to be defined — and increasingly *is* defined — in terms of the spread of advertising media rather than in terms of distribution areas. When an advertiser gears his planning to "the New England market" or "the Southern California market," he is actually conjuring up something which acquires reality only because his particular objectives require it.

The old geographic definition of the market, as a town and its hinterland, has been shaken in this century by two parallel developments: one is the enormous expansion of world population, reflected in highly developed countries by the growth of metropolitan regions and the expansion into vast semi-urban areas along the main lines of transport (exemplified by the English Midlands, the Ruhr Valley, or the almost continuous series of towns that stretch from Portland, Maine, to Norfolk, Virginia). The isolated communities of another period have been replaced by the growth of these vast interurban belts. The geographer

Jean Gottmann sees the shadow of the future in the continuously built-up Megalopolis which extends in a strip along the North Atlantic coast.

The second major development has been the tremendous improvement of systems that permit the movement of people and goods over vast areas with greater speed and less effort. This development carries with it an important implication for the definition of a market. It means that the most effective and economically practicable distribution range for almost any commodity (including even the most perishable) can be extended far beyond the area surrounding the point of production.

Another force is working in the same direction. Modern machinery and mass production techniques make possible the fabrication of identical standardized products not only at different points in time, but at different points in space. It is possible to produce virtually identical cars or tubes of toothpaste or bottles of Coca-Cola working with identical equipment in different towns of the same country or even in different countries.

All this has meant that the problems of distribution for any fair-sized manufacturer are less and less apt to be matters of logistics, shipment, and warehousing. More and more they have become problems of penetration — getting goods into the right kinds of outlets and displayed in the right kind of way. Paralleling this change, the problems of advertising have become less and less those of reaching the people who live where the goods can be bought and more those of pin-pointing effort to reach the people who want the goods or who can be persuaded to want them. Accordingly, markets have increasingly tended to become defined in the minds of manufacturers in terms of consumer characteristics rather than in terms of geography — in terms of what kinds of people the potential customers are rather than where they happen to live. Concepts like the "youth market" or the "Negro market" or the "housewife-with-young-children market" are examples of such non-geographical market definitions.

In the big city, human relations become impersonal and people no longer necessarily know their next door neighbors. Friends are apt to be people who share the same field of work, church, school, political preference, or hobby, rather than the families next door. In the suburbs, community life is re-established, but on a much different basis than in the horse-and-buggy era.

With the growth of suburban shopping centers and drive-in movies and the diffusion of industry to the fringes of metropolitan regions, it becomes possible for people living on the outskirts of the great city to live their lives without ever venturing to its center. And yet, though they tread their way gingerly around the edges, their lives are still part of that fantastic web of tangled human and business relationships that is the modern metropolis.

It is apparent, then, that the bonds which connect people and make them similar as customers are increasingly less apt to be bonds of place than bonds of common character or common interest. It is obvious that an advertising director of a company in New Orleans has more in common with the advertising director of a company in Denver than either has with, say, a baker, a brick layer, or an insurance salesman in his own city.

The modern community can no longer be delimited by the artificially set municipal boundaries drawn with a surveyor's rule half a century or more ago. People in complex modern industrial society live segmented lives in which they are simultaneously members of different communities corresponding to different kinds of activities or interests. We all go through life playing the different roles appropriate to the different situations in which we find ourselves and the people we are with. Similarly, we are members of audiences for different mass media and respond appropriately to each type of media exposure. I am a different person, in effect, when watching television with my family than when reading the newspaper on the bus, and I am a different (though not necessarily a better) man when I read the editorial page than when I read the comics.

To say that media make markets means nothing more than that they create common interests and set common standards of taste. They tend to attract people who are alike socially or culturally or in certain dimensions of personality. The same psychological elements may help to dictate or influence a person's choice of a medium as help to define his use of a product or choice of a brand.

Every advertising medium tries as hard as it can to define a market for itself by making advertisers and audiences alike conscious of something which, for practical purposes, may never before have existed. A radio station may establish itself as "the Voice of Northeast Lower Something," in order to carve out for itself a lucrative area of doing business, even though the people living in that area may have no sense of common identity other than that created by the medium itself. A magazine like *Vogue* or *Sports Illustrated* may actually create in the minds of its readers a feeling akin to that of membership in some kind of secret order. And it is in terms of these characteristics which make for a common life style that advertisers themselves often tend to define their marketing objectives. The choice of a medium thus may influence not only an advertiser's perception of what he has to say to his customers but the whole orientation of his business. This is by no means true of all advertisers, and even among those who depend on selective publications, the term "market" continues to be used with geographical or demographic meanings as well as to refer to markets made by media.

Local markets and national coverage

Media exposure and advertising pressure are not evenly distributed against the entire population. At the very bottom and very top of the socio-economic scale people tend to insulate themselves from the mass media experience in which advertising is embedded. The welfare client may not be a reader of anything much and may not have the cash to repair the TV set. The Brahmin prefers the companionship of books and stereo to that of mass culture.

But there is another kind of unevenness in advertising pressure which reflects both the distribution system in marketing and the pattern of media costs. The bigger the media vehicle, the more economical its rates are apt to be in terms of impressions or exposures delivered. Big local media — television and radio stations, newspapers, and outdoor plant operations[3] — are in big markets. Exposure to all media is bound to be higher in urban areas where there are more competitive media choices among stations and papers. In the rural hinterlands, the educational level is lower than it is in the cities and people read less. They are also less likely to be within the effective same-day distribution range of a newspaper and less likely to get several TV channels with full strength.

Even in selecting the optional stations to add to a basic TV network buy, the media planner is apt to work from the top of the list down. Whether he ranks markets in terms of population, aggregate disposable income, purchase of the generic product or of his own particular brand, or by any other measure of sales potential, he almost invariably puts the big ones on top and the little ones at the bottom. There are strong reasons for him to follow this course of action, apart from the fact that media in the bigger markets offer him a greater economy in cost per thousand. The big-town consumer has more brands available to him when he shops. Economies of scale operate in big markets in warehousing and in the logistics of handling merchandise as well as in advertising. The advertiser's own distribution centers are apt to be in the bigger markets; so are his regional offices and his biggest customers. He has to start where his people are, where his own business is concentrated.

---

[3] The outdoor "plant operator" is one who owns or leases a number of billboards in an area. No substantial advertiser uses a single poster; he buys positions in aggregates or "plants," and aims at a certain "showing" which represents a proportion of the total traffic in the area.

When you start at the top of a list of markets you always have to stop somewhere down the line in making up a schedule. Media lists are not only limited in length, they are also commonly subdivided into A, B, and C components which attribute disproportionate weight to the A markets, sometimes with the rationale that the potential sales volume there is higher, sometimes on the grounds that the media cost efficiency is higher.

It is true, of course, that income in the United States is not evenly distributed. The twenty top metropolitan markets, with 32% of the population, had 39% of the purchasing power in 1966. All 300 metropolitan markets, with 72% of the population, had 80% of the purchasing power. Wealth and purchasing power have concentrated to an even greater degree within the metropolitan markets, gathering especially in the suburbs — which have grown fivefold since 1945. In the big markets, a higher proportion of the work force is engaged in better paying jobs of higher skill than is the case in small cities and rural areas. Family incomes are bigger and spending on consumer products is greater. Thus advertisers have been encouraged to concentrate their marketing and sales promotional pressure on the major areas which account for so heavy a proportion of their total sales. An even higher proportion of all advertising messages go into these same markets than the superiority of their wealth and spending would seem to justify. It is in the development of neglected small town sectors of the market that some regional brands have their strength.

It might appear logical to advertise most where public acceptance of a brand, as reflected in sales, was high. Yet, rarely does a brand's sales pre-eminence coincide exactly with the manufacturer's facilities for physical distribution. There is a tendency for a company to want to support its product with advertising wherever it has distribution, regardless of its share of a given market or of the market's importance in the total sales picture. Thus the mere fact that the product is distributed creates consequences for the planning of advertising and sales promotion. If a product is in the stores, has salesmen calling on dealers, and has wholesalers or distributors who handle it, this means that there are people who must be placated, whose enthusiasm must be aroused or maintained. The manufacturer must convince them that he is backing up the product with advertising support. A similar phenomenon occurs in areas where the product's market position is weak or where it faces stiff local competition; there may be strong pressures to overadvertise, if only to maintain the "presence" of the brand in the market.

Few advertisers distribute their products evenly on a truly national basis, i.e., so that one may be 100% sure of finding them in even the smallest crossroads' general store. Nevertheless, the advertiser frequently aims at national coverage.

Via radio or television, national coverage can be achieved with a standard network hookup of somewhere between 100 and 150 stations whose signals can be heard in most of the households in the country. In practice there is often good reason for an advertiser to add to the network's basic list of stations with optional buys in markets important to him. National coverage of a kind can also be attained through the use of magazines whose dispersion and distribution are national, even though it is not likely to be consistent. Even the biggest national magazines show thin spots in many rural counties on the coverage map. To cover the *whole* United States with a newspaper campaign would require the use of hundreds if not thousands of dailies and weeklies in cities and towns and villages, but the 100 biggest daily newspapers can deliver about 45% of total newspaper circulation.

Why do advertisers commonly think in terms of covering the whole country? One reason is that professional marketing and advertising people move in circles where facts, figures, and concepts tend to be expressed in broad national terms.

Partly this is because United States government statistics are the best available in the world, and represent the yardsticks used by most industries and corporations. The distribution territories of the advertiser rarely coincide exactly with the standard territorial categories of the statisticians (state or county boundaries, Census divisions, or regions). Salesmen's districts are apt to follow the snaking of highways across the landscape and these in turn may be delimited by rivers or mountain ranges, and have very little to do with the standard political boundaries on which Census data are based. (By the same token, sales districts can by no means coincide with the coverage area that represents a TV or radio station's effective signal strength, or a newspaper's circulation.)

Advertising people in big companies express themselves in national terms simply because general conversation usually focuses on prototypes, on "good examples," on averages. When we think of marketing in the United States, we are likely to have in mind the most *typical* patterns of distribution and consumption rather than the full range of patterns.

Another reason why advertisers often think in national terms is that the changing character of the American public has tended to break down the old distinctions among urban markets or trading zones. America has an increasingly mobile population, thanks to wars, the automobile, long vacations, and affluence. A fifth of the households move each year. Regionalisms of speech, dress, manner, and custom tend to become more and more obscure.

The very growth of the mass media has in itself become a factor of profound importance in creating national cultural unity. The advertising carried by these media, like the editorial or entertainment content, has offered the same model of The Good Life, with identical artifacts and appurtenances, to households from Maine to Hawaii. It has helped create a common marketing climate in the new suburban housing developments and shopping centers which present much the same sight from coast to coast.

Local community boundaries might appear to have less and less importance in an era in which downtowns are deteriorating and the motorized housewife looks increasingly to the city's periphery to fill her buying needs. In the typical interurban complex midway between large urban centers, people have a number of focal points to which they can turn for shopping and recreation, but they by no means lose their sense of identity with the community.

In a market which Frank Orenstein and I have called Intercity, we interviewed 500 people regarding their shopping habits, their media exposure, and their total pattern of work and movement.[4] Intercity is a town of under 30,000 which lies within easy access of a dozen other towns and cities, including some major markets. We selected it because it has no daily newspaper or broadcasting station of its own. People read daily newspapers which emanate from half a dozen or more surrounding towns and can watch TV channels from four of those towns.

We found a strong correlation between the towns where people travel to work, to shop, or to visit, and the town where the newspapers they read are published. The relationship held both with regard to general shopping and visiting patterns and to the specific facts of where people made their last major purchase of certain items of clothing or furniture. Those who shop in a town were apt to read the newspaper published there, while their next-door neighbors who did their shopping somewhere else were likely to read the newspaper published in that other town. Thus even in a period of growing urban complexity, each daily newspaper sorts out a market by attracting as its audience those who look to its home community as a place to visit and buy.

Local news of familiar people and places is a strong part of the newspaper's appeal. Independent radio stations, particularly those in smaller towns, very often have this same strong identity with their home towns.

In the case of television, incidentally, we found no correlation be-

[4] Leo Bogart and Frank Orenstein, "Mass Media & Community Identity in an Interurban Setting," Journalism Quarterly, Vol. 42, No. 2, Spring 1965, pp. 179-88. The field work for this study was done by Ilse Zeisel.

tween the location of the station that people watched most and the town where they were most likely to visit or shop. These findings are easy to understand when we recognize that television is perceived by its viewers as entertainment in the main line of show business from New York to Hollywood. Television programming is big time and national, and the local station often has little identity except as the outlet for a network.

In spite of the tendencies toward homogenization in American society, powerful regional differences still exist, some on a scale which marketers and advertising planners rarely recognize. The habit of talking in terms of national averages unfortunately disguises enormous regional and local market differences in shopping habits, in competitive brand distributions and brand standings, in consumer tastes and preferences, and in the actual characteristics of consumers themselves.

Solomon Dutka points out that the 212 standard metropolitan statistical areas (SMSA's) of the United States range in population between 60,000 and eleven million and land area from 45 square miles to 27,308 square miles.[5] Yet these metropolitan areas are often lumped together in marketing and media plans as though they represented a common set of conditions and way of life!

The median ages of the population in the separate SMSA's range from 20 to 37 years, the median incomes from $2,940 to $8,750. The percentages completing high school or more range from 24% to 61%, the percentages of homes with television from 75% to 95%, and the percentage of two-car homes from 10% to 39%.

Dutka points out that between 20% to 30% of the total market for most product categories is made up of local or regional brands. Comparing nationally marketed products, Dutka finds strong variations in the regional distribution of their sales. One food brand has 56% of its sales in the East, another 19%. Of two competing cigarette brands, one had 19% of its sales in the Central region, the other 44%. One of two competing appliance brands has 26% of its sales in the West and the other 3%. Yet the management of both companies think of themselves as "national brands," and are apt to require national coverage in their media schedules.

These kinds of striking local variations provide a rationale for the use of local media by national advertisers, either as a flexible primary force in promotion or to supplement national media with extra pressure in the places that need it.

---

[5] Address before the International Newspaper Advertising Executives Association, San Diego, California, June 24, 1965.

Media attributes and contrasts

Consider two of the most disparate forms of advertising — the classified newspaper ad and the OUTDOOR BILLBOARD POSTER. The newspaper reader who turns to the classified section and looks for a particular kind of ad is ready to buy or sell. The person who passes the outdoor poster is exposed to it on a more or less random basis, since the message is displayed to the world at large.

The outdoor or transit advertiser is not interested in everyone who passes by his sign. There may be some relationship between the location of the billboard and the point of sale for the product, as when a gasoline advertiser places a poster on a highway within a mile of a service station.

Usually the mass media advertiser starts from the premise that the potential customers for his product are widely scattered. He uses a mass medium rather than a specialized one precisely because he assumes that the tastes or interests expressed in the demand for his product or brand do not correspond to those appealed to by any particular advertising medium.

The task of outdoor advertising is to create a quick impression, a reminder that the product exists. The outdoor advertiser seeks to maintain a reference point in the consumer's mind for possible future action, but he can normally do this only by reinforcing the effect of previous impressions from other sources.

In some of its applications, RADIO has taken on these characteristics of billboard advertising used as a reminder of other contacts between advertisers and customers. Twenty-five years ago, radio linked the advertised product to the show-business glamour of program personalities whose activities were avidly followed by the mass audience. When Arthur Godfrey spoke of Chesterfields or of Lipton's Tea, for example, he spoke as a convinced and enthusiastic user anxious to pass on his enthusiasm as a matter of public service.

These advantages of broadcast program sponsorship have been largely usurped by TV. Even though today many disc jockeys seek to preserve the tradition of personal testimonials in their recitation of commercials, how many listeners accept this as more than the merest convention? Most radio messages now resemble buckshot in being widely scattered in their impact.

Studies made by the Bureau of Applied Social Research for NBC and by Dan Yankelovich for ABC closely parallel each other in demonstrating radio's new role as an intimate personal companion. The spectator at the baseball game whose transistor is tuned to the broadcast of the game is seeking an affirmation of his own sensory experience, as well as a better understanding of it.[6] (Presumably if, as is often the case, the radio is tuned to the account of another game, he is extending his horizons!) FM radio is essentially a different medium.[7] And FM radio is undergoing major changes that will differentiate it even more as a result of FCC rulings that it be programmed independently of AM for at least half the broadcast day.

As a source of information and instant orientation, AM radio, with its ubiquity and mobility, has carved out a new and indispensable place for itself in the communications system. As a purveyor of "background music" it permits each individual listener to move about always surrounded by his own wave length of personal sound (occasionally to the annoyance of others). It is the most widely accessible source of instant news.

Precisely because radio is now an individual rather than a group listening experience, it offers special values for the advertiser whose product — accident insurance or athlete's foot remedy — may represent too delicate a subject for TV. The familiar announcer or disc jockey may take the tone of a buddy offering direct personal advice.

The advertiser who echoes the musical theme of his TV commercials on radio may evoke the original visual image as well, at a much lower cost than by added frequency on television.

TELEVISION has three great advantages for the advertiser: (1) of all the media, it comes closest to the intensity of interpersonal confrontation; (2) it generates huge audiences at the same moment in time; and (3) it permits the advertiser to encounter the consumer in a relaxed frame of mind, ready for whatever light entertainment the magic box will bring him, eyes and ears simultaneously engaged.

To a viewer in a passive, receptive state the advertiser can show his product in use, he can evoke empathy with the personality who is his spokesman, he can perform all the tricks of film editing and montage.

The television advertiser can employ animation and special effects which give fantasy a form of expressiveness it can rarely achieve in print. He can get the viewer to project himself into remote realms of the imagination, and have the fantasies taken literally.[8] (A still photograph of the

---

[6] He is also, incidentally, more apt to read a newspaper account afterwards to review his recollections.

[7] Its audience is in large part unduplicated by AM, according to a study conducted in 1963-64 in a ten-market FM coverage area by Quality Media Inc. FM accounted for 5/7 of the total listening time devoted to radio in FM homes, and these tended to be above average in income and education.

[8] A fresh problem arises, of course, when the technique takes attention away from the subject, when the advertising becomes so cute that the viewer misses the point.

Ajax White Knight would look bumptious, a cartoon of him would seem silly, but in television he is part of an intriguing game.)

Television has the unique capacity to create vicariously the illusion of personal experience, of "being there." Millions of people who watched the funeral of President Kennedy were bound together in a sense of common participation in a momentous event and in a universally shared emotion. But this kind of rapt involvement, in which even a slight interruption is intolerable, represents one extreme of a long continuum of TV communications experience. At the other end of the attention scale, television programming may be no more than a casual accompaniment to other activities — a drone of sound and a flicker of light at the far periphery of perception.

The solitary viewer is engaged in essentially a different type of activity than the shared experience of watching (and talking about) a program in the company of other family members.[9] The television audience can comment, criticize, and participate in what it sees; within the home environment it is stimulated to the kind of conversation about content which is not permitted in the theater or the movies.

It is precisely the capacity of television programming to arouse audience involvement that makes the commercial break an interruption. In living room viewing, the commercial break provides the occasion for the kind of remark on what has come before which is inhibited by the theatrical convention of silence at the time the program is on. To this extent, the advertiser may lose as well as gain from the very strength of the medium.

The advertising planner is normally not concerned with such matters as the difference between situation comedy and gag comedy as environment for his commercials. In comparing television with other media, he often tends to think of the advertising tasks to which each medium most typically lends itself. To do this he must deliberately ignore the variations which exist among programs. Yet, programs with different kinds of internal structure (dramatic or episodic) provide settings which are propitious for the advertiser's message in varying degrees.

The integrated commercial, in which the performers stop their antics long enough to tell a product story, is an increasingly rare phenomenon, paralleling the decline in live programming and the general substitution of pre-packaged film.

This alienation of the commercial from the immediate entertainment environment is by no means an unmitigated loss. With integrated

[9] Color television, which one out of seven families owned by early 1967, was bound to accelerate the growth of multi-set households, in which the greatest amount of individual viewing occurs.

commercials the audience is sometimes more absorbed by technique than by substance. Their interest in a known personality may make them less attentive to his words about a product than to his style of talking or to the incidental stage business. And if the performer is a comedian, his serious advice to buy may not always be taken seriously. But such problems of technique are minor indeed in the light of television advertising's unique capacity to capture and hold the viewer's attention and interest.

In contrast to TV, much MAGAZINE advertising is predicated on the belief that an integrated mood or tone between the ad and the editorial environment is desirable. Most people reject the idea of magazines and newspapers without ads. Many others who claim that they would prefer to see publications without ads would probably find them most uninviting. Ads are part of the total configuration of what the reader expects to find.

Four-color advertising in magazines affords the advertiser an opportunity to picture and describe his product faithfully and attractively. He encounters the reader in a situation where useful information can be savored, where appealing pictures and inspired text can set off fantasy, where the reader can be spoken to as an individual in a leisurely reflective mood.

However, the reading situation is not always the rapt, deep-in-the-club-chair type idealized in the promotional literature of magazine publishers. It also encompasses the casual skimming that occurs in a barber shop or dentist's waiting room, where the reader picks up the publication in the expectation (and even the hope) that his perusal will be quickly interrupted.

Just as some types of TV programs leave viewers less prone to distraction, so certain types of magazines demand more intense reading. Text magazines (as *Reader's Digest* and Alfred Politz have shown) are read longer and picked up more often than picture books. Monthlies are kept around the house longer than weeklies are.

It is easy enough to visualize the woman who studies and clips the ads in *Good Housekeeping* to get recipe ideas or food service suggestions, or her sister who buys *Vogue* for the fashion ads, or the man who pores over the pages of *Popular Mechanics* as much for the advertised gadgets as for the how-to-do-it articles. These same people may be in a quite different frame of mind when they go through *Life* or *The Saturday Evening Post*. Reading *Good Housekeeping* may have more in common with reading the woman's page of the newspaper than it does with reading *Life*.

The big magazine success stories since the War have been those of specialized publications, like *Playboy* or *Sports Illustrated*. At the same time, the death of *Collier's* and the shaky health of the *Post* have directly reflected the competition of TV as a general entertainment medium. These trends suggest that any magazine can today handle its assignment best if it attracts a homogeneous hard core of readers who can be clearly defined for the advertiser and whose expectations as to advertising content are directly related to the editorial formula.

Theodore Peterson has written in his historical study of magazines:

> The influence of the minority magazines could not be measured by their circulations. Men accustomed to reaching vast audiences sometimes found their power a little puzzling. Frank P. Walsh once called the *Nation* the greatest mystery in American journalism. He had written an article about railroads for it in the days when its circulation was about 27,000. He had done a series on the same subject which was syndicated by the Hearst newspapers, which then had a total circulation of about 10,000,000. Soon after the *Nation* appeared, he got phone calls from senators, lobbyists, persons of importance. But never, he later recalled, had he ever met a person who mentioned his articles syndicated by Hearst.[10]

The *Post, Life, Look,* and the *Digest* (for all their importance as carriers of the mainstream of U. S. popular culture) cannot present a sharp audience profile any more than the CBS Television Network can. Such general media seek to be all things to all men, women, and children and, accordingly, the nature of their editorial offerings is both varied and diffuse. The advertising content of great national magazines parallels their editorial matter in its attempt at universality. Ads and articles together give these magazines their flavor; they mirror the variety and complexity of the contemporary world. They would be quite different without their miscellaneous ads, which form a succession of striking visual *non sequiturs* in keeping with the flow of the articles and features.

Big or small, a great magazine has *character*, a unique personality that sets it apart from the others which resemble it. The vitality and force a magazine exudes can have great value for the advertiser if he can harness the tone of his message to the large editorial force around it. But few magazine ads are prepared with an individual touch for each publication on the schedule. The typical campaign is designed to be run in the "women's books" or the "shelter magazines" and the expensive engravings are put to multiple use.

Some publishers display genius in making their magazines appear unique in the eyes of the advertiser. Others are less successful. On one occasion a few years ago, three associate media directors and eight buyers

---

[10] *Magazines in the Twentieth Century,* Second Edition, Urbana: University of Illinois Press, 1964, p. 439. The article by Walsh was written in 1921.

from the media department of a large advertising agency stood through several rounds of drinks and sat through a dinner of rare roast beef in a private room over an expensive midtown New York restaurant. The magazine which was paying for this luncheon — as it had done and would do again for dozens of identical luncheons in the same setting — was now about to have its innings. One of the agency men excused himself and hurried off immediately after the meal, pleading an urgent meeting back at the office. The publisher of the magazine stood up to express his appreciation to those still present for their attendance. He had no new research, no facts or figures to report. (This was a good thing, too, because the facts and figures on his particular publication showed a steady decline by every criterion advertisers might consider.) But he did want to talk about the editorial character of his publication which made it unique and gave it a mandatory position on every magazine list. "The *American* magazine," he said gravely, "is everything the name implies." It died soon afterwards.

NEWSPAPER SUPPLEMENTS represent a special form which many media planners find hard to classify. The Sunday magazine (so it is called, although many actually appear on other days of the week) is often considered as part of a magazine budget and evaluated in terms of cost and coverage against *Reader's Digest* or *Life*. For many years, the major syndicated Sunday magazines fostered the concept that they were part of the magazine medium, in spite of the fact that the audience reads them as part of the big diversified Sunday newspaper itself. Supplement ads are commonly adaptations of magazine ads, even though the editorial environment and audience expectations are somewhat different.

In recent years, the nationally syndicated supplements have lost ground to locally edited ones, which are even more closely integrated into the newspaper format. As a medium, the supplements offer the advertiser vast circulation at low cost. They also offer him the opportunity to expose his message at a highly concentrated time, as opposed to the much more attenuated and longer life of a magazine issue's readership.[11] The supplements have also made much of the relaxed and leisurely home environment of Sunday reading and suggest that on this day of rest the buying plans for the strenuous week to come are discussed in family council.

The DAILY NEWSPAPER offers the advertiser great flexibility, both in timing and creative technique. The advertiser can almost always get his ad in the paper on the day he wants and with only a few days' notice,

[11] As with the rest of the newspaper, only a small part of supplement readership is "pass along."

while the broadcast spot on the desired channel and time slot must generally be wangled well in advance. A given quantity of newspaper space can be divided into a very large number of units and shapes, and these can be scheduled to fit the advertiser's needs.

Large space in the newspaper can be used dramatically, with the aid of Run of Paper color or pre-printed high-fidelity color within the paper (Hi-Fi or SpectaColor) or run in special sections. Small space units can be scattered and directed at different buying interests.

The newspaper represents a regular part of its readers' daily experience, with a habitual place and time of reading. This gives it an intimacy and sense of identification on the reader's part as the voice of his home town.[12]

Because the newspaper is perceived as the comprehensive daily directory or encyclopédia of information, no one reader reads it all, nor is he expected to. To be successful, newspaper advertising should reflect the here and now of today's paper and carry the same sense of immediacy which is reflected in the news columns. Although retail advertisers understand how to achieve this effect, the manufacturer and his agency find the task more difficult if they believe their product to be of low interest or have nothing new to say about it.

For such an advertiser, the chief merit of the newspaper medium is akin to that of the billboard; a single message (in most markets) can be put in front of virtually everybody, and — unique to the newspaper — it can be put in front of them when the advertiser wants it there.

On comparing media

Every advertising medium has been used successfully by someone, in some way, and every media salesman has a portfolio full of success stories which can be pulled out at the right moment to convince the wavering prospect. There may be a case history of failure for every one of success, but these are the ones which are rarely publicized.

Horace Schwerin, whose career has been devoted to testing commercials, concludes from a series of comparative studies made by his firm in Germany that the relative merits of print and television advertising vary substantially from one product field to the next. So cautious a

---

[12] A surprising number of people have direct contact with the newspaper as a local institution. Forty-five per cent have placed a classified ad at one time or another, 43% have visited their local paper's offices, 8% have written a letter to the editor. *Cf. The Daily Newspaper and Its Reading Public*, New York: Bureau of Advertising, 1961, p. 48.

statement can hardly be called into question. However, when advertisements appearing in various media are compared in the aggregate, strong advantages do not usually emerge for one medium over the others.

In a study for ABC Radio, Daniel Yankelovich selected 25 matched sets of advertising messages in radio, television, and magazines. These were exposed to and evaluated by matched groups of 50 respondents each, about 500 in all. Yankelovich had each of the ads ranked on 46 measures of "impact" as well as measures of the degree to which they stimulated "buying interest" or favorable brand attitudes. The criteria included such characterizations as "useful," "honest," "informative," "real," "believable," "clear," "sociable," and "intimate." [13] Remarkably, on 42 of the 48 measures, radio, TV, and magazine ads all performed equally well.

For reasons which I shall develop more fully later, research experiments comparing media are almost always comparing other things at the same time, and the results are apt to be inconclusive. Such research generally proves highly frustrating to sponsor and user alike, because the findings are always specific to the individual ads and commercials tested. There is always room for argument as to whether the creative adaptation of the advertising for a second form is honestly comparable to the original ad. Moreover, no matter in what way the residual "impact" of the advertising message may be defined in experiments of this sort — by awareness, information, opinion change, or purchase behavior — the research must almost always be done under laboratory conditions of enforced exposure — in which people agree ahead of time, for a consideration, to expose themselves to the advertising. This has several consequences: it makes the exposure situation an artificial one, and perhaps the abnormality is more to the advantage of one medium than to the other. It ignores the normal scope of coverage of the two media under comparison, against which the "impact" figures must be projected. And it is not generally concerned with the comparability of costs for real-life usage of the media being evaluated.

A typical attempt to equate the residual impact of print and television advertisements was made by W. R. Simmons & Associates for *Life* magazine in 1966. In metropolitan San Francisco, Pittsburgh, Miami, Omaha, and Boston, interviews were conducted with people who had watched prime-time television the preceding evening. Separate interviews were held with people who had read the current issue of *Life* within the past 24 hours. Viewers who had watched a program the previous evening were shown a series of 18 commercials on a portable projector

[13] "The Yankelovich Report, A Media Research Program," Fall 1965. "Brave," "clean," and "reverent" were omitted from the criteria used.

and asked to identify the ones that appeared on the show in question. Similarly, people who had just read the current issue of *Life* were shown 30 full-page advertisements and asked to identify the ones in that issue.

When all the data had been collated, Simmons calculated a "net retention curve" (the difference between the number of commercials or ads which an individual *correctly* identified with the program or magazine and the number *mistakenly* identified). The television commercials received a slightly higher retention score — 17.6%, against 15.3% for the magazine ads. In keeping with the usual pattern, magazine ads scored significantly higher among people of high income — 18% for those with household incomes $8,000 and over, against 12% for those below $5,000 income. The tendency was reversed in the case of TV (15% for those above $8,000 and 19% for those below $5,000).[14]

The advertiser who attempts to project such results to his own problems in comparing media is still faced with the differences between magazines and TV in cost, coverage, and communications capacities other than those involved in ad recall. If he is really sophisticated, he may also ask himself whether a publication which accumulates its full readership over weeks should really be compared with a broadcast which exists at a moment of time.

Electronic and print media

For Marshall McLuhan, space and time are not the most useful dimensions for classifying media. He prefers "hot" and "cool." "Hot" media like radio and newspapers, McLuhan believes, are active, aggressive, crammed with information. A "cool" medium like television must be activated and participated in by the viewer to suck out information and meaning.[15] Such intriguing and arbitrary statements contradict the more conventional distinction made between the broadcast media (to which the audience is passively exposed) and the print media (from which the reader must actively extract information).

Gestalt theory in psychology teaches that if we see an incomplete circle we tend to complete it in our minds. The expenditure of energy

[14] Curiously enough, there was no such consistent pattern when the retention scores were analyzed by educational level. The margin of difference was very slight for women — 14.9% for TV and 14.3% for magazines. For men the difference in favor of TV was greater — 20%, compared with 16% for *Life*.

[15] It almost appears as though McLuhan is contradicting his own major premise about the pre-eminent importance of media form over content. What makes radio and newspapers "hot" may be less the sizzling immediacy of their communications technology than their news informational content. (News items *are* aggressive, when one stops to think of it.) The entertainment *content* of TV seems "cooler" than its steady flow of lighted dots across the sensitized surface of the picture tube.

required to make it seem whole makes us *more* aware of it than we would be if it really *were* whole. The work of the eminenent psychologist B. F. Skinner leads to the conclusion that conditioning is most successful when it is only partially reinforced. We tend to lose interest when a given act always results in predictable consequences. We learn best when there is an element of uncertainty in our learning, when we have to work hard and participate actively. Just these conditions exist during the reading process when the reader himself is an active participant.

The key distinction between space and broadcast communication is often described in terms of the time dimension.[16] But though it takes time to read a magazine or newspaper, this time is under the reader's control and he can scan vast quantities of information very rapidly in order to absorb what he needs. For this reason, the total time spent reading and time spent viewing or listening are simply not to be compared (as they sometimes are) as measures of communication.

The real difference between electronic and print media starts at the point where the message is physically presented to readers or viewers and where the attrition of interest sets in.

Any medium which flows in time begins with a higher probability of dominating the senses on behalf of a given message than does a static medium in which the printed word is scanned and assimilated selectively. This gives broadcast advertising its quality of intrusiveness.

Broadcast advertising demands a higher level of conscious awareness than print. But broadcast messages are for the most part randomly scattered and not (to the same degree as with print) selectively perceived by those who are predisposed to be purchasers of the product.

Several different advertising tasks may be lumped together loosely under the heading of "getting the reader to think about the product." He may use the advertising as a reference point to absorb factual information, or he may use it as a starting point for revery or fantasy, imagining that he owns the product and considering the utility it might have.

In the case of print, revery can set in the moment the reader stops at the ad. When his scanning is interrupted and he stops to read the copy or look at an illustration, he is already, in his own mind, building up an appropriate set of symbolic associations for the interpretation of what he sees. The more physically dominant an advertisement is, the better able it is to attract attention long enough for the reader to become involved in this type of speculative revery or fantasy.

[16] Actually, visual perception does not exist outside of time. A figure must be exposed for 0.003 seconds before it is "seen" with a complete contour, according to H. Werner, cited by William Dember, *Psychology of Perception,* New York: Holt, Rinehart, and Winston, 1960.

In time-bound broadcast advertising, we expect speculation or revery to last for the actual duration of the commercial and to end abruptly when the next commercial or program comes on. Demonstration in a television commercial mobilizes the viewer's fantasies about the use and ownership of the product, but ordinarily, when the demonstration ends, the viewer must cope with the new images and ideas that follow it on the screen.

The media mood

How does the emotional response of audience to medium redound to the advertiser's benefit? It has long been understood that a product can borrow prestige from the media in which it advertises, and much media merchandising has been based on this. The small regional manufacturer who runs space in *Life* can proclaim his product at the point of sale "as advertised in *Life*" much as he can display the Good Housekeeping Seal of Approval. On television the "magazine concept" shows like "Today" and "Tonight" have used much the same technique. (Of course, the personal testimonial delivered by a radio or television showman expresses par excellence the product's opportunity to borrow authority from the medium.)

That editorial context is important finds corroboration in a number of studies relating advertising to its environment. A study conducted for *Life* magazine on "The Effect of Media Context on Advertising" by Nowland and Company in 1962 placed identical ads in *Life* and *Look* magazines and an unmarked portfolio. Each respondent was shown three different advertisements, one in *Life*, another in *Look*, and a third in the portfolio. The respondent was asked to choose one of the three advertisements for each of six different criteria (including interest, believability, and choice of product). The study concluded that "selections of the advertisements when they appeared in *Life* were significantly higher than when the advertisements appeared in the portfolio, on five of the six criterion questions. . . . *Life* selections exceeded *Look* selections by significant amounts on four criterion measures." Each magazine's readers chose the ads in that magazine significantly more often than did readers of other magazines.[17]

---

[17] Before this — in 1956 — *Good Housekeeping* had engaged Burleigh Gardner's Social Research Inc. to demonstrate that the same ad directed to the housewife was more warmly received and better attended to in a woman's magazine than in *Life* or the *Post*. *Cf.* "The Meaning of Good Housekeeping and Its Advertising to Its Readers," *op. cit.*

Research by William Blair of Harper-Atlantic Sales shows that people who give high ratings to the editorial content of a publication are also more apt than other readers to say that they usually look at most of the ads in the publication and find them enjoyable, informative, believable, and creative.[18] The people who read both mass and selective magazines give higher ratings to the advertising in the selective ones.

In television, TvQ — a syndicated service which periodically measures program popularity — has consistently found that people who like a program more than average are also most likely to recall commercials and advertisers. In a series of studies TvQ made for the International Latex Company, 42 commercial tests were conducted for brands in four product categories over a period of a year, with a total of 8,800 respondents. Housewives were interviewed on their choice of brand before and after each new program came on the air. People who liked the program when it appeared switched to the advertised brand 40% more than those who felt the show was "average" and 200% more than those who did not like the show.

In another study, TvQ compared reactions to commercials for "favorites" and "non-favorites" among the premier telecasts of new programs at the opening of the 1962-1963 season. This approach permitted the investigators to get reactions to programs which did not have a history of prior exposure and existing attitudes. The percentage recalling one or more commercials was 27% in the case of those who termed a new program their "favorite," compared with 22% for the "non-favorites." The advantage was even more substantial for the "favorites" with regard to recall of the commercial highlights and key selling points.

In England, two studies — one conducted late in 1964 and one conducted in the Spring of 1965 — measured both presence and attention during commercial breaks. Those who liked a program best were most apt to be viewing attentively, without other distracting activity. Liking the *preceding* program had more influence on determining attention than liking the *following* program, suggesting that a receptive mood carries over but is not necessarily anticipated.

A similar finding comes from a study made by the Bureau of Advertising in 1965. In three three-channel cities, 5,275 telephone calls were made during prime evening time, the numbers being dialed ten minutes after the hour or after the half-hour in order to avoid station-break spot commercials. People watching television were interviewed about the advertising on the program they were actually watching. Remarkably little difference was found in the spontaneous recall of the last in-pro-

[18] *Subscriber Attitudes Towards Editorial and Advertising in Five Magazines.* Harper-Atlantic Sales, Inc., 1966.

gram commercial between those with above-average interest (19%) and those with average interest (18%) in the program they were watching, but recall fell off to 14% in the case of those with less than average interest.

This same research also demonstrated that within television a distinction between primary and secondary audiences could be drawn much like the distinction long recognized as making a difference in attentiveness to magazine advertizing. Viewers were separated first into those who were watching alone and those who were watching with others in the family. Then each group in turn was subdivided — the solitary viewers into those who had planned in advance to watch the program and those who merely kept the set on from the previous show or twirled the dial, and the group viewers into those who themselves selected the program and those who were merely along for the ride as part of the family viewing situation. In both cases, the viewers who had exercised conscious choice of the program were better able (by a three-to-two margin) to recall the last commercial or to name any advertiser on the program.

These planful viewers are, almost by definition, the ones who are most likely to return to the same program week after week. They are thus the most likely to become familiar with the sponsor's commercials and to recognize them wherever they appear. Such a regular viewer is most likely to be the one who has a spontaneous and favorable association between program and product at the point when he makes his purchase decision.

Under these conditions, to paraphrase McLuhan, the program *is* the product; the aura of favorable association with the media vehicle is a significant part of the brand image itself. The housewife standing before an array of packages in the supermarket is subconsciously comparing the appeal of TV programs or magazines as part of her comparison of the attributes of the products themselves. This is not at a high level of deliberation; it is simply part of the whole complex order of comparisons which confronts her at that moment and out of which she makes her spontaneous choice. This kind of automatic identification takes place for all brands whose advertising habitually occurs in a certain context. The more concentrated the advertising is on a particular vehicle, and the more exclusive its dominance of that vehicle (full sponsorship on a TV program, as opposed to spot participation), the richer and more vital will be the texture of associations which carry over from the program to the product.

In 1966, only 7% of evening network shows were under a single sponsorship. The benefits of full sponsorship of a program series by a company appear to be obvious. The program sponsor is able to select the kind of environment in which he wants his message to appear. He can elect to place his commercial at a high-tension point in the show, with the heroine in peril dire, or at a low-tension point when interest may be lower but the audience is less likely to be irritated by his interruption. He can choose to have an integrated commercial, with the show's regular announcer or performers stepping ever so slightly (he hopes) out of character to talk about Our Sponsor's product.

Full sponsorship involves hazards as well as benefits, particularly when the sponsored program is considered controversial or has political overtones.

The prevailing desire of most American corporations is to remain inoffensive to any group of potential customers. An executive of the Coca-Cola Company stated this viewpoint succinctly when he was queried about the company's position on racial matters: "Our problem is to walk a very fine line and be friends with everybody. I've heard the phrase 'Stand Up and Be Counted' for so long from both sides that I'm sick of it. Sure we want to stand up and be counted, but on both sides of the fence. For God's sake, why don't they let us go on selling a delicious and refreshing beverage to anybody who's got a gullet he can pour it down." [19]

In the Spring of 1964, the Xerox Corporation put up $4 million to underwrite a series of 90-minute spectaculars on the United Nations. As soon as the news was announced, protest mail started to come in. The letters ran at a rate of 100 to one against the forthcoming shows. An analysis of the letters found that 61,000 had been written by about 16,000 people. As the management of Xerox became concerned about this project, pro-UN organizations rallied to the support of the company. They stimulated 14,500 letters of approval from 14,500 separate individuals. A survey made for Xerox by Elmo Roper from a national cross-section of 1,500 adults found that more than one out of four had seen, read, or heard about one or both of the first two UN shows, and one out of five had actually watched at least one of the shows. Three out of four called the program "good" or "outstanding," and among those aware of the programs, 31% identified Xerox as the sponsor, in spite of the fact that the corporate identification had been limited to an opening and closing institutional credit. Only 5% termed the series "not a particularly good idea." But more timorous management might have rushed to cancel the show when the first onrush of hostile letters began!

When the advertiser relinquishes full sponsorship and buys a par-

[19] E. J. Kahn, Jr., *The Big Drink,* New York: Random House, 1960, p. 153.

ticipation in a network show, he loses some of these prerogatives.   When he buys a network spot, with his messages spread over a number of different shows, he loses still more.   And when he buys spot TV on a local basis — no matter how courageously his agency's time buyers may negotiate for the best positions next to the highest-rated shows — he has altogether lost his special privileges to control his ad's environment.

The print advertiser rarely has any such special privileges.   If he is a regular advertiser on a long-term continuity schedule, he may win a special position such as Coca-Cola has on the back covers of many magazines and as Campbell Soup had for years at the end of the main editorial section in the *Saturday Evening Post*.

In newspapers, advertisers may specify that they want their ad in the sports pages or the financial section, but they cannot specify that the Giants are to win or lose or the Dow-Jones stock averages are to go up or down, even though this coloration of the surrounding editorial matter may have a profound effect on the way people see their messages.

Media concentration or media mix?

The major argument for concentration of an advertiser's budget within a single medium is that it provides him with an opportunity to dominate that medium relative to his competition.   This dominance applies at least to those prospective customers who are likely to be exposed repeatedly to the medium.

The advertiser who pursues this course expects that his strong impact on a part of the market is translated into greater familiarity with his brand — and thus to actual preference.   This reasoning seems particularly cogent in the case of those packaged goods for which the consumer cannot detect material brand differences.   When it is hard for him to distinguish brands in actual use, he is likely to select the brand he perceives as most familiar and acceptable.   He may identify the brand's apparent popularity with public approval, which in turn he associates with successful performance.   It must be the best if it's the favorite! The sharply concentrated use of a single medium can give a brand this aura of mass acceptance in the eyes of people whose restricted orbit of media exposure coincides with the advertiser's scheduling strategy. There are also several arguments contrary in favor of a mix of media. The principle of "synergism" has often been invoked by media planners and media salesmen alike to justify the advantages of a media mix.   The idea is that the communications effect of two media working together is greater than that of either alone.   The use of two channels of persuasion working together improves the odds of breaking through the defenses which people erect against irrelevant communications. Thus presumably the same effort or investment distributed over two media can work more effectively than it can in a single medium.

Logically there appears to be some confusion in the use of the term "synergism" as applied to a schedule of *different* media. The word suggests that simultaneous pressure is being applied by two forces. This is indeed what happens in television, which combines aural and visual communication.

In what has already become a classic study, Leon Festinger and Nathan Maccoby studied the effect on college fraternity boys of a filmed critique of fraternities.[20] When the sound track was played to the visual accompaniment of an irrelevant and amusing film which lampooned abstract painting, anti-fraternity opinion increased more than when the original film was shown. Perhaps the visual presence of the speaker allowed the boys to justify their rejection of the film's message by finding fault with him as an authority, whereas his disembodied voice did not lend itself to this kind of rationalization. In any case, the experimenters concluded that visual distraction might give a spoken message greater persuasive effect than visual reinforcement. If this were true it would be most important in the design of TV commercials (and in contradiction to the longstanding precept that video and audio should be mutually reinforcing).

It should be noted that when sight and sound are totally unrelated (as in this experiment), the effects cannot possibly be the same as when *related* but *different* messages are conveyed at the same time, creating conflict because neither is clearly dominant. It is interesting to think of the Festinger-Maccoby findings in the light of a Schwerin Research study which compared commercials with superimposed copy or graphics over an existing visual against those without "supers," and found the *latter* to be superior in performance. Such findings about the effects of combining sight and sound within *one* medium tell us little, however, about the use of separate media.

Perhaps the notion of synergism can be extended to describe what happens if a print ad happens to be read shortly before or after a TV message is seen, or when a driver listening to a commercial on his car radio sees a billboard advertising the same product, but it seems dubious to attribute to it to all the virtues of a media mix.

The real advantages of a media mix have nothing to do with synergism at all. One advantage is that a media mix generally extends the advertiser's coverage beyond what he would normally achieve with a single medium. This is not a virtue in and of itself, unless we assume that

[20] "On Resistance to Persuasive Communications," *Journal of Abnormal and Social Psychology*, Vol. 68, 1964, pp. 359-66.

his message with a single medium will be delivered repeatedly to some people (the heavy users of the medium) beyond the point of diminishing returns in persuasion. Instead of continuing to beat these people over the head with a message they may already have absorbed, the advertiser can cut his effort against them and divert part of it to achieving first contacts in new sectors of the market.

A media mix permits the advertiser to segment his audience by delivering different forms of the message with different copy themes or psychological appeals through different media to different kinds of prospective customers. An advertiser can use one approach in *Town and Country* and another in *Woman's Day,* or he can address himself to teenagers on the radio and to sports-minded men or housewives in the newspaper (depending on the section in which he places his ad).

Another advantage of the media mix is that it permits the same individuals to be contacted within different psychological contexts. This presents the possibility of attracting attention in one environment for a product which might not be noticed in another. And by presenting a familiar message in an unfamiliar or different context, it creates possibilities of capturing fresh interest for an otherwise tired subject.

The chances of winning attention increase if there is a touch of familiarity about an ad, with a touch of uncertainty as to why it appears familiar. This is like seeing someone who looks familiar and stopping to speculate as to where one has seen him before. The mind will dwell longer on the person's identity than it would if he were an acquaintance whom one had expected to see. A man may pass the office receptionist ten times a day and each of those meetings will have very little effect on his impression of her. But if he sees her at the theater, well-coiffed and smiling at her boyfriend, she suddenly appears in a different light and becomes a more interesting subject of speculation.

The basic principle here is that of the poetic metaphor, in which the sensibilities of the audience are aroused by an unexpected juxtaposition of familiar images. One of the virtues of the media mix is that a product message received in an unaccustomed media context arouses this kind of small shock of recognition. The product familiar through its radio commercial which is suddenly seen on a billboard will create greater awareness in us than if we hear another commercial for it.

On the other hand, an advertised product must follow the characteristic style of advertising technique for every medium it uses. The constant shifting of creative techniques within a medium, or among media, can create inconsistencies and confusion in the product image and actually inhibit attention.

GETTING THE MESSAGE THROUGH

"Advertisements are now so numerous that they are negligently perused," said Samuel Johnson in 1758. The A.A.A.A.[1] research on consumer judgment of advertising shows that a large proportion of observed ads are not recorded as noteworthy in any way (see pp. 8-11). But even more striking is the small number of advertising messages counted under conditions of hypersensitivity to advertising, i.e., sensitivity artificially induced by the research plan. What a minute proportion the count of 76 observed ads in 12 hours represents in light of the tremendous daily outpouring of messages from all sides and through all media!

Is there a practical physical limitation on the number of stimuli or messages which the human senses can absorb? There is good evidence to the effect that a constant input of fresh stimuli is essential to our mental balance. During every waking moment we are bombarded by an enormous array of sensory impressions. Yet we do not ordinarily lose

[1] American Association of Advertising Agencies.

ourselves in contemplation of the design of the fabrics and furniture around us, the play of light and shadow, the beating of our pulses, the itching of our skins, or the varied sounds which reach us through the open window. We can at any moment selectively concentrate our attention on any of these many stimuli, or we can ignore them. In the same way, the proliferation of communications in our visual and aural environment forces us to be selective in what we recognize and register. To use the terms of Gestalt psychology, we learn to separate "figures" from "ground." We place certain stimuli within the forefront of our attention, while others of equivalent itensity are relegated to the background.

The great film historian, Siegfried Kracauer, refers in his *Theory of Film* to "the blind spots of the mind."

> The role which cultural standards and traditions may play in these processes of elimination is drastically illustrated by a report on the reactions of African natives to a film made on the spot. After the screening, the spectators, all of them still unacquainted with the medium, talked volubly about a chicken they allegedly had seen picking food in the mud. The film maker himself, entirely unaware of its presence, attended several performances without being able to detect it. Had it been dreamed up by the natives? Only by scanning his film foot by foot did he eventually succeed in tracing the chicken: it appeared for a fleeting moment somewhere in a corner of a picture and then vanished forever.[2]

The "blind spots of the mind" may be experimentally located in the psychological laboratory. When, through the use of a stereoscopic device, an upright face is presented to one eye and an upside down face to the other eye, the individual does not see two super-imposed faces; he sees one face right side up. Similar results are obtained when a nude and a clothed figure are presented simultaneously. When a baseball picture and a bullfight picture are shown at the same time to different eyes, Americans see the ballgame, Mexicans the bullfight.

How we perceive

What makes us perceive things as meaningful to us so that they register in our minds? In the words of W. H. Ittelson and F. T. Kilpatrick,[3] "perception is never a sure thing, never an absolute revelation of 'what is.' Rather, what we see is a prediction — our own personal construction designed to give us the best possible bet for carrying out our purposes in action. We make these bets on the basis of our past experience."

[2] New York: Oxford University Press, 1960, p. 53.
[3] "Experiments in Perception," *Scientific American*, August 1951, p. 55.

According to the perception theorist James J. Gibson, "perception involves meaning; sensation does not. . . . Sensations are not the cause of perceptions. . . . Conscious sensory impressions and sense data in general are incidental to perception, not essential to it. They are occasionally symptomatic of perception. But they are not even necessary symptoms inasmuch as perception may be 'sensationless' (as for example in auditory localization). Having a perception does not entail the having of sensations." [4]

The processes of visual perception are extraordinarily complex. J. Bronowski writes:

> The brain asks the eye for information not about points but about objects: their boundaries, their movements and their contrast against the background. This is a much more recondite system of information than we, who are used to television pictures and graph paper, would expect. Moreover, in higher animals it is relayed to either two or three different parts of the brain, which have evolved at different times. In short, the brain (and the retina, which in origin is part of the brain) is concerned from the first moment with integrating the impressions it receives from the environment; it *begins* by discriminating. What it treats as units of information are far more complex assemblies and contrasts than we would think of feeding to a machine.[5]

Derek H. Fender describes the changing of the eye's focus in visual search as a matter of feed-back controls or servomechanisms. One such servomechanism, for example, controls the eye muscles "to position the image of an object on the fovea. Each pair of muscles receives signals proportional to the displacement of the interesting part of the image from the fovea, and the muscles then act together to move the eyeball in such a way as to reduce the displacement to zero." [6]

Through still another servomechanism, the eyes are brought to the correct angle of convergence, making depth perception possible. Similar changes occur in the thickness, and therefore in the focal length, of the lens. The accommodative mechanism of the eye has what Fender refers to as a steady "hunting motion . . . superimposed on it that continually lengthens and shortens the focal length of the lens."

Depending on the location of the object being viewed, a change in one direction will improve an out-of-focus image, and a change in the other direction will worsen it; this information is fed back to steer accommodation in the direction of the sharpest focus. Once the correct lens thickness is found, information about it is fed across to the convergence

[4] "The Useful Dimensions of Sensitivity," *American Psychologist*, Vol. 18, No. 1, January 1963, pp. 1-15.
[5] Review of Michael A. Arbib, "Brains, Machines and Mathematics," *Scientific American*, June 1964.
[6] "Control Mechanisms of the Eye," *Scientific American*, July 1964.

mechanism. The two systems exchange information but are separate and distinct in their modes of control.

Perception is a matter of probability, a probability which increases as the intensity of the stimulus is changed. Change is experienced as a "shock of transition," to use William James' term. Thus we normally think of perception as an activity which involves a reaction to stimuli which are *above* the threshold of consciousness or awareness.

The geometric relationship between stimulation and experience is expressed in Weber's Law, one of the landmarks of perceptual psychology. The stronger or more intense the existing stimulus, the greater the real change required to produce the sensation of change. William Dember points out that Weber's Law deals with variations in the intensity of a given stimulus against a constant background. If the Law applied *regardless* of the original intensity of the stimulus whose strength is being varied, then its detectability would depend only on the relative contrast of target and background. But when the background has high intensity, it is harder for a stimulus target to be distinguished. Conversely, when the background has less intensity, it is easier for a stimulus to be noted. And the bigger the visual target, the easier it is to distinguish it from the background — this holds true up to a critical focal point beyond which it becomes harder again.[7]

A similar relationship of message to background appears to apply to hearing as well as seeing. John Cohen proposes that the apparent duration of a brief interval is influenced by the intensity of the stimuli that delimit it. "The more intense the stimuli are, the shorter the interval seems to be. . . . A reverse effect occurs, however, if the interval is defined by a continuous stimulus and the subject is asked to compare two equal intervals made up of stimuli of unequal intensity. The interval with the more intense sound seems to last longer than the interval with the less intense sound."[8] In short, our perception of what we hear and see is inseparable from the environment of the message.

Another psychologist, Henry Helson, has applied the concept of "adaptation level" to describe the neutral perceptual state of an organism at the moment a fresh stimulus is received. Thus a new sensory impression is always perceived not merely in terms of its own physical strength, but in relation to the stimuli which have preceded it.

We bring to most experience a "set" of expectations about what is to come next. We interpret new stimuli in terms of these anticipations and see, in effect, what we expect to see. People who are hungry or

[7] "Ricco's Law," cited by William W. Dember, *Psychology of Perception*, New York: Holt, Rinehart, and Winston, 1960, p. 359.
[8] "Psychological Time," *Scientific American*, November 1964.

thirsty are more likely to recognize words that pertain to hunger or thirst. When we look for more than one thing at the same time, it is harder to detect *any* of the things we are looking for. Experiments have shown that we recognize familiar words more easily than unfamiliar ones, but that unfamiliar words are detected more rapidly when we are prepared to expect them.

G. S. Blum has shown that at low levels of awareness "the individual would be sensitized to threatening impulses and impulse-related stimuli; but if the stimuli were close to awareness, defense would occur. Thus both vigilance and defense are predicted depending on the level of awareness." [9]

Blum demonstrated his point by showing to his experimental subjects both anxiety-producing and neutral pictures; the subjects were then asked to identify the pictures under two different conditions of exposure, one much briefer than the other. On brief exposure, the anxiety-producing stimulus was identified more often. It was *less* easily identified when the exposure was long enough to permit some awareness of the content.

This finding has interesting implications for advertising dealing with subjects which are essentially unpleasant (like headache remedies, for instance). The suggestion would seem to be that product identity might be more readily established in print (where the reader could abbreviate his contact with the message) than in a TV commercial where the message could not be avoided. Successful experiences in television would seem to belie this.

Scanning and reading

Ulric Neisser has observed that "reading" is an ambiguous word which covers many levels of comprehension. Scanning is a kind of reading which involves a relatively low level of cognitive analysis and which takes place at a rate that seems independent of the quantity of information which must be processed. Neisser describes scanning as it is exemplified in the daily work of people who are accustomed to looking for several thousand targets at once:

> The readers in any newspaper-clipping agency. Such a firm may have hundreds of clients, each of whom wants a clipping of at least any newspaper story in which he or his firm is mentioned; beyond this, many clients will be interested in an appreciable number of different trade

[9] "An Experimental Reunion of Psychoanalytic Theory with Perceptual Vigilance and Defense," *Journal of Abnormal and Social Psychology*, Vol. 49, No. 1, January 1954, pp. 94-98.

names and titles and others will specify their clipping needs in a more general way. . . . It takes a year or more to train a clipping reader to scan newspaper type at well over 1,000 words a minute, keeping watch for all the agency's targets. Error rates are said to be in the neighborhood of 10% for the best readers, and neither the error rate nor the speed seems to change as an agency gradually acquires more clients.[10]

Neisser concludes that "visual search can involve a multiplicity of processes carried out together." He points out that "perceptual analysis, then, has many levels. It seems to be carried out by a multitude of separate mechanisms arranged in a hierarchy, the more complex mechanisms receiving as their input the information that has been assimilated and predigested by more elementary ones." He cites experimental evidence that eye movements may actually be "anticipations" rather than "responses" to stimuli. "This suggests strongly that the eye's control system must be doing something more than reacting to a motion; it must be predicting."

The psychoanalytic concept of repression helps to explain at least one aspect of the scanning process. Ordinarily, the term "repression" refers to the subjugation, below consciousness, of an unpleasant experience or emotion. A newspaper reader sees a photograph of an atrocity and then "forgets" that he has seen it. At a far less intense level of emotion, he represses his perception of an ad for a product with unpleasant brand name associations.

But this psychological mechanism is distinct from the kind of rejection which takes place automatically in the normal reading process. Most of what is seen or heard but not perceived does not represent an active repression of information for which there is an actual aversion. It represents rather an economical response to an oversupply of stimuli. As the reader scans, he inhibits not so much the unpleasant as the merely irrelevant.

The newspaper represents a large, complex array of visual stimuli, and studies of how it is read can tell us a good deal about the general process by which advertising messages come through to us.

Since the eyes are always in motion, the reader constantly confronts new cues that stimulate new interests on an open spread of pages in a magazine or newspaper. His focus of vision is attracted to those areas of potential interest which are glimpsed in the periphery of the visual field.

In the reading process, our systematic scanning is arrested and concentrated when we find something we want to examine more closely. To some extent the reader is engaged in a purposeful search for useful

[10] "Visual Search," *Scientific American*, June 1964.

information. But he also appears to be in a state of hypersensitivity or susceptibility to relevant information that he is neither looking for nor expecting to encounter. All this, moreover, occurs in the twinkling of an eye.

The reader, as he scans, unconsciously tends to simplify things for himself by fitting material into context. To use a concept from Gestalt psychology, the reader seeks for closure: he tries to reduce the environment to the most easily manageable terms; when he looks at the page, he interprets it in terms of its *over-all* meaning.

What attracts our attention

As we go from a small ad to a big one in print, or as we add color to black and white, we increase the probability that the reader's eye will physically alight upon the message in the normal course of the scanning process. We do not comparably increase this probability as we go from a brief I.D. to a longer commercial on TV, although the opportunity for the absent-minded or diverted viewer to return his gaze to the screen is greater if the message is extended in time.

Novelty and complexity attract our attention. However, as William Dember points out, even complex stimuli "should lose their attractive power once they have been thoroughly investigated. The most interesting painting, for example, cannot be viewed interminably. The finest symphony, if repeated often enough, becomes banal and commonplace. The best novel cannot bear continual re-reading." [11]

In an experiment conducted at the University of Manchester, a group of people exposed to a concert of recorded music were asked to signal when they became aware that their minds had been wandering away from the program. As reported by John Cohen, the percentage of inattentiveness rose from 19% after five minutes to 66% after ten minutes and to 82% after twenty minutes. When a similar experiment was run with a lecture instead of music, the proportion rose from 27% inattentiveness after five minutes to 52% after ten minutes and 61% after twenty minutes. Curiously enough, the lecture audience became *more* attentive after a half-hour had elapsed. [12]

Curiosity, the sheer zest for exploration, appears to be an essential human attribute. Human beings (and their brethren, the apes) go "stir-crazy" in a dull monotonous environment. Experiments in "sensory deprivation" — in which extraneous stimulation is kept to a minimum

[11] Dember, *op. cit.*
[12] Cohen, *op. cit.*

— show that people lose many of their normal attributes and capacities under such circumstances. They even create their own excitement through hallucinations.

On the opposite side, extreme stimulation (pain, for instance) can also interfere with the normal workings of perception and intelligence. The optimum condition is stimulation short of the extreme. To quote Daniel Berlyne, a psychologist who has specialized in this subject, "novel stimuli attract more inspection than familiar stimuli. Similarly, human subjects will spend more time looking at more complex or more incongruous pictures, unless complexity becomes extreme." [13]   Stimuli that produce conflict also produce arousal and readiness for action. Attention is stimulated by the presence of the unexpected and the uncertain.

For the advertiser, there is a fine shade of difference between the degree of conflict which produces attention and interest and the degree which people perceive as unpleasant and seek to avoid. No one can state in advance and in general terms where this fine shade of difference occurs, because it is always peculiar to the product and to the advertisement. The "shock effect" of seeing a familiar figure out of context (Bert Lahr with a bag of potato chips) represents a quite different kind of "conflict and arousal" than a grisly photograph of an automobile wreck. Insurance companies which show wrecked cars inevitably show them only slightly wrecked, and the casualties have only superficial wounds. (In its "Kill or be Killed" training films, the Army taught World War II infantrymen the technique of hand-to-hand combat. One film showed the soldier emerging from his gory first battle with his arm in a sling. For the trainee this device created attention rather than utter panic and abhorrence.)

It is quite clear that there are limits beyond which one does not normally want to go in scaring people with the threat of B.O. or halitosis. Filter cigarette ads do not mention lung cancer or heart disease; they don't have to, because it is tacitly understood by advertiser and customer alike that the thought is present in every line of copy that deals with filter action. So we stress fine tobacco and great taste.

The incongruity which whets attention may be created by media scheduling, as well as by the creative theme. It may be done through a media mix in which the product appears in different contexts. Or it may be created by the use of different spatial or time units which make the advertising look or sound different when it is encountered on different occasions.

Norman Mackworth, a Harvard psychologist who studies perception with the aid of a camera that photographs eye movements, makes a key

[13] "Conflict and Arousal," *Scientific American*, August 1966, pp. 82-87.

distinction between "looking" and "attending," activities which he considers closely related but *not* identical. Mackworth points out that the hockey player who must look ahead of him at the other players still manages to attend to the puck at his feet. He sees without looking, through his peripheral vision. The reverse, looking without seeing, is a common phenomenon of everyday life — and the cause of many traffic accidents.

Mackworth finds that when people look at pictures they tend to concentrate their gaze on a small part of the total area (usually less than 10%). The "informative" area to which attention is directed also tends to be the most easily recognized part. A whole scene can often be interpreted or identified from only a small part of it. Because pictures represent more complex visual phenomena than words, Mackworth concludes from his evidence that pictorial information is processed more slowly than words are by (literate) adults.

The "useful field of view" in which visual information is actively being processed varies in size according to the complexity of the information within it. When the material being presented is crowded with irrelevant or unwanted details, or when there is less time to process information, the useful field of view is narrowed, much as the eye's pupil contracts in the presence of too much light.

Mackworth stresses the importance for perception of internal factors which help direct the line of sight. "Every time an individual uses his eyes to perceive, he is making a choice." There is a constant "interplay between external sensory stimuli and internal schemata." He distinguishes two kinds of exploratory behavior in which the individual selectively changes what comes before him. A person can *modify* what he sees through short eye movements — "visual steps." Through longer movements — "visual leaps" — he can bring in new stimuli from sources previously *outside* his field of vision.

Different people examine pictures in a different sequence, and the same people look at them differently on different exposures. Mackworth compares the eye movement tracks to a "random walk." "The fixation point is really an area of regard. Therefore an apparent near miss with the fixation point will often represent a successful attempt to locate a region rich in information."

Mackworth notes how an unexpected incongruity can affect perception: "In reading . . . a visual anomaly such as a misplaced letter may force itself on attention after the eye has moved on and then cause a backward checking glance. This indicates that somewhere the visual pattern has been stored and examined." [11]

[11] Unpublished paper. 1966.

Symbols and perception

There is a basic physiological element at work in perception which arises from the tendency of the central nervous system to avoid unnecessary fatigue and to seek equilibrium. Attention is most likely to be attracted to a visual field which can be apprehended with a minimum expenditure of energy. This occurs when there is adequate framing, good design and layout, and sharp contrast of black and white. Attention is harder to get when there are fuzzy gray areas or different units of illustration or text which fight for attention, as they do in a cluttered advertisement or poorly made-up page.

The appearance or sound of an ad makes it clear or complex — and hence more or less easy for the eye or ear to absorb its meaning. The essential principles of good design apply to TV as they do to print. The "no-clutter" principle is expressed not only visually, but also in the cardinal rule of producing commercials to which I referred on page 113: video and audio should reinforce each other.

Purely physiological reactions to physical stimuli are only partly responsible for the way we perceive advertising or any other form of communication. Perception is also a matter of symbols and the meanings they convey in relation to existing reference points.

Form always carries symbolic associations and meanings, intended or unintended in the case of man-made forms. The interdependence of purely physical and symbolic forces in perceptual attraction is illustrated in a description by Rudolf Arnheim of a Renaissance painting which shows St. Michael weighing souls on a balancing scale:

> By the mere strength of prayer, one frail little nude figure outweighs four big devils plus two millstones. The difficulty is that prayer carries only spiritual weight and provides no visual pull. As a remedy, the painter has used the large dark patch on the angel's dress just below the scale that holds the saintly soul. By visual attraction, which is nonexistent in the physical object, the patch creates the weight that adapts the appearance of the scene to its meaning.[15]

We see and hear things because our eyes and ears are sensitive to light waves and sound waves which the central nervous system is able to organize into meaningful patterns. This can happen because new sensory input can be related to previous significant experience. The constant and instantaneous comparison of new sensation to the meaning of what has happened before makes it possible for us to discriminate one event or thing from another and to separate messages from their backgrounds.

[15] *Art and Visual Perception*, Berkeley: University of California Press, 1954, p. 11.

Like any other vehicle of communication, an advertisement is made up of symbols on many different levels. The shape and contrast of dark and light areas represent letters which individually, in our Western alphabets, stand for sounds and in combination are words which symbolize objects, actions, or properties. Headlines, slogans, text, and logotypes convey symbolic meanings. So do the illustrations of products, people, and backgrounds which evoke whatever associations the advertiser has in mind — and often many that he hasn't.

Advertising for any product will arouse a more intense response from prospects (however these are defined) than from non-prospects. But every ad or commercial uses verbal and pictorial symbols with overtones of meaning that have nothing to do with the product at all and to which different kinds of people are especially sensitive or responsive. This is particularly true of television commercials in which the announcers or models and the background situations lead the viewer into realms of fantasy that do not necessarily support the sales message.

Horace Schwerin, the leading tester of TV commercials, reports that commercials which use maximum exaggeration are preferable to milder "half-way houses of hyperbole." The most effective commercials for a men's grooming product were those in which girls actually swooned when the wearer approached. The most effective commercials for children's sneakers showed a child traveling at a speed faster than sound when he wore the advertised product.

It is obvious that a brassiere ad showing a shapely model will arouse different kinds of product- and non-product-related reactions and fantasies for men than for women. Similarly, though less obviously, an automobile ad that shows a car on a rugged mountain road carries different meanings than an ad showing the same car in the driveway of a stately mansion. Moreover, the relative weight of car fantasy and irrelevant fantasy in each case will vary for people of different temperaments with different life styles and car-using patterns.

The significance of non-product symbols in advertising art and theming is often discussed in the context of copy or motivation research, but it is seldom treated as a significant factor in media planning. The use of a baby, an animal, or a pretty girl to capture the reader's or viewer's attention is a trick way to realize the full potential of the audience. The objective is no different from that of the media planner who tries to maximize attention by using an unusual shape for his ad in the newspaper or by spotting his TV commercial in a particularly favorable adjacency.

Remembering print and TV advertising

When we separate the elements in perception which are predominantly physical from those which are predominantly symbolic, certain innate characteristics of print and television can be better distinguished.

The act of paying attention to a print ad is different from the act of paying attention to a commercial. The broadcast viewer may show inattention by being physically absent (as when he walks out of the room to get a drink of water), by being selectively inattentive (as when he picks up a newspaper or a deck of cards or converses with someone without changing his position in front of the set), or by being mentally absent when, to all intents and purposes, he continues to look at the set but fails to register the message because it does not concern or interest him.

When the reader of a magazine or newspaper opens to a page, however briefly, he can ignore an ad only by being selectively inattentive in the latter sense. He is not going elsewhere. He is simply rejecting the content of the ad as meaningless or inappropriate for him, but this takes place as part of an instantaneous and largely subconscious registration of the ad upon his field of vision.

In broadcasting, we consciously tune in the programs we like and tune out those we do not like. But on the mental level we also psychologically "tune in" those messages which are of relevance, interest, and concern to us and "tune out" those which are irrelevant. (In terms of everyday life, "tuning in" is like hearing one's name mentioned by someone at the other end of the room in a crowded cocktail party; "tuning out" is the typical male's obliviousness to the display in a dressmaker's window which he passes each day on the way to work.)

In advertising research we usually assume that an advertisement registers an impression which, together with an accumulation of other similar impressions, and interacting with other *non*-advertising influences, will imprint itself on the minds of the audience and condition the ultimate buying decision. We generally assume that the strength of these impressions is primarily a matter of *conscious* impact, so that recall and recognition are widely used as indicators of an important intermediary step in the process by which advertising works. Along with the particular impact of a given message, our research methods tend to measure the accumulative impact of all similar preceding messages.

We use measures of recall (in which we ask people to tell us what was in an advertisement) or recognition (in which we actually show people the advertisement) because they are available in a standardized form from readership research services, even though we know that recall of both broadcast commercials and print advertising represents not an accurate report of actual attention at the moment of exposure, but rather the residual capacity to identify the advertisement after time has elapsed. Tests of recognition yield higher scores than tests of recall (which place greater demands on the memory).[16] Recognition scores also show a more gentle rate of forgetting than do measures of recall.

The memorability of television commercials is commonly measured by techniques which require the person interviewed to recall some features of the commercial from his memory.

Print ads are generally assessed by methods which give the ad every possible benefit of the doubt. All anyone has to do in some kinds of interview is nod his head (which comes very naturally for some people). Even by these generous standards, readership scores for individual ads vary all over the lot both in newspapers and magazines, though research on both these media shows that most readers open almost every page and are thereby physically exposed to the advertising.

Readership scores are a curious amalgam of psychological projection ("This interests me so I must have seen it"), original attention value, and the persistent memory of the ad itself. When recognition (noting) scores are projected against audience figures, the resulting numbers reflect product interest as much or more than advertising reach or efficiency.

The memorability of an advertisement reflects only one of the tasks it set out to accomplish. Advertising may function (1) as a reminder of a product, (2) as a source of information about a product, (3) as an argument on behalf of a product, (4) as a stimulus to create an emotional climate auspicious to a product, or (5) as a means of establishing an aura or image of a product. Measurements of the ad's memorability provide no means of gauging the intensity of qualitative performance for all these functions.

[16] We are most apt to recognize people we barely know when we see them in the familiar setting in which we have come to know them than when we encounter them unexpectedly. In listening to a foreign language, we recognize unfamiliar words most readily when they are spoken in the context of a conversation. Recognition obviously covers a greater spectrum than recall. Recognizing the right answer to a multiple choice question is easier than recalling the answer spontaneously without a reminder. We recognize more words in other people's vocabulary or in reading than we normally employ in our own speech or writing. The same principles apply to measurements of advertising. The recognition method commonly used to score print ad performance incorporates a methodological flaw which arises out of respondent fatigue in the interview situation. The same ad will score higher in a thin publication than in a thick one; yet it is characteristically the major, fatter publications which get measured. A variety of experimental studies show that readership scores can be boosted to much higher levels by reducing the time lag between the original reading and the interview or by providing the respondent with incentives to remember advertising messages that at first do not come easily to mind.

Readership studies invariably find that men remember noting ads of interest to men more than those of interest to women and vice versa.[17] In one such study,[18] readers of the *Des Moines Register* were shown two facing pages, one a woman's page and the other a general-news page; practically everyone, men and women, reported opening the general-news page. And practically all the women reported opening the women's page. Yet only three out of five men reported that they had opened that page, even though it was physically impossible for them not to have had it open when they opened the opposite page. This sort of mechanism reflects more than selective forgetting — it suggests that the initial perception was selective. It was hardly surprising to find that women remembered more of the advertising directed at their sex than men did. But they also actually *saw* more such advertising. As items of interest were seen out of the corner of the eye, the reader's focus of attention was more likely to move toward them.

A full-page ad appealing to women was remembered by far fewer men than reported having opened the page (in the context of the opposite page). Yet since there was nothing else on the page with the ad on it, it is inconceivable that a reader could open the page without "seeing" the ad, however briefly.

In research conducted at the University of Minnesota's School of Journalism, people were re-interviewed after an ordinary readership interview and asked to explain why they had not reported seeing certain ads. The readers' most frequent answer was a kind of acknowledgement that the ad had been seen but simply filtered out of conscious awareness: "I'm not interested in that product" or "I don't shop at that store." (Part of the creative problem in retail advertising is exactly this — to intrigue the reader's interest in a store she has never thought of as being "for her.")

In another small-scale experiment, Mackworth's eye camera was used to take a filmed record of what people actually *focused* on when they read the newspaper in a laboratory situation.[19] This actual record of the changing focus of the readers' vision could be compared with what they reported later in a conventional Starch-type readership-recognition inter-

---

[17] This selectiveness also holds true for recall of television commercials. See footnote 39, page 138.

[18] Leo Bogart and B. Stuart Tolley, "The Impact of Blank Space: An Experiment in Advertising Readership," *Journal of Advertising Research*, Vol. 4, No. 2, June 1964, p. 21.

[19] Leo Bogart, "How Do People Read Newspapers?", *Media/scope*, January 1962, p. 53. Another small experimental study using Mackworth's eye camera was made in 1966 for the Bureau of Advertising by Donald Payne and Herbert Krugman. The research suggested that advertisements which are sufficiently complex in structure or content to require a good deal of their area to be scanned are actually not as well remembered as simple ads which receive fewer eye movements.

view (in which they were asked what they remembered having seen or read).

In the past, studies using "confusion controls" have shown that some reports of recognition of ads in any medium are false. (That is, some ads are claimed to have been seen or heard even though they have never appeared.) This reflects not so much outright distortion as "yea-saying" (agreeableness) or psychological projection, arising from interest in the product or familiarity with the brand. In some cases, of course, what appear to be false claims of recognition actually reflect sighting of the same or similar ads on past occasions. In the eye camera experiment, the number of ads focused by the eye and then forgotten by the reader was about thirteen times greater than the number falsely reported though not actually seen.

The readership process was further explored in the Des Moines experiment mentioned previously. Five different versions of the same day's paper were prepared and delivered in the usual way to matched samples of reader households. In four of these versions (on the same page), blank space was substituted for a different size advertisement. Telephone interviews were made the same evening by Eric Marder Associates and personal interviews the next day. Thus there were measures of performance for the empty space of each size and for an ordinary advertisement in the same space.

This research corroborated the eye camera evidence that we see things out of the corner of the eye and then redirect our attention accordingly. A reader who has once stopped at something on the page is more likely to stop and look at other things — including those which he would otherwise screen out as irrelevant in his initial scanning.

When the experimental page was altered by substituting white space for the various ads, the page as a whole was reinterpreted as being of greater interest either to men or to women, depending upon what material now stood out in the changed visual array.

People who opened a page on which a large white space appeared in place of an ad often "saw" and interpreted it as part of the normal advertising environment. Just as bigger ads are noted by more people than small ones, so the bigger white space got more attention than lesser spaces. But the study found that a good advertisement with a good layout for a product of interest to readers could command an attention level many times greater than that which was par, so to speak, for the empty space. A good dishware ad got nearly four times the level of recognition from women that it got from men. This level was also four times as great as recall (by men or by women) of the same space unit when it was left blank.

The space in the medium merely provided a base on top of which the advertiser's creative treatment determined the level of reader attention. Recognition, in effect, appears to be mainly a measure of interest in the product and of responsiveness to the way in which the product is presented creatively.[20] It is not really a measure of the probability that the message will actually be seen by the reader's roving eye. Page opening appeared to be the only measure of readership which remained relatively stable.

Big ads and ads for interesting products start out with a better chance of catching the reader's attention. But the Des Moines findings suggest that the task for both the advertising agency and the advertiser really begins at the point where the reader's eye is caught. From then on, memorability varies with the individual ad.[21] It seems to reflect the ability of the individual advertiser, starting with whatever advantages or handicaps his product gives him, to do a creative job in the space he buys.

Print: opportunity, exposure, registration

The Des Moines experiment suggested that not only does an ad win a certain amount of attention in its own right, it also appears to enjoy an added element of attention derived from the power of other ads and edi-

[20] The relationship of the advertising message to its immediate editorial environment was examined in a study made in Eugene, Oregon, by Galen Rarick with the support of the Bureau of Advertising. Ad position was varied above and below the fold, from right- to left-hand pages, and from the front to the back of the paper. No major changes took place in recognition scores, even though the surroundings of each advertisement were obviously different under these different circumstances.

[21] Ads which are recalled vividly also stay in the memory longer, according to a study made for *Look* Magazine by Audits & Surveys. Print ads and TV commercials which rated high (over 30) in verified recall were compared with relatively low-rated ads. The recall scores for the high-rated ads were just about the same on the third day as on the second and first days after original exposure. On the lower scoring ads, recall dropped by about a third from the first 24-hour recall period to the 48-hour recall period and held at that level after 72 hours. Here, from my own experience, is a specific illustration of how two advertisements with a comparable capacity to win attention may have varying degrees of memorability: on December 10, 1963, the Studebaker Corporation announced that it would cease manufacturing automobiles in the United States; a few days later, Studebaker's Mercedes Benz distributorship in New York placed a full-page newspaper ad reassuring customers that normal service would continue. A full-page ad for another automobile make appeared in the same issue of the paper. Twenty people who were informally interviewed the next day all spontaneously remembered seeing the Mercedes Benz ad, and all recognized it when it was shown to them. Only one or two remembered having seen the other car ad, but they all recognized it and agreed they had seen it when they were shown the paper.

torial items on the page.[22]   The study demonstrates, in sum, how the environment provides cues that can either help or hinder the observation of any particular unit of space.

The Des Moines experiment illustrates an essential principle of Gestalt psychology: that we perceive things always in relation to other things.   We see or hear advertising in the context of other advertising, of editorial matter, or of entertainment.

In broadcasting, as in print, the advertiser confronts innumerable unexpected elements: inappropriate editorial matter or programming in the immediate environment, competing demands or clashing symbolism in other nearby advertisements or commercials.

The advertiser may write into his contract certain demands which eliminate the most obvious and painful contradictions of his aims.   He may refuse to share space or time with competitors.   Airlines generally specify that their ads or commercials should not appear on the same page or news broadcast that reports an airplane accident, and liquor advertisers ordinarily specify that their ads should not be placed next to reports of accidents caused by drunken driving.

But unanticipated problems may arise out of the advertising context.   Subtle incongruities crop up in the language or pictures, in the choice of models, or in the copy themes when ads are juxtaposed even though the products appear to be perfectly compatible.   Accordingly, there are elements of uncertainty and risk in the placement of every ad or commercial.   In short, the degree and quality of attention actually paid to the message bears a variable and unknown relation to the physical opportunity for exposure provided by the vehicle.

In a national study by the Bureau of Advertising, the relationship

[22] This observation carries with it some implications for newspaper makeup. Would it be advantageous to lump together all the advertising for a particular kind of product in one part of the newspaper, as is commonly done with financial ads on the business pages or with food ads on the women's pages? One must answer this question cautiously. Such a grouping makes it convenient for the advertiser to attract that minority of readers who, on any given day, start out in an active search for a particular kind of product information. But it makes it harder for him to attract readers who are not "looking," who might at first glance not consider the subject of interest but who might be held as a result of a second glance directed at something else nearby.

A study made by Million Market Newspapers in association with the Milwaukee *Sentinel* compared ads with a medical or health subject under two make-up conditions. In one version they were spread throughout the paper, in the other they were concentrated on a single page with a number of articles and features on health. This concentration on a single theme added somewhat to the noting scores of the individual advertisements. How much of this represents a real shift in initial attention is hard to say. There is no question that the grouping of related ads and articles made the page as a whole more memorable to the readers and produced better recognition of its components.

between the physical *opportunity* for exposure and the *actual* exposure to advertising was measured for a cross-section of weekday readers of the American press.[23] This study obtained not only a conventional recognition measure of the ads and articles, but also a record of whether these items had been searched for by the reader and of whether or not they were adjacent to other items the reader remembered. These data, together with other information, were handled so as to deal with the readership of advertising as a series of probabilities rather than in the either-or terms of conventional research on ad noting.

The physical opportunity for exposure to advertising, represented by the opening of the newspaper page, remained constant regardless of what products were advertised and regardless of the size of the ads. Interesting and uninteresting products had much the same chance of being within range of the readers' vision, as determined by the proportion of people reading something on the part of the page where the ad was located (and allowing for differences in the size of the typical ad and for different types of products). Yet the *performance* of the advertising, in terms of reported readership and active search for the ads, varied widely depending on the levels of interest which the products themselves aroused in the readers. (These levels were determined in a separate series of interviews with the same people.) By every criterion used, the best prospects were about twice as likely to remember the ads as non-prospects.[24]

Thus, for a product with a thinly spread-out market, the use of small-space print ads would appear to be warranted: the ads would be within the physical range of exposure to a broad cross-section of the public, yet a high degree of selectivity would separate the prospects from the non-prospects in terms of actual readership.

Of the ads for products which consumers rated of *high* interest, 24% were reported seen by the frequent purchasers who opened the pages on which the ads appeared. The proportion was only slightly lower (21%) for the group which included less frequent purchasers and non-users. However, ads for *low* interest products showed a strong contrast between heavy and light users. Twenty per cent were reported seen by the frequent purchasers and only 10% by the other people who opened the page.

[23] Audits & Surveys Company, Inc., *A Study of the Opportunity for Exposure to National Newspaper Advertising.* New York: Newsprint Information Committee, June 1964.

[24] *Cf.* also Stewart A. Smith, "Factors Influencing the Relationship Between Buying Plans and Ad Readership," *Journal of Marketing Research,* Vol. 2, No. 1, February 1965, pp. 40-44. Smith concludes from an analysis of many readership studies made for the Philadelphia *Inquirer* that prospects (by his definition, persons who claim to be "planning to buy or who might buy" a product) read 30% more newspaper ads than non-prospects.

In short, the frequent purchaser is only slightly less likely to pay attention to an ad for an intrinsically uninteresting product than for an essentially interesting one.[25]   An interesting product will draw nearly as much attention to its advertising from light users as from frequent users. But a low-interest product draws only half as much attention from the non-prospect and the occasional or rare purchaser as from the heavy user.

Average readership scores may be misleading.   The tasks, objectives, and strategies being pursued by the ads run on the newspaper pages by different types of local merchants and national manufacturers vary greatly.[26]   Ads for different products differ in their creative appeals and their use of space.

But for every kind of ad, national or retail, and regardless of the type of merchandise being advertised, there were always a proportion of readers who reported that the product involved was one whose advertisements they were actively seeking.   For any particular type of ad, this proportion was always a minority of the total readership of the newspaper, ranging anywhere from 1% to 15%, depending on the ad size and product.   Projected against the total population, however, such percentages represent an enormous number of customers actively in the market and searching for information about values, prices, and features on the merchandise that they need.

TV: attention and inattention

Getting the message across in broadcasting involves different hazards than accomplishing the same task in print, where the dangers of reader inattention are self-evident.   In judging the performance of television advertising, the advertising planner is more apt to deal with program audience ratings than with estimates of how many *people* have seen his commercial.   Some advertisers are naive enough to equate commercial and program audiences on the grounds that, in the face of TV's intrusive power, no one can fail to get the message.   Yet not everyone tuned to the show can be on hand when the commercial comes on; some of those who "see" the commercial will always have their defensive blinders up, and of those who are receptive to the message, some, as in print, are bound to forget it.

On March 12, 1961, at the height of the rivalry between Jack Paar

[25] The gap would, of course, look greater if interest had been classified into more than a simple dichotomy.
[26] Retail and national ads of the same size perform about equally, overall.

and Ed Sullivan, De Forest Television placed an advertisement in the Chicago *Sun-Times* for sets with two or three screens in the same cabinet:

> The great networks are sharpening their weapons — competitive per-formances at the same hour — you simply can't jump all round the dial and take a small bite — there's too much to miss. But De Forest's double or triple screen TV lets you see all — all the time — when you like what you see better on one, you touch your remote button and switch sound only, or flick the super magic infra-red remote for channel changing: head phones for the stubborn.   It's more fun than you dreamed about — try it tonight.   Enjoy it up to 1 year if you like with-out paying anything.[27]

The multi-channel set has proven to be less versatile than the multi-set household.   The advent of color and all-channel receivers has acceler-ated the rate at which people acquire new TV sets even before the old ones are worn out.   By early 1967, about one in every four TV house-holds had more than one set.   Thus TV appears to be going the route that radio went before it, changing from a family medium with its focal point in the living room, to a personal medium located in bedroom or den for the convenience of the individual viewer.[28]

Perhaps the most famous study of TV commercials ever made was the notorious Toledo toilet study in which it was demonstrated that water pressure all over town went down significantly at the time of the station break.   Over the years much more persuasive evidence has been marshalled to demonstrate that not everyone who is watching a TV pro-gram stays on hand for the commercial.   It may be that the absences are not randomly distributed and that people of a given psychological or social type are more apt to leave the room or divert their attention during the commercial, just as some people are likely to read the financial pages of the newspaper or the front-of-the-book section in *Time* magazine, while others habitually miss those sections altogether.

The 1966 Alfred Politz Media Studies report, which is unusual (and unusually accurate) because it bases television data on a "personal coincidental" measurement (the number of people actually watching at the time the interviewer knocks on the door), shows that during prime

[27] Quoted by Daniel Boorstin, *The Image, or What Happened to the American Dream.* New York: Atheneum, 1962, pp. 128-29.
[28] A study made in April 1965 by A. J. Wood Research among 620 people in thirteen major markets saw that 23% of individuals in multi-set families reported both sets in use simultaneously within the past 24 hours.   Fifty-two per cent said both sets had been used at the same time within the past week.   Persons in multi-set homes were heavier viewers than those in single-set homes, though it is hard to sepa-rate cause and effect here.   When the family splits up to watch different sets, the Wood study found that adults tended to be at one set and children at the other. Interestingly, family differences about program preference were higher in multi-set homes (41%) than in single-set homes (30%).

evening time there are about 64 viewers watching during the station break for every 100 watching the program.[29] Politz also found that in about 10% of the cases, when the television set was on in prime time, no one was watching it.

Many other studies have documented the gaps between tuning and viewing, between viewing the program and viewing the commercial, and between viewing the commercial and remembering later what it was all about.[30] One of the most ambitious of these studies was made among housewives by two ad agencies, Foote, Cone & Belding and Needham, Louis & Brorby.[31] In St. Louis, with evening interviews only one hour after the broadcast, content was recalled by women in 19% of the homes tuned to opening and closing network commercials. Mid-program network commercials were recalled by 14%, 20-second spots by 12%, and 10-second I.D.'s by 7%. One-minute spot commercials did just as well on recall of content as mid-program network commercials.

This research found interesting differences in response to commercials for different program types.[32] There were also important differences by product categories. In the daytime, food and beverage commercials were far less well remembered than commercials for soap products, which also had excellent recall in evening hours. One can only speculate as to

[29] W. R. Simmons and Associates in their 1962 study of metropolitan New York for the *Daily News* found a similar proportion (68%) of the program viewers in the room during all or some of the station break.

[30] In 17,470 telephone interviews conducted by the Richmond Newspapers between 1956 and 1964, 80% of the respondents were able to identify the program then playing on their sets; 25% could (correctly or incorrectly) identify at least one commercial, sponsor, or product on the program being watched. Studies made by BBDO show that the average television commercial can be identified by about 35% of a program's viewers and that 24% can play back at least some of the commercial points. Gallup and Robinson figures show about the same ratio. F. Wallace Knudsen of Audits and Surveys analyzed 2,100 interviews with viewers of hour-long evening programs that had an average of six to eight commercials and found that 21% of the viewers could remember *no* specific commercial, 19% could remember one, 17% could remember at least two, and 9% could remember every commercial on the program; cf. his "Is 'Clutter' Too Narrowly Defined?" *Printers' Ink,* Vol. 286, No. 11, March 20, 1964, pp. 42-43.

[31] A first study was conducted in Queens, New York, in March and April 1961, and recorded over 9,000 completed interviews from 17,000 telephone dialings. A second study was made in St. Louis in October and November 1962, with over 10,000 completed interviews from 20,000 calls. Still a third study conducted in Chicago by Needham, Louis & Brorby showed parallel results. In homes tuned to a program, the proportion of housewives who 23 hours later remembered exposure to the commercial was slightly less in the evening than in the daytime. Recall of the content was about a fifth lower (16% for the typical evening commercial and 20% for daytime). These levels were slightly higher for women's interest products and those advertised on women's interest programs in the evening.

[32] For example, among women viewers of Western programs in St. Louis, 10% could remember the average commercial. But that proportion went up to 28% of those watching a general dramatic, detective, adventure, or suspense show. This raises interesting, but unprovable, speculations that the average woman viewer of the Western is merely "along for the ride" with the male members of her family and that her attention level is correspondingly less.

whether the high frequency of repetition for soap and detergent commercials may have influenced this result.   In the evening, automobile and cigarette commercials did particularly poorly (perhaps because they are addressed more to men than to women).[33]

Gary A. Steiner[34] studied the behavior of 183 Chicagoans (mostly women) while they were actually watching television commercials. They were observed and recorded by college student members of their families. The study ranged over one week's television viewing and covered nearly 48,000 observations. Steiner studied only the commercials *within* a program and did not measure the typical concatenation of spot commercials that occurs *between* programs.

Just before a network commercial came on, 70% of the viewers were paying "full attention," in the judgment of their observers, 22% partial attention, and the remainder were not watching television at all.[35] When the commercial came on, 5% of the viewers expressed some form of annoyance, 4% showed some pleasure or relief, and 90% showed no reaction at all. (This general absence of overt reaction is consistent with the findings of the A.A.A.A. study.)   During the commercial, 47% of the audience were reported to have paid full attention, 37% partial attention; 5% were not in the room at all, 6% left the room in the course of the commercial, and 5% stayed in the room but got up and diverted their attention. Eighty per cent made *no* spontaneous comments on the content of the commercial, 7% made some positive comment, 6% a negative comment, and 5% only neutral or ambiguous comments.[36]

In general, commercials following other commercials had less of the audience's full attention to begin with. Atttention immediately before long commercials was greater than before shorter ones, but that was only because longer commercials are more apt to follow entertainment than shorter ones are. Better educated and younger people showed a lower attention level during commercials. This fits in with the evidence from

[33] Eleven per cent of women watching a program in St. Louis advertising cigarettes could remember the commercial. This proportion increased to 29% when the product advertised was a food or beverage. Many of the non-smoking ladies had "tuned off" the commercial without touching the dial.

[34] "The People Look at Commercials: A Study of Audience Behavior," *Journal of Business*, Vol. 39, No. 2, April 1966, pp. 272-304.

[35] In the case of non-network commercials, which often follow other commercials rather than programming, only 58% of the viewers were paying full attention immediately before the commercial came on, and a smaller proportion (42%) paid full attention to the commercials themselves as compared with network commercials.

[36] Curiously enough, long commercials (over a minute) aroused more positive spontaneous comment from the viewers than shorter ones. (A full 21% of those watching a two-minute commercial made favorable comments.)   The nature of the comments very much depended on the product, rather than the artistry, technique, or personalities employed in the advertising. However, individual brands of the same product varied widely in the amount of favorable or unfavorable comment they elicited.

other studies which show that the better educated are most resistant to TV and its advertising. However, since better educated people may also be more adept at learning, they may be able to "get the message" at a lower level of attention. Since the first commercial in the body of a program begins and continues with higher viewer attention than a commercial which follows another commercial, Steiner wondered whether it might create greater annoyance on the part of the viewer whose program had been interrupted. This was indeed so, but only to a very small degree.

The second part of a piggyback commercial — a commercial that advertises two products of the same sponsor — received slightly less attention than the first part, but the difference was no greater than between the first and second commercial in an unrelated sequence. In fact, the second half of a one-minute piggyback outscored the second of two successive full-minute commercials. Steiner concluded that attention waned mostly because of the absolute length of a series of commercials and not because of the number of different products advertised: "One minute is one minute whether devoted to one or to two products."

The piggyback problem has also been studied by BBDO. Recall of two 30-second, back-to-back commercials generally ranged upward from about 50% to about equal that of the same commercials when presented alone. In some cases the back-to-back commercial actually scored higher than it did when run separately. Whether the commercial went in before or after its piggy-back companion made no difference in its recall. However, the BBDO studies found that too close a relationship between the products advertised might be distracting to the viewer. As reported by *Broadcasting*, "An acute similarity of products (coffee and cream, for example) may tend to confuse the audience, while dissimilar but not completely unrelated products (pie and cheese) may heighten the awareness and performance of the commercial by providing a rub-off — that is, by mutually assisting each other." (Note how in this instance as elsewhere, the existence of a tolerable incongruity appears to heighten awareness.)

Charles Allen has gone one step farther than Steiner in actually observing TV viewers during commercials.[37] He used a stop-motion camera called a DynaScope to provide a film recording of what goes on in front of the TV set. The camera (in an unobtrusive black box with a one-way mirror) took pictures at intervals of a quarter-minute whenever the set was turned on. It photographed everything in the room and, through a mirror reflection, the program on the television at the time.

[37] Charles L. Allen, "Photographing the TV Audience," *Journal of Advertising Research*, Vol. 5, No. 1, March 1965, pp. 2-8.

The participating families were conditioned for a week to the presence of the camera before any recordings were made. Although only 100 households in Oklahoma and Kansas were in Allen's sample, the analysis of the thousands of individual frames of film was a major research job.

Allen found that during prime evening hours 35% of the sets in use had no one watching during the average minute and that 36% of the persons viewing were children. This latter proportion went up to 43% children during the average commercial minute (it was 58% in morning hours). Neither Allen's findings nor Steiner's can be projected nationally, but they both are of interest because of the unique observational methods used.

Unfortunately, most of the evidence we have comparing the attention-getting abilities of commercials of different length, position, and subject matter is not a matter of systematic observation, as in the studies of Steiner and Allen. Mostly it represents a reconstruction by inference from what people remember afterwards. This kind of recall is highly prone to variations that arise from the technique of asking questions, and it inevitably reflects selective processes of memory which may have nothing at all to do with the original level of attention a commercial aroused.

The Bureau of Advertising's 1965 study of in-program commercials found that of those watching TV, 24% could name at least one sponsor or advertised product on the show they were watching.[38] (The actual timing and content of the commercials broadcast was monitored as a separate part of this study.) While women watch much more TV than men do, and thus see far more commercials, they showed substantially less recall of the last commercial, or of *any* advertiser, on the program. This would seem to support the notion that the more advertising one is exposed to, the harder it is for any single message to stand out from the rest.[39]

The ability to identify the last commercial faded rapidly, according to the length of time that had elapsed since it was on the air. When the commercial appeared within less than two minutes of the interview, a third of the program viewers identified it. Within two or three minutes,

[38] This research was described earlier on page 109. Thirty-one per cent of the men and women household heads contacted were in the room with the TV set on when the telephone rang. As in many similar previous studies, substantial minorities reported that they were doing other things — like reading and housework — while they watched TV.
[39] That selectivity works in the case of television as well as print is demonstrated by the difference in recall by men and women of commercials for products of interest to their own and the opposite sex. Women recalled 19% of the women's product commercials and 12% of the men's. Men recalled 24% of the men's product commercials, and 19% of the women's.

the proportion went down to 24%. It was 15% in three to five minutes and thereafter held steady at 12%.

It is no reflection on television's fantastic power of communication that two-thirds of the people who have just seen a commercial within the past two minutes are unable to remember it spontaneously. This fact merely serves as a dramatic illustration of the "looking without attending" which characterizes *most* advertising exposure.[10] Altogether, 54% of those who identified the last TV commercial in our study remembered having seen it before. This figure is necessarily an understatement, since many who had seen it before must have forgotten the earlier exposure, just as many who had evidently just seen it were unable to remember it a few minutes later.

This finding has special interest because high production costs[11] have made it standard operating procedure to put commercials on film and to use them over and over again. This is most particularly true of spot television, in which commercials are constantly rebroadcast at different times to reach the widest possible audience. But it is also true today of the longer, more expensive commercials shown on network television shows, which are also broadcast repeatedly.

The heavy viewer who relies more on television and enjoys it more than average not only sees more commercials but is more tolerant of them. He is in fact more apt actually to enjoy them. This would add to the already existing probability that the heavy viewer will be better able to recall particular commercials than the light viewer just because he is more likely to find them familiar.

Clutter

In the 1963-64 broadcast season, one-fourth of the commercials in programs with participating sponsorship were double-spotted next to the commercials of other advertisers. Commenting on this, Howard Eaton, vice president of Grey Advertising, observed, "In the typical hour participating program today, only two out of six commercial minutes actually are presented within the framework of the program. The remain-

[10] Comparable figures of unaided recall for print advertising do not exist for the simple reason that normal magazine or newspaper reading behavior cannot be interrupted by a telephone interview with the same facility that can be done with a broadcast message. Thus measurements of print advertising readership are generally based on aided recall techniques which jog the reader's memory and produce higher scores. They are also usually made at rather long intervals (like 24 hours) after the original reading took place.
[11] The cost of producing a 60-second commercial is about the same as that of buying 60 seconds of network prime time.

ing four minutes are adjacent to non-program material, such as billboards, promos, credits, and station breaks." [42]

The clutter of announcements succeeding one another at and around the station break has caused most program sponsors to time their messages as far as possible within the body of the program rather than at the very beginning or end, as was once traditional. It is clear that a commercial which is surrounded by other commercials enjoys less attention than does one which is isolated by entertainment. But the evidence on how much less attention it gets is inconclusive; most likely the answer will vary from case to case depending on the specifics of the commercial and its neighbors. [43]

Apart from the question of attention level, the proliferation of commercial messages on TV has a much more serious aspect for the advertiser. This is the problem of maintaining clear individual identity for his product in the face of competitive messages which the viewer can hardly distinguish from his own. For example, during the last week in February 1963, the four commercial channels in Chicago carried 172 television commercial positions for 21 brands of packaged soaps and detergents, the total air time being 158 minutes and 35 seconds. [44] The Colgate brands accounted for just about one-sixth of these positions and about one-sixth of the total time. The Lever brands accounted for about one-fourth and Procter & Gamble brands accounted for about one-half.

Here are a series of thirteen product claims for thirteen of the heavy-duty detergent brands.

1 "It's concentrated . . . gets your whole wash cleaner than any powder can . . . puts its strength where the dirt is."

2 "Fortified with whiteners, water softeners, more cleaning boosters than any powder detergent . . . gets clothes lots cleaner looking with lots less bleaching."

3 "I notice that my clothes smell clean . . . new improved . . . adds new freshness to the cleanest wash you can get."

[42] *Advertising Age*, June 22, 1964.

[43] According to Jack Gould, writing in the New York *Times* of November 28, 1966, "writers in particular have complained that artificial intermissions to make room for spots dictated a series of synthetic climaxes and precluded maintenance of sustained moods." Don L. Chapin of the Taft Broadcasting Company suggested in an address made in November 1966 in Chicago, Ill., to the Television Bureau of Advertising that the sense of clutter in television could be reduced without cutting the total amount of commercial time by clustering commercials in series. (This system is actually used in English independent television and a number of services in continental Europe.) Late in 1966 the Columbia Broadcasting System announced that it would begin bunching commercials on plays and serious cultural programs to lessen interruptions.

[44] This analysis was made at the Bureau of Advertising using monitoring reports prepared by Leading National Advertisers.

4 "A brand new heavy-duty detergent formula with more brightener power than ever before . . . and, its safe suds level assures you of super whitening power, too."

5 "Has lower suds for best washer protection . . . cleans best of all, protects best of all . . . get new active . . . new liquid too."

6 "Has extra strength . . . has five extra laundratives to get the toughest wash clean clear through."

7 "Avoid machine failure with safe sudsing . . . the detergent recommended by every automatic manufacturer . . . unsurpassed cleaning . . . works hard cleaning."

8 "Famous blue magic whitener will wash so white you can actually see the difference . . . and when your white things are this deeper, fresher white . . . you can be sure your whole wash is right."

9 "Combines high suds cleaning power and low suds washer protection."

10 "When it's whiteness you're after, reach for the one with the bleach."

11 "Seeks out, soaks out, drives out dirt . . . whitens as never before."

12 "Fluorescent blueing is new . . . it gets things whiter and brighter . . . has the amazing whitener that's . . . bright as bleach . . . safe as blueing."

13 "Guarantees a whiter wash . . . whiter than high-suds powders, whiter than liquids, whiter than any other tablet . . . a brilliant blue whitener."

The housewife is expected by the advertiser to distinguish his claim from the others. An analysis made by Million Market Newspapers finds that the heaviest viewers, who indeed see the most commercials, are best able to identify brand slogans. But their choice of brands is not much different from that of the lighter viewer.

Horace Schwerin says that "it is possible in some product fields to find imitation, borrowing, and conformity create an almost incestuous similarity of execution shared by every brand's advertising." [45] Schwerin points out how the unique vitality of a copy claim may prove to be of transitory advantage:

Let us postulate an advertiser with a simple and demonstrable vital promise of great strength. He mounts a highly successful campaign, varies the basic idea, and carves out his projected share of the market. Time will generally breed two worms in this rose: one the gradual

[45] S.R.C. Bulletin, Vol. 13, No. 7, July 1965.

wearing out of the original vital promise, the other the appearance of competitors who imitate, encroach on, and vitiate the uniqueness of the vital promise — turning it into a generic product story available to all brands.   When *this* happens — when, to oversimplify, we observe the phenomenon that 'all brands are saying the same thing' — the time is ripe for our hypothetical advertiser to consider the so-called 'creative' approach: the *execution* that is sufficiently arresting to revivify (or, if necessary, supplant) the basic vital promise.   This could take myriad forms — optical hyperbole, humor, slice of life, mood, powerful analogy, and so forth.

Thus the Great Creative Idea moves away from the product and into pure gimmickry in order to break through the barrier of inattention.

REACH VERSUS FREQUENCY, AND THE THIRD DIMENSION

7

Media scheduling is essentially a matter of balancing two objectives, reach and frequency, within an available budget. By "reach" we mean the extent of coverage, the percentage of people brought within exposure range of the advertising over a stated period of time. "Frequency" refers to the number of times this exposure takes place. Should we scatter our messages in such a way as to contact the largest possible number of people or concentrate them to deliver repeated impressions to the same people? (By "people" we may mean prospective customers rather than the public at large.)

No advertiser — not even a Procter & Gamble or a General Motors, spending many millions of dollars — can get the maximum of *both* reach and frequency. One must always be sacrificed in the interests of the other.

Media scheduling may be planned in relation to two characteristics of the product advertised: the breadth of the market and the intensity of

the consumer's involvement or interest.[1]   These two elements (each of which represents a separate continuum) are sometimes mistakenly lumped under the same heading of consumer interest.   A moderate over-all level of consumer interest might reflect the strong concern of a relatively small group of customers.   Only a limited number of people suffer from psoriasis or wear false teeth, but for these people any ad (however small) which deals with their problem presumably has compelling interest.   By the same token, it would be rather difficult to attract a person who does not wear false teeth to study an ad for a denture cleanser, regardless of how large a space unit was used to command initial attention.

When the marketer is able to define his target in narrow dimensions, he must pursue a strategy of concentration.   If his best customers are located in a particuiar segment of the population which corresponds closely with the audience profile of a particular medium, then it obviously makes sense to concentrate his budget with repeated mesages in that medium.   This is essentially what industrial advertisers do; they know that if they want to reach purchasing agents they must put the message in *Purchasing Week*.   The consumer goods advertiser who sells ten-bladed pocket knives to boy scouts knows he can reach them in *Boys' Life;* if he sells skin-blemish cream he may use *Seventeen*.

Many products with an essentially narrow market cannot be defined in clean-cut demographic terms.   The market may reflect idiosyncrasies of personal taste.   The psychological traits that lead to consumption may be scattered throughout the population.   They may not necessarily be associated with the basic personality structure of any particular social group.

No single mass medium can single out people who are receptive to product innovations.   No medium can zero in on the users of auto seat covers or the anxious people who respond to snob appeals in automotive copy or the "oral optimists" likely to respond to certain symbols in a cigarette's name or package design.   Mass coverage may be the only way to reach a narrow market embodying a combination of demographic traits to which no medium quite corresponds.   There are magazines which are read by rich women and others which have particular appeal to older women or to small-town women.   But to reach rich old women in small towns, the advertiser must spread himself thin.

When he must use a mass medium to reach a narrow target, the marketer assumes that the audience will be to some degree self-selective. Whether he uses broadcast or print, he expects the potential customers to

---

[1] A third variable might be the degree to which brand differences are perceived as important in the product field, but this would probably affect media scheduling only insofar as it affects over-all product interest.

pay more attention to his messages than the average consumer, even though both groups will be exposed to them at the same rate.[2]

The use of broad mass media may be called for with four very different kinds of marketing targets. Major appliances typify products with a broad market and high consumer interest. Detergents represent a product with a broad market but low interest. Air travel has a relatively narrow market and high interest. Nail polish remover is a product with a narrow market and low interest.

In all four instances, the advertiser must spread his messages to a wide audience. His need for frequent display of his message and brand name may be less in the case of high interest products, regardless of how broad their market is. High-interest products arouse more attention for their advertising and presumably can get along without the constant reinforcement which low-interest items need. The product with a narrow market may require substantial or dominant space or time units to make sure that the message does not fail to come across to any of the relatively few potential customers. To balance these sometimes contradictory requirements takes shrewd and subtle assessment in each particular case.

The third dimension

The third dimension in any discussion of media reach and frequency is the size or length of the message unit. Within any given budget, the smaller the unit, the greater the number of different vehicles that can be used in the schedule and the more often each can be used.

The size of the ad or commercial affects its ability to achieve actual exposure. It is therefore a determinant of true reach (as opposed to potential reach). The larger or longer the message, the more likely that the reader or viewer will be stopped in his tracks long enough to get the point. A larger unit appears to be more important; it can carry more information about the product, it can incorporate more elements of a multi-faceted product appeal, it can use more elaborate devices to capture the interest of the audience, and (in broadcasting) it is better able to evoke empathy with the company spokesman. But if the message can be put well in a smaller unit, it can be run more times for a given sum of money. Thus the smaller unit carries all the advantages of frequency.

Within a given budget, one of these three dimensions (reach, frequency, and the size of the message unit) must always be sacrificed in order to improve the others. To run a campaign of ads or commercials

[2] This is *generally* true, although, as we saw in Chapter 2, there may be substantial variations in advertising pressure for different products which sell at the same price.

of a given size or length, we may plan our expenditure to maximize reach, or we can maximize frequency within the limits of a certain reach. If we want to look important by increasing the size of the message unit, we must reduce either reach or frequency.

Maximum reach of potential prospects is always desirable in and of itself — provided that a particular advertising unit in a given media vehicle is adequate to the task of persuasion. (This latter restriction can be extremely important; below a certain minimum, a unit may no longer convey meaningful information, and the advertiser paying for it will actually be running reminder ads when there is nothing in the prospect's mind of which he can be reminded.)

In print an advertiser can sacrifice attention value for the sake of repetition, or vice versa. A four-color, double-page magazine spread dominates the reader's attention, but it costs the same as a number of half-page black-and-white ads which might be exposed to his attention repeatedly.[3] The ability to buy attention value could be defined in somewhat similar terms for radio and TV. For a given sum of money the advertiser may buy a two-minute showcase commercial in the context of a network show, or he might buy a number of eight-second spot I.D.'s.

The print advertiser must decide whether to buy the large space necessary to control his own environment or whether to take his chances, with smaller space, on appearing in an environment where random and uncontrollable influences are at work and are bound to affect the performance of his ad.[4] (Such random environmental influences are, of course, present in any medium.)

In the case of a product for which nearly everyone is a prospect, but which has mediocre or low interest (shoes or cereal), large space insures the maximum possible traffic and scanning and thereby enhances the likelihood that potential purchasers will be stopped long enough to get the message. A small space unit might be expected to be more likely to win the attention of the reader to whose interests the message is directed, whereas a larger unit might seem to have a better chance of being sighted by less interested readers in their random progress through the

---

[3] The evidence suggests that a tabloid-size ad in a tabloid newspaper is perceived in relation to the total size of the page and that an ad in a magazine of *Reader's Digest* size communicates in much the same way as a full-page ad in a regular-size magazine. However, it does not follow that the communication capacities of full-page ads are the same whatever their absolute size simply because their capacity for winning attention may be comparable in relation to their environment.

[4] Richard Neff's "Peeled Eye" Department of *Advertising Age* makes a specialty of reporting incongruous pictures and headlines. A mild example of two adjacent pronouncements, the first by the United Lutherans: "Faith Gives You Power!" and "Gulf Gives You More Power!"

publication.[5] A small ad next to others for related products may stand a better chance of attracting the reader who has reached the stage of the purchase cycle in which he is actively searching for this kind of information. However, when a small advertisement appears out of context, cheek by jowl with unrelated ads and editorial matter, there would appear to be more likelihood that it will be seen, however briefly, by people who are not "in the market" but who might be nudged a little in the right direction.

One problem in evaluating the relation of ad size to standard readership scores is that different kinds of advertisers (with products of different interest to the consumer) habitually use different ad sizes. In newspapers, the median gasoline ad runs 1,124 lines, beer ads 733 lines, whiskey ads 360 lines, and analgesic ads 125 lines. Thus average readership scores for different items reflect comparative product interest as well as the attention value of different size units.[6]

In the Des Moines study described in the last chapter,[7] we examined the ratio of recall to recognition as a clue to the persistence of the message's initial impact in the reader's memory. We reasoned that although the size of an ad would affect its ability to win attention, it should have no bearing on whether a message is effectively communicated and remembered once the reader's attention is on the ad. (Two ads with identical *recognition* scores presumably are equivalent in their capacity to win the reader's initial attention. But if they have different recall scores, this means that one registered its message more durably.) Our hypothesis was supported by the results.

Clearly, an advertisement's performance reflects the product it ad-

---

[5] This hypothesis has been challenged by Stewart Smith, who uses a different definition of "prospects" than I do. In print, the shape as well as the size of the advertising unit may affect attention value. Daniel Starch has compared single column quarter-page ads in *Life* and the *Saturday Evening Post* against square-shaped ads of the same space: Daniel Starch, "How Does Shape of Ads Affect Readership?" *Media/scope,* July 1966, pp. 83-85. Both noting (recognition) and reported readership of the single-column ads proved over a fourth higher than for the square ones. When Starch compared Lucky Strike ads which appeared sideways with those in which the type ran horizontally on the page, he found noting to be about the same but readership to be higher in the case of the regular ads. However, a similar analysis made on Botany tie ads found no difference either in noting or reading, and an analysis of full-page Jarman shoe ads with a large illustration found a decided advantage for the sideways ads. Thus it would appear that the positioning of the ad may affect readership in relation to the layout itself.

[6] Verling Troldahl and Robert Jones found that size alone explained 40% of the readership of newspaper advertisements, type of product 19%. This left 39% to be explained by the creative elements of the ad itself *Cf.* Verling C. Troldahl and Robert L. Jones, "Predictors of Newspaper Advertisement Readership," *Journal of Advertising Research,* Vol. 5, No. 1, March 1965, pp. 23-27.

[7] See page 128.

vertises as well as the form the message takes, and its ability to arouse attention is at best a crude index of its ability to sell the product.

Message size and performance

"Which gives the better results, a small number of large advertisements or a large number of small ones?" This question was asked in 1914 by E. K. Strong and it is still being asked today. Strong showed 39 people dummy magazines once a month for four months.[8] At the end of that time, the bigger ads got better recall. But recall did not increase in direct proportion to the increase in space; it grew by the square root of the increase. When the time interval between repetitions was later shortened, Strong found that it was more efficient to use small ads. When the time interval was long, large advertisements were better. (Brian D. Copland of the London Press Exchange reported in 1949 that "the square root law" had indeed applied in England before World War II but that since the War, no doubt owing to the stress and strain of those gallant years, attention increased by the cube root!)

The square root law appears to hold for other indicators of performance, apart from remembrance of the advertisements themselves. In 1936 H. J. Rudolph reported that a half page ad produces 70% as many coupon returns as a full page, and Daniel Starch produced identical findings in 1959.[9]

The Yakima, Washington, *Daily Republic and Morning Herald* ran a one-and-a-half-inch ad buried down near the bottom of the paper with the statement, "there are 17 universities in France." When people were called by the newspaper's own classified girls on the following day, 8% had read the ad the night before and remembered the answer. When the ad was increased to two columns by five inches, 12% remembered correctly. A nearly sevenfold increase in the size of the message added only 50% to the memorability of the message, suggesting that there might be a limit to the extent of potential interest in the subject.

In broadcasting as in print, advertising performance does not go up in proportion to unit size. Studies made by BBDO indicate that the recall of a 30-second commercial is about two-thirds that of its 60-second counterpart (again the square root law at work!). Horace Schwerin re-

[8] E. K. Strong, "The Effect of Size of Advertisements and Frequency of Their Presentation," *Psychological Review*, 1914, pp. 136-52.
[9] Cited by Julian L. Simon, "Are There Economies of Scale in Advertising?" *Journal of Advertising Research*, Vol. 5, No. 2, June 1965, pp. 15-20.

ports that compared with 60-second commercials, 20-second commercials yield 83% in effectiveness, 92% in brand name recall, and 71% in sales points recalled.

The recall of TV commercials by length and program slots was studied by William D. Barclay, Richard M. Doub, and Lyront McMurtrey[10] who made a survey of nearly 12,000 telephone calls in the Chicago metropolitan area in the fall of 1963.

The results showed a striking difference in "unaided proven recall" between the 20- and 30-second commercials, but only a small difference between the 30-'s and 60-'s. "Unaided proven recall" was 6% for 20-second commercials, 14% for 30-second commercials, and 16% for 60-second commercials. Total proven recall, including people who had to be "reminded," went from 9% to 18% to 20% as ad length increased from 20 to 30 to 60 seconds. "Claimed exposure," in which the viewer reported she had been watching at the time of the commercial, went up with the length of the commercial, but not in proportion. "Unaided claimed exposure" went from 21% for the 20-second length to 28% for 30 seconds and to 33% for 60 seconds. "Total claimed exposure" went from 25% to 33% to 37%.

Another way of looking at these figures is in relation to recall of the specific commercial. For a 20-second commercial, roughly a *third* of the people who believed they were watching it could really remember it, but the proportion rose to about *half* of those reportedly watching half-minute and full-minute commercials.

It would seem from this analysis that the difference between 20 and 30 seconds is really critical in order to establish a clear identity in the viewer's mind for the message that has been presented. Why should the extra 10 seconds make this much of a difference? It is very hard to say how much of the observed difference represents a real distinction in communications effects and how much (if any) is a mere artifact of research technique. One explanation may be that the 30-second commercial at the time of the station break is the one that stands out in the sequence of other commercials, whereas a 20-second commercial is much more likely to have a subordinate position. It would almost seem that the viewer finds it hard to separate more than a single commercial message

[10] *Journal of Advertising Research*, Vol. 5, No. 2, June 1955, pp. 41-47. *Cf.* also John A. Martilla and Donald L. Thompson, "The Perceived Effects of Piggyback Television Commercials," *Journal of Marketing Research*, Vol. III, November 1966, pp. 365-71. They found that 60-second commercials did not create significantly more product recall than 30-second commercials, but they did create more favorable attitudes. Integrated multi-product commercials were perceived as being shorter than piggyback commercials of the same length.

from its environment once the continuity of his entertainment has been disrupted.[11]

If an advertiser were to act on the basis of these findings alone, he might decide to buy television only on a spot basis, since the 17% added cost of program sponsorship might not compensate him for the additional 60% recall value of an in-program position. And he might never use 20-second spot commercials at all, since 30-second spots would provide double the proven recall at a cost only one-fifth greater. (Actually the 20-second spot is fast disappearing, a victim of piggybacking rather than of these research findings!)

If advertising strategists have not followed such policies blindly, it is probably because of their recognition (1) that generalized findings do not necessarily apply to specific cases and (2) that there are subtle communications values implicit in greater length which are not necessarily reflected by the single criterion of recall. The registration of specific points of information, the solid identification of the product with certain desirable attributes, the imputation to the advertiser of a serious purpose in his message — all of these may indeed result from greater commercial length in ways which have not yet been measured.

Repetition to build reach

The advertiser is ordinarily concerned with the size of his individual ads or commercials only because size relates to cost and because he must deploy his limited resources to best effect. What any one ad can accomplish is usually significant only in relation to a continuing chain of messages in the campaign of which it is a part. Because such campaigns must often be fully planned and developed before they are actually in print or on the air, the advertiser may get tired of his own advertising long before the public is aware of it. E. Lawrence Deckinger, of the Grey Advertising Agency, remembers the following episode:

> The Detroit office of J. Walter Thompson once worked on a new campaign for nine months under Henry Ford's close personal direction. At the final meeting, final proofs of magazine ads, billboards, and what-not were stretched all about the room. Mr. Ford entered and said without looking around, "Boys, I think the public is getting tired of this campaign." Not a single ad in the campaign had yet been run.

[11] The percentage of housewives in the Barclay study who claimed to be attentive (in the room with the TV set on) also went up slightly in accordance with the length of the commercial: from 44% for the 20-second commercials to 47% for the 30-second commercials to 51% for the 60-second commercials. This represents differences in the timing (in-program or spot) for commercials of various lengths, with the shorter ones more likely to be embedded in other advertising to which the viewers are less attentive.

The term "repetition" in advertising means different things from the standpoint of advertiser and audience. An advertiser may repeat his message in order to add to the total number of people he reaches. He can do this because most media vehicles accumulate new audience members with every successive issue or broadcast at the same time that they lose an equivalent part of their old audience.

The various media differ in their characteristic exposure patterns and thus in their ability to expand the accumulated audience when messages are repeated. A magazine with a large pass-along audience (including many casual and occasional readers) adds proportionately much greater reach through repetition than a magazine with a total audience of equal size made up largely of loyal primary readers.[12]

In general, media whose audiences are accumulated mainly as a matter of regular habit (like daily newspapers or technical publications) have a low capacity for extending reach through repetition compared with media to which exposure takes place on a somewhat irregular and random basis, as in evening television.

The retailer puts most of his advertising in newspapers which reach the readers over and over again each day. By contrast, the national advertiser is not out to sell a product, at a particular price, on a particular day, so much as he is trying to get across some points of information and build an image which will serve him well in the long run. Therefore, he compares media not in terms of a single message but in terms of continuing schedules. Most advertising research on television and radio deals not so much with the one-time audience for a program or for a spot position as with the cumulative reach of that program or a schedule of spots over a period of time.

Today's typical television or radio advertiser scatters his messages over the time and program spectrum in an attempt to achieve broad reach. He either buys television time on a spot basis (34% of all 1965 TV advertising dollars went to spot commercials) or through participating sponsorship of a program along with other companies (80% of all network TV dollars), which similarly allows him to spread his messages around through a number of shows. As a practical matter, this kind of scheduling often must be bought with little regard to the nature of the programming in which the messages are to be embedded.

The spot TV advertiser must assume that his messages either will go repeatedly to the same people or will extend his reach to different

---

[12] The *Ladies' Home Journal* and *Time* both had the same total audience, about 15 million in 1966, according to Alfred Politz Media Studies, but 58% of the *Journal*'s audience was classed as primary compared with 38% of *Time*'s audience. The *Journal* inevitably accumulates fewer new readers than *Time* does from one issue to the next.

people in proportion to the total amount of viewing done by various segments of the audience.   When a commercial is repeated to an audience of the same size it reached the first time, the probability that it will reach new people is directly proportionate to the probability of reaching those people with the first broadcast.   (People who watch TV a lot, and who missed the commercial the first time, have a higher-than-average probability of catching it when it is repeated; light viewers who happened to be on hand the first time have a lower-than-average probability of viewing the repeated message.)

"Vertical" and "horizontal" scheduling of prime-time TV spot announcements have been compared by Gallup and Robinson using a system they have called "Total Prime-Time Television" research (TPT).[13] This system is based on recall of the advertised brand on the following day and "registration" (the ability to play back — or describe — the commercial accurately).   They define vertical scheduling as the alignment of station-break commercials within a given station's schedule on a given night.   Horizontal scheduling refers to the alignment of station-break commercials *across* all stations in a market at the same time on a given night.

The conclusion of the TPT research was that vertical schedules are more valuable than had been generally believed, since performance depended essentially on the total number of times a commercial was repeated.   With a horizontal schedule on different stations, the advertiser can expect a high cumulative audience but a low frequency, since his messages are concentrated in time.   A vertical schedule on a single station produces a low cumulative audience but gives a high frequency of exposure.   (The term "exposure," as used by TPT, refers to what we might prefer to call the opportunity for exposure.)

It is common practice in time-buying circles to measure performance in terms of gross rating points: computed by adding together the average ratings of the programs adjacent to each spot announcement.   Each opportunity for exposure is given equal weight, regardless of whether it represents the first or the tenth in a given household.   Gallup and Robinson conclude that exposure may be multiplied against reach directly, without regard to frequency.   Their analysis argues that a given number of gross rating points on spot TV produces the identical yield in communications effect (measured by recall of the advertised brand and "registration" of the sales message), regardless of whether they stem from repeated messages on one station at different times or parallel messages at the same time on different stations.   However, the advertiser who sticks to

[13] *Cf.* Morris J. Gelman, "The Search for Marketing Efficiency in TV," *Television,* Vol. 22, No. 5, May 1965, p. 30.

a "vertical alignment" on the same station gets more for his money because he earns discounts that would not apply if he spread his budget over a number of stations. Unfortunately, the actual evidence adduced by Gallup and Robinson in support of these interesting statements is highly fragmentary and involves extensive correction factors and indices which have never been published.

In practice, the prime-time spot TV advertiser can rarely buy the identical time position for his commercial on all channels in a market. If he uses a number of stations, his scheduling is apt to be "diagonal" (at different points in time) rather than horizontally broadcast (at exactly the same time). If his campaign continues for any substantial number of weeks, the constant flux of the TV audience inevitably must give him approximately the same ratio of reach to frequency with a given number of messages broadcast on one station or on several with the same size audience. And the ultimate effect of the advertising must be the same by any standard.

The "campaign"

In the advertising world, media performance is customarily measured with reference to arbitrary benchmarks. Where actual audience data are not available on the basis of the arbitrary benchmark period, statistical simulation techniques are generally used to develop estimates of what has been achieved in reach and frequency of exposure within the allotted time. Some of the benchmarks arise from the calendar, some from the contractual practices in buying and selling media. Still others have arisen artificially out of the report-scheduling habits of media research services.

The year has four seasons. Even for products with a seasonal sales pattern, few advertising schedules are designed to follow the calendar exactly, except for the vacation months of July and August. Broadcast advertising contracts are often expressed in 13-, 26-, 39-, or 52-week cycles. The advertiser who buys time outside this framework often incurs a cost penalty.

In the magazine field, rate structures are based on the twelve annual issues of a monthly magazine or the fifty-two annual issues of a weekly. To encourage continuity of usage of the publication, the publishers of a weekly magazine usually offer an advertiser a more economical rate scale if he orders thirteen ads (one-fourth of a year, or one issue in four). He is not likely to order eleven or twelve insertions when the cost of the thirteenth is nominal. This simple fact makes thirteen a magic number and forces the advertiser and his agency to calculate the reach and frequency of his advertising in terms of the thirteen-issue period.

The word "campaign" is often used in advertising to describe the advertiser's contractual obligations. A 26-week commitment to co-sponsor a television program is referred to as a "campaign"; a commitment to run an ad in every other issue of *Look* for a year is a "campaign." Implicit in this military nomenclature is the illusion that the advertisements encompassed by such a contract are also perceived by the public as a coordinated and concerted effort. The advertiser often encourages this illusion by publicizing such "campaigns" to his employees and distributors. He "merchandises" them to his dealers.

The word "campaign" may also be used to describe the introduction of a new product, and here the term is normally more appropriate because it suggests a carefully timed convergence of distribution, promotion, and advertising through a number of media. If the product and its promotion are strong enough to catch the attention of the public at large, they may indeed be aware of a "campaign" to impress and interest them.

In estimating advertising performance for an established product, the benchmarks used are often based on practices of the syndicated media measurement services. Broadcast ratings are commonly released on a biweekly basis. Data on audience accumulation and duplication for different programs have, by custom, been analyzed over a four-week period. This has carried over from the relatively simple era of network radio programming to the much more complex epoch of spot TV. The four-week period has thus become another magic number for media analysis. With the development of the intermedia syndicated services based on diaries or self-administered questionnaires, the four-week period has been extended into print media.

The rise of spot television has enormously spurred the tendency of the advertiser to think in terms of the four-week period. This period not only corresponds to the TV measurements which are customarily available, it also has a great practical advantage. The television advertiser may reach only a small percentage of the total public with any given spot announcement, particularly in daytime. He relies on the repetition of announcements to give him the reach he desires. What point in time, then, should he consider to be the outermost limits of that reach? Theoretically, he will keep accumulating additional audiences *ad infinitum* as long as he advertises. He will never put his message before *everyone* because, for a variety of reasons, not everyone is accessible. Yet every message that is printed or broadcast will add something both in reach and frequency to the messages which have gone before.

By the end of four weeks, numbers have accumulated which look large and respectable enough for the agency's media planner to show to a client who dreams of "total coverage" and who might be overwhelmed with anxiety if he were confronted with figures that showed the reach from a single commercial or a single ad.

A time period of four or thirteen weeks may be convenient or politic to use; it may be the way media research data are most often reported; but it represents no reality at all in the psychology of communication or in the world of consumption. People do not customarily buy products in four-week cycles or thirteen-week cycles. In the rare cases where they do, the timing of those cycles can hardly be expected to correspond with the sequence of messages in an advertising campaign. In tracing the effects of a series of advertising messages (except those for new products), the planner must always begin his calculations at one point in a chain of events and end them at another point. Both these points may be reasonable and wisely selected, but both must also be arbitrary in relation to the ongoing process of communication between the company and its customers. This is true even when the advertiser embarks on something which *he* considers to be new, as when he goes into a new media schedule or begins the use of a new slogan or new creative approach. If the same commercial is broadcast repeatedly over a four-week period, we generally assume that with each broadcast its effect on those people who have seen it before reinforces or "builds on" all previous exposures.

But what of the effect the first time the commercial is broadcast? Does it start from scratch, with nothing to build on? Quite the contrary, it reflects and builds on the accumulative impact of *all* the audience's previous exposure to the product: their exposure to its advertising, to in-store sightings of it, to conversations or news about it, to its actual performance through personal experience with it.

When the media planner summarizes the cumulative audience reach and frequency of a series of messages, he perforce performs his calculations as though each message existed by itself. It does, of course, from the standpoint of the advertiser who has to pay for it or the planner who has to schedule it. But from the standpoint of the consumer on the verge of seeing or hearing a new advertising message (but just before it is presented to him), the effects of all the previous messages have, in most instances, already faded and fused into a single image, a composite of mental fragments from all the impressions and imagery to which he has been exposed. The individual messages of the past are undistinguishable.

This is not to say that individual messages may not have had an impact.   Let us consider the housewife who saw, and was startled by, the very first ad which asked, "Which Twin Has the Toni?"   When she saw a different set of twins in the second Toni ad she must have had a feeling that she had seen this very ad some place before.   The third time she saw such an ad she might still have had a specific recollection of each of the two previous occasions.   But as the years went by and the reader saw 20, 30, or 40 similar ads, she could only be left with a residual impression of the slogan and of the product rather than of the individual ads.

The fusion effect in no way weakens the positive achievement of the advertising.   The Toni advertising I cited was, after all, one of the most highly memorable campaigns in recent history because of the brilliant attention-getting device it used.

Within an ongoing series, a single ad may also be highly memorable (like Volkswagen's "Think Small" ad).   Needless to say, the ad that creates individual identity through a technical trick may entail the danger of psychologically submerging the product.   (The housewife may be amused by the blinding dazzle of the wash in the TV commercial and may vividly remember details of the action, but she may have her doubts as to whether the clothes were whitened by Rinso, Tide, or Bold.)

If the consumer were to be asked to recall advertising for Mr. Clean, she would be likely to play back an accurate description of the figure symbolizing this product — the bald giant with the single earring.   Apart from this general recollection, she might even be able to think of specific advertisements or commercials she had seen during the product's advertising life.   But more likely the memory of all the individual ads would have been collapsed into a single composite impression independent of the media background in which each message was originally placed.

As every new advertising message is presented to the consumer, it evokes and reinforces, however faintly, the effects of all the other messages which preceded it.   The extent to which this happens reflects specific content, verbal and visual.   (There are, of course, instances where it is desirable that there be a minimum of continuity and a maximum of incongruity between an old advertising campaign and a new one. Such instances may arise, for example, when a product faces a radically different competitive marketing situation during which its packaging or ingredients undergo modification or replacement, or when a copy theme is "tired" to the point that further repetition may actually produce a negative effect.)

The residual effect of a message always reflects the preconceptions which the consumer brings to the product and brand.   Therefore, the history of earlier exposure to repetitions of the *identical* message is impossible to divorce from the history of prior exposure to all *other* messages for the product, including those which occur not through advertising channels but through product usage, display, news reports, or word of mouth, etc.

The concept of accumulation in advertising properly describes a process: every message works on the base of all the other messages which have preceded it. But this process of accumulation can be measured only in relative terms, never in absolutes. Accumulation must be measured within time limits, and these must be arbitrarily determined. When different media schedules are compared over a given time period, a "natural" time unit for one medium must be equated with an "unnatural" one for another.

Advertising planners find the concept of accumulation too convenient a crutch to discard it merely on the grounds that it has no basis in valid communications theory. Under "laboratory" conditions it may be possible to measure the communications effects of an individual message in a series, in isolation from the effect of all the preceding messages. In real life it cannot be done. Campaigns in advertising exist only in the dreams and schemes of advertising generals.

Dominance

In the mind of every advertising planner is the goal of achieving dominance for his product relative to his competition. He wants dominance in the mind of the consumer, dominance in the total volume and impact of his messages, and dominance in the position of his ads within every medium he uses. Each of these types of dominance involves different strategic problems, although the advertiser often confuses them.

The message which is delivered most often might be expected to be the one which creates the biggest return, by whatever criteria the advertiser chooses to use. But rarely does a brand's share of all advertising messages for the product turn out to be exactly the same as its share of the market. The obvious reason for this is that many other forces besides advertising go into the creation of a market share. A not so obvious reason might also be present, even if advertising were the only force and even if all advertising messages were exactly equivalent in persuasive power. There may be a point of diminishing returns when we increase the number of messages, just as there may be a minimum threshold below which advertising may be too weak to make its mark.

Market research studies generally show that the biggest-selling brand in a field (General Electric or Coca-Cola) or the most prestigious brand (Cadillac) has greater "top of mind" share of mentions as the first

brand that people think of than it has of the market. However, a fascinating study suggests that beyond a certain point of dominance in its
advertising volume, a leading brand no longer gains in its level of public
awareness in proportion to an increased output of messages.

This inference can be drawn from a series of experiments made by
William D. Wells and Jack M. Chinsky,[14] using college students as subjects. In each experiment the student was seated in front of a keyboard
containing two rows of numbers (1 through 5 and 6 through 10). Numbers were read to him through earphones attached to a tape recorder.
After each series of numbers, the student was asked to register one of
the numbers by pressing a key on the machine. In an ordinary sequence,
each number's share of "choices" coincided almost exactly with its share
of "messages." When a given number occurred more often than others,
it continued to be chosen in proportion to its share, up to the point where
it was mentioned three times as often as the number with the lowest
frequency. This pattern changed when a number became completely
dominant. The number with a "dominant" share of 50% of the messages
got less than two-fifths of all the choices. A number with only a 5%
share had about a sixth of the choices. The intermediate numbers had
a share of choices corresponding to their share of messages.

The authors put a great many qualifications on their findings,
modestly pointing out that "they have nothing to say about the product
characteristics that produce or prevent a repeat sale." They do indicate
that "perceived salience, as denoted by choice, can be increased by increasing a message's share of the total message stream. Up to a point
an increase in share of messages produces a proportionate increase in
perceived salience, but at some point further increases in share of messages become inefficient and do not produce commensurate returns."

The Wells and Chinsky findings refer to messages received within
the framework of a given "message stream" (or medium). But in real
life many message streams are flowing at once. An advertised brand may
dominate its product field within a particular medium and still remain
weak within the total market. This can happen if the audience for the
medium is small or substantially duplicated by other media which carry
a large amount of advertising for other brands of the products.

There are substantial benefits for an advertiser who, by his consistent and dominant presence, creates an identification between his
product and a vehicle which has a unique significance for its public.
This is well known and much played upon by "little magazines" or by
radio programs which boast of their small bands of loyal and devoted

[14] "The Effects of Competing Messages: A Laboratory Simulation," *Journal of
Marketing Research*, Vol. 2, No. 2, May 1965, pp. 141-45.

followers.   The implication is that to the reader or listener this is *his* magazine or program in a sense which others are not, because others are for "everybody."

Thus the advertiser is presumed to reap a double dividend, both from the greater intensity of interest and attention with which the audience comes to his message and from the audience's conscious loyalty to the advertisers who support their medium ("Mention our name when you buy from our fine advertisers!").[15]

There are two separate components in the notion of dominance within the medium.   One relates to the short-run experience of a day's TV viewing or radio listening or the reading of a particular issue of a magazine or newspaper.   The other refers to the ongoing and accumulative force of advertising in the medium as a whole within one magazine issue or broadcasting day.   The dominant advertiser is the one who by sheer expenditure of effort or brilliance of execution manages to make his voice heard above the din.   His ability to make his message stand out from all others seen or heard in the same media context will have much to do with the nature of what he is selling and the content of what he is saying.

The concept of dominance must assume that throughout the industry everyone is trying as hard as he can.   Talent and the coming of the Great Creative Idea are unpredictable — part of the luck of the game.   Where control *can* be exercised is over the money to be invested and the strategy of investing it.   One can outspend the competition, if only in the obscure and neglected wedges of the market, and thereby achieve dominance (if only dominance of effort) in selected places and times.

The more advertising messages that are placed before us at the same time, and the more that are presented to us in the same context, the bigger the job becomes of using the interesting and relevant ones and screening out the ones we interpret as meaningless "noise."

This screening process takes place in terms of perceptual units which may or may not coincide with the media units in terms of which the advertiser thinks and by means of which he hopes to dominate the market.   The advertiser may want to dominate today's paper, but if I read the paper on three separate occasions and open different sections or pages each time he may be "dominating" my second reading but not the first or third, which for me are separate media "events."

The advertiser who buys an outsize gatefold ad in *Life* or a colorful Hi-Fi ad in the newspaper is willing to pay a premium because his

---

[15] This is only a step away from the ads extracted from local merchants for the high school yearbook or the fireman's ball program: essentially a ritualized form of tribute rather than a means of promotion.

advertisement will dominate the medium in a direct, tangible, physical sense. People cannot pass it by as part of the scenery. Whether or not the message is convincing, it is bound to stand out. This is dominance of the media unit. The reader's attention has been arrested.

The typical television or radio advertiser does not define dominance in terms of the length of his commercials. Instead, he relates dominance to the question of whether his messages appear in prime evening time, fringe time, or day time. Or — most characteristically — he believes dominance to be a matter of repetition, rather than of physical format, in his messages.

The aim to win dominance rarely is limited to an issue of a publication or to a single sequence of programs on a particular network. It means being the biggest air conditioner advertiser in magazines or the most heavily advertised detergent brand in daytime television. When the advertiser defines the problem of dominance in this broadened way, he is no longer concerned with the job of breaking through the barrier of inattention. He is under no illusion that anyone puts down a finished copy of the *Reader's Digest* with a sigh of pleased recollection of that great ad for Bre'r Rabbit molasses. He assumes that media experiences fade into one another and that few people carry full awareness of the original context with them from one advertising exposure to the next.

The advertiser who seeks to maintain dominance in a whole medium may start with a number of possible assumptions. One is that the medium is exactly right for the product; it has the right audience profile to match product usage. He may also assume that the medium provides the right emotional climate: the housewife consults the newspaper when she makes up her shopping list; her mind is on the subject when she's reading a "shelter book" like *Better Homes and Gardens;* it takes the right kind of beloved, smooth "dee-jay" to kid her into trying this product; the product cries for demonstration on TV.

The advertiser may also start with a wary look at his own resources and those of the competition. No matter how extensive his funds may be, they are rarely big enough to dominate everything. This may cause him to redirect his attention to two different kinds of opportunity for dominance.

First, there are sectors of the market which the competitors are not reaching: the housewives who barely scan the newspaper, never look at *Better Homes*, hate disc jockeys, and don't watch much TV. Our advertiser might concentrate his fire on these neglected people and capture their attention (and undying brand loyalty!).

A second opportunity is often provided by the fact that certain copy points can be made better through one medium than through another, with the result that all the competing strategists have rushed in the same direction and are operating from the same premises. The ensuing clutter of similar claims, the succession of cheerful smiling satisfied housewife models, may have left the public utterly confused on the subject of brand identity. If Our Brand moves to a different medium, the same copy points may stand out with greater individuality; or perhaps different copy points can be used to further differentiate our product from its competitors.

In short, a given dollar expenditure in a minor or secondary medium may win a brand dominance in one area of the consumer's mind, whereas the identical number of messages delivered in the context of a medium dominated by the competition might fail to establish a substantial identity for it.

The advertiser who makes use of this second opportunity is after the same body of potential customers that his competitors want; instead of bucking into the center, he is going around left end, so to speak, and reaching his target in an environment where the competitors ain't. Reach and frequency should never exist as objectives for their own sake; they are meaningful concepts in advertising strategy only in relation to where the customers are and how the competition is getting to them.

THE USES OF REPETITION 8

To many an advertising planner, telling his story over and over again
seems an essential part of persuading the consumer, much as repeated
association of food and a bell was essential in the conditioning of Pavlov's
dogs. Thomas Smith gave classic expression to the theory in his "Hints
to Intending Advertisers," published in 1885, which still represents the
premise on which many advertising schedules are constructed.

> The first time a man looks at an advertisement, he does not see it.
> The second time he does not notice it.
> The third time he is conscious of its existence.
> The fourth time he faintly remembers having seen it before.
> The fifth time he reads it.
> The sixth time he turns up his nose at it.
> The seventh time he reads it through and says, "Oh bother!"
> The eighth time he says, "Here's that confounded thing again!"
> The ninth time he wonders if it amounts to anything.

The tenth time he thinks he will ask his neighbor if he has tried it.
The eleventh time he wonders how the advertiser makes it pay.
The twelfth time he thinks perhaps it may be worth something.
The thirteenth time he thinks it must be a good thing.
The fourteenth time he remembers that he has wanted such a thing for
a long time.
The fifteenth time he is tantalized because he cannot afford to buy it.
The sixteenth time he thinks he will buy it some day.
The seventeenth time he makes a memorandum of it.
The eighteenth time he swears at his poverty.
The nineteenth time he counts his money carefully.
The twentieth time he sees it, he buys the article, or instructs his wife
to do so.[1]

The advertiser's objective in repeating his message may be quite different from that of merely extending his reach. He may want to deliver messages repeatedly to the same people in order to reinforce a message already delivered. His objective may be (1) to remind the audience of a previous message which might otherwise be forgotten; (2) to reinforce or give added emphasis to such a former message; (3) to break through a barrier of psychological resistance that may have inhibited effective communication of the earlier message; (4) to approach the task of persuasion from a different perspective (that is, by varying the creative approach) and thus to exploit more than a single opening into the consumer's consciousness; or (5) to add to the residue of all the advertiser's previous communications and thus to amplify the consumer's existing fund of information or favorable opinion.

Discussion of the effects of repetition in communications usually assumes that the *same* message is repeated. However, no message, inside or outside the laboratory, is ever perfectly repeated. In ordinary experience, its context of editorial matter or entertainment (and other advertising) on one occasion, even within the same media vehicle, is not the same as its context on other occasions. Context may affect the likelihood that a message will be perceived, but it also affects the likelihood that it will be perceived as meaningful, interesting, or relevant. The people who get the message are also different at different points in time; their mood, needs, and circumstances are never exactly the same from one exposure to the next.

Because the advertising practitioner tends to think of repetition from the standpoint of what he is doing rather than of what the public is getting, he is apt to view repetition in terms of a media schedule in which he may buy repeated insertions in the same vehicles. But from the standpoint of the audience, getting messages for a particular product in the same magazine or radio program may or may not really mean getting the same message twice.

Changing the visual or symbolic form of a message within the framework of the same unit and media environment (as when we run a series of magazine or newspaper ads or television commercials) is qualitatively different than repetition of the identical message.

When the form of the message changes, we no longer have perfect reinforcement (the same direct reminder of a previous experience). Of course the memory trace of that initial message may be evoked by retaining certain visual, verbal, or symbolic continuities from ad to ad throughout a campaign. By changing the outer form of the message we can add to the information or appeals we stressed the first time. We can do this either by aiming at a different class of prospective customers or by arousing a different array of psychological motives on the part of people who have already been approached by another tack. In the former instance, we extend the reach of effective communication, since succeeding messages may be caught by people who were not receptive to the first one. In the latter case, we add to the persuasive effect on people already reached by giving them new reasons or incentives to buy the product.

A message may change character completely, depending on its environment. An ad in *Life* may have a completely different effect when seen again in *Time* than it would if repeated in *Life* a second time. The second time the reader comes upon the ad in the same magazine it seems part of a familiar environment. To the degree that he "expects" it, it may not register at all; but when he sees it in a new publication, there is a sense of incompleteness or uncertainty about the familiar look of the ad itself in a changed environment.

Real time must also be a factor in determining the level of incongruity and the extent to which it can force perception of the message up to the level of conscious attention. If an ad is placed in the same week's issues of *Life* and *Time*, the reinforcing effect on the reader who sees both within the space of a few days is bound to be different than if the same ad is repeated in *Life* after a week or a month.

Advertising themes usually do have a limited life span in popular expectations, and an ad repeated after a fairly long time interval is bound to evoke a different kind of response than one which appears at the time when it is "supposed to."

The effect that can be achieved with repetition varies with the specific marketing problem. No two brands of the same product are identical, either in character or in sales objectives. Each brand faces a unique set of tasks that arise from its competitive environment. Each has its own symbolic overtones which reflect its qualities, its packaging and name, its past history of advertising and promotional themes, its established position in the marketplace, and its reputation with consumers.

"Teaching" the advertising message

Regardless of his specific objective, the advertiser is always engaged in "teaching" people something about his product. He repeats a message to the same individual both to make certain that his "lesson" has sunk in and to offset the processes of decay in memory.

The most frequently cited student of repetition is the great nineteenth century psychologist Hermann Ebbinghaus, who studied the processes of memorizing meaningless things like nonsense sequences of three letters. Ebbinghaus' findings take the form of a decay curve which is "negatively accelerated" (becoming less steep as it goes along). The Ebbinghaus curve is often called the "forgetting curve." Actually, the amount and rate of forgetting are different for remembering exact words and for remembering general sense or content.

"Overlearning" occurs when there is continued practice and exposure to information after it is already perfectly recalled. A small amount of overlearning is valuable because it permits longer retention of the already learned material. There is, however, a point of diminishing returns, beyond which further overlearning fails to produce additional results. A critique of the familiar memory curve has been made by Harry P. Bahrick[2] on the grounds that it does not make allowances for such "overlearning." Bahrick observes, "We cannot demonstrate a classical retention curve by the recall measure for the words in the Lord's Prayer or the National Anthem for most adult Americans."

Bahrick points out that measurements of recall may fail to reflect changes that take place in the quality of thoughts that people associate with overlearned information. Thus people may continue to "remember" advertisements a long time after they have forgotten a great deal of their meaningful content. (The great advertising campaigns of the past, whose slogans are still vividly remembered, reflect this kind of overlearning.)

Much of the information we acquire in daily life has no value to us beyond the immediate moment and is retained only long enough to serve its immediate purpose — e.g., dialing a telephone number or re-

[2] "Retention Curves: Facts or Artifacts?" *Psychological Bulletin*, Vol. 61, No. 3, 1964, pp. 188-94.

sponding to a casual social introduction. Short-term memory varies according to the type of material used as well as with the age and general intellectual ability of the individual. It is notably vulnerable to obliteration by distractions, as when we look up a phone number and have to speak to someone before we dial.

Immediate forgetting is a great blessing, since most of the information we acquire is only of momentary value. If we were to retain every minute detail of the things happening around us, says Ian M. L. Hunter, "this would deprive us of freedom to consider the detailed requirements of the present moment." [3]   Because of immediate forgetting, it is hard to compare in minute detail two events which are separate in time. However, the vulnerability of memory presents a particularly difficult problem in advertising because of the furious pace with which messages succeed each other.

Short-term memory becomes more fallible the greater the number of elements or "chunks" that have to be remembered. It is also hindered by the number of similar messages received just previously. The longer the interval between such extraneous messages, the less the interference. But interference from other messages is the prime reason for short-run forgetting. Messages which have really been learned (and are in long-term storage) do not weaken or decay with time, but short-term memories do, even when there has been no interference from earlier messages. One student of the subject, Lloyd Peterson, observes, "Perhaps the decay should be considered a perceptual phenomenon rather than an element in what is traditionally called memory; it occurs before the subject has had time to process the message." [14]

For a given number of messages, a slow rate of presentation makes for better learning than a fast rate. When one or two extraneous pieces of information are introduced between a message and a test of memory, learning is better in those cases where the message is presented twice in rapid succession. However, when the amount of extraneous material is increased, learning is improved if the messages are repeated after a spaced interval. The paradox, in Peterson's words, is that "in order to remember something better you should allow some forgetting to occur."

Explanations for this phenomenon remain for the moment in the realm of conjecture. As Peterson puts it, "Perhaps there is a characteristic of the retrieval process that enables it to work more efficiently after

[3] *Memory,* London: Penguin, 1964, p. 79.
[4] *Cf.* Lloyd R. Peterson, "Short-Term Memory," *Scientific American,* July 1966, pp. 90-95. In the article, Peterson describes short-term storage of information as an "activity mechanism" in the nervous system which dies out if there is no occasion to repeat the experience. He distinguishes it from the long-term storage that takes place in real learning, where a structural change actually takes place within the nerve cells.

an interval of irrelevant activity. A related possibility is that recall itself is a disrupting process, tending to interfere with storage activities."

There is a great danger in analogizing from the kind of induced learning that takes place in laboratory experiments to the much more casual way in which we learn advertising messages in the ordinary course of events. However, there is some implicit support in Peterson's work for the principle of reinforcement which — wittingly or unwittingly — plays an important part in advertising scheduling.

When we repeat commercials for the same product within a given television or radio program, or on different pages of the same issue of a newspaper or magazine, we may profit from the extra measure of learning that comes because extraneous information (entertainment or editorial matter, or other ads) has been interjected between the messages we want to deliver. The advertiser may benefit from this kind of short-run repetition insofar as those he reaches with the particular media vehicle learn his message more thoroughly. However, he accomplishes this at the expense of an opportunity to reach additional people with the same message delivered on an entirely different occasion or with a different vehicle.

Typically, the curves which graph the results of experiments in learning have an exponential shape. Each increase adds a little less than the one that came before. This might lead us to believe that it is more efficient for advertising to strive for maximum reach on a one-time basis than to accept the progressively reduced effect of repeated messages.

But things are not that simple, unless the advertiser's sole objective is to communicate the name of his product once. Normally, his tasks are more complex; he has much more to say, in words or pictures.

B. F. Skinner, some of whose most remarkable psychological experiments have involved training pigeons rather than people, has shown that learning takes place most rapidly when the learner has to "work" at it, when there are gaps that he has to bridge himself — by chance, guesswork, or reasoning — and when he has the opportunity to test his experience again and again in varying contexts. Repetition reactivates the traces of earlier messages. The individual on the receiving end has to "work" by searching his memory and "feeding back" the associations with his past experience. After a certain number of repeated exposures there is a breakthrough in learning: the message has been delivered. (This notion has been applied in programmed learning, in which information is broken up into a number of components, each small enough to be absorbed readily and each representing a logical development from what is already known.)

Essentially, the idea is that we progress in knowledge by *bursts* rather than in a steady stream. It may take a certain number of repetitions to break through the veils of resistance or disinterest. A logical conclusion from this might be that breadth of reach in an advertising campaign is highly inefficient if it is not supported by sufficient repetitions to register a message forcefully.

A fascinating experiment by Hubert A. Zielske[5] of Foote, Cone & Belding produced findings which at first glance might appear to contradict the "burst" theory. He mailed the same thirteen ads to two matched samples of women in Chicago, in one case at weekly intervals, in the other at four-week intervals. At the end of thirteen weekly exposures, 63% of the women could remember the ads, but forgetting took place rapidly when the messages stopped and virtually no recollection remained nine months later. By contrast, the monthly messages provided continual reinforcement and built gradually up to a 48% recall level at the end of the year. Zielske thus demonstrated *both* the need for continuity *and* the efficacy of using bursts of messages to penetrate awareness.

"Flighting" or the repetition of messages in sequence was also studied by Wells and Chinsky in their research on "The Effects of Competing Messages" (see page 158). A number was withheld from the stream of messages for the first part of a series and then fed in at a double rate in the second part. This "flighted" number was chosen at a rate about 50% greater than its share of messages, strongly suggesting that concentrated repetition makes a communication more memorable than the same number of repeated messages strung out at even intervals.

This study offers support for the theory of scheduling advertisements to run in concentrated bursts separated by substantial time intervals, rather than in a continuous series. This is particularly true if the advertiser has a new sales point, and a real one, rather than a mere restatement of the established virtues of his product. Such a message might have a considerably greater effect if it is repeated after a short interval rather than after a long one, simply because the original impression may be more vivid — and thus more readily reinforced.

The value of repetition is often debated in terms of the marketing characteristics of the advertised product: how many people buy it, how often. It is rarely thought of in terms of *what* is being communicated. With a message of extremely low interest to everyone, no amount of repetition may be sufficient to force the point through the audience's protective internal censorship. Conversely, if an advertisement says something vitally significant to the audience, there is no particular value in repeating the message, since almost everyone interested will remember it any-

[5] "The Remembering and Forgetting of Advertising," *Journal of Marketing,* Vol. 23, No. 3, January 1959, pp. 239-43.

way. (When Crest toothpaste won the endorsement of the American Dental Association in 1960, a single press advertisement announcing this fact created a recall level of 42% among women two weeks later, a phenomenal level of retention for a single advertising message.)

This does not mean that people will not forget; they do very rapidly. But reminding people of something they already "know" presents the advertising planner with problems quite different from those he faces when he wants to make sure they are learning the message in the first place.

According to Ian M. L. Hunter, repetition enriches *understanding*. When we have occasion to use information often in different kinds of situations, we have mastered it more thoroughly than if we know it only in a given setting. (This is an important argument for the media mix.)

Hunter points out that repetition also serves a *maintenance* function, since repeated use of what has been memorized favors later remembering. The sooner the repetition follows the original learning the better, since this repetition serves as a review of the originally exposed material.

Hunter observes that "the best rehearsed actor never gives two performances which are identical in every respect." In the simplest task of memorization — memorization of all-digit telephone numbers, for example — individuals assimilate information and remember things in completely different ways. People do not remember even a mere sequence of random digits simply by rote; they notice relationships among them and further try to relate them to sequences (like dates) that are personally significant as numerical reference points. We reproduce memories by reconstructing their context or the series of events which led up to them. Thus we can best recall those things which can be visualized as part of a pattern of associations.[6]

The more complex and the longer the information that is being mastered, the more time it takes to learn it proportionate to its length. (In one experiment a passage of 100 words required a learning time of nine minutes, 200 words required 24 minutes, 500 words 65 minutes, and 1,000 words 165 minutes.) The greater the spacing between periods of study, the less time has to be spent in the actual learning periods, although, of course, there is an increase in the total time required before the learning is completed.[7] This would appear to suggest that with a given amount of advertising effort, short messages which are dispersed

[6] "Anticipation" is the aspect of memory in which we respond, often at a subconscious level, to stages in a familiar pattern of events. When we anticipate something, we are in effect extrapolating a certain outcome from similar experiences we have already had.

[7] This observation is based on experiments made by A. P. Bumstead in 1940 and quoted by Hunter, *op. cit.*

and separated might outperform those which are highly concentrated into single long units — provided that the short messages reinforce each other as parts of a single learning experience. However, there is a profound difference between the process of learning as a purposeful task and the kind of incidental learning which advertising messages represent.

Our memory is hindered most by interference from messages which closely resemble what we should remember.[8] Different processes are involved when we memorize information by rote than when we try to learn it selectively from amidst a body of incidental or extraneous material. The incidental learning of "unwanted" information interferes with the "selective" learning of useful information. The more such incidental or unwanted information is present, and the more it resembles the wanted information, the more interference occurs with useful learning.

From a series of experiments on this problem Eugene Burnstein[9] concluded that the extent to which useful information is retained in the memory depends on how little interference there was in the original learning process. The implications of Burnstein's findings for the advertising planner is that even the best prospects, those who are interested in the message, can be effectively distracted from getting the point because of the vast amount of irrelevant advertising to which they are simultaneously being subjected in the same context.

Behind much advertising theory lies the psychological assumption that there is a kind of reservoir or pool of attention which consumers reserve for advertising messages within the time span they devote to a given publication or to a given block of listening or viewing. Competing brand messages in the same product field naturally crowd and cancel each other out; but apart from the contradictory effect of directly competing messages (for no one is going to switch both to Winstons and Marlboros at the same time), there is another, more subtle, negative effect which derives from the accumulated pressure of *all* other advertising messages. The idea is that the poor human mind can comprehend so much and no more. The theory holds that in effect every advertising message must crowd out some other message; any attention devoted to a

---

[8] In a study made in 1931 by J. A. McGeoch and W. T. McDonald (cited by Hunter, *op. cit.*), university students received a list of adjectives to be memorized, and different kinds of activity were interpolated between memorizing and the test recall. Forty-five per cent of the adjectives were recalled when the interpolated activity was reading jokes. When numbers were shown in between, recall of the adjectives went down to 37%. With nonsense syllables, recall of the adjectives went down to 26%. Learning adjectives unrelated to the originals reduced the percentage to 22%. Adjectives opposite in meaning to the originals brought the score down to 18%. When the students had to learn a list of adjectives synonymous with the originals, they remembered only 12% of the original list.

[9] Eugene Burnstein, "Some Effects of Cognitive Selection Processes on Learning and Memory," *Psychological Monographs*, Vol. 76, No. 35, Whole No. 554, 1962.

message for one product hastens the forgetting of all other messages for all other products.

An analogy could be drawn between the consumer's capacity for information and his limited purchasing power. He can buy either a new alarm clock or a bottle of Scotch; he can hardly afford both. If he holds the Marlboro ad in mind, how can he remember the one for Taystee Bread?

These propositions have a core of truth but suggest a great many false corollaries. Interference does occur in short-term memory when ad messages succeed each other in rapid succession, but messages which have been learned and assimilated are not ordinarily vulnerable to the same kind of interference. There is no evidence from the students of learning and memory to support the notion that new information is acquired at the expense of old established knowledge. One of the most amazing features of human intelligence is its virtually unlimited capacity for acquiring new experiences and new ideas. Old and important memories often have greater vitality than recent ones. So the concept of a pool of product and brand information truly constant in size simply makes no sense at all. Advertising is also only a part, and in some cases only a small part, of the total amount of information we have about consumer products. (How well we remember dad's old car, the brand of shortening mother used, the brand of cat food that the cat wouldn't touch!)

As we become aware of a new brand on the market, we do not forget the old brands — forget in the sense of not being able to recognize them. If the new brand captures our interest and patronage, the old ones may, however, become less salient for us. We may be less likely to think of them spontaneously, or to recall their particular virtues or slogans. But such a switch is not likely to happen unless the new brand succeeds in out-advertising its established competitors from the standpoint of effort, skill, or both.

Although new messages can be learned without our forgetting old ones, this doesn't contradict the principle that all messages are in competition for our interest in the first place, in getting to the point where they *might* be remembered.

It stands to reason that advertising which is useful for any one individual may represent interference for another. The constant progression of advertising messages through all media represents a realistic and significant barrier for the learning of any new message. The presence of similar messages leads to especially strong interference. However, from the standpoint of the consumer, similar messages may be those which are similar in style or technique of presentation, i.e., layout, artwork, models, melody, etc., rather than necessarily those which advertise the same product.

Krugman's theory of how products are perceived

Herbert Krugman, a leading theorist in consumer psychology, has pointed out that our emotional response to repetition depends on what is being repeated.[10]   He finds that six or eight repetitions of a certain style of music make it more acceptable as it becomes more familiar, but that liking does not increase beyond that point. However, with a simpler subject (packages of a washday product) there is no increase in liking after a single repetition of exposure to the design.

Krugman refers to the work of the social psychologist Eugene Hartley,[11] who observes that at the onset of a series of repetitions "we contend with the effective significance of new stimuli, the pleasure of novelty or the gratification of curiosity." As repetition continues, the object benefits from a feeling of conscious familiarity and the response to it improves.   But a time comes when the object is thoroughly familiar and where further repetition "leads to a loss of associative power, a de-differentiation of perception, and boredom, satiation, or negative adaptation." In short, one mint after dinner is fine, two are better, and the twentieth creates disgust.

Krugman observes, "Marketers would like to think that their products were indeed better and/or that consumers believed them to be better. What is often the unrecognized case, however, is that their products are neither liked nor considered better but chosen only because they are adequately good *and* for the pleasure of their recognition, i.e., sheer familiarity." [12]

According to Krugman, advertising represents "information which the consumer recognizes as present but to which he makes no personally relevant connections, i.e., he remains uninvolved."   He defines "involvement" as the number of conscious "bridging experiences, connections or personal references per unit of time which the viewer makes between his or her own life and the stimulus." [13]

[10] "An Application of Learning Theory to TV Copy Testing," *Public Opinion Quarterly*, Vol. 26, No. 4, Winter 1962, pp. 625-34.   Krugman concludes in this article that some individual television commercials are more susceptible than others to an impairment of effectiveness through heavy and long exposure.
[11] E. L. Hartley, "The Influence of Repetition and Familiarization on Consumer Preferences," paper presented at the Convention of the American Psychological Association, September 6, 1961, quoted by Krugman, *op. cit.*
[12] Herbert Krugman, "The Learning of Consumer Likes, Preferences and Choices," unpublished paper delivered July 1966 at Purdue University. *Cf.* also Krugman's "The Impact of Television Advertising: Learning without Involvement," *Public Opinion Quarterly*, Vol. XXIX, Fall 1965, pp. 349-56.
[13] "A Low Involvement Model of Mass Media Impact," a paper delivered before the 1966 Conference of the American Association for Public Opinion Research, Swampscott, Massachusetts. *Cf.* also "The Measurement of Advertising Involvement," *Public Opinion Quarterly*, Vol. 30, No. 4, Winter 1966, pp. 583-96.

He postulates that with low-involvement material there would be an absence of "perceptual defense." In other words, the unconscious psychological mechanisms of self-protection are not aroused by communications which people consider unimportant. Thus the repetition of low-involvement stimuli "can alter the salience aspects of perceptual structure without accompanying changes in verbalized attitudes." When an unimportant message is repeated, the content may seem more *familiar* even though it is not any more consciously *acceptable*. Repeated exposure to ads for a brand builds a potential for seeing it in a new light. "The change process may be over before the customer heads for the store, shopping list in hand."

The potential may be activated at the point of sale when the customer recognizes the brand on the supermarket shelf as something that is already familiar through advertising. Its familiarity may "trigger the actual shift in perception, this shift followed by behavioral change." The behavioral change in turn might give rise to new attitudes consistent with the individual's actions.

Krugman suggests that the television stimulus is "animate" while the observer is "inanimate." Since the rate of "stimulation" (the pace of the communication) is out of the viewer's control, there is a relatively low opportunity for personal "connections" with the advertising message.

In the case of print, however, the quality of the stimulus is "inanimate," while the observer is "animate." Krugman argues, therefore, that print advertising may lead to a shift in opinion at the time of *actual* exposure. Being active, the individual is busy establishing personal "connections" with what he reads, and any psychological defenses that may be called forth are aroused *before* he enters the store. Krugman contrasts this with the "low-involvement" nature of stimulation through TV advertising, which must be activated when the product is seen at the point of sale.

Krugman tested his hypothesis by analyzing the descriptions people give of television commercials and magazine ads for the same products. Looking for the personal "connections" which relate the message to the reader's own interests, he concludes from the data that "direct attention to advertising materials produces fewer and slower connections than when attention is focussed on something else, in this case the more natural focus on editorial matter." The very strength of print advertising may therefore arise from the fact that the reader must be *distracted* from his main line of search in order to get the advertising message.

In Krugman's view, the process of "gradual shifts in perceptual structure, aided by repetition, activated by behavioral choice situations, and *followed* at some time by attitude change" characterizes low involvement products. He believes that high involvement product choices might well be made on the basis of *conscious* opinion change based on a conflict of ideas.

Krugman's intriguing hypothesis continues to stimulate new research. Of course, products cannot be neatly separated into low- and high-involvement categories, each with its own different mechanism of consumption behavior. What is a low-involvement product to one person may be a matter of fairly high involvement to another (soap, for example, is one thing to the slovenly housewife and another to her compulsive neighbor).

It seems plausible that there is a continuum of involvement from low to high, with both conscious changes of attitude and unconscious changes in perceptual behavior taking place to some extent at both extremes. Curiously enough, the classic example of how purchase behavior results in rationalization of attitudes after the fact comes from the automotive field, the very prototype of high involvement. It has long been an accepted dictum in automobile advertising circles that the most intense readership of new car ads is on the part of recent purchasers who wish to reassure themselves that they made a wise choice.

Field experiments in repetition

Outside of the psychological laboratory, studies involving repeated exposure of the same advertising content to the same people have been largely confined to print media because of the greater ease of conducting controlled experiments with print. In general, advertising studies of repetition duplicate the findings of academic research, though most of the experiments are at the same time less rigorous and on a much larger scale.

In its purest form, repeat exposure to an advertisement means seeing or hearing it again in the *identical* context. This can never happen in radio or television. It *may* happen when a magazine or newspaper is picked up for a second time if the reader had not finished it on the first occasion.

Do advertising messages lose their power to persuade as they become familiar through repetition? The evidence suggests that they do. Schwerin reports on an analysis of 118 tests of TV commercials and nine of print ads in which measurements were taken both before and after high-frequency repetition in the normal course of their respective campaigns (in England and Germany).[14] The time interval between the

[14] *SRC Bulletin*, Vol. XIV, No. 8, September 1966.

first test and the repetition ranged between one and eighteen months. (Unfortunately, the exact degree of respondents' prior exposure to the advertising was not measurable in this research.)

In 91 of the 127 cases, the results of the second test (after the message was already generally familiar to the public) were less favorable than on the first occasion, when the message was brand new. (In 27 of these cases, the decline was statistically significant.) In only *one* case were the results significantly *better* for the oft-repeated message.

Aaron J. Spector of National Analysts reports on a study of 127 magazine subscribers, each of whom was shown every page in an advance issue of the publication.[15] Half were exposed only once and the others were shown the same pages again on the following day. A variety of recall measures was used in an interview two days after the initial contact and exposure period. Repeat exposure created 30% more unaided recall, and comparable improvement occurred by some other criteria. This appeared to be true whether memory of the ads was checked one day later or two.

To compare the effects of two magazine advertising exposures with one exposure in the same issue, Charles Swanson, then of the *Saturday Evening Post*, commissioned Alfred Politz in 1959 to interview 150 subscriber-readers of the *Post* in Rochester, New York. (Since a copy of the *Post*, a text magazine, is picked up on more occasions than its picture-book competitors, there was an obvious advantage to demonstrating the value of repeat exposures.)

In each household, an interviewer hand-delivered a specially prepared copy and asked the reader to go through it in the usual way. Questions about the advertising and the brand were asked two days later, and another specially prepared copy of what appeared to be the same issue was left with the reader at the end of the interview. By rotating twelve ads in the specially prepared issues, four were exposed once, four twice, and four not at all to each reader. The final interview was conducted three and a half days afterwards. Which pages were opened was determined by the use of a glue spot which stuck the pages together.

Familiarity with both the brand and the advertising claims and the degree of willingness to buy the brand increased at about double the rate for two exposures as for a single one. Belief in the claim increased three times as much with two exposures as with one.

Some years later, Politz made a somewhat similar study of "Repeat Exposure Value," [16] this time for the *Reader's Digest*, which has a long-standing sales strategy of stressing the advertising value of its long "life"

[15] *Media/scope*, September 1960.
[16] Alfred Politz Media Studies for the *Reader's Digest*, January 1966.

and repeated pickup. He interviewed a national cross-section of 361 adults, divided into four equal groups. Two of the groups were given one day to look through a new copy of the *Reader's Digest*. The other two groups were given a second one-day "exposure" after a three-day interval. The magazines left with the respondents were specially doctored, with half including one set of six test ads and the other half a different set.

When the interviewers returned, they checked the readers' familiarity with each brand and its sales points, their rating of the brand's quality, and their interest in buying it. (Of course, they asked this not only about the "test" brands whose ads were included in the text magazine, but also about the other six "control" brands.)

A single day's reading added 12% to the top-of-mind familiarity, comparing the average brand "advertised" with those not in the magazine received by the reader. With two days' reading, the advantage rose to 21%. Similarly, among those familiar with the advertising claims, the percentage who correctly associated claims and brand went up 15% among those with one exposure and 25% with two. The proportion rating the brand "very highest quality" was 11% higher with one exposure, 17% higher with two. The proportion who said they "would buy" the advertised brand was 15% greater after one day's reading and 26% greater after two.

The two-thirds or three-fourths margin of improvement resulting from a second exposure is thoroughly congruent with other studies on the effects of repetition. However, the findings are hard to apply to the effects of repeated exposure in *different* issues of the same publication. They still leave the media strategist with the problem of whether it is worth doubling his delivery — and thereby his expenditure — of the same messages on the same people, in order to get less than double the residual communications effect.

Unfortunately, the research did not compare the value of repeated exposure for the same issue of the same magazine (as measured) with the possible value of similar repetition with different issues, or with different magazines altogether. It can only be conjectured whether the "shock" of receiving the same magazine after a three-day interval prompted the readers to look at it with a degree of bemused curiosity quite different from their normal interest in an unfinished magazine lying around the house and picked up for a second time.

In another experiment, readers of *Look* magazine were interviewed by Politz' Universal Marketing Research in 1964 on their recall of advertisements and then re-interviewed about a month later on the ads in a second issue. The recall of advertisements accumulated at a faster rate from issue to issue than the audience for the magazine itself. Because of this, an increasing proportion of the audience potential was translated into recall as the campaign progressed.

For example, four issues of *Look* had 24.1 million readers (including those who read several issues) compared with 14.7 million reached by one issue. But while a single ad in one issue might have a recall level of 25% (or 3.7 million of the 14.7 million readers), with four repetitions the number remembering it rises to 11.6 million readers, nearly half of the gross audience. Ads with low recall scores (since their "potential" for conversion is greater) tend to accumulate readers slightly faster than high-scoring ones. Presumably — although the published reports of the research do not offer the evidence on this point — the rate at which the ads were remembered grew faster than the rate at which the magazine accumulated readers because of the weight of the repeated advertisements on the regular readers who saw several issues.

To the advertiser, even more convincing evidence on what happens when the same message is repeated to the same people comes from coupon advertising, where the pull of the ad is directly traceable in the number of orders or inquiries. As early as 1912, William Shryer[17] analyzed thousands of keyed coupon advertisements soliciting mail responses. His conclusion was that "the first insertion of a tried piece of copy in a new medium will pay better, in every way, than any subsequent insertion of the same copy in the same magazine."

According to Julian L. Simon, "virtually all published mail order data corroborate this finding." He cites Victor Schwab's 1950 estimate that if a full-page ad is repeated within 30 to 90 days the second ad will pull 70-75% as many mail orders as the original ad; the third insertion within a short time will pull only 45-50% as much.

However, the national advertiser must hesitate before he infers that mail order ads present a pattern which also applies in his own case. Typically, the mail order advertiser sells to only a restricted minority of the market. He may use up the potential of interest long before most national advertisers do. And he is seldom after the repeat sales on which any packaged goods manufacturer relies to maintain his business.

The time dimension

Repetition has two aspects : frequency and time. Messages repeated at different intervals of time may reinforce each other with varying degrees of effect. Timing on the calendar becomes significant for some advertised

[17] Cited by Julian L. Simon, "Are There Economies of Scale in Advertising?" *Journal of Advertising Research*, Vol. 5, No. 2, June 1965, pp. 15-20.

products if it relates to the purchase pattern. (There are rather subtle aspects to this, as one of the incidental objectives of advertising is to create demand for seasonal products out of season.) For products which are bought evenly throughout the year, the advertiser customarily assumes that if messages are evenly spread, the more often they are repeated, the greater the likelihood that they will hit their target at a time close to the individual purchase decision, when their effect is presumably greatest.

The literature in psychology does not suggest that opinions are most likely to change in response to the latest word on a subject. In purposeful learning, the first items in a sequence are mastered soonest, then the very last items, and the middle items are learned most slowly. This is the famous so-called inverse "J" curve which favors the first messages which come along.

The advantage of being first or last depends on the nature of the argument and varies according to the competitive pressures on opinion. The world would be a strange place indeed if everyone were always convinced by the last argument heard. We would all be incapable of consistent action, and our behavior would change constantly in response to the pressure of incoming information and appeals.

Studies of "the order of presentation in persuasion" by Carl Hovland [18] and his associates indicate that when conflicting or competing messages are presented to an audience in an effort to influence their thinking, there is not necessarily a permanent advantage for the message which is received last. Any such advantage is dissipated within moments, if the message is one of a long series.

This should be all the more true when messages are, as in the typical advertising campaign, part of an interminable series to which the consumer has been subjected over many years in a highly competitive field. Each advertising message in such a product category has a slight reinforcement effect which offsets the slight decay in cumulative effect since the previous message. The timing of the message last exposed to the customer may be of far less importance than the persuasive effect of some earlier message which he perceived as informative or significant.

The closeness of the message to the purchase act can hardly have any significance if the major purpose of repetition is reinforcing the original communication. From the standpoint of delivering cumulative effects, the process of persuasion is really almost independent of the purchase cycle; it exists in a different time perspective.

Except for that minority of advertisements which directly solicit telephone or mail orders, the main object of most advertising is not to

[18] *The Order of Presentation in Persuasion,* New Haven: Yale University Press, 1957.

clinch a sale, but to qualify a product or brand for purchase in terms of the consumer's definition of utility. This may mean defining a brand as one that falls within the range of acceptability as a well-known, nationally distributed product. It may mean getting the consumer to believe that the brand has special features which add to its values and distinguish it from its competition. It may mean persuading the consumer to think of the product in terms of some time-bound sense of urgency ("Available only while the supply lasts." "This week only, $3.99.") This feeling of immediacy, of short-lived opportunity, is, of course, the secret of most retail advertising.

The time factor in consumer decision-making involves two separate dimensions: (1) the *actual* sequence of events, and (2) the *perception* of events.

Certain events in life require corresponding changes in consumption habits. Immediate changes in a family's distribution of its income follow a rise in the wage earner's salary or his loss of employment, but changes also follow the birth of a child, the death of a spouse, the departure of a son for college, the wedding of a daughter. On a much more trivial scale, buying decisions result from circumstances that have little to do with conscious desires: things we use wear out or are consumed and have to be replaced.

The man who has to buy his wife an anniversary present confronts this situation with a different degree of earnestness on the date of the anniversary than he does in the previous weeks during which he may be more or less in the market. The housewife who knows that she is low on meat for the freezer is in a different situation than the one who suddenly finds she has company coming for dinner that night and knows she must buy a roast to cope with the situation. A car owner who has been thinking about getting a new automobile because the old one is starting to burn oil faces a less urgent decision than the one who finds that his rear axle is broken.

A great deal of advertising seeks to create an artificial sense of urgency about the purchase, on the premise that the chance of making a sale is greater in the face of an implacable deadline. This may take the form of a deal, special, bargain price, tie-in offer, or coupon. Or it may take the form of an appeal to changing taste, fashion, or styling, or to the consumer's urge to be first to try a new product. In either case, the aim of this advertising is to force the subject to the forefront of the consumer's consciousness. The assumption is that the consumer is already a potential prospect — one who is either vaguely in the market or who might be brought into the market though he would not otherwise be motivated to buy.

CREATIVE THEME AND VARIATION

"As Long As You're Up . . ."

The Grant's Whiskey campaign developed by Hockaday Associates illustrates in a variety of media (magazines, newspapers, car cards, outdoor) how the same copy line and visual scheme can be effectively repeated. Each repetition arouses at the same time a sense of the familiar or *déjà vu* and of the unfamiliar. This was done first by cropping the original photograph, then by showing the same model in the same pose but in a different costume, and finally by substituting other models. The Eames chair was an essential attention-producing device in the first ad; had it been continued as a feature in the subsequent ones, it might have deflected interest from the essential theme (Grant's means the luxury of being served).

A Great Creative Idea like this one acquires a momentum of its own when its motif becomes common currency. Imitation and parody, which are possible only when it can be assumed that the original is well known, begin, and the caricatures evoke all the original meanings. A relatively unfamiliar brand thus enters the realm of universal familiarity. When the consumer sees it on the shelf, it is a known quantity, "a friend." All the connotations created by advertising are now inseparable from the name of the product itself.

as long as you're up get me a Grant's®

Please. It's the Scotch in that tall, triangular bottle.
Under the Dufy. Why do they call it Grant's 8?
That's the age. Most Scotch is only four years old,
but it really takes 8 years to smooth out a Scotch.
Water? Just a little. Thank you, darling.

The light and legendary 8-year-old blended Scotch Whisky.
Eighty-six proof. Imported to the United States from Scotland
by Austin, Nichols & Co., Inc. New York.   ©1962 Austin, Nichols & Co., Inc.

Please. It's the Scotch in that tall triangular bottle. Under the Dufy. Why do they call it Grant's 8? That's the age. I think it takes eight years to smooth out a Scotch. Water? A little. Thank you, darling. The choice and cherished eight-year-old blended Scotch Whisky. Eighty-six proof. Imported to the United States from Scotland by Austin, Nichols & Co., New York. ©1963 Austin, Nichols & Co., Inc.

Please. It's the Scotch in that tall triangular bottle. Why do they call it Grant's 8? That's the age and I think it takes 8 years to smooth out a Scotch. Water? Thank you, darling. The choice and cherished 8-year-old blended Scotch Whisky. Eighty-six proof. Imported to the United States from Scotland by Austin, Nichols & Co., New York. ©1963 Austin, Nichols & Co., Inc.

Thank you, darling. That kind of service gets you a place on my Christmas list. What's it going to be? Oh, you know. What I give everybody but the kids. Grant's 8. Give the light and legendary 8-year-old blended Scotch Whisky. Eighty-six proof. Imported to the United States from Scotland by Austin, Nichols & Co., New York. ©1963 Austin, Nichols & Co., Inc.

as long as you're up get me a Grant's

© 1964

as long as you're up
get me a Grant's

Please. The Scotch in the triangular bottle with 8 on it.
Why? Because the Grants know it takes 8 years to lighten
a Scotch. Quality takes time. Have one. We'll keep
Grant's in the family. Like the Grant family of Glenfiddich.
86 proof. Bottled in Scotland. Imported to the United
States by Austin, Nichols & Co., New York

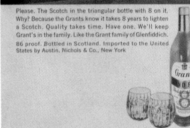

as long as you're up
get me a Grant's

184

as long as you're up get me a Grant's

Please. The Scotch in the triangular bottle. That's right. The one with 8 on it. Yes, Grant's is 8 years old. I guess that's why it has the taste you acquire on the spot. You can't rush quality. Or hurry lightness. So take your time, dear. I'm willing to wait for Grant's.

86 proof blended Scotch Whisky. Bottled in Scotland and imported by Austin, Nichols & Co., N.Y.

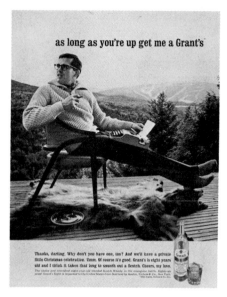

as long as you're up get me a Grant's

Thanks, darling. Why don't you have one, too? And we'll have a private little Christmas celebration. Umm. Of course it's good. Grant's is eight years old and I think it takes that long to smooth out a Scotch. Cheers, my love.

The choice and cherished eight-year-old blended Scotch Whisky in the triangular bottle. Eighty-six proof. Grant's Eight is imported to the United States from Scotland by Austin, Nichols & Co., New York.

as long as you're up get me a Grant's

Please. The Scotch in the triangular bottle with 8 on it. Why? Because the Grants know it takes 8 years to lighten a Scotch. Quality takes time. Have one. We'll keep Grant's in the family. Like the Grant family of Glenfiddich.

86 proof. Bottled in Scotland. Imported to the U.S. by Austin, Nichols & Co., N.Y.

as long as you're up
get me a Grant's

Please. That's right. The Scotch in the tall triangular bottle. Isn't just a little. Thanks, darling. Why don't you have one, too. We'll have our own little Christmas celebration together.

Papert, Koenig, Lois, Inc.

Can a woman who marries a lazy young novelist find happiness with a carpet of Polycrest in the study?

"As long as you're up, get me a sponge," said Ernest, "I just spilled my scotch on the carpet again."

Not that he's sloppy, thought Elizabeth, he's just so absorbed in learning how to type.

Fortunately the carpet was Polycrest olefin—the most stain-resistant kind of carpet you could buy. They picked it out together. The day Ernest sold his new novel to Skin Divers Quarterly.

She wore a path right through the last carpet they had. All the way from the kitchen to Ernest's favorite chair. It wouldn't happen with Polycrest, though. Polycrest is one of the toughest carpet fibers ever devised by man.

She returned with the sponge. Whoosh, the spot was gone. Polycrest was really amazing. She loved that warm color, those crisp patterns, the deep, rich, luxurious pile. It really looked like carpets twice the price.

Ernest interrupted her thoughts. "As long as you're still up," he said, "get me another drinkie poo."

She returned with the bottle and poured it slowly over his head.

Carpet is Callaway's "Skyline"

POLYCREST UNIROYAL

as long as you're up
get me a Grant's

Please. The Scotch in the triangular bottle. That's right. The one with 8 on it. Yes, Grant's is 8 years old. I guess that's why it has the taste you acquire on the spot. You can't rush quality. Or hurry lightness. So take your time with the drink, dear.
86 proof Blended Scotch Whisky. Bottled in Scotland and imported by Austin, Nichols & Co., N.Y.

"As long as you're up, get me a grant."

Joseph G. Farris in Saturday Review

"As long as you're writing, Harry, you'd better lay off the Grant's."

"*As long as you're up, James, get me a Scotch.*"

Herbert Goldberg
Courtesy of Signature, The Diners Club Magazine

"As long as you're Grant, get me a 7-Up."

Such advertising seeks to create new demand, rather than to improve a brand's share of market. There is no logical relationship between the timing of the advertising contact and the "normal" time of purchase. Naturally, the advertiser would like to reach people at a time and in a setting where they are most easily persuaded, but the interval between the message and the impulse to purchase will reflect the effectiveness of the message itself.

A different case exists where people enter the market for a variety of reasons and where the decision to buy stems from circumstances which have very little or nothing to do with advertising. In this case, the advertising message is important as a reminder of the product's utility for the user or of the brand's distinctive merits. The advertiser wants the greatest possible likelihood of exposing his message to those people who at any given moment are faced with the need to buy. This means the broadest possible coverage of the prospects that is consistent with high frequency within a given budget.

The philosophy of the soap companies in their use of daytime TV is to use high frequency for the purpose of achieving dominance rather than to extend reach. At any given point in time the housewife's awareness of Bold detergent versus Fab is only slightly influenced by the accidental fact that a Fab commercial or a Bold commercial happens to be the last one that she saw. The purpose of advertising to her with high frequency is not to increase the chances of having the last word before she departs for the supermarket. It is rather to increase the chances of breaking through the wall of her indifference to learning anything more about a product about which she feels she already knows as much as she wants to know.

To the extent that advertising is actively sought or consulted, its timing is critically important. Theoretically, it is possible for a car manufacturer to concentrate his whole advertising budget in the week of new model introductions. If he did this, he might have a tremendous impact in distinguishing the make both from the previous year's models and from the competition. But as the model year wore on, there would be no way for the prospective purchaser to refresh his memory of this announcement, and the manufacturer's initial advantage would be lost. No car maker could afford to advertise in this way, because car owners are apt to enter the market at any time, and the message must reach them when they are susceptible to influence.

The timing and spacing of messages is one of the most vital strategic problems in the preparation of an advertising schedule, but it involves different considerations in print and in broadcasting.

Consider the problem that remains once we have made the strategic choice between ten large dominant units within a publication and a hundred small units at equivalent cost. Whichever solution we choose, we are still faced with the problem of how to distribute the units we select. We can disperse them evenly one at a time or we can cluster them in groups succeeding each other at short time intervals. We can even place a number of ads within the same publication, reducing the time interval between exposures to a minimum — typically, less than the interval between repeated commercials on a sponsored TV program.

Clustering ads may give us an advantage in creating immediate awareness. Yet we lose the advantage of continuity that we get by spreading ads over time, and we reduce the likelihood of any given message reaching the maximum number of purchasers close to the moment which is psychologically ripe for each.

The broadcast advertiser must concern himself not only with the *number* of occasions his messages are diffused, but also with the *distribution* of these messages in real (clock and calendar) time. He must compare the relative value of scattering messages over an entire broadcast season or concentrating them in brief intense bursts.

A large concentration of commercials within a short period of time adds to the chances of catching the viewer's attention. A special program or spectacular may have the sponsor's three, four, or five commercials successively interrupt the entertainment. The recurrence of commercials is expected to have the same overwhelming effect on the viewers that the print advertiser hopes to achieve by the massive use of space. Within such a framework of intensive exposure, the repeated commercials are intended to produce different results than if they were scattered through an evening on several different networks or spread in the course of a week over different programs on the same network.

The length of the real-time interval between repeated messages is critical to the subject of repetition on TV. An advertisement repeated in a print publication may be exposed to the same people after a substantial time interval. Even if the same ad is inserted in the newspaper every day for a week, a twenty-four hour lag separates one day's reading and the next. With magazines, the interval may be a week or a month.

Even in a 24-hour period, random exposure to a vast number of other messages and experiences occurs, and the residual impact of any single advertisement can be expected to be small indeed unless it vitally touches the reader's material interest, aesthetic sense, or private symbol system.

But on television, if several commercials for a product occur within the same program, each one starts only slightly below the level of awareness created by the last one. Among those viewers who are attentively viewing when the first commercial comes on, comparatively little of what comes through will have been forgotten by the time the second one comes on. (This sidesteps the point that for the typical commercial, communication is far from perfect, even with the attentive viewer.) Repetition used in this way creates high conscious awareness of the advertising message. (It probably also creates strong awareness of the advertising technique being used or of the mechanics incidental to the main sales purpose.) Scattered spot TV messages lose this advantage.

Varying the content

Repeating the identical message in the same media context involves different psychological mechanisms than the repetition of messages which differ in their style or substance. When an advertiser repeats a message in a given media environment, he hopes to recreate some of its original impact and to reinforce its effect on those who saw or heard it previously. He also expects to deliver the message for the first time to those who had missed it before because they were not exposed to the medium, not in physical range of the message, or simply inattentive to it in its original context.

When the same space or time unit in the same medium is used for a new advertisement or commercial, it combines an element of the familiar (e.g., the medium, context, product name, and advertising theme) and the unfamiliar (new art and layout).

Several variations of the same ad or commercial are commonly repeated in a particular publication or program. The process works somewhat differently when the same message, with slight variations, comes to the consumer from several media. A reinforcing effect may be produced when a television jingle is sung on radio. Or there may be carry-over from print to TV (or vice versa) because of the copy, the visual symbolism, or the models used.

In 1916 a pioneer advertising researcher, Henry Adams,[19] prepared a dummy magazine in which a given ad appeared either once, twice, or four times. The second repetition added about 50% to the recollection of the ads, whether it was a quarter-page, half-page, or full-page unit. The four appearances of the same ad represented about two-and-a-half times the value of a single ad. On the other hand, when *different* ads for the same brands were used, instead of repetitions of the same ads, the value of two ads was two-and-a-half times the value of a single one, and the value of four ads was about four times as great.

[19] *Advertising and Its Mental Laws,* New York: Macmillan, 1916, cited by Simon, *op cit.*

The most ambitious published study of repetition in advertising was directed by John Stewart[20] (with the sponsorship of the Bureau of Advertising and the Newsprint Information Committee) and involved the experimental introduction of two new products: a frozen chicken dish (Chicken Sara Lee) and a pre-packaged bleach (Lestare) in Fort Wayne, Indiana. The full advertising campaign for each product was a thousand-line newspaper ad once a week for twenty weeks.

Matched sections of the city were blanked out from exposure to the ads for varying periods. In a control area, no advertising ran at all; in another matched section, advertising ran for four weeks, in another for eight weeks, and in a fourth for twenty weeks. Over a twenty-three-week period, interviews were conducted with matched samples totaling nearly 6,200 respondents.

The design of this research posed a dilemma right from the outset. Since the objective was to study the effects of repetition, it was necessary to repeat the same unit of advertising space. But above and beyond that, it was necessary to repeat the identical ad each time. Any variation in layouts, copy themes, or illustrations of the sort we would normally expect in this kind of campaign, would have changed the very thing which was being measured — repetition of the *same* message.

By any of the measures used (awareness of the new product, information about it, or attitudes toward it), a certain number of successive repetitions (between half-a-dozen times and ten) clearly continued to have an incremental effect. Beyond that point, the major value of repetition was in maintaining the product at the level it had previously attained and protecting it from the immediate attrition that sets in when advertising stops. The more often the ads were repeated, the slower the rate of decay in the effects of the advertising. But the exact point at which the favorable effects of repetition started to wear out appeared to vary with the individual campaign. For one product, the second four ads added more net effect than the first four; the advertising campaign had an accelerating effect as it continued. For the other product, the pattern was reversed; the second four repetitions had a diminished effect.

Clearly, this vital difference must be accounted for by the particular creative strategy used in relation to the product in each case, since the media vehicle, the space unit, and the time interval were the same in both instances. In the first instance, the correct procedure was to repeat the same ad as long as it continued to build up to its maximum effect. In the second case, different ads might well have been used in successive insertions. Some readers seemed to have reached a threshold of psycho-

[20] John B. Stewart, *Repetitive Advertising in Newspapers*, Boston: Harvard University, Division of Research, Graduate School of Business Administration, 1964.

logical resistance when the same ads were shown to them again and again and again. After a certain point, the advertising (in its particular theming and appearance) no longer appeared to register with those who were not potential customers. They had seen it before; it fell into context; it simply did not have to be perceived as the eye scanned by it.

What would have happened to the shape of the curve of net favorable effect if the ad copy and layout had been changed periodically? There is reason to believe that it might have shown accelerated growth with each change. Each new format would have won the attention of some readers who were responsive to the new approach even though they had become oblivious to the old one.

An interesting combination of familiar and unfamiliar elements can be found in a recent Grant's Scotch Whiskey campaign which began with an ad that showed a man seated with a typewriter on his lap in a chair of striking design. In subsequent ads various parts of the same photograph were cropped and then, in a later development of the campaign, other models were shown in a similar situation. Throughout, the same slogan was used ("As long as you're up, get me a Grant's").

Such a procedure reinforces the original message, but at the same time it creates attention and awareness because of the audience's need to close the psychological gap between the expected and the unexpected. The reader is stopped by the incongruity between familiar and unfamiliar elements which he must resolve himself.

The slogan used in this campaign appears to have achieved that greatest and most rarely found criterion of success, a viable existence independent of the advertising campaign itself.

MARKET SEGMENTATION

Who was the genius who first discovered that rich people buy more things than poor ones? Or his equally anonymous successor who discovered that smokers buy more cigarettes than non-smokers, among rich and poor alike? Let monuments be erected in their memory, for every year these startling discoveries are made anew!

Every advertiser wants to use media that will bring him straight to his marketing target. Unfortunately, there is no general agreement on how marketing targets should be defined. The management of an American organization operating in South America once defined three target groups for a big public information campaign. The first was "all literates." The second was "all illiterates"; and the third was "all others."

John W. Burgard, Advertising Director of the Brown & Williamson Tobacco Corporation[1] has criticized

---

[1] In an address to the 1966 meeting of the A.N.A.

the tendency of network research to concentrate on total audience, or
share of audience, largely ignoring the details of audience composition
which are important to the advertiser. It would appear that some advertisers either do not have very good information on audience composition,
or else ignore it; otherwise right now I don't think we would see a cigar
commercial on a show which has a very definite skew to older women.

The question of how many *people* could be reached by a medium
for a given cost was often rephrased to inquire how many *customers* could
be reached. Gail Smith, Director of Advertising of the General Motors
Corporation, put the proposition in these words: "I think the advertiser
will be able to buy a pound of people or a pound of territory as today
you can buy chicken breasts or legs without getting stuck with the whole
bird." [2]

The development of mass marketing in the United States has been
accompanied by an enormous amount of research designed to locate the
best prospective customers for different commodities. The relationships
between market and audience characteristics were readily seen as a
problem of matching, and the ability to put messages in front of prospects
with minimum waste and at minimum cost is often considered to be one
of the chief skills of the advertiser.

Elementary to the alignment of media capabilities and marketing
requirements is the concept of market segmentation. This concept is, in
.effect, being implemented by any company which systematically seeks to
describe its customers and potential customers and to differentiate them
from the public as a whole with regard to such characteristics as sex, age,
income, education, and so on. In their selection of media, advertisers
have long attempted to match the particular profile of their own consumers with comparable media profiles. A manufacturer selling a product to high-income professional families looks for "class" media. An
advertiser selling to young mothers tries to find a medium which is directed at their interests.

In their eagerness to get to the most rewarding segments of the
market, advertisers often succumb to the tendency to use standard definitions, regardless of whether they coincide with the proper target — those
who are ready to be persuaded.

Trapping the heavy user

Who is the elusive prospect that every advertiser seeks, the one whose
defenses will melt and whose deep-rooted purchase habits change immediately, if only our message can reach him?

[2] Speech before the Magazine Publishers Association, June 4, 1964, White Sulphur
Springs, W. Va.

For many knowledgeable marketers, the best prospect can always be defined as the heavy user, the one who buys more of the product in question, faces the purchase decision most often, and is thus, presumably, most sensitized to advertising.   In almost any product category it can be demonstrated that a large percentage of the sales volume comes from a minority of the total public, often from a minority of the product's users.   How logical, then, to seek media whose audiences are made up of just those very same heavy users!

One illustration of this approach comes from an analysis by Dik Warren Twedt[3] of data taken from the Chicago *Tribune* consumer panel on eighteen product categories.   (The 402 families in the *Tribune* panel maintain a continuing record of their purchases which makes possible the comparison of their individual product and brand selections over extended periods of time.)   The heavy users appeared to have lower-than-average brand loyalty.   They did not buy to save on price alone.

The heavy using families were different for different product categories.   Twedt therefore inferred that demographic characteristics are not good predictors of heavy usage.   It seemed to follow that it is more efficient to measure consumption of each product directly — in direct relation to the media habits of the heavy users — than to assume that they fall into any particular population bracket with known media exposure patterns.

Twedt tested this hypothesis by applying a computer program developed by Data Inc. to his marketing data, in order to develop a media schedule for Chicago.   He concluded that "the media vehicles used to optimize our reach among heavy bacon users are not the right ones for reaching heavy instant coffee users. . . .   A television program, for example, may have as many ratings as it has potential sponsors."

While this conclusion is intriguing to anyone prepared to recognize the complexities of the market, the evidence on which it rests is somewhat incomplete.   As in a great many similar attempts to match market and media profiles, the unit of Twedt's analysis was the household.   This makes sense when we analyze consumption because for the most part families consume together, whether or not they buy together.   We know, however, that media experiences are, to a large extent, individual within the family.   The individual who does most of the buying for a particular item in a heavy-using household is not necessarily the same one who does most of the reading, viewing, or listening to the media vehicle which has heavy exposure in the same family.   The products analyzed were all grocery items whose use varied substantially, not merely with income but with family size, composition, and ethnic background (since persons of

[3] Address before the Advertising Research Foundation, October 6, 1964, New York, N.Y.

Italian and Polish descent eat differently even when they have similar jobs and housing).

We are left wondering whether a demographic analysis that used more variables at once might not come up with far better yardsticks of prediction than those which Twedt tried and rejected. The widespread tendency to make measurements in terms of households rather than in terms of people is a by-product of the accidental fact that the Nielsen Audimeter — the most widely used instrument in broadcast audience research — measures set-tuning rather than the actual process of communication, which is always on an individual basis.

It goes without saying that a family's consumption characteristics do not necessarily apply to all of its individual members. In some households, the husband has three beers a day and the wife has none; this is a heavy-using household. Similarly, there are patterns of household *media* consumption which do not apply to individual members. The paterfamilias may remain oblivious to the women's magazines his wife leaves all over the living room; his household is "heavily exposed." In large families, TV viewing is higher than in smaller ones, but the housewife actually watches TV *less*. The kids watch TV while she is slaving over a hot stove to get their TV dinners ready.

The advertiser often faces a tactical question as to whether to aim at the ultimate consumer or at the purchasing agent. His problem is compounded by the fact that when several members of the same family are interviewed, they often disagree as to who controls the brand decision. Media researcher Malcolm B. Ochs[4] points out that almost one-third of all laundry soaps and detergents are bought by men, while among the women interviewed for a *Good Housekeeping* study, 30% reported buying razor blades for their men, and of these, 53% claimed to select the brand without asking the man. A 1958 study made by the Home Testing Institute for *McCall's* found that in a majority of cases involving the purchase of men's apparel (like shirts, slacks, jackets, sweaters, or sportswear) the wife claimed that the idea of buying was hers and that she selected the item purchased. *True* magazine used Starch data to prove that the woman's voice in the decision to buy men's apparel is stronger at lower incomes, whereas the upper-income man is more likely to make his own decision.

In developing any advertising plan, it is of course essential to know who the heavy users are and to determine whether they buy the product for reasons that are in any way different from those of other people, in which case they would demand a different copy approach. However, the most effective advertising is not always that which provides the most

[4] *Media/scope*, March 1966, pp. 77-79.

concentration on users of the product in general, or even on heavy users in particular. Often the advertiser's problem is less to hold on to his existing share of market than to expand the market as a whole by attracting new customers or increasing consumption on the part of light or moderate users. Or, by contrast, in a mature market where there is "saturation usage," like the soap and coffee markets, the advertiser's main marketing task may be to attract customers away from his competition at *every* level of use.

In many product categories, usage is governed by strictly objective material considerations like family size, income, or position in the life cycle, and advertising serves largely to shuffle brand shares rather than to expand consumption per se. The extent to which people can be induced to increase their consumption of soap as a result of advertising is small relative to the increase in consumption which takes place when a new member is added to the family.

There is also a serious technical problem in relating consumption patterns accurately to media use. Most survey data today are subjected to a constant process of adjustment and weighing. The numbers that are ground out of the computer no longer represent straight answers to questions asked of individual people. New techniques of sampling give us more accurate projections for the whole population, but at the same time the sampling error is harder to calculate.

This becomes more of a problem when we compare smaller and smaller subgroups, like heavy users of a given product who read a particular publication or listen to a certain radio program. At this point, any comparisons we make, even when we start with a big sample, are based on a small number of interviews, which means the results may show a large statistical error. This problem gets even more serious when we compare surveys at different points in time. How far should we pursue the heavy user through this jungle of statistical question-marks?

Who is the target?

Paul Klein of NBC recalls visiting an advertising agency handling a large margarine account and delivering a presentation which showed that a particular schedule on his network would reach a very large concentration of the heavy margarine users. After he had finished his presentation, complete with numerous statistics, the account executive told him plaintively, "But we want to reach the heavy *butter* users."

In defining the target, every marketer must decide on the probabilities of converting the people who do not use his product. His tactics

A CONFUSING BUSINESS WHERE DISAGREEMENTS ARE RAMPANT

must necessarily be different for a broad market than for a narrow one. If he goes after current users only, he may lose the chance of winning new customers to the product field. If he goes after heavy users only, he loses the chance of convincing the light users to buy more. If his is the dominant brand in the market, expanding total sales for the product field will redound directly to his benefit. If he has a minority position, his success in getting people interested in the product may either carve out a unique new position for his brand or merely benefit his competitors. Thus the interrelation between defining the target and plotting the advertising strategy can clearly be seen.

The advertising planner must weigh the productivity of converting existing users to his own brand at the same time that he keeps his present customers safely within his camp against the blandishments of the competition.

For toothpaste, the level of brand loyalty ranges from a low of 32% for Listerine to a high of 74% for Crest, according to analyses made by the Brand Rating Index for a six-month period between December 1964 and May 1965. (Brand loyalty was defined by BRI as mention of a brand as the one bought most often at both points in time.) A comparably broad range of variation occurs in many product fields.

BRI's Norton Garfinkle[5] reports that older people and people of lower income and education have the highest rates of brand switching, whereas those of higher income and education are most brand-loyal. However, the brand-loyal people of lower income switch from one *established* brand to another, while the higher educated have the greatest propensity to switch to new products and brands.

Perhaps the most exhaustive comparative analyses of shifts and constancies in brand usage for different products were made in the early 50's by George H. Brown, who, like Twedt, used the Chicago *Tribune's* consumer-panel data.[6] A few years later, Ross M. Cunningham[7] reanalyzed Brown's data for seven product categories. He concluded that there was a significant amount of brand loyalty to individual products as shown by actual purchases (rather than by brand preference, which BRI measures). Cunningham cited instances in which over 90% of a family's purchases for a three-year period had been concentrated on a single brand.

[5] "New Measurements of the Value of Marketing Targets and Media Audiences," a speech delivered at the 12th Annual Conference of the Advertising Research Foundation, October 1966, New York, N.Y.
[6] *Advertising Age,* Vol. 24, No. 4, January 26, 1953. Brown was at the University of Chicago Business School when he did this study, before his move to the Ford Motor Company, where he heads Corporate Marketing Research.
[7] "Brand Loyalty — Where, What, How Much?" *Harvard Business Review,* Vol. 34, No. 1, January-February 1956, pp. 116-28.

Does this mean there is a certain kind of brand-loyal customer whom the advertiser should seek for his very own? Cunningham observes that there is no significant proportion of families who are *consistently* loyal across all types of product categories. Those loyal to a brand of one product may have very little brand loyalty in the case of another product. Cunningham found the highest brand loyalty for headache tablets, margarine, and scouring cleansers and the lowest for canned peas and toilet soap. He noted that many families apparently have a favorite second choice but that this makes less difference the more loyal they are to a single product.

Cunningham discovered "secondary" loyalties which carry over from one of a manufacturer's brands to his other brands. Brand loyalty appeared to be almost impervious to price offers and deals and showed no truly significant relationship to store loyalty or to the size of the consumer's purchase. In the case of the low-priced, frequently purchased items measured, brand loyalty appeared to be unrelated to socioeconomic characteristics. In essence, Cunningham tells us that brand loyalty is real and important, but it is specific to the product category rather than to any particular type of consumer.

Taking a different tack on the same subject, John U. Farley[8] investigated the differences in family characteristics that might account for differences in brand selection. He hypothesized that households which put the greatest effort into gathering market information should, in general, show the least brand loyalty as long as brands are considered comparable with each other. He also reasoned:

"Heavy buyers should thus tend to pay less than light buyers for a given item. If brand preferences are not strong, heavy buyers should also appear less brand loyal than light buyers."

Since people of higher income place greater value on their time, Farley hypothesized that they would spend less time shopping around among different brands which they consider to be comparable and should therefore show greater brand loyalty than those of lower income. On the other hand, he felt that big families who have to stretch their budgets farther would spend more time comparing brands and would therefore show less brand loyalty.

To test his theory, Farley examined 1957 data from the Market Research Corporation of America on the purchases of 199 families in metropolitan Chicago. The evidence supported his thesis that "heavy buyers of a product tend to pay less for a given container size than do light buyers." His other hypotheses, however, were not borne out by the evi-

[8] "Brand Loyalty and the Economics of Information," *Journal of Business,* Vol. 37, No. 4, October 1964, pp. 370-81.

dence. Instead, there was some indication that high-income families tend to be brand-disloyal rather than loyal as he had predicted. (This would seem to be in line with research we did at the Bureau of Advertising in 1965 which showed a higher use of grocery products with store or private labels among the better-off.) Farley concluded that any greater value that high-income (and better-educated) people place on their shopping time is outweighed by the greater efficiency with which they handle information. However, the inconclusiveness of Farley's findings supports Cunningham's conclusion that "it all depends" on the product and that there is no over-all style of brand choice.

A national survey made by the Bureau of Advertising in 1961 came closer than Farley's own analysis to demonstrating some of his original hypotheses. This study found that people of higher income make more active use of advertising as an adjunct to the shopping decision. Low-income people tend to shop around in order to hunt bargains regardless of whether they actually like shopping per se. The higher-income person who doesn't enjoy shopping can afford simply to stick with the store he knows and trusts. Bargain-minded people are more skeptical of the truthfulness of advertising. The most skeptical people are those who consider shopping a chore, but in spite of this, because they tend to be of lower income, they do more shopping around among stores. This research showed that women enjoy shopping; men regard it as a chore and are therefore much more likely to shop at a single store for any particular major purchase rather than to shop around as women do. Men are less bargain-minded than women are; they are more apt to buy on impulse and are less resistant to credit purchasing. Women are more conscious of consulting advertising for information than are men. In general, people enjoy shopping less as they grow older, and this is reflected in the decreasing number of stores they visit on a shopping trip. Findings like these make it clear that the marketer can hardly expect to find all the customers of a certain type clustered together in one place and available to him through any particular advertising medium.

Related conclusions are reported by Herbert Kay from a pilot study[9] among 300 women. Kay defined "prime prospects" as people who use a product, who can be persuaded to switch brands, and who are susceptible to advertising appeals.

Prime prospect status by Kay's definition is not related to the volume of usage or to conventional demographic classifications. In one product category, 33% of the prime prospects he surveyed had incomes under $5,000, while only 13% of the other users were in this low-income

[9] Private communication.

bracket; but in another product field, the proportion of prime prospects and other users with low incomes was the same (about a fifth).

Comparing two products with the same proportion of users who are over 35, Kay showed that one has virtually identical proportions of prospects among both younger and older women, whereas the other has twice as high a percentage of younger women users as older ones who might be persuaded by advertising to switch brands.

Comparing two women's service magazines with an identical four-week cumulative audience, Kay found that the percentage of heavy toothpaste users who read at least one issue of each was identical with that of all the women interviewed (35%). However, one magazine reached 24% of all those users whom Kay classifies as the "prime prospects," the other 44%. Among prime prospects who were also heavy users, the disproportion was even greater.

Kay provides other examples of media vehicles which appear to be evenly matched in terms of audience size and even in the proportion of product users and heavy users who are reached. Yet when he adds in the extra dimension of willingness to switch brands, he finds striking differences in the proportion of magazine readers or program viewers who are prime prospects for conversion. The explanation has to be that certain media vehicles, because of their content, manage to attract more of the persuadable than others do. The evidence is slim thus far, but the concept is appealing.

There is no *perfect* case of media and market matching. Any medium, no matter how selective, will reach some people other than the ones who are prospects for a manufacturer's product. Any market of heavy users, no matter how concentrated, will include many people beyond the reach of a selective medium.

In any attempt to correlate media and consumption habits, some very important simplifications have to be made. To the extent that there is a relationship at all, it is rarely a *direct* relationship between the two. Instead, it usually arises because of the intrusion of a third element which reflects such things as the consumer's age, education, or income, or more subtle matters of personality and taste.

Exposure to any one advertisement is not, of course, randomly distributed among those exposed to the medium that carries it. Within the audience for any medium there is selective sensitivity to different types of advertising content and technique. Not only the media plan, but the very nature of the message, determine whether or not the advertiser reaches his target. Who that target really is is something he must judge for his own unique product; no easy formula can define it for him.

Locating the "interested" prospects

Every advertiser hopes to strike a responsive chord among the people exposed to his message. But how can he decide who will be interested?

A number of propositions emerge both from common sense and from a variety of consumer studies:

1 An expensive item is more likely to arouse the consumer's emotional involvement than a less expensive one.

2 A product about which the consumer feels deeply is most likely to arouse an active, purposeful search for information when he is in the market.

3 A product category in which the customer perceives brands as being very different creates a more purposeful selective interest in advertising than one in which the customer assumes that all products are pretty much alike.

4 Most products which are bought arouse comparatively little involvement. They are likely to be inexpensive and they demand rather effortless or routine decision-making. (This is not true of products that are consumed daily but which serve as symbols of social position or of individual personality or taste — cigarettes are the best example.)

5 The more expensive an item is, the more money is normally expended on promoting the sale of each unit and the greater the total advertising pressure that influences each purchase and seeks to raise the level of consumer interest.

6 The more differentiated the product from others of the same kind, the more informative the function of advertising and the more actively the prospective buyer consults and uses it in making up his mind.

The people interested in a product are not always the best prospects. Some products, like insurance or weed killer, may carry a rather high degree of emotional involvement, and yet this may be a negative feeling. Product interest and frequency of usage were both considered in a national study conducted in 1964 by the Bureau of Advertising.[10] To follow up on a study of daily newspaper readership, a sample of approximately 1,600 people representing a national cross-section was interviewed about a variety of consumer items.[11] It was assumed from

[10] This study was sponsored by the Newsprint Information Committee and conducted by Audits and Surveys.
[11] The items about which questions were asked varied from one interview to the next. They reflected the incidence of newspaper advertisements for the products in question and were not a representative selection of *all* advertised products relative either to consumption or to the total amount of national advertising.

the start that the attitudes and actions which defined an individual as a prospect in one product category might be substantially different from those which defined him as a prospect in some other field. Frequency of purchase was recorded rather than the volume of use (with which it would closely correlate but which is harder to estimate accurately). However, it was not assumed that the frequent buyer could always be considered the best prospect. The survey questionnaire also measured (1) the degree to which the consumer found the product pleasant or pleasant to use, (2) the degree of his interest in reading and hearing of new developments in the product field, and (3) his willingness to talk about the product.

For the typical product, the largest proportion of people interviewed reported that they found it pleasant to use. (A few categories — liquor, cigarettes, air travel — elicited rather sharply differentiated responses from users and non-users.) The next highest proportion of the respondents liked to read or hear of new product developments. Finally, a much smaller proportion liked to talk about the products. (Air travel is an exception, because people are interested in reading or talking about it as much or more as they find it pleasant.)

All three of these measures (pleasantness, interest, and discussion) were combined into a single score of the consumer's involvement with the product. The variation from product to product was striking. For men the proportion with a "high involvement" score ranged from 75% for new cars down to 8% for women's make-up. For women canned vegetables and packaged mixes got a "high involvement" score of 66% and vodka a low of 7%. Even though advertisers often aim their messages only at men or only at women, the study found that the opposite sex often showed a high level of interest in the product. Bread and some other food products aroused high involvement scores from men, while cars, tires, and air travel received high scores from women.

In addition to the questions about "involvement" with the product, people were asked whether they considered the brands in the product field to be all the same or different, and their "brand loyalty" was also investigated. These data were related to the readership of advertisements for the same products, obtained in a separate interview two weeks earlier. The highest level of readership occurred among people who were brand-loyal, but not among the *most* brand-loyal. (Since their minds were already made up, they did not want to be confused with the facts.) Those who think most brands in a given product field are really different pay more attention to advertising for that product than people who think the brands are all alike (and therefore not worth learning more about).

Soft drinks and coffee are among those product categories where blindfold taste tests customarily show that differences among individual brands are difficult to detect. Yet these two categories were tied for second place (after new cars) in the percentage of men who believed that there were important differences among brands.

The extent to which people feel there are important brand differences in a product field has very little to do with their attitudes toward the product as such. For example, 9 out of 10 men and 8 out of 10 women considered bread extremely pleasant to use, but only about 1 in 3 people liked to talk about bread and only half thought that there are important differences among brands of bread. Only 1 man in 4 believed that there are important differences among airlines. Yet, next to automobiles, men reported talking about air travel more than about any other measured product or service.

How does the frequency of using a product relate to attitudes toward it? Different patterns appear to emerge in different categories. For example, in the case of blended whiskey the most frequent purchasers were also those who were most likely to find the product pleasant to use, who were most interested in new developments, most inclined to talk about it, most convinced of differences among different brands, and who showed the highest proportion of brand loyalty.

In the case of bread, a product which almost everyone uses, frequency of purchase appears to have no bearing at all on either brand attitude or purchase behavior or on involvement with the product. This merely reflects the fact that the user of bread is not necessarily the purchaser. His feelings toward the product may have no opportunity at all to be translated into buying behavior.

In the case of airlines there is still another pattern, for the key difference in attitude appeared to be between flyers and non-flyers, rather than how often flyers fly.

The results imply that the most efficient advertising campaign may be the one which reaches not the highest proportion of heavy users, but rather the highest proportion of people who are susceptible to persuasion to use the product more often, or to shift brands. As we have seen, product usage, product attitudes, and brand attitudes do not relate to each other in the same predictable way for every product.

The problem of classification

It is still common in American advertising and marketing for the public to be classified in terms of categories which have long outlived their usefulness. In the early years of marketing research, it was standard practice for interviewers to be assigned quotas of people to contact in what were euphemistically known as A, B, C, and D neighborhoods. How these social classes were defined varied in description from one interviewing organization to the next and each interviewer made her own interpretation, depending on which side of the railroad tracks she herself had been raised.

During the mid-40's and early 50's, the concept of social class developed by W. Lloyd Warner and his school of social anthropologists became widely familiar.[12] Studies made by Warner's disciple, Burleigh Gardner, of Social Research, Inc., were widely popularized by Pierre Martineau, the gifted promotion director of the Chicago *Tribune*.[13]

Warner and Gardner related consumption styles to social class position, of which income was a component but not necessarily the sole determinant.

The classic sociological analysis of social classes, begun by Karl Marx and continued by Max Weber, dealt primarily with power relationships. Warner stressed the idea that prestige, as both a cause and derivative of power, had much to do with an individual's worldly display of possessions and manners of conduct. Warner's scheme of description began with the social class to which a person was assigned by others. In his system, class position was related to the *source* of a person's income as well as its amount. It was further affected by the type of his occupation, his level of education, his racial or ethnic origins and church affiliation, and the type of house and neighborhood he lived in.

Social mobility also loomed large in Warner's outlook. A competitive economic order places a high premium on striving for promotion and achievement. The marketing system and the pressures of advertising all work to arouse appetites for the joys of consumption as the fruit of personal achievement. Warner showed that the way a person spends his income, including his product and brand choices, might in many cases have far more to do with the symbols of social class toward which he aspires than does his original social background.

Although Warner defined six social classes — ranging from Upper-Upper to Lower-Lower — in his famous study of Yankee City (Newburyport, Massachusetts), Gardner preferred to simplify the contrast into that between upper-middle class values and those of the "Middle Majority" which linked the petite bourgeoisie and the solid working-class in banal conformity to conventional virtues.[14]

[12] *Cf.* W. Lloyd Warner, Marcia Meeker, and Kenneth Eells, *Social Class in America*. Chicago: Science Research Associates, 1949.
[13] *Motivation in Advertising*. New York: McGraw-Hill Book Company, 1957.
[14] *Cf.* Lee Rainwater, Richard P. Coleman, and Gerald Handel, *Workingman's Wife*. Chicago: Social Research, Inc., 1959.

The influence of Warner and Gardner's social class analysis waned with that of motivation research. The main line of marketing and media data still uses the traditional demographic comparisons based on income, education, age, and city size. These necessarily lump into a single category individuals who are highly different in their characteristics, outlook, habits, and values. For example, the common practice of classification by education lumps into a single bracket a man with a Ph.D from Harvard and one who has spent a year or two in an academically fifth-rate college. Such individuals probably differ totally in their income, outlook, habitat, and life style, and yet they are lumped together as "college-educated" in most studies that analyze consumption.

Life styles reflect the great complexity of roles which individuals play in an increasingly segmented society. No man is just of middle income and over 35. He may also be a father, churchwarden, union member, Mason, medical patient, and Republican. It is precisely at the intersection point of these varied roles that we find the most interesting deviations from expected patterns of buying.

These roles are not fixed for any individual. As young people leave the dependent world of childhood and become consumers, job-seekers, club members, taxpayers, car owners, and heads of families, their media habits change as well as their activities as consumers. All this has profound implications for the advertiser. He must "teach" each generation of consumers all over again what its parents know.

A consumer's buying style does reflect his measurable demographic traits, but it is also — and in some cases to an even greater degree — an expression of highly individual personality attributes.

One of the problems with consumer surveys in general is that they are seldom made with samples large enough to allow us to classify people in terms of more than one or two dimensions (like income, education, age, etc.). When we compare people in terms of three or four of these characteristics simultaneously, even though we may start with a very large sample, we usually end up with far too few in any one subgroup to make the results statistically conclusive. Thus the market analyst chronically settles for comparisons that are far less sophisticated than those he wants and needs.

When we meet a stranger, we automatically make very complex and subtle assessments which allow us to position him in terms which are meaningful in the sense that they provide us with cues as to how to communicate with him. We make instantaneous judgments from his appearance and manner about his age, social position, urbanity, ethnicity, regional origins, intelligence, and personality. We make all of these judgments simultaneously and in relation to each other. They are subject to testing by our further observation or experience with him.

This kind of delicate differentiation comes as close to the heart of the marketer's problem as anything could. The marketer is always dealing with people's consumption tastes, with their vulnerability to certain kinds of persuasion, and with their media exposure patterns. All of these phenomena correspond to the kinds of highly individual attributes which enter into a first-hand, everyday, informal assessment of personality. Yet the marketer rarely gets his research data in a form which allows him to look at people in terms of these dimensions. He is forced to work with crude generalizations, and with variables which are not sensitive enough to distinguish among key elements in the market.

Consumers are today increasingly differentiated, not merely with regard to the traditional types of demographic characteristics but also in terms of psychological attributes which are in no sense related to such conventional measures as age or income. This may be true in the case of widely used products (like cigarettes or white bread) where brand choice reflects response to symbols rather than to any objective or overt product differences.

Some personality traits do seem to have a relationship to social class and distinctive practices of child rearing. But any such relationship is unpredictable for large populations and certainly of less significance than so simple a matter as whether one is a first-born or middle child.

The importance of individual personality differences in consumption may be suggested by some of the findings from the study of car buying which we described before (page 72). Consumer decisions to purchase automobiles appear to cluster into three major patterns which we termed the repetitive, emotional, and logical. People who follow these different purchase patterns seem to differ more psychologically than in demographic terms.

In the repetitive pattern, advertising mainly fills a supportive function. The purchaser really knows all along what he is going to do and the advertising is a way of reassuring himself that he is correct in staying with his present make and dealer.

In the emotional pattern, advertising is a strong stimulus to fantasy. The prestige and status aspects of car ownership are important to this kind of buyer, and advertising differentiates his image of the various makes.

In the logical buying pattern, advertising has little to do with the decision to buy, but it is actively consulted as a source of information on particular makes and models.

All these people were prospects for a car manufacturer, since they bought cars, yet advertising has different tasks for each group. For the repetitive buyer, advertising serves to create a feeling that the time to buy is right now. It keeps the public informed of new automotive developments, relates the make to the local dealer, and assures the potential purchaser of the value he is getting. For the emotional buyer, the main task of advertising is to build a prestigious brand image. It also creates the feeling that new important improvements are constantly on the way to support this type of buyer's feeling that the car means pleasure, excitement, and adventure. For the logical buyer, advertising must provide the specific factual information needed for reference to compare different makes.

Like users of consumer products, media users may also be distinguished on grounds which go beyond the more conventional classifications. In those cases where the standard demographic characteristics yielded no points of particular distinction, attempts have been made to differentiate media audiences in psychological terms. At one time the *Saturday Evening Post* promoted the concept of "The Influentials" [15] and sought to demonstrate that its readers included somewhat more than the average proportion of leaders of public opinion.

Readers of *Harper's* and the *Atlantic*, matched against non-readers of identical income, age, and other attributes, have been shown to engage in more foreign travel, drink more Scotch, and write more letters to their Congressmen. Media also have turned an apparent handicap into an asset, as the MacFadden publications [16] have done by extolling the marketing virtues of the blue-collar housewives who read "confession" magazines.

On one occasion the media director of an advertising agency pitching for a new business account kept talking about the blue-collar market. He couldn't understand why his colleagues were silently grimacing until he suddenly realized that the only man in the room wearing a blue shirt was the president of the company whose account was being solicited. [17]

Demographic categories and social change

During the 1960's, the realities of a fast-changing American society have made the classic structural definitions of the social order more and more suspect — or even irrelevant. The changing age composition of the

[15] *Study of Influentials*, Philadelphia: Curtis Publishing Company, 1957.
[16] *The Woman Behind the Market*, New York: MacFadden-Bartell Corporation, 1962.
[17] Richard Baxter reports this poignant tale.

population has created new self-conscious interest groups of people in the same age-bracket who have been shaped more by a common historical and social experience than by family income. The post-war generation of adolescents has a strongly felt community of interests, values, and heroes, and a certain community of consumption styles. Much the same might be said of the new and growing group of aged people with con- siderable remaining life expectancy who are modestly affluent as a result of social security, union welfare funds, and company retirement plans — also a post-war phenomenon. The emergence of these two age-interest groups, each with its own special product interests and symbolic focal point, represents a major new development.

Another such development reflects the rapid attrition of the rural sector in American life and the crumbling (by court decree) of the rural political dominance which traditionally kept state legislatures under the control of a conservative and often benighted minority element.

The urgent needs of an urban society in housing, transportation, and recreation are bound to have profound implications for marketing.[18] The growth of the metropolis has come hand in hand with the deteriora- tion of central cities and the spread of the dreary suburban developments that house white working-class refugees from urban cores inhabited in increasing proportions by Southern Negroes. The bitter struggle of the Negro during the mid-1960's has created new tensions within American society.

These developments have shattered traditional community identifi- cations which formerly gave some cohesion to the social order. Their effect on the distribution system is generally understood by big merchants concerned about the future of "Downtown." But they have an equally great effect on people's values and on what they do with their money, as well as with where and how they buy. Yet the impact of significant social change on individual consumption patterns is rarely encompassed by consumer surveys.

The advertising strategist who recognizes that a person's choice of both media and products reflects his particular social environment must also recognize that the meaningful distinctions between one environment and another are not limited to such classical determinants as city size, income, and sex. Anxieties over schools, taxes, and the draft may be the most pertinent considerations.

During the ten years ending in 1966, the number of working wives increased three times as fast as the number of households. (The more educated a woman is, the more likely she is to be at work.) It is esti- mated that two-fifths of family consumer expenditures occur in house-

[18] By 1980, three-fourths of the U.S. population will be in metropolitan areas.

holds where the wife works. Obviously the problem of reaching the busy working housewife represents a different advertising challenge than that of reaching a woman who spends her days at home.

Race and ethnic origin (with its religious associations) may have profound importance for the marketer, and yet these factors are often ignored in market and media analyses. One exception is the "Negro market" which certain advertisers go after. Research has shown that, in addition to special requirements in cosmetics and minor special tastes in food, the average Negro does have some buying habits which are different from those of the average white. Indeed, it would be surprising if this were not the case, since the average Negro's income is lower and must be spent on a different array of purchases. (To illustrate: a four-week analysis of warehouse transfers to supermarkets made by *Progressive Grocer* found that stores in Negro neighborhoods sold only 14% as many olives as the average store, but over twice as much canned milk and 76% more canned peaches..)

The psychological disadvantages that Negroes face seem to account for their heavier than usual reliance on prestige brands. The reputations of particular manufacturers for good or bad race relations have also influenced the position of their brands in sales to Negroes.

By and large, the advertiser reaches far more Negroes through the mass media than he can through *Ebony* or *Jet*, the Negro press, or the Negro radio (which is really owned by whites). But his advertising in Negro media can build for him an identity as a "good guy" which gives his messages in the mass media greater force with the Negroes in his audience.

David North reports that the Negro market loomed large in the calculations of a major wine company:

> For some weeks the company's agency and directors tried to plot a way to get into the middle-class white beer-drinking market — a novel switch since most of this wine firm's sales were made to Negroes. Finally the agency made a proposal for a new product with broad appeal — a light wine with substantially less alcohol than most domestic wines. After he reviewed the program, the president of the firm said with assurance, "Great! Now let's test it in the Negro market first."

Peculiarly enough, the very forces of racial upheaval which have heightened marketers' awareness of Negroes in the 1960's have also inhibited the collection of data which makes intelligent analysis possible. With its chronic hypersensitivity in public relations, American business has always been nervous about asking people's religion or ethnic background in market surveys. Even the interviewer's recording of race as part of the classification data on a questionnaire is now often eliminated on the ground that someone might object!

Yet ethnicity may make tremendous differences in consumption style even in a country where egg foo yung, pizza, and matzo-ball soup are all part of the priceless national heritage. In an analysis of liquor consumption in Ohio, Frederick W. Williams, Jr.[19] demonstrated that bourbon predominates in the rural and small-town counties where the population is of native American stock, while blended whiskey (everybody's type, with its "neutral spirits") is favored in the big cities with their diversified population of more recent immigrant ancestry.

Only rarely have media analyzed their own audiences along ethnic or religious lines, although it is obvious that differences must exist which parallel the different occupational, educational, and political complexions of different ethnic groups in the United States. A 1964 study of New York newspapers found that each of the (then) three afternoon papers drew its readers primarily from a different one of the three major religious groups.[20]

When the advertiser does go after particular ethnic segments, he most commonly uses a creative approach which also has an appeal for the rest of the market he must cover to reach his target. Rheingold beer did this in the New York market with a series of TV and radio commercials, each depicting the brand's popularity among a different breed of New Yorkers. Only the naive advertiser will ignore the fact that foreign language media are not (except in Spanish) any longer the best way to cover any ethnic group, a conclusion brought home by the example of a liquor importer who felt he had to use the Yiddish papers in New York when he learned that Scotch was the preferred type of whiskey among drinking Jews.

The fallacy inherent in this example is not infrequently encountered in other contexts. In one of its sales bulletins, for example, NBC says, "If income were the sole criterion of a medium's value, advertisers of such products as laundry soap and toothpaste would be concentrating their budgets in such media as *The New Yorker* and *Saturday Review*." [21]

A media vehicle may have an audience that is highly concentrated in a certain income or age sector of the population and still fall far short of giving the advertiser adequate coverage of that sector. It may be more efficient for him to use a vehicle that has a more diversified audience, yet which also covers his desired specialized target more completely.

[19] Unpublished research report, Bureau of Advertising, ANPA, 1964.
[20] Unpublished research made by Data Inc.
[21] *What Is the Marketing Value of the Heavy TV Viewer?* NBC Research Bulletin No. 273 (G-R-TV), Marketing Studies, March 18, 1965, p. 1.

Who is ready to be persuaded?

The prototype of a "thin market" is the one which represents a relatively small proportion of the total population but which is distributed among all types of people in all walks of life (the prospective customers for a denture cleaning agent or a dandruff cure might be collectively considered prototypes of this sort of market).

But even the broadest market is thin at any given point in time, as was demonstrated in a study made by the Bureau of Advertising late in 1965.[22] In five markets ranging in size from Cleveland, Ohio, to Rutland, Vermont, two series of interviews were made, seven days apart, with some 10,000 women. The respondents were asked about all their shopping and purchases in the previous week for all general merchandise items. (Grocery and drug items were deliberately excluded from the questioning because of the sheer number of purchases and the great frequency with which such items are bought.) Similar questions were asked about shopping intentions for the following week.

The comparison of purchase intentions and actual shopping demonstrated both the thinness of the market for most items and also the enormous extent of turnover in consumer demand. For almost any item, a very small percentage of people accounted for all the large retail sales volume chalked up in a given week. Seven per cent of the women were in the market for a dress (the most frequently mentioned item); 3% said they would buy one within the next week. In the following week only 5% of the women actually shopped for a dress and 3% bought one. (These tiny numbers add up to a $37 million dress market every week.) However, the women who had shopped and bought were not necessarily the same ones who had had a dress on their minds a week earlier. In fact, 63% of the dresses bought were purchased by women who had not, even after repeated probing, mentioned a dress as something they were planning to buy only a week earlier. The proportion was the same even in the case of expensive items like major appliances. Altogether, three-fourths of all the buying that took place was unanticipated a week earlier.[23]

[22] *The Retail Customer: How, When, and Where She Shops and Spends*, Bureau of Advertising, ANPA, 1966. This study was conducted by Opinion Research Corporation and sponsored by the Newsprint Information Committee.
[23] This jibes with studies done at the University of Michigan's Survey Research Center, using a much longer time interval between interview and reinterview. For example, of those planning to buy a car within the next year only half had actually bought one a year later. Two-thirds of the cars bought are sold to people who had not stated an intention of buying one a year earlier. *Consumer Behavior of Individual Families Over Two and Three Years*, studies edited by Richard F. Kosobud and James N. Morgan. Monograph Number 36, Survey Research Center, Institute for Social Research, Ann Arbor: The University of Michigan Press, 1964.

Offsetting the influx of new customers into the market was the substantial attrition in the plans of those with intentions to buy.[24] Women who had not reported shopping for an item which they had mentioned a week earlier were specifically reminded of their earlier intention. In some cases the plans still existed — they had merely been deferred. In other cases, however, the plans had simply been dropped. This was true of 28% of the intended washing machine buys, 29% of the bedroom furniture, and 45% of the raincoats. Something else had come along.

Naturally there are substantial differences from one product to the next in the turnover within the market from week to week. Big-ticket items like furniture and major appliances are dreamed about for a long time before the customer actively enters the market and does something about her buying intentions. The fantasy which surrounds such products can wax and wane in intensity and even in consciousness over a long period of time. As a lady told us in another study, "I'm very seriously thinking about buying a dishwasher, and I must say I've been seriously thinking about it for quite some time. For several years."

By contrast, an inexpensive article like hosiery may be bought when a woman sees it on sale or gets a run in her stocking. Certain merchandise has an almost inflexible demand: infants' wear, for instance. When baby needs new shoes, mama will get them — and quickly; the buying plans will not be dropped.

Unanticipated purchases are not necessarily made on "impulse." We become conscious of new needs every day. There is wear and tear on the things we own, so they must be replaced; ever-changing demands are made of us; we have ever-rising expectations; and we are constantly being reminded by promotion, by advertising, by merchandise on display in windows or stores, of new things we might enjoy using and owning. Obviously, the smaller and less expensive the item, the more apt we are to buy it without advance thought. But we also respond most to products which stimulate our imagination and which are out of the ordinary, which are fun even though they may be frivolous.

If half the major appliances bought in a week are sold to people who had not been planning a purchase a week earlier, it would seem to follow that package goods purchases show an even more spontaneous character. Most housewives claim to take a shopping list to the supermarket for their main trip of the week, but it can hardly be comprehensive. A survey of

[24] An analysis of different types of stores and among individual stores of the same type uncovered substantial differences in the ability to convert shopping trips into sales once the customer was inside the store. This merely documented the difficulty of evaluating advertising, whose mission it is to attract the customer, but which can rarely clinch the final sale.

7,147 shoppers in 345 representative supermarkets was made by IDE Associates, Inc. for the DuPont Company.[25]   Shoppers were asked what they intended to buy as they entered the store and then reinterviewed a second time to find out what they had actually bought.

The results show a wide range of variations among product categories in the proportion of purchases which are specifically planned ahead of time, planned in a general way, and decided on while the customer was in the store itself.

To illustrate: 48% of the purchases of soap flakes and detergents are unplanned.   Impulse purchases account for 82% of the magazine and book sales, 80% of the toy sales, and 74% of the soft goods purchases. Three-fourths of the white bread purchases, it was found, were planned ahead of time, but only two-fifths of the rolls.   In the fruit and vegetable department, half of the purchases of oranges were planned, but only a fourth of the berries.   Three-fourths of the meat buys are planned, but only half the fish.   For branded packaged goods, the variations are just as striking.

One customer enters the store with a shopping list and a set of product decisions in which brand choice is already involved.   The other customer makes her selection when she is confronted with an array of packages, each with its own connotations and memories, vivid or faint. Is the function of advertising the same for both?   The constant turnover in the market merely pinpoints the problem faced by the national advertiser in determining who his customers are and how he can reach them. The target he faces is a shifting target.

If we think of the market not on a week-to-week basis but as something that changes day by day, the number of active customers is smaller still.   On the average shopping *day,* 5 women in 1,000 actually buy a dress; 3 in 10,000 buy a refrigerator.   We can look beyond the general merchandise categories covered in the Bureau of Advertising study and extrapolate similar estimates from sales data.   In any given week 5 families in 1,000 buy a car, which means 8 in 10,000 on the average day that most dealer showrooms are open.

How many families are in the market for every one actually buying? Our study found that only 5 in 100 are in the market for a major appliance.   For every 100 planning to buy, only two actually do buy on a given shopping day.   Studies made at the University of Michigan show that at any given moment 15% of the families are in the market for a car (at least they say they expect to buy one within a year).   This suggests that for every 100 people with at least the glimmer of a car purchase intention today, there are only five actually buying.

[25] "Supermarket Buying Decisions in the U.S.," 1965.

Even when we go to the packaged goods field, the concept of the thin market still holds true. In any week, 34% of the households in the U.S. buy a staple like canned coffee: this means 6% on the average shopping day. Twenty-three per cent buy cornflakes within the course of a week — 4% on an average shopping day. Cheese spreads and cocoa — huge product categories — are bought by about 1% of the families on any average day. Even when we make allowances for the concentration of food shopping on certain days, the principle still applies.

In the case of grocery products the amount of advance planning, reflection, discussion, and fantasy which precedes purchase is, of course, negligible compared to most general merchandise items. Even for products which we normally consider to represent a big, broad market, the proportion of people who are sensitive, alert and interested in the subject is extremely small. Yet to the advertiser there is nothing more precious than the few people who are in the market and ready to buy right now. The data we have presented suggest some serious limitations to the utility of the concept of the heavy user, because the few people in the market for any item at any given moment are apt to be widely scattered throughout the population. We are not likely to find them all clustered in one place.

The degree to which the customers are dispersed is often obscured by market analysis in which percentages are based on the "independent variable" (like sex or age) on which consumer actions or attitudes are assumed to depend (rather than the other way around). This technique aims to establish cause-and-effect relations. If we think rich people buy more of a product than poor ones, we look at purchases income group by income group, so that the percentages are based on 100% of the rich, compared with 100% of the poor. When this is done, comparatively small differences between the profile of users and that of the general population blow up into what appear to be large differences.

For example: A Simmons study[26] finds that usage of frozen vegetables goes up directly with income. In one week they are bought by 41% of the families with incomes of $8,000 and over but by only half that proportion, 23%, of those with incomes of $3,000 and less. This is a substantial difference. But let's consider the actual distribution of users in relation to total population. Twenty-six per cent of the users are in the $8,000 and over category compared with 19% of the total population. At the other end, 20% of the users have incomes of less than $3,000 compared with 26% of the population. Now the differences in profile look far less overwhelming. In the gigantic middle-income group, the proportions are the same — 54% versus 55%.

[26] *The Women Behind the Market*, 1963.

In the Bureau of Advertising study, also with a one-week time-span, we found that the big middle-income half of the population made half of all the product purchases recorded — half the women's wear, half the home furnishings, half the major appliances. Of course, people of higher income buy fancier clothes and furniture. And, of course, they make more purchases in the course of a year, which raises the chances of their buying, or being in the market on any given week or day. But in the very thin market as it exists on any given day, the actual buyers are very widely scattered through the income, age, and educational spectrum. And they are not easy to pinpoint.

When the advertiser aims his effort at heavy users, he tries to match their profile against the profiles of various media audiences to deliver as many messages as possible against the most rewarding targets. The assumption is that if he can only get to these people, he can use all the powers of *persuasion* to get them to buy his brand. He must keep pounding his message home so that he attracts their attention and pulls them over to his side. But we have seen that at a given moment in time only a very small number of people have a potential interest in what he is trying to sell them, and these few people are usually not clustered together within easy reach.

Some of these people are looking the other way. They have lowered the iron curtain of indifference. Almost nothing the advertiser can say to them can possibly rouse their attention, much less persuade them. Some of the people out there have cautiously turned their heads. They may have some faint flickers of responsiveness or interest in the product. But within that cold and abstracted crowd, there are a few, a precious few, who right at this moment have turned around. Some are actually coming his way. Be they heavy users or light, they *are* actively in the market; they *are* ready to buy; they *want* to know what he has to tell them. The marketers might well be more sensitive to the mood of these real prospects, and to their desire for information, and not try quite so hard to *persuade* the many others who are simply not to be persuaded on the day he speaks to them.

THE CONCEPT OF "AUDIENCE" [1] 10

For a number of years the term "audience" has been essential to the vocabulary of media and communications research. The measurement of media audiences has absorbed vast effort and expense; the findings obtained have become an indispensable component in every advertising plan. The fundamental validity of the audience concept has rarely been called into question. Yet can it be taken for granted? There are in fact five good reasons to be wary of this concept.

1 The word "audience," in the vocabulary of today's advertising, means something quite different from its original meaning and has been applied for quite different reasons to the consumers of broadcasting and print.

2 Audience measurements represent far-from-certain estimates which are in no sense comparable among media.

[1] Adapted from an article in the *Journal of Marketing,* Vol. 30, January 1966, pp. 47-54.

3 Audience data are intangibles and abstractions, but are often dealt with by marketers as though they corresponded to real "things" or physical objects.

4 The preoccupation with audience size has led to erroneous decisions in the management of media content.

5 The energy devoted to audience measurement has deflected concern from more useful research into the communication process.

Until modern times, the term "audience" was associated mainly with the theater. Recently, however, by a process of gradual extension, it has come to be applied in connection with those mass media which interest the marketer. In the classic tradition, drama exists only in relation to the audience. Murmurs, rustles, coughs, and laughs communicate reactions back to a cast long before the curtain provides the signal for applause. Such an audience has collective characteristics, apart from those which characterize its members as individual spectators. An audience, in the classical tradition, must be conscious of itself, of its presence and purpose in being where it is, and of its own reactions. There is a social cohesion among the members of the audience, but this arises out of the spectacle. Drama arouses the Aristotelian feelings of awe and pity only to the degree that it can play on those universals in human experience and aspiration which are intensified in a collective setting.

It was only with the motion picture that the term "audience" began to be applied generally to a mass medium. The cinema theater is, after all, superficially identical with the legitimate theater in its seating arrangements, its fixed spatial relationship between spectacle and public, and its rule that the audience must sit in darkness and silence. But in the motion-picture experience there is no feedback, except for the long-run effects of box-office receipts, fan mail, and articles by the critics. Essentially, the communication flows in one direction.

Audience and the mass media

It was logical for the term "audience" to be applied directly to radio and (later) to television, which, like the movies, reach people who cannot play back their reactions directly to the performers. As in the movies, there is often a time lag between the original performance of a program and the time of exposure. The listeners to a particular broadcast (and, in a different way, the regular listeners to a series of broadcasts) share a common experience and a certain consciousness of each other's presence.

Quite early, the studio audience was introduced as a device to promote empathy on the part of the scattered listeners.

Audience as a *measurement* concept for radio evolved some years after the term "radio audience" had become a conventional part of the broadcaster's vocabulary. At a time when broadcasts were on the air for only a few hours a day and only a few people owned wireless sets, it was indeed logical to assume that anyone with the equipment to experience the miracle would naturally put it to use each evening. But when networks of stations (connected by telephone lines) were formed in the United States in the early 20's and programming developed on a regular basis, it became imperative to distinguish the audiences of individual shows from one another.

The number of letters received by a broadcasting station provided only a crude indication of the number of its listeners. The volume of mail varied from program to program depending on whether it was solicited, whether attention was focused on individual performers, whether these were strong or popular personalities, and whether there was any departure from an established or conventional pattern of listener expectations.

As more and more radio stations crowded the airwaves, it could no longer be possible for a station to reach every listener within its signal range. Stations began to vie with each other in their claims of listeners, just as newspapers or magazines vied with each other in claims of circulation.

The units of air time which stations and networks sold to advertisers appeared to be fixed in quantity. Actually, they varied greatly in the size and character of the listener groups they yielded. The advertiser was not really buying an hour of time so much as the opportunity to present a sales message to a certain number of listeners. He knew that the number would vary according to the signal strength and popularity of the station and the timing and appeal of the programming in which his message was embedded.

Thus the survey method — to which advertisers had already grown accustomed in marketing research — became the source of listener estimates. As advertisers made larger investments, the need for accurate measurement of what they were getting led to greater innovation in research techniques, larger samples, and more frequently repeated surveys, not only on a national basis but also for individual markets. The "ratings" industry became big business. Measurement now consisted of estimating an intangible — "the listening experience" — rather than making a count of tangible objects — radio sets or letters to the station.

Uncertainties in audience measurement

What was encompassed in the term "audience," as it now came to be used in relation to the modern media, could only be defined pragmatically in terms of statistics yielded by particular research methods. Thus, "audience" could be the number of people who said they "ever" listened to a particular show, the number who said they had listened to that show last week, or the number who reported they were listening at the very time they were interviewed. It could be the number who selected the show from a roster, or who listed it in a radio-listening diary.

"Audience" could encompass not only the respondents who were the source of information but other members of their families — on whose listening the respondents also reported. "Audience" could be the people who listened to *any* part of the program, those who listened to at least five minutes, or only those listening during the average minute.

Paradoxically, the most widely used and most objective broadcast audience measurement instrument available today, the Nielsen "Audimeter," is the furthest removed from the reality of communication. Since this device mechanically measures set-tuning, it leads to audience data expressed in terms of households (or "homes," as Nielsen somewhat sentimentally puts it), rather than in terms of the individuals who are actually listening or viewing.

But the very ubiquity of Nielsen ratings based on the Audimeter — their undisputed place in the whole power structure of advertising — has led to widespread use of the household concept in other media-audience measurement (even marketing surveys). The use of the household as the unit of coverage becomes particularly open to question when household audiences are treated comparatively as "duplicated" (reached by more than one media vehicle) or "unduplicated" (reached by a single vehicle only), when the media vehicles in question may reach different members of the family.

Over the years, an enormous range of ratings statistics has been produced by a variety of definitions and research methods. Yet all these statistics represented the *same* thing, not only to laymen but to most non-research people in broadcasting and marketing. The true practical value of the measurements lay not in the absolute numbers, but in the program-to-program comparisons obtained by *any* given measure, regardless of its validity.

Each measurement assigned a single quantitative value to the term "audience"; yet what was being measured represented more than a single kind of listening experience. When the manager of a theater counts the house, he knows that there are a certain number of people in the auditorium. He also knows that they are, with few exceptions, present from the beginning to the end of the play.

In broadcasting, the count of the house may also be treated as a simple matter, but this does violence to reality. The members of the audience are unknown to each other; they are continually drifting in and drifting out; some of them are more attentive than others. In short, "audience" measurement requires that a rather considerable variety of media-exposure patterns be lumped together only for the sake of convenience.

All this had a profound effect upon the study of print media, where the established criteria of measurement involved that most tangible of yardsticks, paid circulation.

Until the establishment of the Audit Bureau of Circulations (A.B.C.) in 1914, circulation was a nebulous term which reflected the claims that rival publishers made in order to assert their own importance and prestige.

In 1869, Rowell's *American Newspaper Directory* employed the following symbols to designate the reliability of its data:

> The so-called *Z* attachment indicates that the paper finds it impolitic or impossible to make a circulation statement that will hold water; a *Y* means that the publisher finds it better to make no statement at all; the double question mark means that the rating is unsatisfactory, but facts to warrant a better rating cannot be got at; the plus and minus sign, indicating that two statements of circulation received from the office, covering the same period, give different figures; the double exclamation marks indicate that there is something about the paper that the advertiser ought to know before he spends too much money in it; the double daggers indicate that the publisher is a kicker from whom little information can be extracted; the white pyramids indicate that the paper may be dead; the black spheres indicate that the paper says it ought to have a higher rating, but is shy about furnishing facts to warrant the accordance of such a claim; the so-called doubt-marks, not to put too fine a point upon it, indicate that the publisher has been putting out circulation statements that were false, and got caught at it.

The A.B.C. represented a great milestone in media research simply because it replaced an intangible criterion with a tangible one. The tangible criterion was a verified, audited, checked-out count of actual copies of publications which people had paid money to buy.

When radio audiences came to be measured in terms of people listening, rather than by the possession of sets, the resulting figures were of an order of magnitude which few newspapers or magazines could match in circulation. There was an immediate competitive need for a measure which acknowledged that a newspaper or magazine normally had several readers for every copy printed and placed in circulation.

The evolution of marketing concepts made advertisers and agencies more and more conscious of the need to direct advertising to the best prospects for their products. Questions about the kinds of people various publications reached were conventionally answered through subscriber surveys, but for widely circulated magazines and newspapers it became possible (during the 20's and early 30's) to use a sampling survey of the general population to locate readers and then to compare the total numbers from one publication to the next.

The application of the term "audience" to the readers of a periodical probably had its origins with the formation of the Magazine Audience Group in 1937. *Life* and *Look,* as picture magazines, had much to gain from the use of a measurement concept which incorporated the "pass-along" readers, giving them equal value with those who had subscribed or paid for the publication. But text magazines like the *Saturday Evening Post and Collier's* also benefited from a media yardstick which produced figures in the millions, rivaling those projected by the radio rating services.

Not all magazine publishers recognized the advantage of the new concept with equal speed. The following advertisement, a full page spread in the New York *Herald Tribune* of Wednesday, December 7, 1938, is worth reproducing in its entirety for its sheer quaintness:

To Advertisers and Advertising Agencies
....A CORRECTION!
Data from a survey purporting to show the number of readers reached by the four leading weekly magazines are now being shown to advertisers and agencies.

This survey credits Collier's with an amazing average of 15,900,000 people "who see, open, and read some part of each issue. . . ."

Despite the flattering total of readership found, we wish to make clear that Collier's had no part, financial or otherwise, in the conduct of this survey.

Nothing in our experience, during the nineteen years we have owned Collier's, in any way justifies an assumed readership of 15,900,000 people per issue.

A national survey recently made by our own circulation department among 166,600 people indicated that Collier's might have as many as 7,032,454 readers for every issue.

We believe, however, that any rating of magazine values by readership estimates, no matter how conscientiously compiled, is unsound and confusing; and harks back to the dark ages of advertising before the Audit Bureau of Circulations was established as the quantitative appraiser of circulations.

And until some standards better than those of the Audit Bureau are available, we will continue to claim for Collier's only its net paid A.B.C. circulation — 2,633,878 average for the third quarter of 1938; and an intimacy and influence with the most Active Audience in the national market.

THE CROWELL PUBLISHING COMPANY
Publishers of: COLLIER'S * WOMAN'S HOME COMPANION * THE AMERICAN MAGAZINE * THE COUNTRY HOME MAGAZINE

It was only a few years before *Collier's* also leaped on the bandwagon, too late to save its life.

The first studies which applied the term "audience" to magazine readership were concerned primarily with the evolution of techniques which would make it possible to validate the reader's claim that he actually had read the magazine in question.[2]

Through the growing influence of the Advertising Research Foundation, the prevailing standard of readership validation eventually became the disguised readership test — in which the reader is asked to leaf through a copy of the publication, asked his opinion of the different articles or features, and only at the end confronted with the question of whether he happened to read that particular issue.

As more audience studies of print media were completed, rival sets of data emerged measuring what appeared to be the same thing. Such variations resulted from a combination of ordinary sampling errors, differences in statistical adjustment procedures, and divergences in sampling and interviewing techniques. They also arose from different limitations placed on the universe to be sampled in terms of geography or age (for example, all individuals over 10, over 15, over 18, or over 21).

In most individual readership surveys of magazines and newspapers, the publications which order and pay for studies have different objectives than those who ultimately use the findings. This contrasts with the common practice in market research, in which the survey specialist works directly for a client who has certain questions he wants answered. (It also differs from the practice of the broadcast ratings services, to which the advertiser and agency must subscribe, even though the broadcasters pay the lion's share of the cost.)

Advertisers and *agencies* are the ones who eventually put media research to work in preparing plans and allocating budgets, but it is the *publisher* who picks up the check — both because it is expected of him and because he hopes to promote the findings in such a way as to demonstrate the desirability of his publication. There is, of course, just one magazine which can claim the largest number of readers, but it is only an exceptionally unimaginative advertising manager who cannot discover

[2] A pioneer study using this technique was the *Life Continuing Study of Magazine Audiences*, Report No. 1, New York: Time & Life, Inc., 1938. For a recent authoritative defense of the total audience concept see Darrell B. Lucas, "Can Total Magazine Audience Be Ignored?" *Media/scope*, November 1964, pp. 64-72.

or define some criterion of readership or some category of magazines in which his publication will rank first, whether in terms of circulation or of size or quality of audience, "accumulative audience," "primary readership," "cost per page," "cost per thousand," "cost per ad readership opportunity," "time spent in reading," "reading days," "length of time in the household," "number of times picked up," "ad page exposures," or in terms of "reader heat," "depth of reading," "reader impact," and "reader loyalty," as demonstrated by either the *high* percentage who buy it on the newsstand, or by the *low* percentage who buy it on the newsstand.

The highly competitive character of the publishing business is reflected in its research. Each publication has its strong and weak points, and so it orders the type of study which is most likely to produce a good case. At the very least, a duplication of effort results when separate surveys use slightly different methods to measure readership of the same magazines. Sometimes sampling or analytic techniques have been used which contain a built-in bias that reduces the value of the results.

Thus we have had surveys of high school students claiming to be "nationwide" that were based on a sampling of 29 high schools (only one in a major metropolitan area). We have had studies based on panels of "1000 *typical* readers selected from women who have written the beauty editor for help and advice." A magazine which ranked seventh in circulation and fifth among magazines with a preponderantly female readership once advertised a new survey of 3,500 women shoppers that put it immediately after *Life* among "magazines received in the home" and ahead of *Life* and everyone else among "magazines read regularly." The fourteen stores at which shoppers were interviewed were not representative of anything except themselves, but the statistics look very impressive.

The "validation" of a sample may be as spurious as the sample selection itself. In a report that once reached my desk the researchers had apparently selected a sample from their returns to conform with the circulation distribution of their magazine — an admirable procedure. Their statement read: "Well over 3,700 questionnaires were filled out and returned from all parts of the nation, but only 2,600 were used in this report. How closely the returns paralleled the actual circulation distribution by geographic divisions and city size groups is shown in the comparison on the next page." Thus the very method employed to overcome the biased response to their survey was quoted as evidence to support its validity.

Cases of this type have become less frequent in recent years, and usually reflect the overenthusiasm of salesmen rather than a lack of research skills or standards. Only because the great bulk of readership surveys are well and honestly done is it possible — even common — for one magazine or newspaper to build a sales presentation around research done by its competitors. There is a high premium on statistical accuracy in print media audience studies today.

New sources of data

During the 1960's, the advent of the computer brought into the forefront a number of new syndicated research services which periodically offered data on a great variety of media and products based on a single set of interviews. These intermedia services provided what to the layman could easily appear to be essentially the same information, although as services they were (and are) conducted by substantially different methods.

W. R. Simmons and Associates uses personal interviews to collect information on magazines and newspapers and a diary to get television information. The same combination of methods was also used by the *Nielsen Media Service*. (This service represented the first move by the A. C. Nielsen Company, the biggest broadcast-ratings firm, into the measurement of print media. Nielsen disbanded the service after several years of operations.) Standard Rate & Data Service, the largest data collecting firm in the field of media rates, circulation, and marketing information, also abandoned a subsidiary, *Data Inc.*, after an expensive and unsuccessful attempt to break into this new area with services that would gather audience data and also provide computerized media decisions. Data Inc. used personal interviews to obtain all its data on product consumption and print media, but added a roster[3] to measure audiences for a selected list of TV programs. The original *Politz Media Service* was designed and promoted but never instituted; it was revived several years later, relying entirely on personal interviews for TV as well as magazines. By contrast, the *American Research Bureau* conducted local experiments with an all-media diary and *Sindlinger* with all-media telephone surveys; but in neither case did these experiments lead to the establishment of a major syndicated intermedia service. *Brand Rating Index* uses a self-administered report form to measure newspaper and magazine readership and the viewing of a roster of TV programs. This simple method is a far cry from the highly elaborate techniques evolved

---

[3] A "roster" is a list of programs, usually arranged by time periods and identified by channel or network, which the respondent looks at as an aid to his memory. Among the regular ratings services, *Pulse* is the principal user of this technique.

in thirty years of effort to assure accurate audience measurement. The great success of BRI arose from its extensive reporting of product use and brand choice in many merchandise categories.

All of the intermedia services, successful and unsuccessful alike, solicited audience data on a great variety of media vehicles, more than was previously considered feasible for inclusion in a single omnibus survey. In addition, they incorporated a considerable number of questions on product usage and brand choice for a wide array of packaged goods.[4]

Even when two organizations use what appear to be identical research methods, their findings are apt to look dissimilar because of their differing field forces, sampling procedures, and interviewer instructions. Needless to say, if they use different questioning procedures and timing, the variations in their results are apt to be even larger. Unexplained differences in media audiences often appear from one survey period to the next, even in the reports of the same research organizations. When the data are expressed in their original form as percentages of the total population sampled, the variations in results obtained by the different methods are often fairly small.[5] However, the same variations are exaggerated — in terms of hundreds of thousands or millions of customers — by the practice of making statistical projections from survey results.

Three studies of the adult audiences (18 and over) of leading magazines were made between the late Fall of 1964 and the Spring of 1965 by Politz, Simmons, and Data Inc.[6] *Better Homes & Gardens* appeared to have 17,480,000 readers according to Simmons, 19,200,000 according to Politz, and 21,451,000 according to Data Inc. *Woman's Day* had 10,957,000 readers according to Simmons, 13,310,000 according to Politz, and 15,543,000 according to Data Inc. *McCall's* was credited with 16,598,000 readers by Simmons, 21,750,000 by Politz, and 20,221,000 by Data Inc. *Family Circle* was credited by Simmons with 12,435,000 readers, by Politz with 15,550,000, and by Data Inc. with 16,536,000.

The variations in these figures, arrived at by different organizations at about the same time, are matched by the variations in the figures found in successive surveys by the same organization, even when circulation figures remain constant.

When the Advertising Research Foundation evaluated — and gave a clean bill of health to — the 1964 Simmons study, telephone interviews were made ten days later with a subsample of those originally interviewed. The breakdown by percentages of those in the group who have

[4] The implications of this omnibus questioning are developed in Chapter 12.
[5] This lack of major variation might be interpreted as giving an advantage to the least expensive method.
[6] *Advertising Age*, August 16, 1965.

different answers to various questions in the two interviews could be projected into enormous figures. For example, car ownership figures changed by 7%, which projects to 4,000,000 families nationally. In the second interview, 5% of the answers on smoking were different from those given in the first, which is equivalent to "switching" on the part of 6,000,000 adults. This kind of variation is no reflection on Simmons' methodology or field work. It does reflect the standard problems of interviewing people at two points in time.

William S. Sachs[7] called attention to the differences between an Audit Bureau of Circulations check of respondents interviewed in Politz's 1964 magazine audience survey and the names on the magazine subscription list. (Since some magazine copies go to business establishments, libraries, and so on, the sample might be expected to show a lower penetration than circulation as a percentage of total population.) Of the people Politz sampled, 10.2% reported that someone in their household subscribed to the *Saturday Evening Post*, and this turned out to be exactly the same proportion uncovered by A.B.C. In the case of the *Reader's Digest*, the figures were relatively close — 21.6% for the sample, 22.4% for the publisher's statement. In the case of *McCall's* and *Look*, however, there were discrepancies — 10.7% for the sample and 12.6% for the actual subscriber list in the case of *McCall's*, and 9.6% for the sample and 11.8% in the publisher's statement in the case of *Look*. These variations are within the normal range of chance sampling error, but when they are projected they can look frightening to anyone who assumes that the estimates produced by surveys represent reality. When we recognize not only that these estimates are approximations subject to human error, but also that at best they mirror phenomena which are constantly changing, we must be far less willing to take the term "audience" at its literal meaning.

Are broadcast ratings here to stay?

Estimates of broadcasting audiences vary even more than those from print media surveys because samples are generally much smaller, and because program ratings are produced on a continuing basis, rather than the once or twice a year of the intermedia services. As usually happens when different measurements are available to describe the same phenomenon, ratings have been raised as banners by the rival networks and have often become a matter of claims and counterclaims.

[7] *Media/scope*, March 1966, pp. 60-63.

Over a period of time, parallel rankings of programs emerge, with minor variations, from all the ratings services. But the absolute levels of audience size reported are to a considerable extent functions of the individual measurement techniques used. In 1966, several different methods were compared by the All-Radio Measurement Survey (ARMS), partly in response to the questions raised by a Congressional Committee and partly because of a widespread conviction in radio circles that the medium had been shortchanged by inadequate measurement of out-of-home listening. The ARMS committee, consisting of a group of distinguished broadcasting researchers, took as its standard a coincidental telephone measurement, which showed the average in-home quarter-hour radio audience between 7:00 A.M. and 10:00 P.M. to be 11% of the adults in the homes called. The comparable figures generated by other measurement techniques ranged from 7% with a telephone-solicited four-media diary[8] mailed in every week, to 14% for a personally placed radio-only diary mailed in daily. The total "all-places" quarter-hour listening figures found by these two methods ranged between 18% and 10%, and the daily net-reach-of-radio figures (the percentage listening at all on a given day) ranged from 90% to 63%.

The essence of the ratings system is that there must be a way of getting comparable measurements day after day and week after week. When the objective is to get figures on a program's or station's *share* of audience, a different kind of measurement method must be used than if the objective is to get the most accurate figures possible on a one-shot basis.

The Nielsen Television Index, which provides the most widely used ratings, has the great merit of measuring set tuning every week, on a continuing basis. It does this with a permanent sample of 1,160 households, which yield under 1,000 usable Audimeter records on an average day. There are obvious difficulties in making and keeping a permanent sample or panel representative of the whole population. Not everyone is willing to let a gadget be attached to his set. (For that matter, not everyone is willing to keep a diary of viewing for weeks on end, which Nielsen's local ratings and other services require.)

The most accurate method of measuring the *amount* — as opposed to the daily trends in *share* — of viewing is generally considered to be the "personal coincidental method," in which interviewers go out to a fresh cross-section of households, ring doorbells, and find out, if people

---

[8] A "diary" in broadcast ratings parlance is a record of viewing or listening, by day and time period, kept by families which agree to cooperate with the research, usually for a period of several weeks. The diary method of rating television program is used by the American Research Bureau and Mediastat. The "four-media diary" covered newspaper and magazine reading as well as radio and TV.

are home, whether they have a TV set on. This was the method employed in the November 1965 survey of over 12,000 households by Alfred Politz Media Studies. Politz found 41% of the households with sets turned on at the average evening minute (between 6:30 and 10:00 P.M.) and 37% with someone watching. The equivalent (January 1964) Nielsen figures commonly quoted show 58% of TV households (55% of all households) watching. Politz found 24% of the adults (over 18) watching TV in the average evening minute. The Nielsen figure generally used is 41%. (All audience figures fluctuate in the course of the viewing year, and the evening hours covered by Nielsen and Politz are slightly different. But both sources reflect the heavy-viewing season.) The discrepancy between 24% and 41% represents a 71% difference in audience size and cost efficiency, but publication of the Politz study created no mad rush to investigate which numbers are right.

All broadcast ratings are relative to the competition. The show "The Man from U.N.C.L.E." doubled its audience share when its time changed. The same pattern has been found in many cases where a network's lineup has been varied to bring its programs up against less effective competition.

Herbert Maneloveg, BBDO's director (and student and critic) of media, has called attention[9] to the peculiar effects of the March broadcast ratings reports prepared by both Nielsen and the American Research Bureau (ARB), the two leading ratings firms. In 1965, 178 of the 228 Nielsen city reports were compiled only twice a year, one of those times in March. Similarly, 189 of ARB's 236 reports were compiled twice a year, and one of those times also was in March. The media buyer, Maneloveg points out, often makes the assumption that those ratings carry through for the entire year (in fact they do not), and stations often attempt to influence the ratings reports for March by manipulating the programming for that period.

In radio, where ratings reports are issued even less frequently than for television, the spot buyer is just that much more painfully subject to error when he assumes that the ratings for one period are applicable throughout the year. The very small samples used in most local markets produce results subject to a wide margin of statistical tolerance (plus or minus approximately four percentage points, 95 times out of a 100, with a rating of 10 and a typical sample of 300). This merely adds to the likelihood that the week in which interviewing takes place, with its own peculiar balance of seasonal, weather, and competitive forces, is not

[9] *Advertising Age,* April 19, 1965.

typical of the whole year.   Yet the data are used as if they were typical.
They have to be.

Television audience composition figures disguise substantial differences between the audience in the Eastern time zone and that in the
Midwest, particularly during early evening hours.   Jack Gould, television and radio editor of the New York *Times*, points out that "by
around 8:30 or 9:00 o'clock in the Eastern time zone, the majority of
youngsters between 2 and 11 years old have retired from the parlor and
adults are left in full control of their TV sets.   But in the Middle West
it is only 7:30 or 8:00 Central time, and children are still a factor in
family decisions on what shows to watch.   The consequence is that a
show that may attract adults in the East can find its national rating
depressed by the different TV preferences of youngsters still awake and
watching in the Middle West."   (In the case of the Pacific Coast where
programs are rebroadcast from tape, this problem does not exist.)

The traditional Nielsen "total audience" (sets tuned for six minutes
or more) runs from 10% to 25% higher for half-hour shows than the
Nielsen "average audience" (based on the average moment of time recorded on the Audimeter tape, which moves continuously as long as the
set is in use).   This differential increases for full-hour and hour-and-a-
half programs.   The "total audience" for a program is larger than the
audience at the time of any given commercial.

Edward Papazian, BBDO's scholarly vice president for media
research, points out that television audience composition figures are
based primarily on diary data which reflect the *total* audience of a program (or of a 15-minute segment, in the case of Nielsen's audience composition reports), rather than the audience during the average minute.
Since the total audience is bigger than the average-minute audience, an
advertiser's projection from homes tuned in (Audimeter) to people
watching (diary) is bound somewhat to overestimate the number of
individuals actually viewing (diary) if it is applied against the total
audience rather than against the average audience.

Not all the people in a family who watch any part of the program
are going to be watching it at the average minute, since family members
move in and out of the room while a show is on.   And although many laymen think that a Nielsen rating represents the percentage of people
watching a program, it doesn't mean that at all — and couldn't, unless
all households had television, and everyone in the households tuned to
a program were watching.   There is bound to be a growing disparity
between the percentage of people watching a program, as the presence of
extra sets in the home makes television more of an individual medium.

The confusion is compounded because when Nielsen calculates

program ratings based on tuning of sets in multi-TV households, he counts every set that is tuned to a different program just as though it were located in a different household altogether. The disparity between tuning and individual viewing gets bigger at the upper-income level. In the families with income over $10,000 there are 63% more adults than in families under $5,000, and *half* these high-income families have more than one set.

Such statistical niceties as these are generally rejected with impatience by advertising people for whom research methodology is a big, complicated bore and who want to deal with research data in simple, common-sense terms. However, the tolerance of inflated numbers may in at least some cases coincide with self-interest and an unwillingness to rock the rather large boat.

Criticism of the ratings services reached a climax in 1963 during an extensive probe by a Congressional investigating committee.[10] The emphasis in the committee's hearings was on charges of interviewer cheating and improper or inadequate sampling. These charges got the headlines and were easy for the major ratings firms to dispel, since their stock in trade is integrity at the level of data collection and processing. But the most interesting revelation in the hearings was that of the ratings services' major point of vulnerability: their stance of certainty.

The hearings suggested that the illusion of exact accuracy was necessary to the ratings industry in order to heighten the confidence of their clients in the validity of the data they sell. This myth was sustained by the practice of reporting audience ratings down to the decimal point, even when the sampling tolerances ranged over several percentage points. It was reinforced by keeping as a closely guarded secret the elaborate weighting procedures which were used to translate interviews into published projections of audience size. It was manifested in the monolithic self-assurance with which the statistical uncertainties of survey data were transformed into beautiful, solid, clean-looking bar charts.

Such practices were derived from the traditions of store auditing, a field in which the leading broadcast rating firm first established its mark. When measurements are made of the actual movement of goods across the shelf in a store, the figures must be presented in a way that approximates the reality of goods shipped, stocked, inventoried, and sold. The figures have to look "hard." But this way of looking at the figures as "hard" unfortunately has been carried over into the realm of survey research on audience behavior. For example, a release of January

[10] *Broadcast Ratings:* Hearings before a Subcommittee of the Committee on Interstate and Foreign Commerce, Eighty-Eighth Congress.

5, 1967, from the Television Information Office points out that upper-income ($10,000+) TV households using television in prime evening time showed "an increase" of half a percentage point between 1965 and 1966. A difference of as much as *eight* percentage points would not be statistically significant (i.e., explicable on the basis of random probability 95 times out of 100) between two separate samples of 200 each. (Nielsen has 201 upper-income households in his panel.)

The appearance of oracular infallibility is especially unfortunate because audience measurements as they are made today (in print as well as broadcasting) involve a tremendous number of statistical adjustments and weightings after the data are gathered.

In spite of their importance, ratings are not themselves rated highly as a subject of general interest. On July 12, 1965, CBS broadcast a documentary on the subject of TV ratings, and Arthur Nielsen, Jr., was one of the authorities interviewed. Remarkably enough, this program had a rating of 20.8 in New York according to Nielsen and of 11.7 according to ARB.

The elemental principles of sampling continue to remain a mystery to many intelligent laymen. William Weilbacher reminds us that the Senate had investigated the rating services on a previous occasion in 1958:

> The Founder, Arthur Nielsen, Senior, went down to Washington to tell the Senators all about sampling and sample size. He took with him a monumental Nielsen presentation on this subject. The presentation went on for three hours and covered every conceivable technical subject that might interest the Senators, as well as many that would not. In addition, all kinds of statistical gods and the Census Bureau were invoked repeatedly during the presentation. Mr. Nielsen finally concluded. Senator Mike Monroney of Oklahoma, who was presiding, thanked Mr. Nielsen profusely for coming down and making such a great presentation, and then made two extended remarks, the essence of which was: "I just do not understand how you can measure the listening habits of the American people with a sample of only 1,050." Mr. Nielsen's response was simply, "I am afraid you are reaching the wrong conclusion, Senator."

The naiveté of those in high places in the broadcasting world itself is illustrated by FCC commissioner Robert E. Lee's suggestion that ratings be provided by the Census Bureau, even though he personally does not believe in them. In April 1966, the commissioner reported that he had recently been impressed by a "contrivance that might be more accurate than the rating systems — a device installed in a vehicle that can determine the channels householders are watching while the vehicle is cruising the streets." [11]   Even if this "recent" contrivance, which had been around for twenty years, were amenable to systematic sampling — and it isn't — it would be used to produce . . . ratings!

Most advertisers in the United States today use television as a means of scattering messages (through spots or shared sponsorship), rather than creating the traditional type of sponsor identification with a program or broadcasting personality.   The communications context of the message is as much left to chance as it is to the advertiser who runs an advertisement in a thousand newspapers from coast to coast, never knowing what news or advertising will surround it from one paper to the next.   Yet the rhetoric of audience measurement, as applied to "rating points" in a spot TV schedule, arises from the assumptions applicable to network radio in the 50's.

Numbers versus communication

Audience measurement has moved further and further away from the kind of first-hand submersion by the researcher into his own data which characterizes the best of analytical research.   In the latter tradition, a sensitive observer conducts his own interviews or observations and then pores systematically over the evidence, refreshing his insights with recollections of the original reporting as he himself gathered or experienced it.

In current audience-research practice, by contrast, a huge apparatus is called into play.   The numbers ultimately spewed forth — by a computer usually — no longer represent a straight count of the number of people who answered "yes" or "no" to an interviewer's inquiry.   Interview data transferred onto punchcards may be weighted in accordance with the "nights-at-home" formula in order to produce a projectable probability sample.   They may be weighted further in order to make the sampling results coincide with known criteria of validity.   They may be adjusted and weighted further to eliminate inconsistencies between bodies of data gathered by one method, such as a diary, and by another method, such as an interview or a mechanical recording of set-viewing time.   A research firm's trade secrets may lie in its complex manner of manipulating data to attain projections of greater accuracy.

The preoccupation with audience measurement reflects the status of advertising as a business investment which is expected to yield a sales

[11] *Advertising Age,* April 26, 1966.

return much like any expense incurred in product improvement, distribution, packaging, or promotion.[12] For the advertiser who wants to maximize the yield on his investment, media audience statistics are vital for evaluating alternative courses of action.

In literature, the ascription of human attributes to inanimate objects is known as the pathetic fallacy. In advertising, we are guilty of a pathetic fallacy in reverse when we take the process of human communication and reduce it to numbers to which we foolishly ascribe the attributes of things. These "things" go by different names: messages delivered, rating points, exposure opportunities, impressions.

Businessmen are accustomed to working with numbers which represent concrete ideas, whether these are monetary units, units of raw materials, or finished products. Media-audience figures are easily imbued with the same degree of independent reality as statistics which represent dollars or francs, cartons of cereal, or cans of beans. They are no longer accepted for what they are — projections from surveys — which reflect the vicissitudes of sampling and the basic problems of response validity.

Such uncertainties are, of course, the last thing in the world that the businessman wants to worry about. But the problem of evaluating communication effects is extraordinarily expensive and difficult when it is attacked with seriousness and sophistication. Over the past generation, the research world has been strewn with the bleached skeletons of innumerable unsuccessful attempts to measure accurately the specific effects of a specific advertising campaign.[13]

The very difficulty and cost of accurately measuring advertising effectiveness led to an emphasis on audience measurement as a poor but useful substitute. The underlying and unvoiced assumption is that the sales yield from an advertising campaign is somehow or other in proportion to the number of people it reaches.

Implicit in the use of the audience concept is the assumption that audiences for different media can be isolated, that they can be considered in separate compartments, much as publications or TV programs can be thought of as separate.

Audience data are compared not only as to the extent of exposure

[12] For illustrations of this approach, see Kristian S. Palda, *The Measurement of Cumulative Advertising Effects*, Englewood Cliffs, N.J.: Prentice-Hall, Inc., 1964, and Robert S. Weinberg, "Sales and Advertising of Cigarettes," in *Report of the Third Meeting of Operations Research Discussions Group*, New York: Advertising Research Foundation, 1960.

[13] For a general discussion of this subject, see Harry Deane Wolfe, James K. Brown, and G. Clark Thompson, *Measuring Advertising Results*, Studies in Business Policy, No. 102, New York: National Industrial Conference Board, 1962, and Darrell Blaine Lucas and Steuart Henderson Britt, *Measuring Advertising Effectiveness*, New York: McGraw-Hill, 1963.

to media, but also as to the characteristics of those reached by one medium or another.

The desire to go beyond total numbers was inherent in the very first decision to reject circulation as the criterion for comparing different print vehicles. Common sense led to the conclusion that two publications with identical circulation might attract very different kinds of readers according to their relative emphases on entertainment or information, on subjects of specialized or general interest, and so on.

This distinctiveness of reader profiles was borne out by the first subscriber surveys. Similarly, radio listening studies quickly distinguished the listeners of daytime serials from those of symphony concerts or discussion programs. However, in recent years it has become more difficult to differentiate the audiences of the major American mass media. In the course of one month in 1964, 41% of the adult population reportedly looked at least one of four issues of *Life*, 32% at one of two issues of *Look*, 29% at one of the four issues of the *Saturday Evening Post*, 32% at the single issue of the *Reader's Digest*. No wonder the readership profiles of these mass-circulated magazines resemble each other remarkably!

Since newspapers are read in 87% of all households, it is not surprising to find that, outside of those big cities that have a highly competitive press, there is a virtual identity between the characteristics of the general population of a town and those of the readers of the leading local newspaper.

Since most evening television programming is leveled at the broad mass of viewers, there are amazingly small differences in the actual audience profiles for programs which run the gamut of formats and appeals, even though *preference* profiles do show differences.

There are variations in the appeal of programs to different income groups, according to TvQ, which measures interest levels and not actual viewing patterns.[14] In January 1965, a western, "Bonanza," had a 50% higher preference level in the lowest income sector than in the highest sector (over $10,000). Another western, "Gomer Pyle," had a similar difference between the lowest income sector and the middle and high income groups. "Mr. Novak," a "situation comedy," had a TvQ score of 28% among those of highest income, but in the lower and middle income groups the level was identical — about 23%. The "Dick Van Dyke" variety show aroused a higher level of interest at the upper-middle and upper income brackets than in the lower-middle and lower income brackets, but it was no greater among the highest income than among the upper-middle income people (37% and 38%).

[14] *Media/scope*, March 1965.

An April 1965 TvQ report examined the top ten evening network program TvQ scores for three different educational groups. Four programs — "Bonanza," "Walt Disney," "The Fugitive," and the "Red Skelton Show" — were among the top ten in preference for people with grade school, high school, or college educations, although their respective ranking was not the same in all three groups. Two additional shows — "Saturday Night Movie" and "Andy Griffith" — were on the top ten list for both the grade school and the high school education groups. Otherwise, the programs remaining on the list were different for every educational group.

While such measurements of program interest may be important to the sponsor, actual viewing is defined by what is available and by family decisions in which people "go along for the ride," as well as by positive preferences.

There are, of course, individual shows which in their timing or content are specifically beamed to children, housewives, male sports-enthusiasts, intellectuals, and other definable groups. But setting such special programs aside, audience composition in terms of age, sex, income, education, and city size shows remarkable consistency on the average for drama, comedy, quiz, audience participation, mystery, western, and other popular programming types.

This lack of sharp differentiation seems to reflect the role of television viewing as a pastime. Until now (though this is changing), viewing has tended to be a matter of shared family experience in which the wishes of first one family member and then another may prevail in the selection of programs. The desire for a variety of fare reinforces the tendency to "watch TV" as an activity regardless of what happens to be on.[15]

Audience measurements and media content

In an economy in which the mass-communications media are operated privately for profit, measurements of audience size must inevitably be the basis of decisions that affect media content.

Let it be granted that American mass media are, by and large, controlled by responsible people who take their civic duties seriously. Such people would properly resent the charge that what they put into their

---

[15] Gary A. Steiner, *The People Look at Television: A Study of Audience Attitudes.* New York: Alfred A. Knopf, Inc., 1963; "1963-64: TV's Sick Season?," *Broadcasting,* Vol. 66, No. 24, June 15, 1964, pp. 58-62; Leo Bogart, *The Age of Television.* New York: Frederick Ungar, 1958, pp. 85, 93.

publications or broadcast time represents prostitution to the demands of advertisers. Yet advertisers' demands often coincide directly with the internalized demands that arise from the goal most mass-media operators set for themselves: namely, to provide, within the framework of a given editorial or entertainment formula, offerings which appeal to the greatest possible number of people. Other things being equal, most mass-media operators seek to broaden rather than restrict their appeal. Obviously they would prefer their influence to be greater rather than less.

The cost per thousand of any media vehicle almost always goes down as the size of its audience increases. Advertising decisions are invariably influenced, if not actually determined, by cost per thousand. Thus media operators are sensitive to all indications of shifts in public taste and often follow research findings in adapting their fare to maximize audience size.

The "illnesses" and deaths of great mass media are linked inextricably with advertising decisions — in which both audience data and unsupportable hunches about audiences play important parts. In November 1964, the *Saturday Evening Post* was switched by its publishers from weekly to biweekly publication, in spite of the fact that 6.5 million families had indicated with an outlay of cash their interest in receiving it every week. The previous year saw the demise of the second largest newspaper in the country, the New York *Mirror*. As with the other New York newspapers which followed it into oblivion, the concentration of advertising as a result of media judgments represented a key reason for the *Mirror's* failure.

It is easy to be philosophical about such changes and to assume that they reflect the same inevitable pressures of the competitive marketing world that are manifested in the life cycle of any consumer product. But should the criteria applicable to manufacturers apply in the field of mass communications?

An analysis of the large newspapers which have merged or ceased publication in recent years shows that while all had suffered substantial declines in advertising revenues, on the whole their circulations in the years before their discontinuance had remained relatively stable. Clearly, from the public's standpoint they filled a need, just as *Collier's* filled a need for an undiminished number of nearly 4 million families each week before it "died" in 1957 for lack of advertiser support. More recently, other magazines which have been hard-pressed on the advertising front have also continued to maintain their audiences.

The perception of the advertising decision-maker as to what the public wants changes far more drastically than the tastes or motivations of the public itself. The public may have gradations of feeling. The media decision-maker responds in terms of either-or. To the extent that he is responsive to changes in the audience, he tends to overreact and exaggerate. If he feels that a medium has lost 5% of its vitality or appeal, he does not cut his budget for it by 5%; he may cut it by 50% or may get out altogether.

Audience response is more than a matter of the number of people "exposed" to a publication or program. Consumers have different kinds of responses to different media, depending on how these media fit into the pattern of their interests and daily activities. They have different degrees of involvement, of identification, of a sense of possession. Subtle shifts in the quality of this response may occur at a level different from those revealed by audience measurements, or at a considerable lead in time over them.

The life-and-death effect of audience estimates is most clearly seen in the broadcast industry. The over-all reliance on ratings in policy planning naturally encourages a tendency for tastes to be leveled to a common denominator. Certainly there is no collusion among the TV networks in determining what goes on the air, but all three networks use the same criteria in selecting programs.

David Mahoney, then executive vice president of Colgate-Palmolive, engaged in the following colloquy with one of the House Committee's investigators in 1963:[16]

Mr. Richardson.	If you are going to renew on a show, does, let's say, CBS, bring you a brochure, or someone within your company a brochure, showing you how the ratings have been throughout the year on that show?
Mr. Mahoney.	Yes.
Mr. Richardson.	In other words, they talk ratings a great deal?
Mr. Mahoney.	Yes, they do.
Mr. Richardson.	They sell by ratings?
Mr. Mahoney.	I think so.
Mr. Richardson.	As far as your company is concerned . . . is it the basic sales tool, in your opinion?
Mr. Mahoney.	Yes.

Mahoney also observed, "In my opinion, they base the price of the show on what they think the implied rating is."

Thomas W. Moore, president of the ABC Television network, has noted how the three chains have struggled for supremacy in ratings, ending up each of the last few broadcast seasons in a close heat. "We do resent having the ratings — our own bookkeeping tool — used to carve

[16] *Broadcast Ratings,* Part I: Hearings before a Subcommittee of the Committee on Interstate and Foreign Commerce, Eighty Eighth Congress, p. 376. (Mahoney moved to the presidency of Canada Dry late in 1966.)

us up before the public on the very occasions we elect to rise above the competitive entertainment fare." [17] Yet though every network management feels tyrannized over by the ratings, none is willing to risk playing the game by any other rules.

In mid-1965, 58% of total station operating hours were devoted to network programming, 12% to syndicated material, 13% to feature films, and only 15% to locally produced programs.[18] These over-all figures are misleading because network hours almost completely take over in the evening, when audiences are biggest. (Of the locally produced activity, 40% was in news programs, 26% in children's programs, 16% in variety, panel, or music shows, 8% in religious programs, 7% in women's service programs, 6% in sports, and 5% in farm programming. Less than half of the stations — 47% of them — carried play-by-play sports.)

The scheduling of shows, which has largely passed out of the hands of the advertisers and into those of the network managements, is governed by the desire to build a strong lineup which will hold the greatest possible number of viewers over the longest possible period of time, against the attractions of the competing networks.

In 1966, only 14% of evening network shows had been on the air for seven years or more. In the 1964-65 television season 40% of the previous season's network programs were discontinued and replaced, and a like fate befell a similar proportion the year before. This remarkable attrition from one season to the next demonstrates the direct application of audience-rating statistics in programming practices.[19]

The interoffice memoranda of television officials produced in evidence before a Senate subcommittee investigating the causes of juvenile delinquency in 1964 offer interesting insights.[20] The evaluation on one script reads, "Not as much action as some, but sufficient to keep the average bloodthirsty viewer fairly happy." Commenting on a script for "The Untouchables," Quinn Martin, an ABC official, wrote, "I wish we could come up with a different device than running the man down with a car, as we have done this now in three different shows. I like the idea of sadism, but I hope we can come up with another approach to it." On another occasion, the same gentleman warned the producer of the program (who was subsequently fired) of the need for "maintaining this action and suspense in future episodes. As you know, *there has been a*

[17] *Advertising Age,* April 26, 1966.
[18] Based on a typical cross-section of 232 U.S. TV stations reporting to *Television* magazine. The figures do not add to 100% because some programs were classified under more than one heading.
[19] *Cf.* "Image Builders Go Back to Print," *Business Week,* No. 1835, October 31, 1964, p. 70; and Harold Mehling, *The Great Time-Killer,* Cleveland: World, 1962.
[20] "Television and Juvenile Delinquency," Interim Report of the Subcommittee to Investigate Juvenile Delinquency, 1964.

softening in the ratings, which may or may not be the result of this talkiness, but certainly we should watch it carefully." (My italics.)

In defense of the policy of using ratings as a basis for programming decisions, the broadcast industry has argued that this makes eminently good business sense. As Sylvester Weaver, late of pay TV and formerly of NBC, told the Congressional investigators of ratings,

> We who are in the business I am sure all know they are estimates, but again, with all the other problems, you do not go around trying to persuade your client that the one reliable thing that looks like it is safe, that you can talk about, is not safe, either. It is not human nature to work that way.[21]

The broadcasters have also raised the cry of "cultural democracy." The programs which prove popular with the greatest number of people are, according to this argument, the ones that most deserve to be on the air. The counter-argument is that there is a two-way process at work, and that public tastes merely reflect a preference for what is made *available* and familiar by the media.[22] It is interesting to note that both the *pro* and *con* sides of this "great debate" tend to take for granted both the ratings figures and the underlying concept: an undifferentiated and attentive body of viewers moving from one program to the next.

A vital question raised in the discussion is whether the commercial system of broadcasting is to be blamed for whatever may be wrong with the state of the television arts, or whether the free choice of the viewer is instead responsible. As David Sarnoff, board chairman of RCA, once phrased the case for the media, "We're in the same situation as a plumber laying a pipe. We're not responsible for what goes through the pipe." [23]

FCC commissioner Lee Loevinger calls TV "the literature of the illiterate; the culture of the low brow; the wealth of the poor; the privilege of the underprivileged; the exclusive club of the excluded masses. . . . A demand that popular entertainment conform to the taste and standards of critical intellectuals is mere snobbishness." [24]

Certainly educational television (ETV) has not been able to attain massive audiences in competition with commercial TV. According to the National Educational Television *Fact Book* for 1966, only 10% of the people in areas covered by ETV watch it at all in the course of a week.

---

[21] *Broadcast Ratings, op. cit.,* Part I, pp. 176-77.
[22] Bernard Berelson, "The Great Debate on Cultural Democracy," in Donald N. Barrett, ed., *Values in America,* South Bend, Indiana: University of Notre Dame Press, 1961.
[23] Quoted by Harry J. Skornia, *Television and Society,* New York: McGraw-Hill, 1965, p. 54.
[24] *Advertising Age,* October 17, 1966.

Countries with a state-operated system of broadcasting face the continuing problem of balancing programs aimed at social uplift with others that will assure the presence, night in, night out, of a large body of attentive viewers.   The task becomes even more complicated when commercial and state-operated or educational channels exist side by side.   A kind of Gresham's law of popular preference operates, leaving no more than a minority available for an educational or elite-interest program when it competes with less demanding amusements.   The BBC radio's famous "Third Programme" draws 1% of the audience.

Leo Rosten, a sociologist and editorial adviser to *Look,* says, "When the public is free to choose among various products it chooses — again and again and again — the frivolous as against the serious, escape against reality, the lurid as against the tragic, the trivial as against the significant." [25]

The highest-rated program in the first two years of the Hartford test of pay TV was the first Liston-Clay prize fight, which drew 83% of the subscribers, according to CBS' economist David M. Blank.[26]   The subscribing households were above average in income and education. In total, 84% of all pay TV revenues in Hartford came from viewing of motion pictures and 11% from sports.   For such special cultural events as plays, operas, ballets, and concerts, the average rating was about 9%. For educational features it was less than 1%.   Of 599 programs offered, the lowest rated was entitled "Presidential Leadership" and it had no viewers at all.   The next lowest drew one household out of 4,717 and was entitled "You and the Economy."

When both CBS and NBC televised the 1966 Senate Committee on Foreign Relations hearings on U.S. Asian policy, these two networks lost 55% of their normal daytime audience.   When John Schneider, the new president of CBS Television, ordered the return of "The Lucy Show" after four days, the network's great news director Fred Friendly resigned amidst fireworks and a fleeting moment of soul-searching in broadcasting circles.   The whole debate over ratings was crystallized in this one episode.   Network management took the position that the sheer number of sets tuned in represented a measurement of communication taking place. There was no recognition of the special character of a unique experience, the depth of meaning communicated by it, its memorability, or the chances of its being incorporated into the permanent residue of a listener's life experience.   It takes as long to brush one's teeth as to vote in a presidential election, and on election day more people brush their

[25] Quoted by *Television,* July 1965.
[26] "The Quest for Quantity and Diversity in Television Programing," a paper delivered before the American Economic Association, December 28, 1965.

teeth than vote. This does not make toothbrushing on that day more important. Who will stand up against the most popular choice?

Audience measurement or communications research?

The emphasis on audience measurement in American media research has deflected attention from the process of communication.

"Audience" has been used as a term which aggregates units of equivalent value, so that the major research interest has been in counting these units rather than differentiating them. Audience figures for print and broadcast media are dealt with comparatively as though communication in space and time could somehow be reduced to a common basis; and audience figures for each medium have been lumped together without regard to the frames of reference of different people or the different qualities of communication for different groups.

The conventional kind of audience figure for a TV program lumps together the woman who turned the show on because she wanted to see it, the man who stayed in the living room because he had no place else to do his reading, and the son who came in for a few minutes to ask permission to use the car. They might all be classified as part of the viewing audience, but the concept of total audience is meaningless as long as these three people are given equal weight.[27]

Some of the most interesting research being done today on mass-media audiences represents an attempt to define such audiences in more differentiated terms than those provided by traditional measurements. An illustration of this kind of refinement is a study made by Alfred Politz Research for the *Reader's Digest,* which distinguished the character and reading habits of primary and secondary magazine readers.[28] The study confirmed that the secondary, or "pass-along," readers of a magazine have lower income and education, are less likely to have an interest in the publication, and spend less time reading it than those who paid for it. But at least some part of the casual pass-along readership may never be counted. On behalf of another group of magazines,[29]

[27] The radio audience can be classified into four components, Peter Langhoff, president of the American Research Bureau, told the 1966 conference of the Advertising Research Foundation. He found from surveys in St. Louis and Washington that about one in six home listeners could be described as doing concentrated listening; half the audience were "listening with incidental activity" (a routine chore like housework). A small group were involved in some other activity while incidental listening took place. About a fifth of the total were doing only "incidental hearing."
[28] *A Study of Primary and Passalong Readers of Four Major Magazines,* Alfred Politz Research, Inc., Pleasantville, N.Y.: Reader's Digest, 1964.
[29] *Reader's Digest, National Geographic,* Harper's-Atlantic.

Eric Marder compared readership as it was observed in a dentist's waiting room with readership as it was pictured by the answers given later in a conventional magazine audience survey. He found, according to William Blair,[30] that over half the observed readers of the smaller publications would not have been counted at all by conventional survey techniques — they were screened out on the opening question, "Have you looked into any issue of this magazine in the last six months?" Evidently they answered in terms of their usual reading habits rather than in terms of their actual (and exceptional) experience as pass-along readers.

Since World War II, radio has changed from the major vehicle of general entertainment into a portable, personal instrument. Today, TV is undergoing a similar transformation. Yet qualitative changes of this kind are not reflected in audience data. Just as readers may be differentiated according to whether they have purchased a publication or have picked it up casually to kill time, so viewers might be differentiated between those who select a program because they want to hear it and others who merely happen to be around when other family members or friends are watching it.

Listeners tend to identify with radio stations whose character is "right" for them. Every parent of a teen-age child is aware that certain radio stations specialize in the music of a particular subgroup in the teen-age spectrum. As the child progresses in age and interests, he moves from one station to another as his 24-hour-a-day favorite.

Any person who has had his normal routine broken by illness, unemployment, vacation, or some other change in his usual daily schedule has had the experience of turning on the radio or television set at an unaccustomed time and, perhaps, to an unfamiliar station. He then suddenly discovers the existence of a world previously unknown — unkown not only in its entertainment formula but also in its advertising pressures. Long-forgotten brand names suddenly spring back to memory. Perhaps it will dawn on him that "out there" is a part of the public for whom this particular station and time is "home," for whom there is a personal identity with the music, the disc jockey, the announcer, and also with the advertiser who regularly uses that station and time.

The intensive cultivation of a small sector of the total population such as that discovered by the unaccustomed listener is the basis of much advertising strategy. By a concentration of effort, the advertiser seeks to attract the loyalty of a limited public rather than to spread himself wide but thin.

Audience research in the future must go further in the task of

[30] Address before the Advertising Research Foundation, October 1966, New York, N.Y.

examining the *quality* of media experience rather than the numbers who experience it, and distinguish among different kinds of communications experiences which are now included together under the heading of total-audience figures. A serious attempt along these lines will lead inevitably to an emphasis on analysis rather than measurement as the proper pre-occupation of advertising research.

Much of our current understanding about how we acquire information is based on the behavior of the white rat. Indeed, the white rat has much to teach us about ourselves. But the white rat lacks a soul. Since he is not, like us, a symbol-building animal, he lacks a capacity for identification with the thoughts, goals, interests, and motivations of others, which is the basis of all communication among human beings.

While we communicate by gesture and touch, our main means of interacting with each other is through language. Language is a symbolic device by which we can put ourselves in someone else's place and infer what he means to tell us. This process of communication cannot be reduced to stimulus and response. It defies mechanical explanations. And it entails a set of objectives and methods completely different from those which dominate most audience research.

The most telling criticism that can be leveled at the audience concept is that it deals with the process of communication as though it could be broken down into units or bits — which in advertising are commonly referred to as "impressions," "impacts," or "exposure opportunities," as though they were somehow objects which exist in the real world. Behind this choice of vocabulary is a view of human behavior as something which *can* be reduced to stimulus and response. In such a mechanistic psychology, the audience becomes the passive recipient of messages; its members are as gray and faceless as Orwell's "proles."

Audiences for different media are thought of as discrete, as though they consisted of different individuals, when in fact they represent different aspects of the same individuals at different points in time and in different contexts.

How remote this conception is from the idea of the audience for the classic Greek drama, who were individually and together as one with the actors and with the heroes whose *personae* the actors briefly assumed! And how remote, too, this conception of the audience is from the theory of communication as a process of symbolic interaction, which entails the uniquely human capacity to empathize and to infer what other people mean.[31]

[31] Hugh D. Duncan, *Communication and Social Order*, Somerset, N.J.:   Bedminster Press, 1961.

The measurement of audiences has deflected energy, attention, and resources away from the major unsolved problems with which students of the mass media might more properly be concerned: the processes of perception and learning through which readers, listeners, and viewers filter and acquire information, relieve their boredom, and expand the horizons of their personal experience.

COST PER THOUSAND WHAT?   **]]**

Like other businessmen, advertising people have always been highly cost-conscious. E. Lawrence Deckinger recalls that the late E. J. K. Bannvart, the Biow Company's new-business specialist, once reported to the agency's head about a meeting he had had with the then president of Lever Brothers. "Their President is the smartest man I ever met," Bannvart began. "I resent that," Mr. Biow replied, without a moment's hesitation. Mr. Bannvart insisted: "He's a bachelor. But he earns $100,000 a year." "Of course he's not married," exclaimed Biow. "Who can afford to get married on such a salary?" (A salary of $100,000 may seem piddling today but twenty years ago it was a lot of money.)

The cost of advertising can be defined simply enough when the advertiser thinks in terms of units of *diffusion*, without regard to what goes on at the receiving end. What does it cost to advertise? Here are a few specific figures that appear on the standard rate cards for 1966.

A four-color page in *Life* costs $53,200, in *Reader's Digest* $58,900.

A full-page, black-and-white ad in the Chicago *Tribune* cost $4,791 for a national advertiser earning maximum discounts and delivers a circulation of 845,000 copies. A 1,000 line black-and-white ad in a single newspaper in each of the top 100 markets costs $162,000.

A schedule of twenty 60-second radio spots on WRC in Washington can be bought for $1,300, while a minute of network radio time ranges in price between $600 on Mutual to double that sum on CBS. One minute can be run on a leading radio station in New York for $140. A minute announcement during the peak driving time of early morning or late afternoon in the top 100 markets costs about $3,000.

On television, 10-second spots on KNBC in Los Angeles cost $600, and one-minute participations $1,320. A 20-second spot announcement on a leading New York television station costs about $2,500. A prime-time spot in the top 100 markets costs $32,000. A half-hour of time on an average television network of 132 stations costs $66,000 when included as part of a normal continuing schedule.

The costs of preparing a one-minute television commercial run about $5,400. Production charges are a significant part of the broadcast advertiser's total expense. (By contrast, engravings and other production costs for newspaper and magazine advertising represent, on the average, about 9% over the space costs.) The cost of sound consultation work for a one-minute commercial runs between $1,000 and $5,000 on TV, and between $500 and $3,000 on radio. Advertisers have paid up to $12,000 for rights to a 5-second sound track. Even before a musical jingle is arranged, recorded, and edited, costs can range between $2,000 and $5,000; and certain jingles for the Hertz rent-a-car commercials are reported to have cost as much as $50,000 to produce. Packaging on products may have to be especially redesigned so that they look right to the camera. Name stars like Claudette Colbert and Edward G. Robinson are said to have received $100,000 for their parts in Maxwell House Coffee commercials.

Apart from the cost of producing commercials, the costs of program sponsorship have always been significant to the broadcast advertiser — averaging as much as his network time costs. These costs show no signs of decreasing. Between the 1958-59 and the 1964-65 television seasons, continuing talent and production costs rose 65% on "The Ed Sullivan Show." They rose 292% for "Wagon Train," which had also been on the air continuously in those years. During the same period, production costs on "The Perry Mason Show" nearly doubled and network time costs went up by about one-fourth.

The costs of new programs are keeping pace. The production cost of a new one-hour program rose from an average of $106,700 in the

1962-63 season to $155,000 in 1966-67.[1]   The cost of an average new half-hour show increased from $58,000 to $74,000 in the same period. And these unit costs do not reflect the substantial cost of the "pilots" through which new program ideas are sold.   Advertisers often call for pilot films to test program ideas before they commit themselves to a series, and these pilots are fearfully expensive to produce.   A half-hour pilot may cost $250,000 for a program which will cost $70,000 per episode when it gets on the air.   (The lavish and painful trial-and-error tinkering with plot, personalities, settings, and talent involved in such a pilot are hilariously described in *Only You Dick Darling* by Merle Miller and Evan Rhodes.

Richard Cox, vice president in charge of television and radio programming for Young & Rubicam, stated recently:

> One of the reasons costs have risen so much is that advertisers have been buying participations and scatter plans and leaving the program development role to the networks, whose basic interest is to bring in a show at a marketable price but who are not as cost conscious as the people who eventually pay the bills.   Cost rises tend to be granted because they can be passed on.   Everything mushrooms.

Within a generally inflationary economy, the absolute dollar cost of time or space in all media continues to increase.   The cost of a four-color page in *Life* increased 62% between 1955 and 1966; the cost of 1,000 lines in the ten largest dailies increased 19% in the same time period.   But rising circulation figures compensate for much of this increase; on a cost-per-thousand circulation basis, *Life's* charges rose 24% in this period, the newspapers' 13%.   Similarly, during television's great growth period, a substantial number of the medium's rising charges have been offset by the growth in the number of people viewing the average program.

Costs separate and unequal

Every advertising medium, like most other businesses, offers discounts as an incentive to heavy and continuing use.   Such discount structures tend to "lock in" the advertiser within specified units.   (It may cost him virtually the same to buy twelve monthly issues of a magazine as to buy eleven; so of course he will take twelve.)

National advertisers who use a magazine's full circulation may pay less than what a regional advertiser would theoretically have to pay if he

[1] *Television Magazine,* June 1966.

bought most of the sectional editions on an individual basis. In the average paper in the top 100 markets, a national advertiser pays 61.7% more than the retail merchant for the same space, according to a 1966 study of rate differentials made by the Association of National Advertisers. A good part of the differential is accounted for by the fact that the advertising agency's 15% commission, a 2% cash discount, and a representative's commission of about 5% must be subtracted from the newspaper's receipts for national advertising. Moreover, retailers can sometimes effectively use only part of a newspaper's total circulation, while the national advertiser is expected to use it all. The historical justification which newspapers offer for the differential, however, is that the local merchant, day in and day out, is their bread and butter, and has to be kept in the paper at the lowest possible cost.[2]

Intense competition in the broadcast industry has made it more and more difficult to keep accurate track of time charges to the advertiser. On smaller radio stations it is not uncommon for merchandise to be bartered for time, or for the station to accept a share of the advertiser's take from a direct offer. On network TV, separate negotiations with the network on time and with a producer for programming have often been replaced by a package deal with the network. As one agency executive described it, the official rate cards (which list the network's time charges) are "simply a beginning point for bargaining." [3]

Gene Accas of the Leo Burnett Company estimates that the package form of TV advertising accounts for more than half of the nighttime sponsorship dollars. He disputes the notion that it is possible to purchase TV advertising packages at lower unit costs than the advertiser customarily pays, or that the advertiser who waits until the last minute can get a bargain price from a panic-stricken network.

The deft footwork required of the TV advertiser and his agency today is manifest in Accas' advice on the importance of "having constant communication with other agencies, so that at a given instant you may be able to consider, in soliciting a package for your client, not only network availabilities but also such 'sell-off' requirements that other advertisers may seek." Accas goes on to list other elements in the expertise of the TV buyer: "a continuing knowledge of the market situation — who is

[2] In a doctoral dissertation on the subject, James Ferguson has suggested that newspapers have held retail rates down because retail ads are informational and offer as strong an incentive as editorial matter to building circulation. Unfortunately, he ignores the fact that retail and national ads of the same size and product type get equivalent readership scores; cf. his The Advertising Rate Structure in the Daily Newspaper Industry, Englewood Cliffs, New Jersey: Prentice-Hall, Inc., 1963.
[3] Gerald T. Arthur, former senior vice president in charge of media for Donahue & Coe, in testimony before the Senate Antitrust Subcommittee, June 2, 1966, as reported in Advertising Age, June 6, 1966.

buying; what is being bought; the pricing that prevails; those shows in which there is flexibility, and those in which prices are cast iron; having an intimate familiarity with the efficiency levels at which packages are being bought and sold — and above all, being realistic in every aspect of the art." [4]

Gerald Arthur, formerly media head for Donahue & Coe, observes that "Certain time periods as well as new programs are offered to small advertisers only after larger, more consistent advertisers have an opportunity to buy. . . . As a matter of fact, certain time periods have nicknames bearing the names of the advertisers, such as General Foods time and the P & G bloc, and are commonly referred to in this fashion in the trade." [5]

The increased use of television by the multi-product advertiser has brought about "piggybacking," the placement of messages for two unrelated products of the same company back to back in an effort to use larger units of time most efficiently. (Piggybacks saw their beginnings in 1961 when Alberto Culver launched a commercial that combined VO5 Hair Dressing and VO5 Hair Spray.) And this in turn has brought new problems in its wake. [6]

The National Association of Broadcasters' Code, adopted September 1, 1964, requires that the products or services advertised be related in character, purpose, or use; that they be treated in such a way as to appear to the viewer as a single announcement; and that the commercial be constructed so that it cannot be divided into two or more separate announcements. In spite of the Code, according to *Television Magazine* (May 1966), non-integrated commercials have achieved dominance because they seem "to fit in more with the facts of life of present-day advertising."

The multi-product advertiser's ability to use TV more efficiently was the subject of an influential article in the July 1965 issue of the *Yale Law Journal* by Harlan M. Blake and Jack A. Blum. They found that price concessions "deprive top big advertisers of flexibility but give them substantial advantages over smaller competitors." Network volume discounts gave the largest advertiser obvious direct advantages over

[4] Speech before the Association of National Advertisers' TV advertising management seminar (reported in *Advertising Age,* May, 30, 1966).
[5] Gerald Arthur, *op. cit.*
[6] Sam B. Vitt, media director of the Ted Bates agency, reported in an address before the 1966 meeting of the Association of National Advertisers on a special problem which piggybacking creates for the multi-agency, multi-product advertiser. "The problem of maximizing discounts and controlling budgets always existed. With piggybacking, it assumed frightful proportions. If brand A is combined with B, should A's or B's agency make the buy? How should the paper work be managed, and the billing? And should a handling fee be involved? And what about trafficking and talent payments, and relations with the station representatives, etc., etc., etc.?"

his smaller competitors. The author pointed out that a multi-product company could combine advertising for all its products and take full advantage of the discount structure but that two advertisers were not allowed to purchase time jointly in order to take advantage of discounts.

Blake and Blum described several other peculiarities that result from network rate structures and from the fact that television is characterized by relatively high fixed costs and low variable costs:

> The fact that large advertisers are under strong pressure to concentrate their entire television advertising budget on one network means that the competition tends to be an "all or nothing" affair. . . . It seems likely that this feast or famine tendency provides fertile soil, not only for the well-advertised Madison Avenue ulcer, but for forms of wheeling and dealing not entirely consistent with traditional standards of competition. . . .
>
> The loss of a large advertiser to another network might substantially impair a network's chances in the all-important annual race for viewer ratings, in part because his support of costly high-rated programs would be lost. This in turn would reduce the attractiveness of adjacent times. Smaller advertisers do not wield so potent a bargaining weapon.

Blake and Blum maintain that were it not for the network discounts which cause advertisers to use marginal time periods and to broadcast during the summer months, some of the advertising resources "now coerced into supporting daytime and summer programs might find their way into increased program diversity during the hours of greater viewer demand."

The authors expressed the opinion that the network television discount policies also encouraged corporate acquisitions by giant companies such as Procter & Gamble, General Foods, and Bristol-Myers, to whom advertising represents a substantial expense item. In buying up a new company, a big advertiser could introduce discount savings which would add to the profitability of the business it has acquired.

The U.S. Senate Antitrust Subcommittee pursued the problem in hearings conducted in the Spring of 1966. One small manufacturer, Ivan Combe, reported that his firm had sold the rights to a successful product because of apprehensions about the advantages available to larger competitors using TV. "Large companies with vastly different divisions can share a minute through the use of piggyback, but small companies can't combine with each other to buy a minute." In the same hearings, Jeno Paulucci, president of the Chun King Company, alleged that his company's charges for a Stan Freberg special on ABC were twice as much as they would have been for a giant advertiser.

The advertising manager of Hudepohl Brewing Company, Bertrand

A. Schloemar, reported that his company had spent over a million dollars since 1959 to develop a radio and television audience for games of the Cincinnati Royals Basketball team in its marketing area.   However, when the ABC network began national broadcasting of basketball, a national brewer (Pabst) bought time in Cincinnati, Dayton, Columbus, and Indianapolis.   To continue its broadcasts in Cincinnati and Lexington, Hudepohl would have had to buy a full regional network, including such cities as Pittsburgh, Steubenville, Wheeling, and Akron where it had no distribution.

In a statement prepared for the Subcommittee, David C. Melnicoff, vice president of the Federal Reserve Bank of Philadelphia, alleged that "a manufacturer with a buying advantage for advertising is tempted to — and may, in fact — proliferate brand names and product concept variations, and by this means, attempt to crowd his competitor's products off the supermarket shelves. . . .   Television is the ideal medium for the effectuation of such a strategy.   Not only is it an extremely potent selling device, but its availability is limited.   An initial cost advantage in its use might, therefore, become self-reinforcing, as access to its less favored competitiors is preempted or restricted to inferior time periods."

All three networks announced that discounts would be virtually eliminated from their rate cards by the Fall of 1967, and that time charges for different evening hours would be set on a more complex basis than formerly.   Hearings before the Senate Antitrust Subcommittee in December 1966 raised strong doubts as to whether the elimination of rate-card discounts on network time would really lead to changes in the final costs of TV "package buys" which often include talent and production charges as well as time, and which encompass commercials scattered through a number of different programs.   In these hearings, network spokesmen took strong issue with the allegation that advertisers had concentrated their television budgets in a single network in order to enjoy discount benefits.   At the same time they acknowledged that the rate cards are merely a starting point for hard negotiation.   In terms of program packages and time periods, the big advertiser of course still retained the standard advantages of being the best customer — advantages which are hardly unique to the advertising business.

The search for a yardstick

Every medium of communication yet invented can inform people, can persuade people, can sell merchandise and services.   And every medium has its own file of success stories to prove it.   Moreover, every one of our modern mass media can be used in a remarkable diversity of ways both with respect to scheduling and to creative treatment. From this arsenal of options, each advertiser must select the right use of the right media to solve his own unique marketing problem. He must ask himself at every point in his planning what his strategy is accomplishing, how effective it is in meeting his objectives. He may be initially motivated to be concerned with the *cost* of his advertising effort only insofar as this might allow him to calculate the profits or losses involved in generating each unit of additional sales. However, Robert Weinberg has suggested, in an analysis of the cigarette market,[7] that in many product fields the effects of advertising can never directly manifest themselves in sales until a certain level of expenditure is passed. A company must, regardless of its size and share of market, exert a certain minimum amount of pressure if only to maintain itself above the threshold of consumer awareness and thereby stay in business. If this is an acceptable point, then one additional way of judging media is in terms of their capacity to achieve that irreducible minimum of market coverage and subtle invisible psychological pressure on the consumer.

An advertising investment is a *means* of achieving the desired end of profit; it is not an end in itself. It follows that the efficiency of advertising can never be gauged by any criterion other than the ultimate *effect* it produces, regardless of whether this is accomplished by reaching many people a few times, by reaching a few people many times, or by merely triggering off other reactions within the complex mechanism of distribution and merchandising that ultimately lead to increased sales. The important question is *where* the advertiser gets, not how he gets there.

The measurement of advertising exposure and the determination of advertising costs make perfect sense as long as they are used as part of the description of an advertising *plan*. For a given budget in any medium, the advertiser knows what volume of space or time is at his disposal. In newspapers and magazines, he knows the number of copies printed and he can estimate from research the number of people through whose hands they will pass. In the case of broadcast media, his researchers can make some preliminary guesses regarding the number and kinds of people who will watch or hear his messages, and he can check these guesses afterwards by means of estimates based on the rating services and other surveys.

[7] Robert S. Weinberg, "An Analytical Approach to Advertising Expenditure Strategy," a paper prepared for the Association of National Advertisers, Inc., 1960.

Why cost per thousand?

Cost per thousand refers to the common practice of calculating advertising costs on a comparative basis by dividing the budget allocation for each media vehicle by the total number of units of its advertising delivery or performance.[8]

Many different units have been used to derive cost-per-thousand figures: circulation, audience, impressions, gross rating points, viewers, cumulative reach, prospects, sets in use per commercial minute. We can apply cost per thousand three ways:

1 in comparing different scheduling applications of a particular media vehicle (a program or publication);
2 in comparing different vehicles within the same medium;
3 in comparing different media.

The use of cost-per-thousand measurements is taken for granted throughout the advertising industry. In 1956, testifying before a Congressional subcommittee, Frank Stanton of CBS presented the prevailing viewpoint clearly, as shown in the following quotation:

> I do not think that we can legislate an advertiser into an uneconomic purchase, and unfortunately the facts of life are such that on a cost-per-thousand basis — and I believe the advertiser makes his choice on that basis — I think these moves can be justified . . .[9]

This viewpoint was echoed in 1963 by Thomas Moore of ABC who told another Congressional hearing:

> The most common yardstick against which many advertisers evaluate their purchases is the cost per thousand of the viewing homes. . . . This is understandable from the point of view of an advertiser who is interested in the advertising values which the medium offers in order to maximize the sale of his product or service at the lowest possible cost.[10]

Cost per thousand (or CPM, as it is referred to by the cognoscenti) is the common coin of the advertising realm, but its convenience and general acceptance should not be confused with true value. The

[8] *Cf.* Roger Barton, *Media in Advertising*, New York: McGraw-Hill Book Company, 1964, pp. 219-22; Darrell B. Lucas, "The Cost-per-thousand Dilemma," *Media/scope*, Vol. 1, March-April 1957, pp. 29-32; *Reader's Digest* Symposium, "Cost-Per-Thousand Prospects Emerges as Buying Criterion," *Advertising Age*, June 8, 1964, p. 3.
[9] Testimony before the Antitrust Subcommittee, Committee on the Judiciary, Eighty-Fourth Congress, Second Session.
[10] *Broadcast Ratings*, Part I: Hearings before a Subcommittee of the Committee on Interstate and Foreign Commerce, Eighty-Eighth Congress, p. 67.

use of CPM as a basis for comparing media leads to problems in a number of areas:

1 At what level of communication should the performance of a medium be evaluated?

2 Can communications be treated as units identical in impact or quality, as the CPM concept assumes?

3 Is it correct to ignore the large variations, many of them unpredictable, in the performance of any medium at different times and places?

4 Are there any fair generalizations that can be made in advance about equivalent units of communication in different media?

These questions must always be confronted when specific CPM comparisons are made, and CPM has no meaning at all except as a comparative measure.

Levels of communication: the A.R.F. model

At what level of functioning should advertising media be measured to provide cost-per-thousand data?   A model of the advertising process was described in 1961 by a committee of the Advertising Research Foundation headed by Seymour Banks, vice president of the Leo Burnett Company and an outstanding media theorist.[11]   This model has six stages, all of which relate to a medium's capacity to present a message to people who will be persuaded to buy the product.

1 On the first level is the *distribution* of the vehicle.   This refers to its physical circulation or distribution into households, where it becomes available for communication.   In only some of these households are there prospects for the advertised product.

2 At the second level, the *vehicle* must get actual *exposure* to people; it must have an audience of live human beings, some of whom are prospects.   If the television set is on, this is considered "distribution."   If people are watching the program, this is media "exposure."   If a copy of a publication is delivered into the household, this is distribution; when that copy is read by an individual, it has had exposure.

3 At the third level, the *advertising* itself must get *exposure*.   The

---

[11] *Toward Better Media Comparisons,* A Report of the Audience Concepts Committee of the Advertising Research Foundation, 1961, p. 15.

message must achieve an actual physical presentation within the attention range of the individuals in the media audience. Not all the people exposed to a program, magazine, or newspaper are physically exposed to a specific advertising message. They may be out of earshot when a commercial comes on, or they may skip the particular page where an advertisement appears.

Up to this point, the A.R.F. description primarily concerns the advertising vehicle and its distribution pattern. Media research measurements at the first three stages deal with the capacity to put the message in front of a certain number of people.

4 At the fourth stage, which the A.R.F. committee calls *advertising perception,* the intrinsic capacities of the vehicle begin to interact with what the advertiser and his agency do with the time or space they have bought. There is apt to be a sharp differentiation between the physical exposure to the message (at stage 3) and conscious awareness of it on the part of people who might have a potential interest in the product itself or in the advertising appeal.

5 At the fifth stage, that of *advertising communication,* the sense of the message is persuasively transmitted to the recipients. Again this effect is selective; more prospects than non-prospects "get the message."

6 At the final stage, *sales response* represents what the individual does as a result of a persuasive advertising message. Since he has been influenced to buy, this defines him automatically as being on the prospect side of the line.

The calculation of cost per thousand can yield different results at each of these six different stages.

The fungibility of impressions

A few years ago, psychologist Gerhart Wiebe resurrected a wonderful term, *fungibility.*[12] Something is *fungible* if it is fully replaceable by an identical item; examples might be dollar bills, hamburgers, hogs going through the line in the packing house. When we think in terms of cost per thousand, we must, of course, think of human beings as fungible; we must think of their reactions to advertising as fungible. There is nothing particularly distasteful or immoral in this. We do this sort of thing all

[12] Gerhart D. Wiebe, "Public Opinion Between Elections," *Public Opinion Quarterly,* Vol. XXI, No. 2, Summer 1957, pp. 229-36.

the time when we speak of the population of Cincinnati, the readers of *McCall's*, or any other convenient designation of people in the mass. But this way of thinking is not very useful if we are trying to understand the processes of communication, persuasion, or selling.

There are no available measurements of true "exposures" or of advertising "impressions." These are not things or events with constant properties, but psychological processes which have no exact counterparts in definable behavior. We are forced to rely either on exposure opportunities (as represented crudely by broadcast audience ratings and page opening data) or on recalled or remembered exposure, which is subject to all kinds of inaccuracy, bias, and contamination from other exposures previous to the one ostensibly being measured.

There is no acceptable common impression unit on which to base comparisons even within the framework of the *same* medium, because in evaluating the psychological processes through which messages are received and ingested, we cannot separate the vehicle from the way it is used to transmit a particular idea from a particular source.

Today, few advertising media planners start with exposure opportunity rather than exposure as the unit for the CPM yardstick. The varying nature of communication achieved by the separate media appears to make exposure opportunity an unsatisfactory criterion. Such media as outdoor and transit advertising produce vast numbers of exposure opportunities at very modest costs (many of them, of course, represent, the same messages repeatedly confronting the same people). But these media are commonly presumed to promote only a relatively low level of conversion of "opportunity" (the physical presence of the message somewhere within visual range) into actual exposure or conscious perception. Other media, whose exposure-opportunity costs are much higher, are presumed to be much more powerful in their ability to get the message into the consciousness of the audience and are therefore more economical in the final analysis.

As it is conventionally calculated, cost per thousand represents an average which treats all impressions alike, regardless of whether they are delivered to different people or repeatedly to the same people. So long as the value of a repeated message is assumed to be equal to that of a message which is delivered for the first time, cost per thousand automatically gives an apparent advantage to a medium which reaches a concentrated audience over and over again.

The problem is most acute with television. On the average weekday, 17% of all adult women in the United States account for 45% of all the television viewing hours, according to a 1964 survey by W. R. Simmons. At the opposite end of the scale, 44% of the women account for only 8% of the total viewing hours. However, brand shares among heavy viewers are not substantially different from what they are among the consuming public generally.

The same cost per thousand may represent very different kinds of advertising values. It is possible to arrive at an equivalent CPM with 10% of the people reached 10 times, 100% of the people reached once, or 1% of the people reached 100 times. Yet these three conditions represent very different values for advertisers with different objectives and different problems of persuasion that arise from the very nature of the product.

A low cost per thousand based on an average impression may disguise poor cost efficiency in reaching key segments of the market. It may be far more economical in terms of results to spend more money to present a first message to hard-to-reach potential customers than to spend less inundating the already much-exposed. It follows from this elementary logic that every advertiser must judge media impact in terms of his own unique problems and objectives.

With a given number of impressions, the advertiser can, of course, concentrate his fire or spread it out, regardless of what media or media combination he uses. However, conventional cost-per-thousand measures give the same weight to every message whether it reaches a consumer for the first time or for the hundred and first. Useful though the concept of cost per thousand may be to advertising men in a hurry, it can lead to errors of judgment when it causes them to consider communication as something that exists out of context with the media environment.

When we reduce the effects of advertising to quantities of delivered impressions, we ignore the most essential nature of the communications experience. The user of cost per thousand may be quite aware that he can communicate only as well as he is permitted by the *character* of the vehicle which carries his message and by the specific *setting* it offers him. But the logic of events is such that he tends to use this understanding to *qualify* or *rationalize* cost differences between schedules *after* he has done his arithmetic. (This kind of rationalization, incidentally, is quite different from the considered judgment, at the outset of any cost-per-thousand comparison of media, to select a particular space or time unit in one medium as "comparable" with another kind of unit for another medium.)

Variations within a medium

Tremendous seasonal, regional, and other kinds of variations occur in the audiences of many media which are not always reflected in their rate structures. These enter, but do not ordinarily dominate, the many considerations involved in deciding whether a medium is right for a particular product in terms of the marketing characteristics of the people it reaches or of its psychological suitability as a form of persuasion.

A medium is only a means of communicating with the prospective purchaser of a product. Its value for the advertiser may depend not on the total number of people to whom it is exposed, but on the number of good prospects among them for the product advertised. There is an enormous range in the quality and efficiency of creative use to which a medium can be put. The same space or time may be used to win high attention and to deliver a message that carries strong appeal and conviction, or it may be utterly wasted.

Within any medium there are tremendous variations in cost per thousand by the standards that are commonly used, which are not sales standards. A TV program with a national Nielsen or ARB rating of 25 commonly has market-by-market ratings as high as 40 in some places and as low as 5 in others. In the case of broadcast media, the creative aspect is further complicated by the fact that there is a wide range in creative efficiency not only in the handling of the commercial, but also in the handling of the surrounding broadcast time. The broadcast advertiser seeks to reduce risk by placing his commercials (whether in a program or in spot) at a time period during which the average number of sets in use is of a known size. But there is no foolproof way to predict network program ratings, and with spot the problem is compounded.

The rate at which television audiences accumulate follows the shape of an exponential curve, with each successive repetition adding somewhat less to the unduplicated audience than the previous one. A commercial with a rating of 20% (that is, placed between two shows whose ratings average 20%) would have to be repeated twenty times before 80% of the households had tuned in to it at least once.

Within print media, translating circulation into total audience produces uneven consequences. Of the total reading of newspapers, 94% represents the primary audiences of people in families where the paper was actually delivered at home (as it is in seven cases out of ten) or bought on the newsstand, and only the remaining 6% is pass-along. For *Life*, the primary audience is 39% of the total, pass-along 61%. Newspaper audience figures represent readers reached almost all on the date of publication, while the most commonly used audience figures for magazines reflect a six-week buildup of readership for a particular issue of a weekly.

Print media also accumulate readers from one issue to the next at widely varying rates which reflect differences in their exposure patterns. For magazines, the importance of pass-along readership is reflected in substantial accumulation of audiences over repeated issues. While a single issue of *Life* is looked at by 26% of the adult population, the proportion rises to 51% who see at least one issue in six. Eighty-one per cent of the adults read one or more newspapers on a single weekday, but the five-day accumulation is only 90%.

Individual magazines differ substantially in the extent to which their readership is concentrated in the days immediately following publication. Edward Papazian[13] has estimated that *Life* magazine's first-day audience accounts for 20% of the total audience of its issue life, which he projects over five weeks. *The Saturday Evening Post* and *Look,* which are biweeklies, attract 18% and 17%, respectively, of their total issue audience the first day. For *Reader's Digest* it is 20%, but for *McCall's* only 10%. Papazian estimates that *Life* reaches 60% of the audience for any one issue during the first week after publication, whereas the proportion is 45% in the case of *Reader's Digest* and 40% in the case of *McCall's.*

Examining further differences among individual publications, Papazian points out that *TV Guide* has a relatively small pass-along audience. It is thrown away by many of the purchasers after seven or ten days, so that it reaches perhaps 40-60% of its audience on the first day after it arrives in the home and about 90% of its total issue audience during its first week. In contrast, specialized publications like *Business Week,* *The New Yorker, Sports Illustrated,* and *Newsweek* deliver only between a third and half of their readers in the first week, because of their high pass-along rate.

The first readers a publication reaches are its subscribers and a portion of the newsstand buyers. The next groups, in chronological order, are the remainder of the newsstand buyers plus some pass-along readers. Since primary readers are higher in income and education than secondary readers, the weekly audience profile of a magazine changes during its issue life.

In short, the variations among vehicles within any one medium are far, far greater than the differences between different media. This merely underlines the importance of attempts to find good measurements of the *end* results of advertising, rather than of the *middle* range of data on audiences and costs.

Intermedia comparisons

As a measure of efficiency, cost per thousand is only as good as the data it is based on, which may or may not be accurate. An executive of a large agency recently presented to a media research group a comparison

[13] *Media/scope,* January 1966.

of the cost per thousand people in the 18-49 age group reached by two network programs. Based on ratings, Program A had a cost per thousand of $4.17 and Program B had a cost per thousand of $4.11. When the programs were compared on viewer preference TvQ scores, the comparative CPM's were $8.21 and $8.92, respectively.

This comparison was presented to illustrate the dilemma which confronts the media specialist who must decide whether audience ratings or preference ratings are a better criterion for comparing programs. Actually, by either standard (ratings or preference scores), the differences between the two shows were trivial. In both cases, differences which fell within the ordinary tolerance limits of random statistical error were made to seem important when they were projected in terms of dollars and cents.

When we compare vehicles within the same medium — different newspapers, television programs, or magazines, for example — it may appear reasonable to use the same yardsticks of efficiency. Really serious problems arise when we seek to compare the efficiency of advertising through different media which communicate in different ways. Everyone talks about the impossibility of making intermedia comparisons, and everyone continues to make them nonetheless. Agencies issue dollars and cents comparisons of outdoor "impressions" based on traffic estimates, broadcast "impressions" based on households tuned to programs, and print "impressions" based on advertising recognition tests.

Some years ago Halsey V. Barrett, then Director of National Sales of the Television Bureau of Advertising, compared media cost efficiency for a one-minute television or radio commercial versus a full-page black and white ad.[14] He used the following criteria in this comparison:

> Broadcasting: "one person exposed to a one minute commercial as measured by Nielsen Average Audience Ratings."
> Print: "one person noting the average black and white full-page ad in magazines and newspaper supplements, the average black and white ad in newspapers, as measured by Daniel Starch."

In sophisticated media research circles such comparisons were not considered kosher at the time (1958) and are less so today. Yet, countless unsophisticated time salesmen still use similar yardsticks, and untold numbers of unsophisticated clients and agency executives see nothing wrong. Comparing impressions delivered by the various media has been likened to the problem of comparing apples and oranges. More often it is like the problem of comparing watermelons and grapes; not only are there differences in size and in kind, but there are different ways in which each can be sliced and served.

[14] *Television,* June 1958.

Real time represents different relationships in broadcast and print communication. A radio or TV signal lasts a moment. A billboard or car card may be on display for months, gradually acquiring new readers but also exposing the message to many of the same people over and over. Periodicals have the same capacity to put a message in the readers' hands again and again. Each issue of a newspaper is picked up on the average of 2.4 times by each reader; each issue of the longer-lived *Reader's Digest* is picked up on nearly five different days. Almost all the people who read a daily paper read it on the very day it is published. With magazines the audience for any one issue grows over weeks, as we just observed.

The fact that communication works differently in space and in time creates peculiar problems when print and broadcast campaigns are compared. For a given dollar expenditure, the audience levels reached by the media vehicle that carries the message may appear to be far larger for print than for television. But this balance is sharply redressed when value judgments are made about the extent of conversion from "audience" to "exposure opportunity" and then to "actual exposure." The relative cost advantage of a medium at one level may be reversed at the next. It is precisely in the hazy area of value judgment over the rate of conversion that the disparities in cost efficiency between print and television often emerge.

Units of space and time

One familiar approach to advertising media costs is that of the cost accountant who computes the expense of materials and labor in production and of the various services in selling as a basis of calculating the rate of profit on each item that is made and sold. This method is most directly applicable to product sampling. A sample is a unit, it is a *thing*, we can exactly calculate the cost of making and distributing it. If we know what one product sample costs, we know what a thousand samples cost, just as we know what it costs to make a thousand units of the regular product.

This way of thinking (in bookkeeping terms) carried over very logically into advertising as long as the accepted unit was a thing: one copy of a handbill, newspaper, or magazine containing an advertisement. But an advertiser using a publication does not buy *all* of it; he buys particular units of space in particular issues. Not only did he have to weigh the relative merits of alternative ways of using his money to buy space in a particular media vehicle, he also had to weigh the comparative merits of different vehicles. Simple bookkeeping considerations no longer produced automatic answers for his decision. He was no longer working with *things*. He was working with *communication,* with human perceptions, motives, and beliefs. Yet cost per thousand represents a holdover of the bookkeeping method to problems which are essentially *psychological* in nature.

In terms of real communication, does cost per thousand per commercial minute mean the same thing when there are three one-minute commercials on a half-hour program as when the time is divided between a two-and-one-half-minute and a 30-second commercial? Can the cost per thousand for a 50-second spot be compared with the cost per thousand for a 30-second spot or an 8-second I.D.? Is a double-page spread exactly twice as good as a single-page ad? To all these questions, the answer can only be, it depends.

Cost per thousand, as defined in terms of *audience* size, does not remain constant if we vary the size of the advertising unit. This is true whether we use measures of potential, like page traffic or broadcast ratings, or recall measures, like noting scores or sponsor identification. By the usual methods of evaluating advertising, the smallest unit of space or time almost inevitably appears to have the lowest cost per thousand.

When total audience figures are discounted to get down to measures of residual advertising effect like recognition or recall as measured by Starch or Gallup and Robinson, the results are never in direct proportion to the size of the advertising unit. The *intensity* of communication through different space or time units is not normally reflected in cost-per-thousand measures. Exposure to the medium, opportunity for exposure to the message, actual exposure, and recognized or recalled exposure all bear different relationships to each other in different media.

An expansion in the unit of advertising space or time is not always translated into a proportionate increase in the number of those who remember the message. Its impact may be expressed qualitatively through more effective persuasion of those exposed.

The size of the unduplicated audience is not doubled from a half-hour to a one-hour television program, nor is sponsor identification. Cost per thousand people exposed to the message does not remain constant as between a 30-second spot commercial and a one-minute one. We can never double page traffic, and we rarely double the number of noters or readers, though we *do* double our costs as we go from a single page in magazines to a double-page spread, or from a 300-line newspaper ad to a 600-line ad. It is customary in calculating the cost efficiency of TV programs to use the fiction of three separate commercial minutes for a half-hour telecast to arrive at "cost per thousand per commercial minute."

This assigns each "minute" equal weight and efficiency, even though we know that a half-minute commercial will carry a weight qualitatively different from that of a two-minute commercial.

When different broadcasting schedules are compared on a cost-per-thousand basis, the time span selected for consideration may determine the results. Consider a half-hour television program in which the sponsor broadcasts three one-minute commercials for the same product. He would normally calculate his cost per thousand based on the number of program viewers exposed to each of the commercials. But if this same sponsor chose to split his three minutes of allotted time into two 90-second commercials rather than three of 60 seconds, the cost efficiency might appear to be much less even though he would be reaching only slightly fewer people for exactly the same length of attentive exposure time. The same spurious difference applies when an advertiser must decide whether to buy a page of magazine or newspaper space as a single unit or to divide it up into two half-page units in different parts of the publication. Superficially, it would seem that at half the space cost, each of the small advertisements is being placed before the same size audience as the bigger one, even though it may attract the attention of fewer readers.

Any intelligent attempt to compare different units within a medium has to be framed in terms of specific applications, rather than in terms of universal laws or generalities. The numbers have to be interpreted and tempered by qualitative judgment. The efficiency of a medium must be seen not only in the number of message units it delivers, but in its capacity to reach into areas where competitive advertising is weak.

Qualitative judgment enters, for instance, in determining, for a schedule in a given medium, what size of standard space or time unit — and what size of investment — to put into each market on the list.

The spatial distribution of media may affect, or apear to affect, their comparative cost efficiency. In any local medium, certain basic costs of doing business remain much the same regardless of the size of the market or the number of people reached. Therefore, the small town paper or station cannot possibly provide the same number of readers or listeners per dollar expended on space or time as its big-city contemporaries. Of course, it costs a great deal more to buy a minute of prime television time or a full newspaper page in a city like New York than it does in Rapid City, South Dakota, but this absolute cost is more than compensated for by the far larger audience that the advertiser can reach with the vehicle in a larger market.

The small-town paper or station can legitimately take issue with the advertiser's assumption that it is fair to apply a constant yardstick of cost. For example, the small newspaper, with its fewer pages, may argue that a smaller unit of its space is equivalent to a larger unit in a larger paper, since there is less competition for the reader's attention. Any small-town medium might claim that its advertisers command a special degree of the community's loyalty, attention, and interest. This argument seems to be supported by the conventional advertising practice of using A, B, C, and D schedules in local media, which we discussed in Chapter 5. Such schedules are ordinarily based on the several markets' size or importance to the particular advertiser. In each category the use of the medium can be varied in the length of the commercial or the size of ad or in the total number of messages run.[15] (In newspapers, for instance, four color may be used in A markets, two color in B markets and black and white in C markets. Thus, if per capita weighting is heavier in the A markets than in the C markets in terms of messages delivered, it may still be kept equivalent in terms of expenditures.)

The difficulties of comparing different units within one medium are compounded in intermedia comparisons. The problem becomes particularly acute when a decision must be made as to what space unit is directly comparable with what unit of time. This type of comparison is conventionally made in terms of common or standard-size dimensions — 20 seconds or 30 seconds or 8 seconds versus 1,000 lines or a full-page black and white or a four color. It is never expressed in precise terms: $18\frac{1}{2}$ seconds versus 526 lines. But the use of standard units in making value judgments on media impact has a curious consequence. If the judgments are even slightly off they are perpetuated throughout all of the subsequent arithmetic on cost efficiency.

Cost-per-thousand comparisons made on the basis of any given unvarying units of space or time inevitably work to the advantage of some media and to the disadvantage of others; this is due in large part to the different patterns of physical distribution for each medium. Most newspaper circulation areas do not radiate as far from their central cities as television station coverage. On the other hand, the competition among vehicles is different from one medium to the next; there are far fewer television stations than newspapers, just as there are far fewer newspapers than radio stations. A strong radio signal covers a much larger area than VHF television, which in turn covers a broader area with the same signal strength than UHF. The trucks that deliver morning newspapers travel on uncrowded roads at night and generally deliver to a broader area than their evening competitors.

---

[15] This additional complication may in some cases help to keep media lists short. The smaller the number of markets in which the agency media department has to buy space or time, the less work and trouble it has.

In 1966 the advertiser who bought full sponsorship of a half-hour program on the CBS television network added only 2.5% in time charges by purchasing all 11 optional stations over and above the 92 which had to be bought in the "basic" network.   But when he bought a page of advertising in *all* the daily newspapers in the United States, his costs were 84% higher than if he had bought a page in all the papers in the top 200 markets.[16]

It is the unusual advertiser who buys a full page in every newspaper. Suppose he buys smaller space units in middle-sized and smaller markets than he buys in the larger ones. On what basis is his cost per thousand to be compared among the various newspapers? And how should he compare the *average* cost per thousand for his varying-size newspaper ads against the average cost per thousand for his varying-length television announcements? Such questions must be answered in daily practice, but the guesswork and judgment that go into the answers are often forgotten when the numbers emerge at the end of the assembly line.

An alternative approach

A few years ago, an important (but subsequently ignored) report entitled "Evaluation of Statistical Methods Used in Obtaining Broadcast Ratings" was prepared by a very able committee appointed by the American Statistical Association on behalf of the Congressional Subcommittee on Legislative Oversight.   According to this report, "The type of measure called 'dollars per thousand' is biased and has a large variance especially if the rating and effective sample size are both small."   ". . . The question that we wish to raise is whether it might not be preferable, instead of referring to dollars per thousand homes, to refer to homes per hundred dollars, or perhaps even better, audience per hundred dollars and to include not only the estimate of homes but also the estimate of people and the composition." [17]

This recommendation is based on the simple statistical fact that "in computing dollars per thousand homes, the estimated rating" (which is subject to large variance) "is in the denominator of the equation" where it will, of course, carry the greatest weight relative to the presum-

---

[16] The typical national spot TV list — and the typical newspaper list — seldom goes beyond the top 50 markets.

[17] "Evaluation of Statistical Methods Used in Obtaining Broadcast Ratings," a report of the Committee on Interstate and Foreign Commerce, 1961, p. 27.

ably more accurate cost figure. But more important, I believe, is the implicit recognition in this observation that one must start with the over-all cost of the advertising investment and *then* use judgment in interpreting what he is getting in return.

The media planner who is forced by his unfeeling, dull, and conventional clients and associates to use CPM to compare media should first calculate the cost of exposure opportunity for each medium and message with the reach and frequency needed to make contact with prospective customers. ("Exposure opportunity" can be defined in the terms of the A.R.F. model, with the advertising message present within the individual's range of potential perception by sight or hearing.) Only then, and with the aid of any available evidence, should he make the qualitative judgment of what he can achieve with words or pictures in the appropriate units of space or time in converting exposure opportunity into exposure.

We can easily calculate what rates of conversion for two different media (each used as we would prefer to use it) would make their cost efficiency come out equal when translated into exposed message units. At this point we are immediately faced with the consequences of any faulty value judgments we may have made on the subject of impact, and we can reconsider our assumptions if we decide we have erred in the direction of greater generosity toward one medium than the other.

A given medium must be judged differently within the over-all mix of media than it can be judged when taken in splendid isolation. Media can, of course, reinforce each other in their coverage of the market, in time scheduling, and in their creative aspect. Where a mix of media is used, the cost-minded advertiser should pass judgment on the efficiency of the combination rather than on each medium by itself.

The advertiser who thinks in terms of cost per thousand is like a military strategist who tries to compare the cost of a thousand men, a thousand planes, a thousand submarines, and a thousand guns. We know today that there are military situations in which it is more efficient to use a patrol than to drop a hydrogen bomb. The military planner must start with an over-all budget, but he distributes it among various weapons in relation to the appropriate tasks he assigns each of them to reach his objective, and *not* in relation to any arbitrary cost criteria.

THE COMPUTER: FRIEND OR FOE? 12

Today, any discussion of advertising media strategy occurs in the shadow of the computer. Computers have won a firm place in automating clerical operations in advertising: calculating rates, estimating, ordering, billing, and the like. In performing these functions, computers are essentially substituting for the standard mechanical punch-card processing equipment which many agencies have used for years.

Since media rates, circulations, and audiences are constantly changing, the use of electronic data processing to store relevant information represents a possibility for large-scale savings of time and money.

The purchase of newspaper advertisements and of television and radio spots entails many hundreds of individual contracts and arrangements with individual newspapers and stations. The average transaction in buying spot TV involves only $350, in a schedule which may add up to millions. The administrative cost of handling such schedules is substantially greater than the cost of placing the equivalent billings in network television or magazines, so here the savings made possible by the computer are particularly important.

Availabilities have always represented a major headache in buying broadcast spots, since most advertisers want their announcements placed by the same criterion, i.e., in the time spot with the greatest possible audience. When a computer is hooked into a teletype system, it offers the opportunity for instantaneous checking of available buys (by station and time) in much the same way that computers are used to check seat reservations on the airlines. Several of the leading station representative firms are acquiring computers for this purpose. The Central Media Bureau offers an across-the-board service which checks availabilities and also handles billing and ordering.

By 1967, some fifteen U.S. agencies had established their own computer installations. (This is in addition to the much more widespread use by agencies of outside service houses.) Al Norelli, an IBM expert on computer systems for advertising, estimates that three-fourths of the computer time used by agencies involves administrative routines.[1]

The big interest in computers does not lie in the area of automating routine operations as much as in media planning and decision-making. The computer does not itself actually make decisions, about media or anything else. However, it can make more knowledgeable decisions possible by its ability to rank or compare media according to specified instructions and (on the basis of its ability to do arithmetic) to apply logic and to distinguish like from unlike — all with great speed. The computer makes it possible to relate different pieces of evidence mathematically to generate a series of probable consequences for alternative courses of management marketing strategy.

It takes time before a computer begins to pay off in any business. Norelli cites a review made by McKinsey & Company, the management consultant firm, of the experiences of eighteen companies who had spent at least a million dollars apiece on their installations. Only a third of them had programs which were judged successful. Norelli believes that "exaggerated and premature claims produced misunderstandings that are only now subsiding. . . . The negative impact of that storm possibly set back computer use in advertising by at least two years. Extremely effective media professionals found themselves justifying their planning techniques against a phantom."

[1] Address to the British Institute of Practitioners in Advertising, 1965, Brighton, England.

While the first wave of hullabaloo over computers can be interpreted as a phase in the cycle of intellectual fashion in the advertising world, the concept of electronic decision-making is not just a fad; it is a development with profound implications, and it is here to stay.

The rush by many agencies to get on the bandwagon was followed in some cases by a rapid disenchantment. Yet, those people in advertising who still minimize the potential of the computer as a tool of business decision-making are like those who dismissed the prospects of space travel just a few short years ago.

Computer models as learning devices

To instruct or program a computer to compare media, we must first have a mathematical model by which our data can be organized. The fundamental assumptions behind such models must be evaluated, not in terms of mathematics, but in terms of how well they actually hold up in the light of what we know about man and his acts and about the process of communication. In science the great value of a model is that it permits a systematic statement of the theories or assumptions which bear on the explanation of a set of events in a way which permits those theories to be tested and evaluated against actual experience. The model provides a rationale for giving order and shape to the evidence. But when the evidence turns out to be inconsistent with the model, the model itself must then be reexamined and altered to bring it in closer alignment with reality.

Models are essentially, therefore, a *learning* device, rather than a means of explaining phenomena or of deciding what to do. They represent a problem only when they are taken literally, as a true depiction of the real world, rather than as a technique for better understanding the principles which underlie the things which can be measured and observed. Media selection models in advertising, like other models in marketing, have great value insofar as they force practitioners to make their assumptions explicit and to think through to logical conclusions the guesses, hunches, and estimates which advertising men generally make as a matter of course but rarely can articulate. This process of making things explicit goes far beyond the problems of media — even beyond advertising — and covers the much broader subject of consumer decision-making.

The computer provides the mechanism by which models can be tested in relation to a great variety of evidence and also in relation to various alternative ways of assessing the same evidence. It can force the practitioner to confront the consequences of changing his opinions about the market, the effects of advertising, or the capacities of the communications media. For example, he can be made to realize that the introduction of new ideas into his conceptions of the purchase cycle, the value of repeated messages, and the qualitative impact of one medium versus another can have certain measurable repercussions on his ultimate decision.

Used in this way, the computer is a tool by which the advertising planner can sharpen his thinking and clearly define the areas of his own uncertainty and ignorance so that they may be examined and studied. Like any useful tool, it may be misapplied. This might happen in media planning if the computer is expected to *make* decisions rather than to indicate what the consequences of alternative decisions might be. The few agencies which by now have gained extensive experience with computers in media selection have learned to use them as an aid to judgment. But many of the advertising layman's notions are still defined in terms of the old idea of the robot or thinking machine which produces infallible judgments all by itself.

In electronic data processing we put certain arrays of information into the machine and expect to get back rearrangements of this information. We start with a certain input in the form of resources. We have a given number of dollars which we can spend in a number of alternative ways. We put dollars in one end and out the other end come measures of comparative efficiency. We usually hope that efficiency reflects the comparative sales yield of these differing strategies of investment.

To be sure, we don't ordinarily project the end results in terms of sales dollars (although this too can be arranged); we usually project them instead in terms of "audience impressions delivered" or "ad exposure opportunities" or some other fancy term. But the underlying assumption is that communication can be reduced to units and that different types of communication, with different objectives and in different media, can somehow be reduced to comparable units. This means that a communications campaign must be thought of as an assemblage of units which can be arranged in different combinations. We think of these units — "impressions" or "exposure opportunities" — as though they were things because they all have dollar values.

The conception of human communication as something made of inputs and outputs is compatible with the most mechanistic kind of stimulus-response psychology and can be highly useful for certain purposes. But it is quite different from an attempt to understand communication as a *process* involving the exchange of symbolic meanings that cannot be measured. The computer merely compounds the problems which were reviewed at length in the previous chapter.

What assumptions underlie the creation of a computerized media selection model? A great variety of assumptions have been employed, and the whole field has undergone enormous changes just within a half-dozen years. E. A. Rawes, Manager of Consumer Research for ICI Fibres, Ltd., presented a model of his company's media selection program to the Institute of Practitioners in Advertising. He used both audience data (which he defined as "opportunities") and readership data (defined as "impacts"). One of his assumptions was "that the probability of an individual noting an advertisement is constant, regardless of whether or not he has already noted an earlier insertion." [2] This kind of assumption, if incorrect, can wreak havoc with many of the conclusions that subsequently emerge with the authority of "The Machine" behind them.

The place of advertising in a model of the total marketing system has been described as follows by a British O.R. expert, B. T. Warner:

> Advertising has a short-term effect on predisposition to purchase, and a longer-term effect which is measured by cumulative advertising exposure. The magnitude of the short-term effect was assumed to depend on both the cumulative advertising exposure and the purchaser's attitudes toward the brands in the product group. These attitudes arise from both advertising and previous use. It was assumed that only favorable attitudes arise from advertising, but that attitudes from use may be favorable or unfavorable.[3]

Warner's statement of his assumptions illustrates the problems implicit in a model which reduces the actual complexities of consumer response to only a limited and manageable number of dimensions. For example, he does not allow for the possibility that advertising may have no effect on people's attitudes or that it may have a negative effect. Warner illustrates his assumptions with a series of geometrical diagrams illustrating relationships for such things as the number of advertising impacts, short-term effects on the predisposition to buy a brand, and cumulative advertising exposures. He also presents charts simulating marketing situations that might arise from various strategic moves on the part of the advertiser.

The progress of these hypothetical events evolves from game theory and from the "scenarios" used in contemporary military strategizing. The brand manager plays much the same role as the field marshal of an army. The number of opponents is known, even though the extent of their resources may be a matter of conjecture. Not only may competi-

[2] *Computers in Advertising*, London: The Institute of Practitioners in Advertising, 1965, pp. 63-66.
[3] *Ibid.*, p. 52.

tive counter-moves be predicted (on the basis of survey data), but also consumer responses to a manufacturer's actions. As the model comes more and more to resemble the real world, more and more information must be fed into it. It becomes more elaborate and sophisticated, and the interaction of all the elements becomes more and more difficult to trace without the help of a computer. Real life is seldom as crisp or simple as game theory almost inevitably assumes it must be. Brand X cannot always expect that only its well-known adversary, Brand Y, will be in the picture when it makes its next move. Other manufacturers may enter the field. New developments may cause the whole product category to become obsolete, or it may be bypassed in public interest for other reasons.

However, even though game theory rests on simplified and idealized notions of the real world of competitive marketing, this type of marketing "game" is very useful for the business-school training of managers and future managers. It provides an invaluable discipline to the marketing strategist who wants to intelligently anticipate the consequences of his own moves in relation to the other forces in the market.

Linear programming

The first and most widely publicized system of applying the computer to media selection involved the use of linear programming. "L.P." (as it is commonly referred to) is an operating procedure which had already been applied widely to making business decisions in other fields where complex data had to be manipulated and arranged to arrive at the best solution among a great array of possible alternatives. Perhaps its first application to media selection was made by Alec Lee and John Burkart, then of British European Airways, in 1958.

Linear programming is a mathematical technique which permits the comparison of a great many alternative combinations in terms of a single criterion (normally cost efficiency). The alternatives are checked through in a logical sequence by a technique called "iteration," which first takes two combinations at random and compares them, then compares the better combination with another random selection and continues to play the game until one particular combination keeps winning. The procedure allows us to limit the number of comparisons actually calculated and to focus only on those which represent likely possibilities.

Linear programming lends itself to the solution of problems in which the elements being compared differ in their characteristics and capabilities and in their inherent restrictions or limitations. L.P. does not provide *ideal* solutions, but only the best solutions possible under the circumstances, given the existing means and restrictions. Although linear programming can be handled mathematically by hand or with ordinary calculating machines, the amount of information that has to be processed and compared in making most advertising decisions is so great that a computer is essential for practical reasons. Because it is a mathematical procedure, linear programming depends on numbers. Qualitative judgments must be translated into mathematical terms which the machine can accept and manipulate. D. H. Philips, media director of S. H. Benson, a British agency, points out that in his own work "large numbers of media selected by the computer for a specific schedule are insensitive to variations in weights used to reflect qualitative attributes — but enough sensitivity remains to require further work on this problem." (The "sensitivity" or insensitivity refers to the degree of effect which the qualitative weights have on the outcome. This of course depends on the design of the model, as well as on the numbers fed into it.)

The first step in the procedure is the bringing together of all relevant information regarding each alternative under consideration. In media planning, the basic data required by the computer might include (1) the available budget,[4] (2) the number of people that can be reached by each vehicle, both exclusively and in combination with others, (3) the characteristics of these people expressed in terms that reflect their values as marketing targets, (4) the cost of buying a certain unit of space or time (with all of the discount contingencies built in for each vehicle), and (5) a set of estimates which reflects the conversion of gross audience into effective communication, predicated on the use of that particular space or time unit. The purpose of the last set of estimates is to adjust the raw audience figures by judging how suitable the vehicle is for the objective of the particular advertising campaign, the creative opportunities it affords, the compatibility of the media environment, and the communications impact. Since there is not much relevant existing data with wide applications across the board, these estimates customarily represent subjective judgments made by experts.

An essential feature of linear programming is that it accepts constraints which may represent realistic outer limits to certain choices. In planning menus for example, certain foods, however nourishing, may be served no more often than once a day, or even once a week. In media planning, limitations on the use of a vehicle may arise either from the advertiser's arbitrary judgment that he must use certain vehicles and

---

[4] Since two alternative schedules rarely cost exactly the same number of dollars and cents, the computer is programmed to provide a reasonable amount of leeway in making comparisons.

use them only in certain ways or from the inherent requirements of the vehicle itself. It is obviously impossible to buy 13 issues of a monthly magazine in the course of a year or 53 issues of a weekly. The constraints may be self-imposed, for example, by a policy judgment that it would be imprudent to buy a particular weekly publication more often than once a month.

With all of the relevant information stored in the computer's "memory," the program can be activated to successively rank and combine media vehicles in various combinations in terms of whatever criteria are considered relevant. In practice, the key criterion is apt to be "efficiency," which may represent a restatement of cost per thousand expressed in a new language. The objective may be stated in terms of maximum coverage, reach, or the number of impressions delivered. These figures are limited by the budgetary constraint on the selection of available vehicles. Thus maximum coverage or impression delivery of predesignated products still has to be expressed at a given price — in cost per thousand.

In the simplest form of linear programming, every repetition of a message through a given medium might be considered to have a value exactly equivalent to that of every previous repetition. But linear programming does not require an assumption of linearity in the way that advertising works. (Linearity would mean that two advertising exposures were twice as good as one, four were four times as good, etc.) Linear programming can be used in a non-linear way, following any assumption desired about the greater or lesser value of successive exposures of advertising messages to the same individuals. There would still have to be an orderly progression implicit in this description, so that it could be described algebraically; for example, the second exposure might be worth half the first, and the third half the second — ordinarily it could not be made worth *more* than the second.

A media decision model using linear programming need not be written in a simplistic way to provide a single "optimum solution." It may aim for "suboptimization" — something practical, though less than ideal. The computer may be instructed to provide a variety of solutions ranked in order according to predetermined criteria. The computer can be instructed to print out relevant information (on reach, frequency, and cost efficiency) for alternative schedules so that a skillful analyst can inspect them in the old-fashioned, reflective way, holding his qualitative judgment in abeyance until the straightforward statistical comparisons have been made. This can be done by separating the computations which reflect the effects of qualitative weights or subjective assessments of media impact from those which reflect the harder information on costs and audience size and composition. Thus linear programming provides the media planner with a procedure not only for comparing alternative schedules, but for testing his own assumptions and improving his understanding of their consequences.

Simulation

The advent of computers coincided with the growing information demands of market planning and resulted in a great demand for detailed data on media audiences which could be related to usage patterns of particular products. Local newspapers and radio stations were bewildered when they received letters from big advertising agencies asking for a breakdown of their audience by education and A, B, C, D Nielsen county groups.[5] The new syndicated research services moved in to offer this kind of information that the local media were not equipped to supply.

But not everyone rushed to subscribe to the new services. Some researchers contended that consumer profiles of media audiences could be estimated by statistical simulation without the need for new research.

Simulation is a mathematical technique whose application has been greatly facilitated by the computer's capacity to sift rapidly through vast masses of data. It can be readily used in association with linear programming to provide useful data in the form needed to make intelligent decisions. However, simulation is not in itself a way of comparing alternatives or of arriving at a "decision."

As the word implies, simulation is a way of extrapolating from existing information in order to estimate the shape of an unknown real world. This can be done by utilizing the computer's capacity to relate evidence from different sources in a random way, by what is appropriately known as the Monte Carlo method. One form of simulation occurs in business "games," in which the consequences of various kinds of decisions on pricing, warehousing, and promotion can be traced against imaginary consumer response and competitive reactions.

The kind of simulation which is relevant to media strategy commonly entails the use of survey data derived from many different separate investigations of the same population. (Surveys are, of course, being conducted all the time using somewhat different interviewing and sampling techniques but aimed at describing very much the same universe or population.) Ideally, the media analyst would like to obtain, using a

---

[5] This is a classification which Nielsen uses to differentiate counties by the degree to which they are urbanized.

single study of the same good sample of people, full information on consumption patterns for his product and on the rate of exposure of all his prospective consumers to all the media vehicles he might conceivably consider using. In practice, learning this much from one survey is not often possible.

All numbers projected from surveys represent estimates of the true proportions which exist in the population at large. The statistical errors of sampling in any one survey are constant. When marketing and media questions are asked of the same people, the interrelationships between them have a basic integrity which can only be approximated when the data are combined from two separate sources. But the answers do not necessarily have any inherently greater accuracy than answers separately obtained from two samples. This fact provides the essential rationale for the use of simulation.

The evidence that we get from public opinion surveys becomes less and less valid as we try to get more and more information about different things in a longer and longer interview. This, of course, is a growing problem as the syndicated research services add additional questions and measurements. In compensation for this possible lessening of accuracy, the longer interviews do provide their users with the opportunity to make all kinds of cross-tabulations without the considerable effort and expense of developing a simulation to solve every marketing or media mix problem. Even the best and most brilliantly planned syndicated research service cannot measure every individual media vehicle with exactness. And it can hardly anticipate all of the vast data requirements of different advertisers with different products to sell, different marketing and advertising objectives, and a different array of advertising budgets within which their media selections might be made. Simulation represents a procedure by which the best available information on each useful item can be put together in order to arrive at a conclusion. In other words, if one survey tells us that the best customers for rock and roll records are girls between the ages of 12 and 15, we don't need to get our media data from the same survey. Instead, we can use other samples of girls in the same age group and find what they watch, listen to, or read. Then we can use statistical estimating procedures to put the marketing and media data together. Needless to say, the validity of this procedure depends on the real relevance of the criteria by which the data are matched, and in some cases the unmeasured personality differences may be more important than the demographic measures which are readily available.

One of the first important uses of simulation was made in the political arena in connection with a forecast of the 1960 presidential election.   Ithiel de Sola Pool, an M.I.T. sociologist, working together with a group of political scientists and mathematicians, constructed a statistical model of the United States based on Census population data for every county, the past political voting records of each county, and public opinion poll data showing the propensity of various kinds of people to vote Democratic or Republican.   A great many earlier studies of the electoral process had shown that people's voting habits could be predicted from their age, income, religion, occupation, and so on.   Thus the computer (under sage instruction) could combine the existing pieces of evidence derived from various sources to predict how the political pendulum was going to swing.

Through the Simulmatics Corporation, Pool and his associates sought to apply the same processes of statistical reasoning to the realm of marketing and media decision-making.   Their system put together information from the best available media and marketing surveys to estimate the comparative virtues of various media combinations.   Unfortunately, Simulmatics was handicapped from the start by a scarcity of data, since much of the best research on media came from the syndicated services which were understandably less than enthusiastic about passing their findings along to their new competitor.

Almost all major surveys classify respondents by sex, age, income, education, and so on.   One survey may break people into three income groups, another into four; and one may classify people into three age groups, another into ten.   Simple statistical procedures may be used to produce estimates that resolve these differences.   The computer itself can be used to rearrange data in different intervals than those assembled in the original field survey.   Once all the relevant information on markets and media has been sorted into a convenient set of bins, the simulation technique makes it possible to recombine the information as though it had all been gathered from the same individuals at the same time.

For example, men under 35, with incomes over $10,000 a year and with at least some college education, living in the suburbs of metropolitan cities, can all be regarded as a single marketing group with a characteristic likelihood of using various products and of exposure to different media vehicles.

Mediametrics

The first media-planning computer model to receive wide publicity was the "Mediametrics" system developed in cooperation with CEIR, the EDP firm, by Batten, Barton, Durstine & Osborn.   In the Mediametrics procedure, media and media units are first accepted or rejected by the planners on the basis of their feasibility for a given advertiser. For example, it may be decided that transit car cards should not be used for an institutional advertiser, that an 8-second I.D. is too short to provide a product demonstration, or that a 100-line newspaper advertising unit would be too short for the lengthy "reason-why" copy.

Within a given medium, some units might be considered feasible and some might not, but a number of different feasible units are brought into the comparison for each feasible medium.

The computer is fed a "static input" of (1) data giving a demographic profile of the consumers, based on available market research, and (2) demographic data on the people and households reached by a single exposure of each media unit. The problem for the computer to solve is essentially one of matching and maximizing economical exposures to the best customers. This requires detailed data on the characteristics of media audiences on a basis comparable from one vehicle to the next (though in the case of local media it is often not available on any basis at all).

The procedure also requires that there be comparability in the message units for each medium under consideration. Here Mediametrics relies on the expert (but subjective) judgment of the agency's media, research, creative, and contact men on the individual account. With the special needs of the product in mind, they judge the appropriate message unit in each medium in terms of its suitability for telling the story of the product, the quality of reproduction, the media environment, and "merchandisibility" to dealers and the trade. The resulting "impact" value is given a quantitative weight.

Thus a weight of 7.5 might be assigned to a 60-second TV commercial in one program while a weight of 5.0 might be assigned to a four-color ad in a particular magazine. This would mean that the average person exposed to the TV commercial would be judged to have received 50% more impact than the average reader exposed to the magazine ad.

A measure of "exposure probability" is next applied against the results of the previous calculations. In the case of TV, program ratings are projected both to households and to individuals and are then discounted by a measure of "effective perception" derived from BBDO's TV-copy research experimental setup, "Channel I." (Effective perception is set at 60% of program audiences for a one-minute commercial and 45% for a 30-second commercial.) For print advertising, the audience of the publication is discounted with a rule-of-thumb procedure identical for magazines and newspapers. (This credits the ad with an "effective perception" which generally runs 50-60% higher than the Starch noting score.)

The end result of the previous calculations is called a Rated Exposure Unit (REU). The computer then extends this single unit value for each vehicle to the full extent of a media cycle. Into this program can now be built restrictions that incorporate such factors as publication frequency and programming availabilities as well as minimum and maximum budget levels within which the medium can be used with each unit under consideration.

The result of these comparisons is to produce an optimum combination of media (which might be different than a combination of the best media). The objective is to maximize the number of REU's that can be bought within budgetary and other constraints. Substitute schedules can now be compared with the optimum to see what advantages they might offer in terms of aggregate reach, frequency, or cost efficiency. Finally, a "sensitivity analysis" makes it possible for the media analyst to see how various elements (including the qualitative ones) affect the final combination. In effect, it is possible for the media planner to judge whether a change of five or ten percentage points in his subjective judgment of a medium (or in his assessment of the relevant data) would bring the medium back into the schedule after it had been eliminated.

The original Mediametrics model was widely publicized as the pioneer application of linear programming to the media selection problems of a major agency, and it illustrates the complexity of the operations involved even in a comparatively simple system. Mediametrics did not solve the problem of how media *selection* and media *scheduling* should interact. Early in 1967, BBDO unveiled a radically new system, LP II, which represented an even more complex model that took into account the degree of evenness, as well as frequency, with which messages can be delivered to the desired target in a given period of time. Thus the computer moved from the task of helping evaluate media to the task of comparing alternative allocations of effort within the framework of a given media mix.

Iteration

Data Inc., the data processing subsidiary of the Standard Rate & Data Service, made a strong effort during its brief three-year life span to promote the "iterative solution to optimize media schedules." It defined "iterations" as "successive approximations to an optimum mathematical solution in which each successive iteration improves the solution over the results of the preceding iteration." (This is, in effect, the conventional style of optimization used in linear programming.)

Starting with a given list of media vehicles, Data Inc. calculated first the *total* number of "heavy users" of a product in the audience of each vehicle and then the number which each vehicle would reach exclusively, without duplication from the other media being considered. A vehicle was positioned on the schedule when it contributed a substantially unduplicated reach, and at that point the remaining vehicles could in turn be examined for duplication.

In one published illustration of its procedure, Data Inc. compared all the households using two food products, designated as A and B.[6] The profiles of these households were found to be identical in family income, geographic area, family size, race, type of neighborhood, home ownership, and age of the youngest child. In spite of this absolute identity in user household characteristics, the model developed two completely *different* schedules for optimized reach of female household heads in the *heavy*-using households for each product.

Altogether, 132 media vehicles were considered: 73 prime-time television shows, 40 daytime shows, and 19 magazines. One schedule called for the use of a daytime television show, "Love of Life"; five prime-time programs, "The Ed Sullivan Show," "The Beverly Hillbillies," "Peyton Place," "Bonanza," and "The Huntley-Brinkley Report"; two magazines of general interest, *Look* and *Reader's Digest;* and two magazines directed toward a more specific audience, *Woman's Day* and *McCall's.* For product B, the model also called for the use of "The Huntley-Brinkley Report" and *McCall's* magazine, but every other media choice was different — the "Lawrence Welk Show," "Bewitched," and "Gomer Pyle," *Reader's Digest, Life,* and *TV Guide.* This analysis allowed for the possibility that the optimum schedule might contain nothing but prime-time TV. It unrealistically assumed unlimited money and complete availability for all prime-time TV shows. (The lack of realism was a function of the input and not the model itself.)

The implication of this comparison was that there is something about the characteristics of product A's users which makes them prefer a completely different type of media exposure than the users of product B, even though the two groups of people may be exactly identical in terms of all their significant sociological traits. However, it is also quite possible that the vicissitudes of sampling were what produced a different set of relationships between product usage and media choice for each product and that purely chance relationships were immortalized in the

---

[6] *Data,* Vol. 1, No. 12, October 1965.

computer program. A sophisticated simulation based on the demographic characteristics of the households might have recommended identical media lists for both products.

The objective of Data Inc.'s procedure was to produce a "combination of the fewest media vehicles which delivers the most comprehensive coverage of . . . the heavy-user market." Coverage, of course, was expressed in terms of the audience reached and not in terms of exposure or impact, so the problem of spreading an advertising budget among vehicles with widely varying communications capabilities remained. The solution to this problem was achieved by means of a technique that boiled down to an affirmation of old-fashioned, intuitive media judgment. Describing the final stages of its "iteration" procedure for one product, by way of illustration, Data Inc. wrote in its bulletin:

> The creative judgments on this product established one-minute commercials as necessary on TV, four-color pages as necessary in magazines and supplements, and 600-line ads as necessary in newspapers. Using these creative requirements, detailed schedules for a one-year period were established. . . .

Thus, in this instance, the solution prescribed by the computer flowed directly from the subjective assumptions made by the analysts.

Dynamic High Assay, and others

Shortly after BBDO announced that it had an operational media decision-making system, Young & Rubicam unveiled its own "High Assay Models." This incorporated a "Data Breeder," which took existing media and marketing data from outside services and from the agency's own research files and extrapolated new data for the media evaluation.

While the original Mediametrics model represents a straightforward alignment of media and marketing demographic data, the Y & R scheme includes information on the habits of consumers in the market. Thus, Y & R is concerned with the timing and spacing of advertising pressure as well as with its total distribution to different groups of potential customers.

The Y & R system incorporates yet another virtue. It makes it possible to evaluate how the different subjective value judgments which are incorporated into the media comparison affect the final outcome. As I suggested earlier, this kind of "sensitivity testing" focuses the attention of the media planner on the more questionable areas of his own judgment.

The Y & R agency uses a pluralistic approach; they speak of models (in the plural), suggesting that different procedures may apply to different problems. The planning process breaks down into four steps: (1) strategy selection, in which objectives are defined; (2) assumption testing, which reviews the fundamental picture of the brand and the market; (3) one-time media efficiencies, in which media are ranked according to their efficiency on a single exposure; and (4) integrated advertising planning, which looks at consumption behavior and multiple media exposures extended through time.

As this brief description suggests, the Y & R procedure is oriented primarily to the assembly of the best evidence and guesses of all the relevant marketing information on the purchase cycle, brand switching, the value of repeated exposure, and the effect of copy appeals on holding present customers and attracting new ones.

For any given product, the market may be separated into different segments which differ in their value to the advertiser. An estimate is made of the cost of gaining an additional sale from within the prime target segment, assuming that the more repeated advertising exposures the people in this group receive in a given time period (up to a point), the more likely they are to buy the product. Media can then be evaluated in terms of the efficiency with which they accomplish the objective. When additional advertising messages no longer profitably yield additional sales from the prime target segment, the computer repeats the cycle of analysis for the next best segment of the market, and so on.

Y & R and BBDO gave their computer models more early publicity than other agencies, but they were by no means the only ones active in the field during the early 1960's. Benton & Bowles sponsored significant research in the simulation of market behavior. In England, the London Press Exchange developed its own linear-programming model.

With remarkably little fanfare, Interpublic developed its Marketing communications Investment Decision Analysis Systems (MIDAS), which represents a battery of models applicable to different problems rather than an attempt at a single global solution to all problems. The procedures break down into four steps:

1 Analysis of existing practice and strategy for a product.
2 Generation of potentially superior alternative strategies. MIDAS uses a model called FAST (Frequency Aimed Selection Technique) which aims to deliver "balanced" message frequency at minimum cost in a given time period.
3 Evaluation and modification of the computer's "proposals" by the marketing experts who can add their judgments to the computer results.
4 Final evaluation of the modified alternative strategies. A com-

puter simulation of media usage by different population groups is frequently used at this stage.

The MIDAS procedure can be applied to different kinds of marketing targets. It can be varied to produce data based on total audience or on exposures defined in any manner desired with various kinds of weights built in — e.g., distinguishing primary and secondary audiences.

The techniques provide for vehicle selection within a medium with or without intermedia considerations, thus making it possible to avoid the pitfalls involved when these considerations are completely integrated into the system.

COMPASS (Computer Optimal Media Planning And Scheduling System) has been developed by a group of major New York and Chicago agencies in a cooperative venture. Theirs is a flexible model with broad application, which makes use of simulation, decision functions, and "search" procedures akin to those used in iteration and High Assay. The model explores a wide range of feasible media schedules, evaluates each in terms of stated reach and frequency objectives, and finally arrives at an "optimal solution." Scheduling of the optimal plan is also considered.

The model can employ qualitative media vehicle weights, relative marketing target weights, and media discount structures. Detailed reach and frequency documentation is provided for each target group. The contribution of each vehicle in the optimal schedule and the potential contribution of all other vehicles is analyzed and reported on during the computer run.

In the words of Bernard Lipsky, a prime mover of the project, "COMPASS is designed so that a media planner is given broad options on an extended set of decision points in advance of a computer run. These decisions are expected to vary from product to product as well as from campaign to campaign for a particular product." [7]

The "broad options" on which the sophisticated media planner insists are a far cry from the notion of the computer as a "thinking machine" which might be the planner's replacement.

Cost per thousand and the computer

"In the final analysis," says Foote, Cone & Belding's W. A. Joyce, "cost per thousand is the major factor in determining the inclusion or exclusion from a specimen schedule of any one media vehicle." Much the

[7] Private communication.

same conclusion emerges from a forthright exposition of the adventures involved in applying computers to advertising written by Frank M. Bass and Ronald T. Lonsdale.[8] They defined the problem of media scheduling by computer as one of selecting the "best" set of alternatives among various media and within media (in terms of page size, color, etc.) with a given budget. To prevent the most efficient vehicles from "running away with the program," the authors introduced the usual operational restraints: (1) No more than one advertisement may be allowed to appear in any one issue of a medium; (2) an advertiser may arbitrarily decide on the maximum share of his budget to be allocated to a particular medium (even though he is uncertain as to what vehicles to use within the medium); or, (3) he may allocate a given number of exposures to different segments of the market, in proportion to their worth. Bass and Lonsdale first estimate the "adjusted audience" of each vehicle, excluding people who are not prospects for the product. They then weight the audience figures by an exposure factor, by a subjective evaluation, and by their congruity with the market distribution of potential customers. Their exposure factor is "arrived at by applying typical Starch or Nielsen ratings for advertisements of product types being considered." Equating set tunings for TV and ad recognition scores for print in this fashion is grossly inaccurate, but it is not wholly unlike the kinds of comparisons which some practicing media planners make. The subjective evaluation is made by an "advertising expert" who evaluates "the appropriateness of the vehicle's editorial content, tone, etc., for the product advertised" on a scale of zero to one.

These authors considered a total of 63 media vehicles, using 33 different linear programs. They came up with very similar results regardless of the system employed to adjust audience figures in terms of "quality" or composition, and they concluded that "the weighting system has very little influence on the solution." Thus "sophisticated weighting systems tend to be 'washed out' in linear models. This suggests that cruder models such as cost per thousand will produce media schedules not very different from those produced by linear models. It is possible, of course, to study the sensitivity of solutions to various weighting systems, but the results suggest that this sensitivity is not great." [9] These conclusions naturally reflect the particular degree of emphasis which the authors placed on the qualitative elements in their program. A different set of assumptions (about the value of a second exposure, for instance) might have yielded quite different results.

[8] "An Exploration of Linear Programming in Media Selection," *Journal of Marketing Research*, Vol. 3, No. 2, May 1966, pp. 179-88.
[9] *Op. cit.*, p. 183

Bass and Lonsdale intelligently observe that in most (non-advertising) applications of linear programming,

> The restraints are imposed by the physical environment. In applying linear programming to media selection problems, however, restraints are imposed by the decision-maker based on judgment, essentially because he lacks faith in the linearity assumptions in linear models. . . . [By the "linearity assumptions" the authors mean the assumptions that there are stable, fixed, and predictable relationships among the elements of the model so that, for example, cost efficiency always goes up in direct proportion to the number of messages delivered.] The peculiar result is that the attempt to improve efficiency of programs by adding restraints, necessarily reduces the value of the objective function. One might add in defense of linear programming that it does produce schedules which appear usable on a judgment basis. Solutions are not very different from those one might derive from judgment alone. . . .
>
> [Attempts] to impose meaningful restraints on the linear model would probably be unfruitful. When only the budget restraint and operational restraints on each vehicle are employed, the model is reduced to a simple cost-per-thousand model. . . . Assumptions about the nature of response to advertising cause most difficulties in models of the type examined in this article.[10]

In sum, the use of the computer to arrive at *solutions* carries with it the danger of perpetuating media selection in terms of cost per thousand. The computer's real value for the advertising planner is its capacity not to supply pat solutions, but to force him to think his problem through to a higher level of sophistication, and thus to arrive at his own solution.

Computers and communication

Computer models of media selection work on the basis of input and output; they work on the premise that an advertising campaign may be thought of as an assemblage of units which can be arranged in different combinations.

Because of its capacity to organize complex data, the computer opens up new possibilities for the analysis of media in relation to known facts about product distribution, consumption patterns, and competitive forces in the market. This very capacity has already pointed out the inadequacy of our present knowledge about how to arrive at a schedule within a media mix; it is forcing the advertising business to do more and better research on the effects of repetition, on the effects of varying time

[10] *Op. cit.*, pp. 183-84.

intervals in exposure, on the comparative effects of concentration and continuity, and on the effects of changing the size of the message unit. Until we have more hard evidence on such matters, the analyses we get from the computer can be no better than our best estimates.

The repetition of an ad in *Life* against a given individual might be given a weight of 50%, the second repetition a weight of 25%, and so on. It might be possible to assume that with *Look,* the respective weights are 66%, 44%, etc. But what of the man who is exposed to the ad first in *Life,* then in *Look?* The computer can perform all the necessary calculations, but of course it cannot evaluate the assumptions behind them. The computer offers the potential opportunity to compare the outcomes and interactions of many different assumptions and to take into account the vast stores of information which may be relevant to a marketing problem.

In point of fact, a realistic model would have to be even *more* involved. Successive repetitions might reasonably be expected to add increasingly to the value of the first message if they bring the message closer and closer to the point of breaking into the consumer's awareness. Beyond that point, however, further repetitions might have progressively less value. The point at which the curve shifts direction might well be a function of whether the message was repeated in identical form or with variations. As a practical matter, any assumption about diminishing returns may be applied to second exposures across the board regardless of whether the initial message was delivered through the same vehicle or through another with quite different communications characteristics.

The media planner might want to assume that the repetition of a magazine ad added 50% and a 20-second television commercial 75%, but at the present time he would have to base any such assumption on *judgment.* He cannot base it on *evidence,* because there isn't any. And this takes us back to the subjective weighting of one vehicle against another, which has always been the media analyst's stock in trade.

A value judgment based on personal opinion or on an opinion poll of five account executives is no less a value judgment when it is printed out by a big machine, and that value judgment introduces an enormous range of possible error. Let me hasten to add that subjective judgments, quantified, have been widely used in other fields of computerized decision-making, and that quantification does have the merit of forcing awareness of the premises on which decisions would normally be based without a computer. But where in the decision process should these judgments enter in?

For all their virtues, computers have one inherent limitation. Their operations are performed in sequence, one after the other, even though they are performed so fast that many things seem to be happening at once. A computer cannot integrate, cannot synthesize, an experience in the way that the human mind can grasp the shape and flavor of an experience all at once. This is a critical point, because decision-making in the field of media has one profound difference which distinguishes it from decision-making on inventory control, airline scheduling, or ballistics.

When we talk about media analysis or any other aspect of advertising, we are talking about communication, which is in no sense reducible to a series of discrete events. An advertising plan is a whole thing in which the choice of media, scheduling, themes, and creative expression can never be isolated from one another. Communication is a matter of symbols, and symbols are of a different realm than science. The basic shortcoming of the computer in media evaluation is really, therefore, the inherent shortcoming of the scientific method applied to the study of persuasion.

ON MEASURING EFFECTS [1] 13

An automobile manufacturer once took a large sample of the subscribers to a particular magazine (100,000 of them) and, for a period of several years, eliminated all its advertising from the copies these subscribers received. As Elmo Roper describes the experiment, the car registrations for the subscribers in the sample were then compared with those for a similar list of people who had received the normal dose of advertising in the magazine.[2] The results showed statistically significant differences between the two samples in the percentages owning the manufacturer's car. Translated into the dollar value of the additional sales, the difference made it apparent that the advertising had paid off.

This is an extraordinary story, because the experiment was so

---

[1] The most comprehensive review of the evidence on this subject is Joseph Klapper's *The Effects of Mass Communication,* New York: Macmillan (The Free Press of Glencoe), 1960. Klapper is only incidentally concerned with the effects of advertising, however.

[2] *Public Pulse,* October 1965.

simple and the results so clear. It stands as a perfect example of what every advertiser hopes for in evaluating his efforts — hopes for, but almost never gets.

There is no one question which management is apt to raise more often, or with better reason, than the question of what return it is getting on its advertising investment. And there is no one question more likely to send cold shivers down the spine of any researcher who has tried before to answer it conscientiously.

William Weilbacher recalls this episode:

> A callow advertising agency researcher once completed a ninety-eight page analysis for a packaged goods brand meant to prove conclusively that television advertising expenditures cause sales. This paper created a considerable stir throughout the advertising agency, and in due course it reached the desk of the agency board chairman. Dynamo and states-man that he was, the chairman rarely bothered with research reports, but on this occasion, much to everyone's surprise, he took the report to the farm for the weekend and read it in detail. At 9:15 A.M. the fol-lowing Monday morning, the researcher found himself in the sumptu-ously appointed office of his board chairman, who said, "I have read this report from cover to cover and I disagree with your finding. I believe that this report proves conclusively that sales cause advertising, and not that advertising causes sales. Is my interpretation correct?" The re-searcher replied immediately and without flinching, "No." "Do you walk on water, too?" asked the board chairman, and signaled that the meeting was over.

It is easy enough for anyone to "prove" that advertising pays. All one has to do is compare the brand opinions or choices of people who claim to have seen or heard the advertising with those of people who haven't. The former are always more favorable, and why shouldn't they be? The people who pay most attention to us are the ones who like us in the first place. The point is illustrated in an anecdote reported by Curtis Grove:

> The scene is the dancefloor of a posh country club on the outskirts of a major mid-western city, as the president of a manufacturing firm bounces across the floor almost in time with the Welkian bubbles of music from the orchestra. Another couple bounces by, and the man (a neighbor, fellow-businessman, socialite, and fellow-club-member) exclaims, "Say! I saw your new commercial on TV last night. It was great! And the kids had a *fit* about that fat little character." "Thanks very much. Glad you liked it," glows the manufacturer, warm with the satisfaction that comes only with the conviction that the new $12,000 spot *is* good.

But few businessmen are satisfied to evaluate their advertising by what the neighbors say. They want more convincing evidence, expressed in quantitative terms, that their efforts are productive. And agencies generally recognize what Interpublic's Marion Harper, Jr., calls their "accountability" to their clients. Unfortunately, the more sophisticated the methodology employed, the harder it generally appears to be to find any statistically satisfactory measure of the effect of advertising in a complex competitive market. Furthermore, sophisticated methods are expensive because they require that very large samples of people be checked at repeated intervals and that the resulting data be extensively manipulated and analyzed.

Advertising, like any communication, does have effects, and these effects *can* be measured. But the expense of proper measurement cannot usually be justified in relation to the cost of the advertising being evaluated. In practice, marketers who want to check effects insist on keeping the cost of doing so in proportion to the advertising budget. This almost always means cutting corners on the research and winding up with frustrating and inconclusive results.

The effect of advertising on sales can be most accurately measured in the case of a unique advertisement that makes a specific offer which could not come to the attention of the consumer in any other way. This description could be true of mail order advertising, or in fact of any solicitation which provokes direct inquiry in person or by mail or telephone. It may be true of a retail ad where the promotion is not also supported at the point of sale.

A product which is advertised over a long period of time does not show wide fluctuations in sales in response to changes in advertising strategy, according to a long-term analysis by Kristian Palda of the sales of Lydia Pinkham's Vegetable Compound.[3] At any moment in time, the sales of a product are influenced by the whole past history of its advertising and of competitive advertising, rather than by just the campaigns of the moment.

Most advertising being evaluated is not an isolated venture, but part of a continuing promotional effort, offset by a similar continuing effort on the part of the competition. Its total impact may be expected to register gradually. It is obviously a much simpler matter to measure the kind of major change in attitude or buying behavior that can be accomplished by an all-out effort (as in the case of a Procter & Gamble launching Gleem tooth paste with a twenty-million-dollar advertising budget for the first year).

[3] Kristian S. Palda, *The Measurement of Cumulative Advertising Effects*, Englewood Cliffs, N.J.: Prentice-Hall, Inc., 1964.

How General Motors does it

The national advertiser who is both brave and big *can* study the effect of whole campaigns on a national scale.   For several years, General Motors has been engaged in a continuing study of advertising effectiveness.   This is of special interest both because of its scope and because it uses the ANA's "Dagmar" approach (described in Chapter 2), which begins by "Defining [specific] Advertising Goals for Measured Advertising Results." [4]   The questionnaire developed for this purpose by Audits and Surveys, Inc. deals with automotive preference levels by make; it goes on to investigate product image, advertising message registration, market behavior, and product inventory.   All this information can be analyzed in relation to demographic data and media habits.

To illustrate the painstaking detail of the G.M. project, the problem of the product's image alone is the subject of 35 different questions for every brand the respondent regards as being in his buying class, and each of the questions is evaluated on a seven-point scale.   The research includes a benchmark wave of interviews each September and five subsequent waves throughout the year.   These follow at irregular intervals because of the bunching up of the advertising investment during the first two quarters after the new models are introduced.

A second round of interviews is conducted with all those who say they "definitely" intend to buy a car or "probably will buy" one, with a third of those who say they "probably will not buy," and with 17% of those who say they "definitely will not buy."   This makes it possible to compute the probability that an individual who gave each type of answer will actually visit a dealer and buy the product.   It is even possible to compute the probability of purchase for the very large class of individuals who are not even aware of a particular make.

In the case of one make, 84% of the people who consider it their first choice go on to visit a dealer and 56% of them actually purchase the car.

Says G.M.'s Gail Smith,

We assume that in order to move a person from one preference level to another, it is neeessary to change his attitude regarding the product. Furthermore, the attitude must be relevant to the way he considers and evaluates cars.   In addition to that consideration, we must cope with the distinct posibility that certain attitude changes may affect movement from one level of preference but have actually no effect at other levels.[5]

---

[4] Address before the Association of National Advertisers, Chicago, May 11, 1965, by Gail Smith, Director of Advertising and Market Research at General Motors.
[5] *Ibid.*

Various opinions about the car and its features are related to the preference level.   In some cases an unfavorable opinion does not relate to preference.   In other cases it does.

Advertising can be evaluated in terms of the Dagmar scheme by measuring changes in the proportion of people in the audience of each medium who hold a particular opinion, attitude, or point of information about a make of car.   Within the framework of each medium, it might be possible to calculate the cost of making people aware of the product. Looking ahead, Smith suggests that it will eventually be possible to set even more stringent criteria, for instance by limiting the analysis to those prospective buyers reached by each medium who not only include the make in their purchasing range but *also* have a low opinion of its trade-in value.   Smith offers a specific illustration.   The difference in awareness of a certain car before and after the test period was 15%.   The "cost-per-thousand accomplishment" projected to $83 (i.e., $83 were spent for each thousand aditional prospects who mentioned that car as an acceptable buy).   However, in a two-media campaign, 9% were reached by medium A only and 33% by medium B only.   Medium A produced a net change of 3%, which worked out to $220 cost-per-thousand accomplishment, while medium B changed 11% at a cost-per-thousand accomplishment of $57.   Smith observes, "The analysis, as you can see, leads to the conclusion that we would probably have been better off to spend our entire budget in medium B.   The conclusion, however, is based on the way we executed this particular campaign and assuming the use of a different creative approach, the results might have been quite different."

Smith's research colleague at General Motors, Donald Batson, points out that with a continuing study of advertising effectiveness it is irrelevant to inquire as to the specific contribution (or demerits) of the creative theme or its execution, the media choice, or the scheduling strategy.   What is being evaluated is actually the total campaign as the agency produces it, with every element inseparable from the others. Thus, eventually, the only criterion becomes the contribution of the *total* advertising plan to the sale of the product, as measured *over time* by the purchase records of people with different levels of exposure to the advertising.   (Differences in the purchase habits of the exposed and unexposed groups may be compensated for by establishing a base period before a change in advertising strategy occurs.)

The GM project has been estimated to cost over three-quarters of a million dollars a year, an extremely modest expenditure for a company which aims to get maximum efficiency from an annual advertising budget which was $173 million in 1965.   But the deeper question remains as to whether what is good for General Motors is necessarily good for the average advertiser, whose research problems may be every bit as complex but whose total sales and advertising volume can hardly justify such an expense. Unfortunately, the costs of researching a given problem are the same for a small company as for a big one.

Do retailers know when advertising pulls?

National advertisers commonly labor under the assumption that, while the effects of their own advertising may be very difficult to measure, the retail merchant doesn't face this problem since every ad he runs is tested by the hard ring of the cash register. Alas, this assumption is an illusion. The retailer can indeed judge whether his ad has pulled mail or phone orders, but he rarely knows how much of the sales of an advertised item are due to the immediate direct effect of the ad itself, how much reflects store traffic generated by ads for other merchandise, and how much represents the delayed effect of past advertising for the same item.

In a recent study,[6] all advertising for women's dresses run by a major department store over a six-month period was carefully analyzed in relation to the sales of the merchandise for three days after each ad ran. The ads themselves were then examined to determine what characterized the ones that pulled best. Sales appeared to reflect the character of the individual advertised item far more than variations in such attributes of the advertisement as the type of illustration, layout, choice of models, or copy.

The retail market is in a constant state of flux, a condition which reflects the interaction of innumerable factors: competitive merchandising and buying practices, seasonality, weather, economic conditions, and the obscurely motivated shifts in customer psychology. Even if advertising were not a factor in retailing at all, one would expect variations from week to week in a store's business in particular merchandise categories. Over the long haul, a store's good weeks and bad weeks should work out to an average from which there are no dramatic variations. Taking any two consecutive weeks, one might expect to find a net improvement from the first week to the second in some cases, a net loss in others, and no change in still others. Such might be the sales pattern for small neighborhood retail establishments which do not advertise.

When we look at bigger stores, however, we would expect advertising to provide some measurable net plus. If the store had suffered a loss

---

[6] Unpublished research analysis, Bureau of Advertising, ANPA.

attributable to factors other than advertising, the net plus from advertising might still leave an over-all loss — though one of less severity than if no advertising had run at all. The dimension and origin of the fluctuations in these other factors cannot normally be measured or traced. Thus we cannot assume that retail advertising has had no positive effects even in cases where a store sold less of a given item in a week of heavy advertising compared with a week of lighter advertising.

In these instances, the pay-out period must be clearly defined. This still leaves a large twilight area for the retailer's judgment on what his advertising is bringing it. From a practical standpoint, one would not expect an advertisement today to result in a sale five years from now; yet it might very well result in a sale tomorrow, next week, or possibly even the week after.

The major function of retail advertising is to retain the position of a store in its market, since this reflects a long-standing reputation in which a continuing advertising program is an important component. The relative week-to-week stability of total advertising by most merchants is mirrored in the week-to-week stability of consumer's mentions of individual stores as the places to buy particular items. Where a store does shift its total advertising direction from week to week in terms of the linage devoted to individual products, the most immediate effects are felt by the people who are already on the verge of buying.

A two-week analysis of all advertising in five retail categories was made in the study of women's shopping behavior which I described in Chapter 9. In this highly intricate analysis, it was found that stores which increased their linage for a given item from the first week to the next produced a 12% greater conversion of purchase plans for the items into actual shopping visits to those stores, compared with the stores whose advertising for the same items did not increase. For major stores the conversion rate was 18% greater.[7]

In the short run, retail ads appear to be most successful in converting an existing purchase intention into an actual shopping trip. They are next most successful in redirecting a continuing purchase intention toward the store which advertises, especially in the case of substantial and consistent advertisers. It is hardest to demonstrate how retail advertising creates new demand for the products themselves, if for no other reason than that the complex forces of national advertising are at work at the same time.

But while advertising can bring the customer into the store, it

[7] "How, When, and Where the American Woman Buys, Shops, Spends," Bureau of Advertising, ANPA, New York, 1966.

cannot make the sale.　An analysis has been made of 2,000 cases in which customers walked out of the store without buying the item they had shopped for.[8]　It shows that women who may be brought into the store by an ad may fail to buy the item because the styling or sizes are not right, the merchandise does not meet expectations, or the customers cannot get waited on.

The technique of measuring change

The effects of advertising can best be measured when there is no prior history of promotion which might still be having a delayed influence on an existing product in a competitive marketing situation.　When we select test-markets we can ascertain the cumulative impact of past advertising from research done before the test begins.　But it is much more difficult to assess the interaction (the harmony or incongruity) between the messages of the past and the message we are currently delivering.

Sales result from an accumulation, over time, of impulse, opinion, and information in the consumer's mind.　This means that under ordinary circumstances, with an existing product, we cannot trace sales back to any one of a particular series of advertising messages.　They may in part reflect the impact of previous messages, just as the particular messages which interest us may have a continuing or delayed effect on future sales.

In a great many product fields, the advertising efforts of one brand may be small compared to the competitive marketing forces.　Specific sales results are hard to relate to specific advertising causes when there are only small changes in over-all sales volume for the whole product category, as measured by factory shipments or store audits.　To meet this problem, researchers turn to a different type of study, in which exposure to advertising messages can be related either directly to purchases, or to some measure of product or brand awareness and attitude that is assumed to correlate directly with purchases.

Consumer opinion research is the only way of getting data through which the specific effects of a company's advertising might in any sense be distinguished from the effects of trends in the market as a whole.　The technical problems we face in trying to measure the effects of advertising are analogous to those of measuring the effects of any other form of communication.

[8] J. F. Borden and F. A. Brooks, *Store Walk-outs:　What Do They Cost?　How Do They Occur?　Can They Be Reduced?*, New York:　National Retail Merchants Association, no date.

When sales effects are inferred from the product usage or purchases reported by respondents in consumer surveys, the relationship of sales to brand attitude generally appears closer than if store or pantry audits are used to measure sales. One reason for this is that questions on product usage and on brand attitudes are asked of the same people at the same time, whereas audits are made at different points in time and by altogether different research methods.

Survey research people are always trying to impress on their managements the fact that one should never draw conclusions from the totals in a survey, because detailed analysis may either turn them topsy-turvy or introduce some important qualifications. One cannot conclude that there is a tremendous untapped market for trousers because nearly half of the American adult public does not wear them every day — a finding that can be interpreted a little more intelligently if the responses for men and women are tabulated separately. This is an elementary thought, but one the sight of which is lost too often in designing studies to measure advertising effects.

The findings of social research in the area of attitude change all point to the same conclusion: the more specifically one states the problems, the more confidently one can state one's findings.

The simplest way to study the effect of any communication is in the laboratory, using an experimental group of students, soldiers, employees, or any other bunch of people whose opinion or behavior can be measured at various intervals of time and whose exposure to any persuasive effort or communication can be carefully controlled. Suppose, in such an experiment, we find that 50% of the people like Our Brand. We show them a commercial. If we come back on the following day and ask identical questions, we might find that the proportion in favor had risen to 70%. There would have been a net gain of twenty percentage points.

If we find only 40% favorable to Our Brand in the second interview we have encountered a "boomerang effect." Our commercial must not only have been unconvincing; it must somehow have irritated the audience and produced the reverse effect from that intended. (The "boomerang effect" is by no means a hypothetical matter. In a study for ABC of 75 "roughly representative" radio commercials, Daniel Yankelovich found that three out of ten were doing an effective job, three out of ten might be doing more harm than good, and the rest were deficient in one important way or another. Eric Marder, who has made many studies of advertising's effects on brand top-of-mind awareness and purchase intention, finds that some ads seem to alienate more customers than they win over. This finding shocks many advertisers, but it should surprise no one who has encountered salesmen who antagonize the very customers with whom they are trying to ingratiate themselves.)

The effect of our message is not necessarily stable and lasting. In the case where our message had a positive effect, we might come back after a couple of weeks have elapsed and again survey the group to find out what has happened to these newly acquired opinions. Suppose we found that 70% were still favorable as they were at first. We could thereupon conclude that the effect of the message had persisted. We might find on the contrary, that the favorable proportion had actually increased to 80%. This would point to a so-called "sleeper effect": the message took a while to really sink in, and some of the people who did not change their minds immediately after seeing the commercial, on later reflection may have been influenced more than they were at first. Or, finally, we might find that the proportion favorable to Our Brand had dropped to 60%. This would still leave a net gain of 10%.

This kind of study can be done in the laboratory far better than in the market place. Actually, to talk of people as if they all fit into one of two categories — favorable or unfavorable to Our Brand — is greatly simplifying reality, since in life one normally makes choices among many possibilities, not between just two. Apart from the group which has *no* opinion, there may be many shades of favorable or unfavorable opinion, and there may also be many degrees of conviction with which a given shade of opinion is held. To add to the complexity of the matter, it might be possible to go back and survey at repeated intervals of time to find out what further changes, if any, occur, as people are exposed to still more new advertising messages.

Another, more sophisticated way of looking at the effects of a communication is to use comparable matched groups. This is what we normally do in test marketing. If we survey two identical groups of people we would presumably find that both of them are favorable to Our Brand in the same degree, let's say by a proportion of 50% in each case. Suppose we now showed Group A our commercial and showed Group B two minutes of Smokey the Bear extinguishing forest fires. Taking our survey afterwards, we would presumably find that the group that had seen the Smokey film (our control group) would not have changed its attitudes toward Our Brand, whereas the group that had seen the commercial might be more favorable than before.[9]

[9] The job of persuasion becomes harder as the proportion of already persuaded people grows. If only 25% of the population now like Our Brand, then 75% of the public remain to be convinced. If half the public already are on our side, then half remain to be convinced. If opinion is 75% favorable, then 25% represent the potential for persuasion.

Some very important implications follow from this very simple concept. Suppose that our objective is to win over 10% of the unfavorable or unconvinced group. If our

Such a favorable effect may be the result of various causes besides our commercial, however. Suppose that Our Competitor launches a clever campaign to discredit Our Brand between the showing of our commercial and the second survey. The favorable proportion in the control group may fall from 50% to 40%. The group that *had* seen the commercial might show the same percentage favorable as before, 50%. We should still conclude that the commercial had had a favorable effect, if it offset the unfavorable effects of other messages working in the opposite direction.

Or suppose that we have unexpected good news — an unsolicited endorsement of Our Brand by the World's Leading Authority. We might find on our second survey that the Smokey group is more favorable than it was and that the others are even *more* favorable, 90% compared with 70%. In this case, we would say that the effect of our message was felt over and above the favorable trend.

The foregoing examples are of course a simplification of reality, in which many competitive pressures and influences are constantly at work. There are endless combinations of residual effects, sleeper effects, and boomerang effects which have to be sifted out in a real-life comparison of groups with different degrees of advertising exposure. Moreover, when we leave the artificial conditions of the laboratory test, we must match groups of people in terms of sex, age, income, and all the many other social characteristics which might by themselves influence brand opinion or buying behavior.

This matching job is important when we conduct repeated samplings of a given population. At the same time, the researcher always works within margins of statistical error, and samples have to be large enough to keep these down to a minimum. To handle this situation, survey technicians sometimes go back a number of times to the same sample of people. (This group is referred to as a *panel*, whether they are questioned only on two occasions or enlisted to cooperate for a lifetime.) Suppose a survey among members of a panel shows 50% favorable to Our Brand, as in the previous illustration. Then we put our commercial on the air and ask our panel members to watch it. Exposure to it would still be purely optional and voluntary. If we survey the same people tomorrow, we may again find 50% who like Our Brand. We

---

original "share of mind" or share of market is 25%, achieving our new objective means that we move substantially forward, reaching a new share totaling 32½%. If our original share is 50%, however, a 10% rate of persuasion brings in a smaller number of new converts, raising our position from 50% to 55%. If 75% of the public are already on our side, then we move only to 77½% if we succeed in convincing 10% of the unconvinced. The stronger our brand position, the harder it is for us to make advances in our total share of the market. Gains are always relative to the starting point.

could easily conclude that the commercial had no effects. Actually, its effect may have been different with different members of the group, and these changes may have cancelled each other out. Everything we know about the market indicates that people are constantly testing ideas and goods; they are constantly switching loyalties, allegiances, and attitudes. Unless we are aware of the dynamic movement that goes on within the public mind, the fact that repeated surveys show no change may lead us to wrong conclusions.

Analyzing further, we might find, if we considered only the people who on the first wave of our survey had shown themselves to be favorable to Our Brand, that 70% were still favorable but that 30% had switched to an unfavorable position. We might find, conversely, that 30% of those who had been unfavorable before the commercial had switched in a favorable direction. In other words, it might seem that the commercial had convinced 30% of those previously unfavorable but at the same time had a boomerang effect on 30% of those who previously had been favorable. This again would be a logical, but a wrong conclusion.

People who are already predisposed to take a particular position tend to expose themselves more to messages which favor that position. Ford owners are more alert than Chevrolet owners to Ford advertising. We would expect those who favor Our Brand to be more cooperative about watching Our Commercial. We should therefore compare the proportions that saw the message among those who were favorable and those who were unfavorable on the first wave. We might find that 4 out of 5 of these previously favorable people had seen it. And we might find that 2 out of 5 of those who were previously unfavorable had also seen it. Accordingly, we must look at the matter in still greater detail, dividing up our sample not only in terms of what people thought on the first survey, but also in terms of whether they had been exposed to the message.

We might find that, of those who had been exposed and were originally favorable, 75% were still favorable on the second survey, whereas 25% had changed their minds. Among those who were previously unfavorable but who had seen the commercial, 50% might now be favorable and 50% remain unfavorable. We might find the same proportion among the smaller group who were previously favorable but who had not seen the film. Among the group which had previously been unfavorable and which had not been exposed to the message, only 17% might have switched.

In other words, there are two proportions which we have to consider. One is the contrasting percentages of change within each group originally holding an opinion for those who were exposed and for those who were not exposed to the message. The other is the percentage which each of these subgroups represents within the total population.

A real advertising campaign program is an extended process, and people can seldom be divided into either/or groups according to whether they have experienced exposure or non-exposure. To come to serious conclusions about advertising effects, we must measure the varying *degrees* of exposure. We must measure exposure not only to our own messages, but to the various competitive messages which work as counter-influences. Ideally we must measure these changes at intervals of time. Although the use of a panel has technical advantages in this respect, it also has an important limitation. Surveys themselves are communications; they sensitize people to the subjects about which questions are asked and thereby independently influence attitudes or behavior between one round and the next. This is the so-called "panel effect." Thus, in practice, a panel study is often combined with repeated surveys of different cross sections of the public at large.

In sum, it is not easy to measure the effectiveness of a given advertising campaign. It is easy to take measurements, and it is easy enough to find differences which can be interpreted as effects, but to come to conclusions that can be justified by scientific criteria requires elaborate and intelligent research design and large samples. All of this is frightfully expensive, and it is not unusual for an analysis to take so much time to complete that the results, when they come in, may no longer have much relevance to a changed situation.

Profit and peril in market tests

The marketer limits the number of variables which affect his research results when he conducts his studies within the framework of a single market — or a few selected markets — in which he has better control over his own brand's input and is better able to observe what his competitors do.

Such market testing is common enough in introducing innovations in the product itself, in pricing, or in packaging. Different advertising strategies are often compared by the same technique — or even as part of a study with broader objectives, before a national campaign is launched.

In measuring the effectiveness of advertising, four elements must be considered: first is the level of advertising pressure which will yield the greatest volume of profitable sales; second is the medium or media mix which will yield the best results; third is the scheduling of particular units of space and time through particular vehicles within a medium;

and fourth is the creative treatment most appropriate to that use of that medium at that level of expenditure. When we embark on a study of advertising effectiveness, we should be clear in our minds as to which of these four elements we are measuring. In practice, most studies of effectiveness are intended to be evaluations of media, but end up measuring everything else at the same time. Therein lies their great weakness.

Different media require different minimum investments. For a given creative approach and a given frequency schedule, there is probably an optimum investment in each medium. Moreover, to do a given job different media might yield different rates of return at different levels of investment. To illustrate: Outdoor advertising might yield $5 of new sales for every dollar of advertising investment regardless of whether that investment was at the rate of $1,000 or $10,000 in a market. Another medium, say, radio, might show a yield of $3 of sales for every dollar of advertising investment when only $1,000 was being expended in the market, but this might go up to $8 of sales per dollar of advertising at the $10,000 investment level. With still another medium — e.g., direct mail — the pattern might work in reverse. It might be that spending at the rate of $1,000 per market on direct mail will bring in $10,000 in sales. But spending at the rate of $10,000 might yield only $20,000. Such differences, while they seem plausible enough, must be stated as hypothetical examples, because there is no published evidence which covers the range of media uses at different expenditure levels for different marketing objectives.

In practice, most market tests of advertising involve comparisons of media, expenditure levels, or both. But for every expenditure level in every medium there are a great variety of possible forms and strategies, and an even greater number of creative alternatives. All too often the tester is willing to believe that his results measure the media or budget factors that he wants to measure, when his scheduling or theming may have far greater effects on the outcome.

Market tests have another limitation: a change in the existing pattern of advertising creates a certain effect of its own in combination with the previous pattern. The so-called "bicycle theory" of media planning argues for periodic changes of the media mix in order to shake up the consumers and make them more aware of the product. In a famous study of the Hawthorne Western Electric plant a number of years ago,[10] two industrial psychologists (Fritz L. Roethlisberger and William J. Dickson) began by varying the physical conditions under which a group of girls were working. They found to their surprise that

---

[10] *Management and the Worker,* Cambridge: Harvard University Press, 1939.

even when the working conditions were made less pleasant, productivity continued to rise because the experiment was indirectly building the morale of the group. Something like this often happens in test-market situations when the sales force, dealers, and local media knock themselves out in support of the promotion because they are interested in the test. Their level of performance could simply never be achieved on a national scale. Yet the fine results of the test may be attributed to the advertising alone.

Valid market tests depend on proper controls, which must exist not only in space but also in time. Enough markets must be used as tests and controls to wash out the effects of unpredictable local conditions. We must have an adequate benchmark period, and we must consider seasonal sales variations. If the test period is too short, we may miss the long-run sleeper effects. If it is too long, the results we are looking for may be completely dissipated under the pressure of competitive activity.

Actual sales are the only meaningful criterion of success, and every marketer watches his own sales figures anxiously. But factory or ware-house shipments to the retailer don't necessarily reflect "sell-through" (retail sales to the consumer) nor do they generally reflect it within a territory that coincides with an advertising test market. Sales measurement presupposes good controls over advertising coverage, controls in time and in geography, and controls over such non-advertising elements as the level of distribution, point-of-sale display, and dealer support or other merchandising efforts.

It is easier to design a study to measure the effectiveness of adver-tising for a new product than for a product which is already in the mar-ket. Too often in this latter type of test, the product itself and the distribution method are being evaluated along with the advertising. In evaluating an advertising campaign to launch a brand-new product in a highly competitive market, however, the question of whether or not to go ahead must often be answered on the basis of a qualitative judg-ment long before the research results are in. The soap companies provide an exception; their decisions about new products are made with great deliberation. But in many cases of less affluent advertisers the decision to pour more money into promotional support of a new product is made fairly early in the game, under the pressure of anxiety about competitive counter-moves. Long before the store audit results have been tabulated, an assessment may have to be based on informal reports of salesman, dealer, and customer reaction.

Where an advertising campaign has the objective of improving the sales and brand position of an existing brand in a competitive market, the only conclusive test is the long-run sales curve. But few items are bought by consumers so frequently that store movement shows a rapid response to advertising which is not supported by unusual promotional effort. Most companies do not have the resources or the patience to wait a long time for results to show. Because of the pressure of time, market tests are often conducted on the basis of unrealistic levels of advertising expenditure. There is a strong incentive to overspend in order to get significant measurable effects over a short period. Unfortunately, this kind of concentration of advertising does not necessarily give us a good basis to predict what will happen when advertising is run at a level the company can afford in a wider market.

To promote a particular product, spending $3,000 in a market in one month might be as effective as, less effective than, or more effective than spreading it out over three months. Spending at the $3,000 monthly rate might be more efficient, less efficient, or as efficient in terms of the yield per dollar of advertising investment as spending at the monthly level of $1,000. The problem is different for different products with different consumer purchase cycles. It also varies according to the position of the advertiser in his field and the brand share he begins with.

Market tests often employ a media mix that is very different from any that would be used in a national campaign. Certain media, like newspapers and radio, lend themselves more readily to testing than do others, like network television and magazines, simply because the production costs represent a smaller share of the budget. Can one really generalize (as I have seen done) from the test performance of newspapers as a print medium to the national use of magazines or supplements; or from the test performance of local spot television to the performance of a network program?

A further difficulty with market tests stems from their character as just one more weapon in the competitive struggle. When Procter & Gamble test-marketed a new Duncan Hines cake frosting in Phoenix, General Mills rushed into the same stores with a test of a similar product. General Mills' Betty Crocker brand did well and was taken out for broader distribution. The Duncan Hines brand was withdrawn. The marketing manager of another company complained about his competitors to a reporter: "They make special price deals on their own products with the stores, they expand their advertising heavily, and they'll even do things like yanking the number one brand off the shelves temporarily just to foul up sales comparisons. One firm even bought up most of the available radio and TV spots when word leaked out we were going into a city for test marketing." [11]

[11] *Wall Street Journal*, May 24, 1966.

A coffee company raised the price of its premium grade product and put it in a fancy canister for a market test. The canister was copied by a rival firm, which used its cheapest grade and cut the price in the same market, thereby effectively ruining the test. According to the *Wall Street Journal,*

> The heightened competition in test markets has become disquieting to many marketing men. They fear it is distorting the sales results obtained in these experiments, thereby reducing the effectiveness of an important research tool widely used by makers of consumer products; far too many products that presumably have done well in test markets are proving to be busts in general distribution, they note, and failures in the test-market phase itself are too frequent.[12]

In the time interval between test marketing and introduction of and distribution of a product on a national scale, consumer tastes and the competitive picture may both change substantially. For this reason, some companies (for instance, in the cosmetics field) are willing to assume greater risks of failure with a new product if by doing so they can gain a time advantage.

In short, test marketing's principal headaches arise from the often contradictory requirements of being scientific and being practical. A market test run on the timetable and spending level of the national market carries with it the risk of not having significant findings soon enough. And always the question remains whether the experiment is *really* controlled, whether extraneous forces have not intervened!

The pitfalls of test marketing are always surmountable, at a price. An extraordinary facility designed to overcome all the ordinary problems of matching test markets was set up in 1964 by the Milwaukee *Journal.* This "Milwaukee Advertising Laboratory" makes it possible to combine rigorous experimental controls with the advantages of testing in a real-life field situation. The result is achieved by a combination of ingenious techniques: first, the division of the Milwaukee metropolitan area into a checkerboard pattern totaling up to A and B markets with virtually identical population characteristics; second, a controlled pattern for distributing all newspapers and a substantial number of magazine subscriptions in terms of the two areas; third, a "muter" device attached to the television sets in a sample of 750 A homes and 750 B homes. (The muter, silently controlled by a special signal from the transmitter, turns off test commercials on sets in the designated sample.)

Consumer purchases of packaged goods are recorded through a weekly diary record filled out by consumers. The uncontrollable forces of competitive activity, weather, distribution, and the like that plague conventional test marketing obviously do not apply in the Advertising Laboratory, since they are always identical in Markets A and B. This makes it possible to measure the direct sales effects of different expenditure levels, media strategies, and creative approaches.

There seems to be little doubt that the Milwaukee Laboratory offers a unique opportunity to study the effects of advertising, at least for the kinds of packaged goods whose purchases can be conveniently recorded with a consumer diary. The Laboratory successfully anticipates and meets most of the objections which have been raised in our preceding discussion. Yet the Laboratory is set up to run no more than fifty or sixty tests at a time, and it can accommodate only a limited number of clients.

The Laboratory is one of the best resources yet developed for investigating both the general and the particular unknowns in advertising strategy. But for the small or middle-sized advertiser who is impatient to measure specific aspects of a campaign, the Laboratory still may be unable to supply all the answers at a price consistent with the investment in advertising itself. The experimenting advertiser, for any given product, must still measure the effects of only one strategic variation at a time, whether it be budget, media mix, media scheduling, or creative treatment. This painstaking manipulation of the advertising and measurement of sales is not easy or inexpensive.

Test marketing is, of course, here to stay; it has innumerable uses, and presents the illusion of great simplicity. But it can offer clear answers to advertising questions only when it is carried out meticulously and on a large scale. As in all forms of advertising research, the value of information must be weighed realistically against the risks of getting faulty information through an inadequate research investment.

Attitude and action

Every evaluation of advertising effects through consumer surveys must sooner or later come to grips with the question of how the things that people tell interviewers relate to their actual buying behavior.

The relationship between attitude and action has been given considerable study by social psychologists, and it has become a favorite subject of marketing theorists as well. Robert C. Lavidge and Gary A. Steiner hypothesize the existence of a "hierarchy of advertising effects" ranging from awareness, comprehension, and conviction to knowledge and purchase of the product.[13] Brian Copland [14] looks at the hierarchy of effects as a series of probabilities. The higher up people are on the ladder (from awareness to acceptance of the product claim), the greater the likelihood that they will be buyers. The same view is implicit in the assumption of General Motors' Gail Smith that "attitudes and/or knowledge affect behavior." Smith considers this one of the three basic assumptions of advertising, and reports, "We have examined this assumption through our Advertising Effectiveness Program and, as far as automobiles are concerned, we have found it to be true." [15] The evidence Smith cites — for an "average brand" of car — relates preferences to actual purchases made within the following six months. Among those purchasers who earlier listed the make as their first choice, 56% bought it, compared with only 22% of those who "would consider it favorably," 9% of those who would merely consider it, and 3% of those who said they would not consider it.

"A direct and close relationship between existing levels of preference [for a brand] . . . and their relative purchase by housewives" was reported by Seymour Banks, who interviewed and reinterviewed 465 housewives.[16]

His conclusion that brand attitudes are good predictors of product use was verified by Cornelius DuBois of Foote, Cone & Belding.[17] Incidentally, DuBois found how a brand's market share can remain constant at the same time that there is considerable turnover in brand usage. The proportion using the brand was exactly the same in the three interview periods. However, 11% of the women stopped using the brand during the period studied, and 11% shifted to the use of the brand; only 17% were users on both occasions. (The remainder did not use the brand at all during the period studied.)

Summarizing 27 studies made by the Grey Advertising Agency,

---

[13] "A Model for Predictive Measurements of Advertising Effectiveness," *Journal of Marketing,* Vol. 25, October 1961, pp. 59-62.

[14] Talk to the 1963 meeting of the Advertising Research Foundation, New York, N.Y.

[15] Address made on June 14, 1966, to the American Marketing Association, Chicago, Ill.

[16] "The Relationships Between Preference and Purchase of Brands," *Journal of Marketing,* Vol. 15, No. 2, October 1950, pp. 145-57.

[17] "The Story of Brand XL; How Consumer Attitudes Affected Its Market Position," Foote, Cone & Belding, New York (no date). Dubois interviewed a probability sample of women in April 1958, then reinterviewed half in June and half in October. Among the users who had called the brand "one of the best" at the time of the first interview, 68% continued using it. Among users who called it "good" in April, 50% continued using it; among the small number who gave it a less favorable rating, only 28% continued using it. Among non-users, those with more favorable attitudes were more likely to become users in the subsequent months. DuBois lays stress on the differences in attitude patterns among different brands and differences in the proportion of users who keep on using it.

whose research department he heads, Alvin Achenbaum[18] has reported that the more favorable the attitude toward a product, the higher the incidence of usage; the less favorable the attitudes are, the lower the usage. The more unfavorable people are toward a product, the more likely they are to stop using it. However, people who have never tried a product have attitudes which are distributed in the shape of a normal bell-shaped curve around the average. Achenbaum found that for a beverage brand "the retention of users is extremely high among people who have very favorable attitudes and much lower among those with unfavorable attitudes," and that the brand's ability to attract former non-users was greatest among those who were most favorable at the outset. Achenbaum analyzes how attitudes on specific attributes relate to the general attitude toward a brand, and concludes that "no one set of specific attitudes is universally applicable to all products. Each product category has its own unique set of factors by which people evaluate the desirability of the product."

Not all the evidence, however, is clear cut.[19] Jack Haskins[20] has examined seventeen studies reported in *Psychological Abstracts* (1954-1963) in which knowledge and attitude or behavior were correlated. Thirteen of these studies showed no conclusive relationship between the two, and the other four were evenly divided between positive and negative relationships.

In a notable presidential address before the Social Psychology division of the American Psychological Association, Leon Festinger reviewed a number of experiments in which attitude was changed by persuasive messages and in which some measure of *actual* behavior was also available.[21] He concluded that "we cannot glibly assume a relationship

---

[18] "Knowledge Is A Thing Called Measurement," in Lee Adler and Irving Crespi, *Attitude Research at Sea,* Chicago: American Marketing Association, 1966, pp. 111-26, and "An Answer to One of the Unanswered Questions About the Measurement of Advertising Effectiveness," address before the Advertising Research Foundation, October 1965, New York, N.Y.

[19] Reviewing the evidence from a number of studies, Kristian S. Palda concludes that changes in brand attitude are not necessarily directly related to changes in awareness. Cf. "The Hypothesis of a Hierarchy of Effects: A Partial Evaluation," *Journal of Marketing Research,* Vol. 3, No. 1, February 1966, pp. 13-24.   Horace Schwerin finds no consistent relationship between "playback" or unaided recall of TV commercials and "effectiveness" as measured by changes in brand preference as a result of forced exposure. "Commercials that eschew logic in favor of emotion — and in so doing fall into the twilight zone of 'mood sell' — are often impervious to playback analysis. People may be sold by the vital promise but they can't articulate the reasons for this conversion." Cf. *Schwerin Research Bulletin,* Vol. 13, No. 5, May 1965.   Arthur Wilkins has described a comparison of an established commercial and a brand new one which got a higher level of recall, but had less effect in increasing awareness of the brand (private communication).

[20] "Factual Recall as a Measure of Advertising Effectiveness," *Journal of Advertising Research,* Vol. 4, No. 1, March 1964, pp. 2-8.

[21] "Behavioral Support for Opinion Change," *Public Opinion Quarterly,* Vol. 28, No. 3, Fall 1964.

between attitude change and behavior." As an example he cited a study (made by Nathan Maccoby, A. K. Romney, J. S. Adams, and Eleanor Maccoby) of "critical periods" in seeking and accepting information. Here a group of mothers were experimentally induced to change their opinions about the proper time to start toilet training for infants. Between the first and the second interview, the mothers who had been "persuaded" did in fact change in their expectations as to when they would start toilet training. By the standards commonly in use, the persuasive effort would therefore be deemed successful. Festinger took a second look at the evidence on when the mothers *actually* started to toilet train their children, however, and found that there was, if anything, a *reverse* relationship between attitude change and behavior. The mothers in the experimental group started toilet training later than they had thought was right before they were "persuaded," but this was also true of mothers in the control group who were never under "persuasion" at all.

Festinger suggests that

> When opinions or attitudes are changed through the momentary impact of a persuasive communication, this change, all by itself, is inherently unstable and will disappear or remain isolated unless an environmental or behavioral change can be brought about to support and maintain it. . . . [In] order to produce a stable behavior change following opinion change, an environmental change must also be produced which, representing reality, will support the new opinion and the new behavior. Otherwise the same factors that produced the initial opinion and the behavior will continue to operate to nullify the effect of the opinion change.

Festinger's data have been reanalyzed by Alvin Achenbaum,[22] who points out that the conclusions are based on very small samples and that Festinger fails to take into account the substantial evidence from the field of market research which links opinion and behavior. Whether or not Festinger drew the correct inferences in his highly influential paper, a real question remains as to whether the levels of motivation involved in such significant actions as a mother's treatment of her child are qualitatively comparable with the processes involved in brand selection.

Another eminent social psychologist, Milton Rokeach,[23] has recently pointed out that there is a difference between one's "attitude toward the object" and one's "attitude toward the situation" in which the object is encountered. Thus changes in verbal opinion are not necessarily translated into redefinitions of a situation in which action is called for. From the standpoint of the advertiser, this analysis has a

---

[22] Address before the Advertising Research Foundation, October 1966, New York, N.Y.
[23] Paper before the World Association for Public Opinion Research, September 1965, Dublin. *Cf.* also his "Attitude Change and Behavioral Change," *Public Opinion Quarterly,* Vol. 30, No. 4, Winter 1966-67, pp. 529-50.

number of interesting implications. It suggests that the measures that researchers conventionally use to gauge advertising "effects" may be in the comparatively abstract realm of brand opinion which does not necessarily reproduce the competitive environment in which products are encountered in the store and buying choices are made. It helps explain why consumers may be more motivated to change their buying actions when there are real changes in the product than as a result of advertising alone. And it places advertising, which seeks to persuade people to change their opinions, into the framework of the total marketing environment, which includes distribution and shelf-facings, and which must be propitious for opinion change to result in action.

One of the most ambitious published tests of advertising media effectiveness was made for Lucite paint and has been reported by Malcolm McNiven,[24] former advertising research director of the DuPont Company, and now serving in a similar post with the Coca-Cola company. Before and after the campaign 10,000 persons were interviewed by phone in 27 test markets divided into nine three-market groups. Each of these three-market groups was exposed to one of five levels of expenditure in either TV or newspapers. For example, one group received no TV and moderate newspaper advertising, and a second had no newspapers and moderate TV. Each of the remaining seven groups had a different combination. McNiven found that in this instance TV advertising best communicated knowledge about Lucite but did not significantly affect its sales. The newspaper ads used in the test appeared to be unsuccessful in communicating knowledge of the product, but increased sales significantly.

In this case, as in so many similar experiments, one is left puzzled as to whether the apparent inconsistency between attitude change and behavior change reflects a real discrepancy or a communications effect which occurs below the threshold of conscious awareness or beyond the measurement capacity of the questions asked.

Commenting on McNiven's study, advertising psychologist Charles K. Ramond[25] points out that attitude change often appears to follow a sales change merely for the artificial reason that an attitude survey commonly occurs after a purchase is recorded in a sales audit:

> The interval between communication receipt and purchase is usually shorter than the interval between the before and after phases of the typical survey. . . . By the time the after survey gets around to the prospect, he may already have become a buyer. And by that time ex-

[24] Speech before the National Industrial Conference Board, September 1963, New York, N.Y.
[25] "Must Advertising Communicate to Sell?" *Harvard Business Review*, Vol. 43, No. 5, September-October 1965, pp. 148-59.

perience with the product has affected his attitudes ten to 1,000 times as much as his exposure to the advertisements or commercials.[26]

Ramond reports the case of a company's advertising director who said publicly that market tests are worthless, because of his experience in two matched markets. The one without increased advertising had considerably higher sales. "Upon investigation, he learned that the entire month's distribution of his product to the test city had been lost in a train wreck." While Ramond cautions against the use of less than three test markets, he does cite the findings of a number of smaller scale market tests which showed significant changes as a result of advertising in only one or two markets. He concludes that "as measures of marketing effectiveness, sales and communication together are preferable to either separately, because one does not always reflect the other."

Qualified findings are also advanced by Valentine Appel [27] of Benton & Bowles on the basis of an experiment he made to measure the relative effectiveness of two plans involving equivalent advertising expenditures. This research used eight groups of three matched markets each. Within each of the 24 markets, 200 users of the product category were interviewed on the telephone regarding brand awareness, attitude, and usage. Appel concluded that, with either plan, the advertising had only negligible effects in *changing* attitudes toward the test brand, but that the initial *level* of attitude was clearly related to whether the advertising had any effect on usage. Those consumers whose attitudes were least favorable to start with were least affected in product usage by exposure to the advertising. The advertising had its greatest sales effect among people who already were *somewhat* favorable to the brand rather than on those with the *most* favorable attitude who may have had little room for improvement.

The fact that the advertising could not be directly related to an attitude change in Appel's painstaking study does not mean that it wasn't working. Obviously, the people who were favorable to the brand must have been made favorable by something in the past, and this may have been earlier advertising campaigns or actual experience with the product. If advertising does nothing more than remind an already predisposed individual to buy the product it must certainly be having an effect, albeit one which is related to the product's need to "tread water" to maintain its position in the market place.

John Stewart's Fort Wayne study of repetition in newspaper advertising (see page 183) found that information, awareness, and attitude

[26] *Ibid.*, pp. 151-52.
[27] Valentine Appel, "Attitude Change: Another Dubious Method for Measuring Advertising Effectiveness," in Lee Adler and Irving Crespi, editors, *Attitude Research at Sea, op. cit.*, pp. 141-52. *Cf.* also *Media/scope,* May 1966, p. 59.

toward the test products did not relate directly to sales at any point in time, although there appeared to be a general relationship. Growing awareness was accompanied by a sharpening of information retained and by more favorable attitudes. More people became aware of the advertised products as the campaign progressed, and those people who were aware of them tended to become better informed and more favorable.

The findings in Fort Wayne suggest that we must think of the effects of advertising as extending for some time after a campaign ends. Thus not merely the *level* of effect, but its *duration* must be considered in any evaluation. Through a gimmick, an ad message may win a momentary but high level of awareness. Another may make a lasting impression on a smaller number of people. A fair comparison of different media strategies requires that measurements be made at various points during a campaign and afterwards.

The attitudes that people form toward products like the ones tested seem to be much more dramatically influenced by actual usage and experience than by any amount of advertising exposure. Consumers in Stewart's study who at the point of sale ran across a product they had not seen advertised and who were nonetheless stimulated to buy and try it, became more sharply and favorably aware of it than consumers who perceived and bought it as a run-of-the-mill advertised product.

The Fort Wayne study forces us to consider the function of advertising in perspective along with all the other elements in the marketing mix. New products were deliberately chosen by the researcher so that there would be no preconceptions in people's minds and so that the situation could be controlled as much as possible. Nonetheless, active competitive pressures continued while both campaigns were on. Each of these products was differently priced relative to its competition. Users of the one were more satisfied with it than users of the other. In spite of the best efforts of the two companies involved, the distribution of one product never got up above the half-way mark, while in the case of the other product it was almost complete.

In the face of marketing forces as powerful as these, the influence of advertising is limited. Consider just two marketing variables studied by Stewart: the consumer's education and her general familiarity with brands in a product category. Awareness of one of the test products was 7% among consumers in the bottom half of the educational scale who showed low brand familiarity. It was 44% for better educated, brand-familiar respondents. Advertising has the task of imposing an influence above and beyond major influences from the life cycle or life style such as these data reflect. When we understand this, we can appreciate the difficulty of isolating its specific effects.

Experiments and creativity

There is an imbalance between the amount of laboratory experimentation on advertising effectiveness and the amount done in the field. Most studies of advertising effects are done in the field, and too often they suffer from inadequate design and inadequate controls. For every dollar of research money expended, advertising efficiency can often be increased more by pre-testing creative approaches than by studies of completed campaigns in actual operation. Laboratory experiments are more likely to come up with significant differences that lend themselves to meaningful interpretation and that can be translated into realistic action.

The cost of truly scientific investigation of the problems that most advertisers want to research under the heading of effectiveness is very often out of all proportion to the cost of the advertising itself. If such research is to be done, it should be honestly done in the name of science, and not justified in terms of its practical utility to the decisions of advertising managements.

However, there is an aspect of advertising whose effectiveness lends itself to extremely profitable research, with a pay-out that is much more immediate than any comparison of media. This is the creative aspect.

Carl Hendrikson, a leading market researcher, reports on an experimental study on the comparative effectiveness of print and radio advertising, made just before the TV era began. An advertising message was prepared for a brand of toothpaste in two forms: a print ad and a recorded commercial. There were two make-believe brands of toothpaste used in this comparison. Each person interviewed saw the print ad for one brand and heard a recording of the commercial for the other brand. He was then offered a tube of toothpaste and given his choice of the two brands in question.

Offhand this sounds a good deal like many of the experimental intermedia comparisons that have been made over the years. But the results were tabulated as soon as they came in, in groups of 25. In the first few groups, the recorded message enjoyed an advantage over the print ad. In subsequent groups, the two were about equal. Later on the print message did much better. In other words, as the study progressed, the print message did progressively better and the recorded message did progressively poorer.

The explanation for this became clear when the recording as it sounded after many playings was compared with the quality of a fresh pressing. It still sounded pretty good. But something of the resonance, the tone values, the subtle qualitative inflections of the announcer's voice had deteriorated with the repeated playing of the record. This new variable completely reversed the position of the two media which were being compared. Minor variations in the creative handling of a message may have more to do with the nature of what is communicated than the difference between media.

The knowing practitioner of advertising is under no illusion that copy tests, whatever ingenious or devious devices they may use, can substitute for talent, taste, or insight. Herbert Krugman points out that ads are tested and compared once, but that in real life we encounter advertisements many times, and our responses change in the process.

The variations in performance within a medium are far greater than those among different media. Any time that several ads or commercials are tested, one is apt to come away with a lion's share while the others creep in with only a small percentage of favorable response. Just as copy tests show how ads and commercials differ widely in their power to persuade and convince, so standard readership and commercial recall services document the variations in the power of ads or commercials to register conscious remembered impressions upon the mind of the reader or viewer.

For instance, the median 1,000-line newspaper food ad gets a Starch noting score of 32 among women, but it can get as low as 15, or as high as 61. The median liquor ad of 660 lines is noted by one out of five men readers, but some of the ads get only a few per cent noting and others get over 50%.[28]

Consider two outdoor campaigns with an identical number and quality of billboard displays in the same community. The one for Standard of Indiana showed an 82% higher recall than the one for Shell.

With a recall measure which demands more of the audience's memory, the gap between the strongest and weakest advertising looks even greater. Gallup and Robinson report that 15 best remembered TV food commercials score 39 times better than the lowest 15. Studies by Kenyon and Eckhardt show variations of the order of 30 to 1 in the holding power of different TV commercials.[29]

An Art Carney TV show and a Bob Hope show a few years ago

---

[28] Daniel Starch & Staff, in a 1957 report on "Tested Copy," analyzed 3,395 food ads (of over 50 lines) in 198 newspaper studies conducted in 1952-54. The smallest ads had a median noting score of 9%. Ads of 1500 lines and over (30 or more times larger) had a median score which was five times as great — 45%. However, noting for the smallest size ads ranged up as high as 34%, whereas the highest noting score for a big ad was 78%. Thus the smallest ads received, on the average, only one-fifth as much recognition from women as the standard large ad, but the best of the small ads received nearly 50% as much recognition as did the very large ads.

[29] Cf. Joseph C. Franklin, "Using Quantitative Order to Reduce Qualitative Confusion in Creating TV Commercials Which Communicate More Effectively," paper read at American Psychological Association meetings, September 6, 1960, Chicago, Ill.

had almost the same talent and network time costs.   The rating of the Carney show was 17; the rating of the Hope show was 41.   There is no report of a national rating service in which one cannot find fantastic variations in the size of audiences delivered by programs with identical production and time costs.

Sponsor identification studies show similar variations in the ability of viewers to associate commercials with the programs they view.   In one comparison, 51% of the viewers of the Danny Thomas show could identify its sponsor, compared with only 19% of the viewers of the Perry Mason show.

In a series of studies done by Benton & Bowles, Arthur Wilkins found that in some cases 50% of the TV commercial audience was just viewing TV while the program was on, while in other cases fewer than 30% were just watching.   This type of variation would not be revealed by any rating figures, yet the level of commercial recall in the attentive segment averaged 60% higher than in the less attentive segment.

Studies on the creative side of advertising lend themselves far better to exact experimentation of the laboratory type than do studies which compare media.   When we make media comparisons in the laboratory, we measure something different from the normal kind of media exposure which takes place in real life.   The medium's strong and weak points, relative to other media, are not necessarily in proper proportion. When we confine our comparisons to alternative creative approaches within a medium, the conditions of exposure can be held constant and the planner can concentrate on the variations in the message itself.   This is the area in which research investments to improve the effectiveness of advertising can have the greatest leverage on the final results.

CONCLUSION 14

The cartoon figure on the television screen who pops up from the back of the cereal box is meaningful to a child because it symbolizes emotions, wishes, and needs which are stirred in him but are left unsatisfied by the real persons in his life. The imaginary creature enters his fantasies and dreams, becoming a part — small, perhaps — of the vital experience through which the child defines himself as a unique human being. To reduce the process by which all this happens into a series of "exposures" and "impressions" is obviously nonsensical, and yet advertising men — we great experts in "communication" — go through this nonsense every business day.

Because the mass media are so largely supported by advertising, they cannot help being shaped by the kinds of judgments and assumptions which advertisers make. As long as many of these assumptions rest (as I have tried to demonstrate they do) on the crude mechanistic notion of communication as a series of events, advertising decision-makers will be mainly concerned with numbers rather than with meaning. And the search for numbers — for big, demonstrable, measurable numbers — inevitably must be reflected in the attitudes of those who operate the mass media for profit.

The publisher or broadcaster (when he takes off his green eyeshade and slips on his toga) has always proclaimed his responsibility to mediate the complexity of the world for a broad public in the form of either information or art. Some media operators come close to fulfilling this ideal; many don't bother to try. It may be that the very notion of mass media is incompatible with the highest levels of intellectual or artistic achievement — not because of the deficiencies of the mass audience, but because mass media require production on deadlines and in massive quantities. The pool of talent available to the publisher or television producer may be utterly insufficient to permit him week after week to perform at the highest level of his responsibility or of his medium's potential. But if there are flaws in the quality of mass media, far better that they be flaws of inadequacy than flaws of intent. The intentional flaws — which arise from a cynical view of the audience — go with a philosophy which makes quantity rather than character the criterion of success.

Decisions about advertising have important implications for other decisions made by a business organization. They represent a deployment of resources which could be used in other ways; they involve expectations of profit. Businessmen want to solve advertising problems as they solve other business problems, using comparable techniques of assessment, evaluation, and research. But while decisions involving evaluation and research are also business decisions, standards of research are essentially a non-business matter.

A good many advertising men are uncertain about advertising research's status as science. But even those who are the most contemptuous of its integrity show no hesitation in using it when it serves their purpose. Advertising costs money and there is a constant clamor to find out whether that money is being returned with interest. To satisfy this clamor, numbers — any recent and possibly relevant numbers — are in great demand. New circulation reports, audience figures, noting scores, and innumerable other statistics pour forth each week; they are the staff of advertising life. Who in American marketing refuses to take the importance of these numbers for granted? Who digs into their meanings, questions their usefulness, asks whether the emperor really is wearing clothes?

A century ago, strategy problems in advertising revolved around the question of what to say rather than over the technique of expressing it or the choice of means by which to say it. Advertising skills primarily entailed the manipulation of words and their meanings.

Today the term "advertising" is subsumed under broader headings. For the retailer it is part of merchandising; for the manufacturer it is part of marketing. In either case, the preparation of advertisements is subordinated to a larger objective and is part of a larger planning process in which product design, pricing, selling tactics, and other considerations must enter and may, in fact, predominate.

Marketing (or merchandising) presupposes planning, order, time tables, schedules, and synchronization of activities with other time-dependent business operations — investment, product research, production, distribution.

These requirements of orderly planning are fundamentally at odds with the nature of the creative process. To be sure, creative geniuses (Mozart, for example) *can* work on schedules and meet fixed deadlines. The application of sustained effort over time may result in productivity, but it will not always yield inspiration. And most advertising does indeed represent the productive output of advertising "factories" rather than inspiration.

One of the things that makes advertising an unusually interesting field of activity is that it involves a perpetual state of tension between its aspect as business and its aspect as art. I have suggested throughout this book that in advertising the Idea has *primacy*, whether it be Great or otherwise.[1] But it should not necessarily have *priority*. Just as the Idea must be framed to fit the requirements of the product, so it must often be chosen to reach a particular marketing target and directed to suit the requirements of a medium. The Idea is not merely a matter of *what* is said. Everything depends on the encapsulation of the message in a phrase, a picture, a headline, a juxtaposition of images which is unique and memorable.

In advertising, as in conversation, it is sometimes better to say nothing than to say something not worth saying, either because it has been said before or because it makes no sense. The company which cannot be distinctive in its product field might do well to cancel its advertising until it *does* have something to say.

The reader who has come this far may be somewhat disappointed to find that there is no set of do's and don't's at the end of these pages, no

[1] It is the failure to understand the primacy of the Idea, of content over technique, that sometimes leads to delusions of grandeur on the part of those innocents who proclaim that advertising men could win "The Battle For Men's Minds" if only they were unleashed on the international propaganda front!

list of guidelines for action on his particular problems. In advertising, as in chess or war, strategy does not consist of rules or principles, for if these existed the opponent would have a predictable counter-move for every move made. Strategy consists rather of a posture (of wariness and guile) and a method of approaching problems.

Advertising planners can indeed call upon a vast body of existing information to help with the decisions they face today, but the way in which past experience may be applied to present problems is always unique to the product, the company, the competition. To say that "it all depends" is not to say that it all depends on chance or faith. While both these factors may influence the way the planner arrives at the solution which turns out to be correct, the solution itself most often consists of the right combination of unrelated principles.

Market analysis, like psychoanalysis, may create sensitivity to the consequences of one's acts. Psychoanalysis may make an individual more tactful, more alert to other people's reactions and expectations, but it cannot endow him with intelligence, charm, or spontaneity. Similarly, market analysis and research may tell a company who its best prospective customers are, what they think, and even what arguments might be most persuasive to them. But it cannot tell the company how to embody this knowledge in great advertising.

A television version of "Hamlet" performed by the Old Vic Company was once run through an audience reaction test, which found the action parts of the play to be more "involving" than the great speeches. The study's author, Jack Roberts, later reported that "from other test results, we'd probably be told the killing of the king doesn't come soon enough and there's too much talking with all those soliloquys." [2]

Just as a great play is more than the sum of its individual lines, so The Great Idea in advertising is far more than the sum of the recognition scores, the ratings, and all the other superficial indicators of its success; it is in the realm of myth, to which measurements cannot apply.

Communication is a process, not a thing. It involves people, not material objects. It embodies in even its most trivial aspects the total outlook, expectations, and values of the protagonists. A company can no more stay in business without advertising today than an individual can exist without communicating with others. By gesture, intonation, rhythm, stance, and style we give overtones to all the words we utter. They reflect our unique personalities. By the same token, every company too is unique, because of the people in it. Some are dull and some have flair. Their advertising tells it. We *feel* the difference.

[2] *Schwerin Research Bulletin*, Vol. 13, No. 3, March 1965.

BIBLIOGRAPHY
A Guide to Further
Reading and Inquiry

Periodicals

The most trenchant commentary on American advertising unquestionably appears in *Mad* magazine, but the reader who wants to keep up with the profession on a continuing basis has other choices open to him. *Advertising Age* is the well-edited and authoritative weekly newspaper in the field. The two other advertising publications of general interest are *Printers' Ink,* a biweekly which specializes in background stories on individual products and companies, and *Madison Avenue,* a monthly which features personalities and is slanted to agency creative people. *Media/scope* and *Media Decisions,* also monthlies, are directed at media buyers and sellers and deal knowingly with many of the subjects discussed in this book.

Editor & Publisher is a news weekly that covers all aspects of the press (including non-advertising subjects). Its counterpart in television and radio is *Broadcasting. Sponsor* and *Television Age,* biweeklies, concentrate on news and feature stories of broadcast advertising. *Television* is an excellent slick monthly which includes commentary on advertising matters and commercial production, as well as on the state of the TV arts and the TV business.

The serious student of communications as a field of social psychology keeps up with the literature through such publications as the *American Psychologist,* the *Journal of Personality and Social Psychology,* the *Psychological Bulletin,* the *Psychological Review,* the *Journal of Social Psychology, The American Journal of Sociology,* and the *American Sociological Review.* Far less technical are the *Journalism Quarterly* and the *Television Quarterly.* All these journals cover a lot of ground; most articles may be of slight interest to the advertiser, but others present new research findings and statements of theory which are vital to understanding the subjects covered in the middle chapters of this book.

For those whose interests are more sharply focused on advertising, the key publication is the *Journal of Advertising Research*, published by the Advertising Research Foundation; the Foundation's annual conference proceedings and occasional publications are also always relevant to our subject. The *Journal of Marketing* and the *Journal of Marketing Research*, published by the American Marketing Association, often include articles on advertising. So, less frequently, do the *Harvard Business Review*, *The Journal of Business* (published at the University of Chicago), and the *Journal of Retailing* (published at New York University). *The Public Opinion Quarterly*, organ of the American Association for Public Opinion Research, reflects the viewpoint of applied social science and is usually the most readable publication of the lot.

Books

I have already had occasion throughout the text to refer to some of the most useful books that bear on problems of advertising strategy, and I shall not refer to them again here. However, there are a number of other writings I have not mentioned that I commend to the enterprising reader.

The most careful and comprehensive examination of advertising's place in the economy is Jules Backman's study (sponsored by the Association of National Advertisers), *Advertising in Competition* (New York: New York University Press, 1967). Until this publication, the classic study on the subject had been Neil H. Borden's book, *The Economic Effects of Advertising* (Homewood, Ill.: Richard D. Irwin, Inc., 1942).

One of the most thoughtful statements on the subject of advertising is by a British economist, Walter Taplin, *Advertising: A New Approach* (Boston: Little, Brown and Company, 1960). The only sociological study of the advertising profession is also British — Jeremy Tunstall's *The Advertising Man in London Advertising Agencies* (London: Chapman & Hall Ltd., 1964). There is a good symposium of essays on advertising's place in society edited by C. H. Sandage and Vernon Fryburger, *The Role of Advertising* (Homewood, Ill.: Richard D. Irwin, Inc., 1960). A highly readable account of the workings of advertising institutions is Martin Mayer's *Madison Avenue U.S.A.* (New York: Harper and Row, Inc., 1958). The A.A.A.A. study which deals with the public's attitudes toward advertising is presented in Raymond A. Bauer and Stephen A. Greyser, editors, in collaboration with William M. Weilbacher and Donald Kanter, *Advertising in America* (Cambridge: Harvard University, Division of Research, Graduate School of Business Administration, 1967).

The standard textbook on advertising agency operations is Otto Kleppner's *Advertising Procedure*, 5th edition (Englewood Cliffs, N.J.:

Prentice-Hall, Inc., 1966). Two excellent texts that deal with forms, systems, and procedures in the media field are Roger Barton's *Media in Advertising* (New York: McGraw-Hill Book Company, 1964) and Lyndon O. Brown, William M. Weilbacher and Richard S. Lessler's *Advertising Media* (New York: Ronald Press, 1957). Certainly any reader who deals or expects to engage in the actual practice of media buying should know what is in these books; I have not tried to duplicate their content.

For years the outstanding textbook on the application of psychology to advertising has been Darrell B. Lucas and Steuart H. Britt's *Advertising Psychology and Research* (New York: McGraw-Hill Book Company, 1950). Another authoritative work (which is also unfortunately now somewhat outdated) is Melvin Hattwick's *Psychology for Better Advertising* (Englewood Cliffs, N.J.: Prentice-Hall, Inc., 1950). Edgar Crane's *Marketing Communications* (New York: John Wiley & Sons, Inc., 1965) is a useful review of social science concepts relevant to advertising, directed at the undergraduate.

On the subject of measuring attitude change, the single most significant book of recent decades was Carl I. Hovland, Arthur A. Lumsdaine, and Fred D. Sheffield, editors, *Studies in Social Psychology in World War II, Volume III: Experiments in Mass Communication* (Princeton: Princeton University Press, 1949). This summarizes the experiments made by Hovland and his collaborators in connection with the Army's information and education program. It is interesting to compare this work with the later refinement of Hovland's theories in his postwar studies, such as Carl I. Hovland, Irving L. Janis, and Harold H. Kelley, *Communication and Persuasion* (New Haven: Yale University Press, 1953). An excellent recent summary of all the experimental studies in this area is Arthur R. Cohen's *Attitude Change and Social Influence* (New York: Basic Books, Inc., 1964).

The most dispassionate book no the motivation studies of the 1950's is Harry Henry's *Motivation Research* (New York: Frederick Ungar Publishing Company, 1958). Joseph Newman's book *Motivation Research and Marketing Management* (Cambridge: Harvard University Press, 1957) is of interest because it presents specific case histories as well as general theories.

The grand old man of advertising research is Daniel Starch. No one interested in such research should miss the summation of Starch's notable studies over the years, embodied in his book *Measuring Advertising Readership and Results* (New York: McGraw-Hill Book Company, 1966).

A number of outstanding social psychologists contributed their speculations and knowledge to a symposium on *Psychology in Media Strategy* (Chicago: American Marketing Association, 1966), which I edited and therefore recommend. An earlier interesting summary on the subject of repetition is James Playsted Wood's *Advertising and the Soul's Belly* (Athens, Ga.:   University of Georgia Press, 1961).

There is hardly any part of the vast literature in marketing that does not in one way or another impinge on the subject matter of advertising strategy.   The influential work of the Marketing Sciences Institute is demonstrated in Michael Halbert's *Meaning and Sources in Marketing Theory* (New York: McGraw-Hill Book Company, 1965).   An advanced approach to the construction of theoretical models of the marketing system is also to be found in *Models, Measurement & Marketing* (Englewood Cliffs, N.J.: Prentice-Hall, Inc., 1965), edited by Peter Langhoff for the Market Research Council.   This publisher has brought out another work by a mathematically oriented social scientist, Francesco Nicosia: *Consumer Decision Processes* (Englewood Cliffs, N.J.:   Prentice-Hall, Inc., 1967).   The systems-oriented reader should look at *Marketing and the Computer* by Wroe Alderson and Stanley J. Shapiro, editors (Englewood Cliffs, N.J.:   Prentice-Hall, Inc., 1963).

For a distribution-oriented perspective from one of the most imaginative students of marketing, see E. B. Weiss's *Management and the Marketing Revolution* (New York: McGraw-Hill Book Company, 1964).   Also relevant but reaching beyond the narrow subject of advertising are two volumes edited by Lincoln Clark, *Consumer Behavior: The Dynamics of Consumer Reaction* (New York: New York University Press, 1954) and *Consumer Behavior: The Life Cycle and Consumer Behavior* (New York; New York University Press, 1955); *Understanding Consumer Behavior*, edited by Martin Grossack (Boston: Christopher Publishing, 1964); and Nelson Foote's *Household Decision Making* (New York: New York University Press, 1961). The only book I know about test marketing is in German: Hans Sittenfeld, *Der Testmarkt* (Munich: Verlag Moderne Industrie, 1966).

I did not have occasion in my text to bring up four fine recent publications of the National Industrial Conference Board: *Evaluating Media* by Harry Deane Wolfe, James K. Brown, G. Clark Thompson, and Stephen H. Greenberg (1966); *Setting Advertising Objectives* by Saul S. Sands (1966); *Measuring Advertising Results* by Harry Deane Wolfe, James K. Brown, and G. Clark Thompson (1962); and *Pretesting Advertising* by Harry Deane Wolfe, James K. Brown, Stephen H. Greenberg, and G. Clark Thompson (1963).   These reports include numerous histories and interesting statistical tables.

Advertising Measurement Services

Media/scope publishes a monthly barometer of advertising costs for the various media.   The standard estimates of total advertising volume are prepared monthly for *Printers' Ink* by McCann-Erickson, Inc., and by

Charles Y. Yang annually for *Advertising Age*.   These estimates, prepared by somewhat different methods, come up with figures which are
not too disparate, but advertising expenditure data involving television
talent costs, radio, and the miscellaneous minor media are extremely
difficult to evaluate precisely and may well be overstated by both sources.

Detailed advertising expenditure figures are based on measurements
of magazines and supplement ads prepared by Leading National Advertisers, Inc. (P.O. Box 525; Norwalk, Conn.) for the Publishers Information Bureau (575 Lexington Avenue; New York, N.Y.).   The LNA also
measures network television broadcasts and prepares cost estimates.
Media Records, Inc. (370 Seventh Avenue; New York, N.Y.) measures
advertising linage and estimates expenditures for newspapers in 135
cities in the U.S. and Canada. Broadcast Advertisers Reports, Inc. (750
Third Avenue; New York, N.Y.) measures network and spot television
advertising.   The N. C. Rorabaugh Company, Inc. (347 Madison Avenue; New York, N.Y.), owned by the LNA, prepares estimates of spot
television advertising for the Television Bureau of Advertising.

Media Research

The organizations which provide continuing weekly program ratings are
the A. C. Nielsen Company (2101 Howard Street; Chicago, Ill.) and
the American Research Bureau (4320 Ammendale Road; Beltsville,
Md.).   For television, both these organizations provide national ratings
and also local market ratings.   The Pulse, Inc. (730 Fifth Avenue; New
York, N.Y.) uses a personal interview with a roster of programs for both
local radio and TV. Mediastat (509 Madison Avenue; New York, N.Y.)
uses the diary method for radio.   C. E. Hooper, Inc. (750 Third Avenue;
New York, N.Y.) makes telephone interviews to measure radio audiences.   Sindlinger & Company, Inc. (Sindlinger Building; Norwood,
Penn.) also uses the telephone to conduct media studies.

W. R. Simmons and Associates Research, Inc. (235 East 42 Street;
New York, N.Y.) and Alfred Politz Media Studies (527 Madison Avenue;
New York, N.Y.) conduct research on the major media annually, personally interviewing large samples.   (Simmons also leaves a TV diary
for his respondents to fill out.)   Once a year, The Brand Rating Research
Corporation (745 Fifth Avenue; New York, N.Y.) measures media and
product preferences, using a self-administered questionnaire.   TvQ (50
Maple Place; Manhasset, L.I., N.Y.), which publishes monthly program
popularity scores, is an affiliate of the Home Testing Institute, which
maintains a large panel of families who answer questionnaires on marketing subjects.

Other Research Organizations

Many organizations, large and small, are engaged in studying sales and consumer attitudes. It would be impossible to list even all the good ones. Here are some which offer periodic reports on a subscription basis:

The leading organizations which provide continuing data on product movement and brand share through the store audit method are Audits & Surveys, Inc. (One Park Avenue; New York, N.Y.) and A. C. Nielsen Company. The Market Research Corporation of America (122 East 42 Street; New York, N.Y.) provides continuing market studies based on a panel of households that keep diaries of their purchases.

Daniel Starch and Staff (Boston Post Road & Beach Avenue; Mamaroneck, N.Y.) researches advertising performance in television, magazines, and newspapers. Carl J. Nelson Research, Inc. (176 W. Adams Street; Chicago, Ill.) does readership research on both ads and editorial matter in newspapers. Readex, Inc. (140 Quail Street; St. Paul, Minn.) does readership studies, primarily on industrial publications.

Gallup & Robinson, Inc. (Research Park; Princeton, N.J.) tests both television commercials and print advertisements. The leading organization in the field of testing television commercials is Schwerin Research Corporation (270 Madison Avenue; New York, N.Y.). Audience Studies, Inc. (711 Fifth Avenue; New York, N.Y.) uses the psychogalvanometer to find out how people react to commercials. Marplan (605 Third Avenue; New York, N.Y.), the research affiliate of the Interpublic Group of Companies, studies commercials by measuring pupil dilation.

The services of these firms are, of course, sold to subscribers, but a number of them publish promotional bulletins that include research observations of high general interest.

INDEX

174-75
brand decisions complicated by, 62
breaking the inattention barrier with 62
building reach through, 150-53
effects of, 163-65
emotional response to, 172-74
field experiments in, 174-77
Krugman's theory of, 172-74
"teaching" through, 165-71
timing aspect of, 177-82
varying content and, 182-84
Research:
  media, 45-48
  motivation, 3, 46-47
  operations, 3, 47
  services, 227-29
Retailers:
  advertising objectives of, 14-16
  and pull of advertising, 296-98
Rhodes, Evan, 250
Richmond Newspapers interviews, 135n
Roberts, Jack, 321
Robinson, Edward G., 249
Roethlisberger, Fritz L., 304
Rokeach, Milton, 311
Romney, A. K., 311
Roper, Elmo, 111, 291
Rosten, Leo, 243
Rudolph, H. J., 148

Sachs, William S., 229
Sales Management survey, 40-41
Salesmen, media, 48-49
Sarnoff, David, 242
Saturday Evening Post, 101, 102, 112, 224
  audience figures, 229, 237, 262
  becomes biweekly publication, 239
  Politz study for, 175
Scanning, 119-21
Scatter plans, *see* Television
Schloemar, Bertrand A., 253-54

Schneider, John, 243
Schwab, Victor, 177
Schwerin, Horace, 104
  commercials study, 113
  on the effectiveness of commercial length, 148-49
  on the effectiveness of exaggeration, 125
  repetition study, 174
  on similarity in brand advertising, 141
Sevin, Charles H., 30, 31
Shryer, William, 177
Simmons (W. R.) and Associates, 105-06, 135, 217, 227, 228, 229, 259
Simon, Julian L., 177
Simulation, 278-80
Simulmatics Corporation, 280
Sindlinger, Arthur, 227
Skinner, B. F., 107, 167
Skornia, Harry J., 33
"Sleeper effect," 300
Smith, Gail, 196, 294, 295, 309
Smith, Stewart, 147n
Smith, Thomas, 162
Social Research, Inc., 207
Space, unit size of, 145-48
Spector, Aaron J., 175
Spot television, *see* Television
Sports Illustrated, 92, 101, 262
Standard Rate & Data Service, 227
Stanton, Frank, 46, 256
Starch, Daniel, 56, 83, 148
Steiner, Gary A., 136, 137, 138, 308
Stewart, David, 40
Stewart, John, 193, 313, 314
Strong, E. K., 148
Studebaker Corporation, 130n
Swanson, Charles, 175
Symbols, and perception, 124-25
"Synergism," principle of 112-13

Taste, problems of, 8
Television:

A
B
C
D
E
F
G
H
I
J

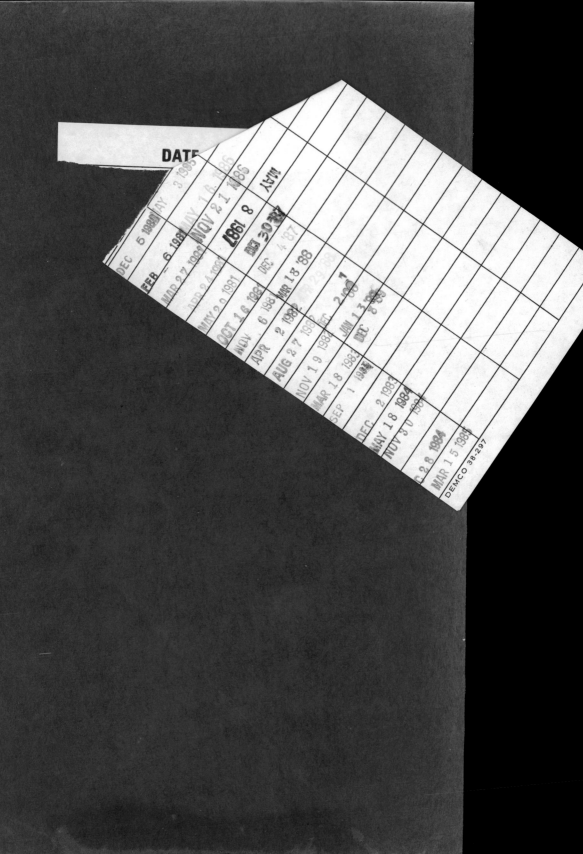